# Lecture Notes in
# Business Information Processing

287

Series Editors

Wil M.P. van der Aalst
*Eindhoven Technical University, Eindhoven, The Netherlands*
John Mylopoulos
*University of Trento, Trento, Italy*
Michael Rosemann
*Queensland University of Technology, Brisbane, QLD, Australia*
Michael J. Shaw
*University of Illinois, Urbana-Champaign, IL, USA*
Clemens Szyperski
*Microsoft Research, Redmond, WA, USA*

More information about this series at http://www.springer.com/series/7911

Iris Reinhartz-Berger · Jens Gulden
Selmin Nurcan · Wided Guédria
Palash Bera (Eds.)

# Enterprise, Business-Process and Information Systems Modeling

18th International Conference, BPMDS 2017
22nd International Conference, EMMSAD 2017
Held at CAiSE 2017, Essen, Germany, June 12–13, 2017
Proceedings

 Springer

*Editors*
Iris Reinhartz-Berger
University of Haifa
Haifa
Israel

Jens Gulden
University of Duisburg-Essen
Duisburg
Germany

Selmin Nurcan
Université de Paris 1 Panthéon - Sorbonne
Paris
France

Wided Guédria
Luxembourg Institute of Science and
    Technology
Esch-sur-Alzette
Luxembourg

Palash Bera
Saint Louis University
St. Louis, MO
USA

ISSN 1865-1348                    ISSN 1865-1356   (electronic)
Lecture Notes in Business Information Processing
ISBN 978-3-319-59465-1          ISBN 978-3-319-59466-8   (eBook)
DOI 10.1007/978-3-319-59466-8

Library of Congress Control Number: 2017941500

Printed on acid-free paper

This Springer imprint is published by Springer Nature
The registered company is Springer International Publishing AG
The registered company address is: Gewerbestrasse 11, 6330 Cham, Switzerland

# Preface

This book contains the proceedings of two long-running events held along with the CAiSE conferences relating to the areas of enterprise, business-process and information systems modeling: the 18th International Conference on Business Process Modeling, Development and Support (BPMDS 2017) and the 22nd International Conference on Evaluation and Modeling Methods for Systems Analysis and Development (EMMSAD 2017). The two working conferences are introduced below.

## BPMDS 2017

The topics addressed by the BPMDS series, in conjunction with CAiSE (Conference on Advanced Information Systems Engineering), are focused on business processes and their IT support. This is one of the keystones of information systems theory beyond short-lived fashions. The continued interest in this topic on behalf of the information systems community is reflected by the success of the past BPMDS events and by their promotion from a workshop to a working conference.

The BPMDS series produced 17 events from 1998 to 2016. From 2011, BPMDS has become a two-day working conference attached to CAiSE. The basic principles of the BPMDS series are:

1. BPMDS serves as a meeting place for researchers and practitioners in the areas of business development and business applications (software) development.
2. The aim of the event is mainly discussions, rather than presentations.
3. Each event has a theme that is mandatory for idea papers.
4. Each event's results are, usually, published in a special issue of an international journal.

The goals, format, and history of BPMDS can be found on the website: http://www.bpmds.org/.

BPMDS solicits papers related to business process modeling, development, and support (BPMDS) using quality, relevance, originality, and applicability as main selection criteria. As a working conference, BPMDS 2017 aims to attract *full research papers* describing mature research, *experience reports* related to using BPMDS in practice, and visionary *idea papers*. To encourage new and emerging challenges and research directions in the area of business process modeling, development and support, BPMDS has a unique focus theme every year. Papers submitted as idea papers are required to be of relevance to the focus theme, thus providing a mass of new ideas around a relatively narrow but emerging research area. Full research papers and experience reports do not necessarily need to be directly connected to this theme.

The focus theme for BPMDS 2017 idea papers was "Enabling Business Transformation by Business Process Modeling, Development and Support." For the 18th edition of the BPMDS conference, we invited interested authors to engage during the two days of BPMDS 2017 in Essen, and to take part in a deep discussion with all participants about the challenges of business transformation in the digitally connected world and the ways business process modeling, development and support may provide capabilities to deal with those challenges. The challenges result, among others, from the impacts of the ubiquity of the actors, social networks, new business models, the co-existence of flexibility, exception handling, context awareness, and personalization requirements together with other compliance and quality requirements.

Practitioners are producing business process models, researchers are studying and producing business process models, and they are also producing new modeling languages when they consider that existing ones are not sufficient. What is beyond? Which kind of analyses can we make using these process models? How can we complete and enhance these process models with annotations, with data coming from everywhere out of the immediate process environment? How can the understanding we gain by working on these models in a sandbox help or facilitate the undergoing business transformation?

BPMDS 2017 received 24 submissions from 18 countries (Algeria, Australia, Austria, Egypt, France, Germany, Hungary, Italy, Luxembourg, The Netherlands, New Zealand, Russia, Singapore, Spain, Sweden, Switzerland, UK, USA). The management of paper submission and reviews was supported by the EasyChair conference system. Each paper received four reviews from the members of the international Program Committee. Eventually, 11 high-quality full papers were selected; among them one experience report and one idea paper. The accepted papers cover a wide spectrum of issues related to business process development, modeling, and support. They are organized under the following section headings:

- Non-functional Considerations in Business Processes
- New Challenges in Business Process Modeling and Support
- Testing Business Processes
- Business Process Model Comprehension
- An Experience Report on Teaching Business Process Modeling

We wish to thank all the people who submitted papers to BPMDS 2017 for having shared their work with us, as well as the members of the BPMDS 2017 Program Committee, who made a remarkable effort in reviewing submissions. We also thank the organizers of CAiSE 2017 for their help with the organization of the event, and IFIP WG8.1 for the support.

April 2017                                                                                    Selmin Nurcan
                                                                                              Jens Gulden

# EMMSAD 2017

The field of information and software systems development has resulted in a rich heritage of modeling methods and notations (e.g., ER, ORM, UML, ArchiMate, EPC, BPMN, DEMO). This canon of methods and notations continues to be enriched with extensions, refinements, and even new languages, to deal with new challenges. Even with some attempts to standardize, new modeling methods are constantly being introduced, especially in order to deal with emerging trends such as compliance and regulations, cloud computing, big data, business analytics, the Internet of Things, etc. These ongoing changes significantly impact the way information and software systems, enterprises, and business processes are being analyzed and designed in practice.

Evaluation of modeling methods contributes to the knowledge and understanding of their strengths and weaknesses. This knowledge may guide researchers toward the development of the next generation of modeling methods and help practitioners select the modeling methods most appropriate to their needs. A variety of empirical and non-empirical evaluation approaches can be found in the literature: feature comparison, meta-modeling, metrics, paradigmatic analyses, contingency identification, ontological evaluation, surveys, laboratory and field experiments, case studies, and action research. Yet, there is a paucity of such research in the literature.

The EMMSAD conference focuses on evaluating, as well as exploring and enhancing, modeling methods and techniques for the development of information and software systems, enterprises, and business processes. The objective of the EMMSAD conference series is to provide a forum for researchers and practitioners interested in evaluation and modeling methods for systems development to meet and exchange research ideas and results. It also provides the participants with an opportunity to present their research papers and experience reports, and to take part in open discussions. More details can be found at http://www.emmsad.org/.

EMMSAD 2017 received 25 submissions from 18 countries (Australia, Austria, Bosnia and Herzegovina, Canada, France, Germany, Hungary, Israel, Italy, Luxembourg, Morocco, Norway, Portugal, Sweden, Tunisia, USA, UAE, UK). The management of the paper submission and reviews was supported by the EasyChair conference system. Each paper received four reviews. Eventually, 11 high-quality papers were selected: nine full papers and two short papers. The accepted papers cover a wide spectrum of issues related to modeling languages and meta-modeling, the process of modeling, integration of models, evaluation and comparison of modeling languages, techniques and tools, and empirical studies of conceptual modeling. The accepted papers are organized into four sections:

- Evaluation and Comparison of Modeling Languages and Methods
- Modeling Approaches to Support Decision-Making
- Behavioral Specification and Business Process Modeling
- Modeling Languages and Methods in Evolving Context

We wish to thank the EMMSAD 2017 authors for having shared their work with us, as well as the members of the EMMSAD 2017 Program Committee for their valuable reviews. We also thank the organizers of CAiSE 2017 for their help with the organization of the event, IFIP WG8.1 for the support, and Sérgio Guerreiro for his help during the review and decision phases.

April 2017

Iris Reinhartz-Berger
Wided Guédria
Palash Bera

# BPMDS 2017 Organization

## Program Committee Chairs and Organizers

Selmin Nurcan     Université Paris 1 Panthéon - Sorbonne, France
Jens Gulden     University of Duisburg-Essen, Germany

## Steering Committee

Ilia Bider     Stockholm University and IbisSoft, Sweden
Selmin Nurcan     Université Paris 1 Panthéon - Sorbonne, France
Rainer Schmidt     Munich University of Applied Sciences, Germany
Pnina Soffer     University of Haifa, Israel

## Industrial Advisory Board

Ilia Bider     Stockholm University and IbisSoft, Sweden
Pascal Negros     Arch4IE, France
Gil Regev     EPFL and Itecor, Switzerland

## Industrial Track Chairs

Rainer Schmidt     Munich University of Applied Sciences, Germany
Jens Gulden     University of Duisburg-Essen, Germany

## Program Committee

João Paulo A. Almeida     Federal University of Espirito Santo, Brazil
Eric Andonoff     Université Toulouse 1, France
Judith Barrios Albornoz     University of Los Andes, Venezuela
Kahina Bessai     Loria University of Lorraine, France
Ilia Bider     Stockholm University and IbisSoft, Sweden
Karsten Boehm     FH KufsteinTirol, University of Applies Science, Austria
Lars Brehm     Munich University of Applied Science, Germany
Dirk Fahland     Technische Universiteit Eindhoven, The Netherlands
Claude Godart     Loria University of Lorraine, France
Renata Guizzardi     Universidade Federal do Espirito Santo, Brazil
Jens Gulden     University of Duisburg-Essen, Germany
Amin Jalali     Stockholm University, Sweden
Paul Johannesson     Royal Institute of Technology, Sweden
Marite Kirikova     Riga Technical University, Latvia
Agnes Koschmider     Karlsruhe Institute of Technology, Germany

| | |
|---|---|
| Marcello La Rosa | Queensland University of Technology, Australia |
| Jan Mendling | Vienna University of Economics and Business, Austria |
| Michael Moehring | Aalen University of Applied Sciences, Germany |
| Pascal Negros | Arch4IE, France |
| Jens Nimis | University of Applied Sciences Karlsruhe, Germany |
| Selmin Nurcan | Université Paris 1 Panthéon - Sorbonne, France |
| Oscar Pastor Lopez | Universitat Politecnica de Valencia, Spain |
| Elias Pimenidis | University of the West of England, UK |
| Gil Regev | Ecole Polytechnique Fédérale de Lausanne, Switzerland |
| Manfred Reichert | University of Ulm, Germany |
| Hajo Reijers | Vrije Universiteit Amsterdam, The Netherlands |
| Iris Reinhartz-Berger | University of Haifa, Israel |
| Colette Rolland | Université Paris 1 Panthéon - Sorbonne, France |
| Michael Rosemann | Queensland University of Technology, Australia |
| Shazia Sadiq | The University of Queensland, Australia |
| Rainer Schmidt | Munich University of Applied Sciences, Germany |
| Stefan Schönig | University of Bayreuth, Germany |
| Samira Si-Said Cherfi | CEDRIC, Conservatoire National des Arts et Métiers, France |
| Pnina Soffer | University of Haifa, Israel |
| Roland Ukor | FirstLinq Ltd, UK |
| Barbara Weber | Technical University of Denmark |
| Matthias Weidlich | Humboldt-Universität zu Berlin, Germany |
| Jelena Zdravkovic | Stockholm University, Sweden |
| Alfred Zimmermann | Reutlingen University, Germany |

## Additional Reviewers

| | |
|---|---|
| Aa, Han van der | Knuplesch, David |
| Andrews, Kevin | Schunselaar, Dennis |
| Aysolmaz, Banu | Steinau, Sebastian |

# EMMSAD 2017 Organization

## Program Committee Chairs and Organizers

### Co-chairs

| | |
|---|---|
| Iris Reinhartz-Berger | University of Haifa, Israel |
| Wided Guédria | Luxembourg Institute of Science and Technology (LIST), Luxembourg |
| Palash Bera | Saint Louis University, USA |

### Advisory Committee

| | |
|---|---|
| John Krogstie | Norwegian University of Science and Technology (NTNU), Norway |
| Henderik A. Proper | Luxembourg Institute of Science and Technology (LIST), Luxembourg, and Radboud University Nijmegen, The Netherlands |

### Program Committee

| | |
|---|---|
| Palash Bera | Saint Louis University, USA |
| Sjaak Brinkkemper | Utrecht University, The Netherlands |
| Tony Clark | Sheffield Hallam University, UK |
| Dolors Costal | Universitat Politècnica de Catalunya, Spain |
| Sybren De Kinderen | University of Duisburg-Essen, Germany |
| Rébecca Deneckère | Centre de Recherche en Informatique, France |
| John Erickson | University of Nebraska-Omaha, USA |
| Neil Ernst | Software Engineering Institute, Pittsburgh, USA |
| Christophe Feltus | Luxembourg Institute of Science and Technology (LIST), Luxembourg |
| Peter Fettke | German Research Center for Artificial Inteilligence (DFKI) and Saarland University, Germany |
| Kathrin Figl | Vienna University of Economics and Business (WU), Austria |
| Mohamad Gharib | University of Florence, Italy |
| Jeff Gray | University of Alabama, USA |
| Wided Guédria | Luxembourg Institute of Science and Technology (LIST), Luxembourg |
| Sérgio Guerreiro | Instituto Superior Técnico, University of Lisbon, Portugal |
| Giancarlo Guizzardi | Ontology and Conceptual Modeling Research Group (NEMO)/Federal University of Espirito Santo (UFES), Brazil |

| | |
|---|---|
| Stijn Hoppenbrouwers | HAN University of Applied Sciences, The Netherlands |
| Jennifer Horkoff | Chalmers and the University of Gothenburg, Sweden |
| Timothy Lethbridge | University of Ottawa, Canada |
| Lidia Lopez | Universitat Politècnica de Catalunya (UPC), Spain |
| Pericles Loucopoulos | University of Manchester, UK |
| Florian Matthes | Technische Universität München, Germany |
| Raimundas Matulevicius | University of Tartu, Estonia |
| Jan Mendling | Vienna University of Economics and Business, Austria |
| Owen Molloy | NUIG, Ireland |
| Haralambos Mouratidis | University of Brighton, UK |
| John Mylopoulos | University of Toronto, Canada |
| Andreas L Opdahl | University of Bergen, Norway |
| Hervé Panetto | CRAN, University of Lorraine, CNRS, France |
| Oscar Pastor Lopez | Universitat Politecnica de Valencia, Spain |
| Robert Pergl | Czech Technical University, Czech Republic |
| Anna Perini | Fondazione Bruno Kessler Trento, Italy |
| Barbara Pernici | Politecnico di Milano, Italy |
| Anne Persson | University of Skövde, Sweden |
| Nuno Pombo | University of Beira Interior, Portugal |
| Jolita Ralyté | University of Geneva, Switzerland |
| Iris Reinhartz-Berger | University of Haifa, Israel |
| Camille Salinesi | CRI, Université de Paris 1 Panthéon-Sorbonne, France |
| Alberto Silva | INESC-ID/Instituto Superior Técnico, Portugal |
| Sase Singh | Elizabeth City State University, USA |
| Monique Snoeck | K.U. Leuven, Belgium |
| Il-Yeol Song | Drexel University, USA |
| Janis Stirna | Stockholm University, Sweden |
| Arnon Sturm | Ben Gurion University of the Negev, Israel |
| Dirk van der Linden | University of Haifa, Israel |
| Steven van Kervel | Formetis BV, The Netherlands |
| Carson Woo | University of British Columbia, Canada |
| Michael Wufka | Douglas College, Canada |
| Marielba Zacarias | Research Centre for Spatial and Organizational Dynamics, Universidade do Algarve, Portugal |
| Anna Zamansky | University of Haifa, Israel |
| Jelena Zdravkovic | Stockholm University, Sweden |

## Additional Reviewers

| | |
|---|---|
| Angelopoulos, Konstantinos | Hernandez-Mendez, Adrian |
| Aubry, Alexis | Kleehaus, Martin |
| Avezedo, Sofia | Koop, Lody |
| Ergin, Huseyin | Stadzisz, Paulo |

# Contents

**Non-functional Considerations in Business Processes**

Towards a Data-Driven Framework for Measuring Process Performance .... 3
  *Isabella Kis, Stefan Bachhofner, Claudio Di Ciccio, and Jan Mendling*

Supporting Secure Business Process Design via Security Process Patterns ... 19
  *Nikolaos Argyropoulos, Haralambos Mouratidis, and Andrew Fish*

NFC-Based Task Enactment for Automatic Documentation
of Treatment Processes ................................. 34
  *Florian Stertz, Juergen Mangler, and Stefanie Rinderle-Ma*

**New Challenges in Business Process Modeling and Support**

Discovering Social Networks Instantly: Moving Process Mining
Computations to the Database and Data Entry Time ................. 51
  *Alifah Syamsiyah, Boudewijn F. van Dongen,
  and Wil M.P. van der Aalst*

Re-evaluation of Decisions Based on Events ...................... 68
  *Luise Pufahl, Sankalita Mandal, Kimon Batoulis, and Mathias Weske*

Requirements Framework for Batch Processing in Business Processes ...... 85
  *Luise Pufahl and Mathias Weske*

**Testing Business Processes**

Performance Comparison Between BPMN 2.0 Workflow Management
Systems Versions ...................................... 103
  *Vincenzo Ferme, Marigianna Skouradaki, Ana Ivanchikj,
  Cesare Pautasso, and Frank Leymann*

BPMN-Based Model-Driven Testing of Service-Based Processes ......... 119
  *Daniel Lübke and Tammo van Lessen*

**Business Process Model Comprehension**

Cognitive Insights into Business Process Model Comprehension:
Preliminary Results for Experienced and Inexperienced Individuals ........ 137
  *Michael Zimoch, Rüdiger Pryss, Thomas Probst, Winfried Schlee,
  and Manfred Reichert*

Eye Tracking Experiments on Process Model Comprehension: Lessons
Learned . . . . . . . . . . . . . . . . . . . . . . . . . . . . . . . . . . . . . . . . . . . . . .      153
   *Michael Zimoch, Rüdiger Pryss, Johannes Schobel,*
   *and Manfred Reichert*

**An Experience Report on Teaching Business Process Modeling**

Teaching and Learning State-Oriented Business Process Modeling.
Experience Report. . . . . . . . . . . . . . . . . . . . . . . . . . . . . . . . . . . . . . . .      171
   *Georgios Koutsopoulos and Ilia Bider*

**Evaluation and Comparison of Modeling Languages and Methods**

On the Requirement from Practice for Meaningful Variability in Visual
Notation. . . . . . . . . . . . . . . . . . . . . . . . . . . . . . . . . . . . . . . . . . . . . . .      189
   *Dirk van der Linden, Irit Hadar, and Anna Zamansky*

Balanced Scorecard for Method Improvement: Approach and Experiences . . .      204
   *Kurt Sandkuhl and Ulf Seigerroth*

Modeling Exchange Agreements with DEMO/PSI and Core Component
of Communication. . . . . . . . . . . . . . . . . . . . . . . . . . . . . . . . . . . . . . . .      220
   *Duarte Gouveia and David Aveiro*

**Modeling Approaches to Support Decision Making**

Towards a Decision-Support System for Selecting the Appropriate Business
Process Modeling Formalism: A Context-Aware Roadmap. . . . . . . . . . . . . .      239
   *Afef Awadid, Selmin Nurcan, and Sonia Ayachi Ghannouchi*

Designing a Decision-Making Process for Partially Observable
Environments Using Markov Theory . . . . . . . . . . . . . . . . . . . . . . . . . . . .      257
   *Sérgio Guerreiro*

Know-How Mapping – A Goal-Oriented Approach and Evaluation . . . . . . . .      272
   *Arnon Sturm, Eric Yu, and Sadra Abrishamkar*

**Behavioral Specification and Business Process Modeling**

Controlled Experiment in Business Model-Driven Conceptual Database
Design. . . . . . . . . . . . . . . . . . . . . . . . . . . . . . . . . . . . . . . . . . . . . . . .      289
   *Drazen Brdjanin, Goran Banjac, Danijela Banjac, and Slavko Maric*

Incorporating Data Inaccuracy Considerations in Process Models . . . . . . . . .      305
   *Yotam Evron, Pnina Soffer, and Anna Zamansky*

Structured Behavioral Programming Idioms . . . . . . . . . . . . . . . . . . . . . . .    319
    *Adiel Ashrov, Michal Gordon, Assaf Marron, Arnon Sturm,*
    *and Gera Weiss*

## Modelling Languages and Methods in Evolving Context

A Security Requirements Modelling Language to Secure Cloud Computing
Environments . . . . . . . . . . . . . . . . . . . . . . . . . . . . . . . . . . . . . . . . .    337
    *Shaun Shei, Haralambos Mouratidis, and Aidan Delaney*

On Valuation of Smart Grid Architectures: An Enterprise Engineering
Perspective. . . . . . . . . . . . . . . . . . . . . . . . . . . . . . . . . . . . . . . . . . .    346
    *Iván S. Razo-Zapata, Anup Shrestha, and Erik Proper*

**Author Index** . . . . . . . . . . . . . . . . . . . . . . . . . . . . . . . . . . . . . . .    355

# Non-functional Considerations in
# Business Processes

# Towards a Data-Driven Framework
# for Measuring Process Performance

Isabella Kis[✉], Stefan Bachhofner, Claudio Di Ciccio, and Jan Mendling

Vienna University of Economics and Business, Vienna, Austria
isabella.kis93@gmail.com, s.bachhofner@me.com,
{claudio.di.ciccio,jan.mendling}@wu.ac.at

**Abstract.** Studies have shown that the focus of Business Process Management (BPM) mainly lies on process discovery and process implementation & execution. In contrast, process analysis, i.e., the measurement of process performance, has been mostly neglected in the field of process science so far. However, in order to be viable in the long run, a process' performance has to be made evaluable. To enable this kind of analysis, the suggested approach in this idea paper builds upon the well-established notion of devil's quadrangle. The quadrangle depicts the process performance according to four dimensions (time, cost, quality and flexibility), thus allowing for a meaningful assessment of the process. In the course of this paper, a framework for the measurement of each dimension is proposed, based on the analysis of process execution data. A trailing example is provided that reflects the expressed concepts on a tangible realistic scenario.

**Keywords:** Business processes · Process analytics · Devil's quadrangle

## 1 Introduction

According to a survey conducted by Müller in 2010, a majority of the questioned companies saw a direct correlation between Business Process Management (BPM) and corporate success [13]. To be able to conduct BPM successfully the performance of a process needs to be measured. Nonetheless, studies have shown that business process analysis has long been neglected in the field of BPM [16,19], as BPM devoted most of the research endeavours on the aspects of process discovery, and process implementation and execution. To be able to analyse a process properly, process performance has to be measured first. A well-established paradigm in that sense is dictated by the so-called devil's quadrangle [4,8]. It shows process performance based on four dimensions: time, cost, quality and flexibility. Those four factors for performance measurement influence each other in a way that it is not possible to improve performance of one dimension without affecting other dimensions, either positively or negatively [4]. An advantage of the approach of measuring process performance with the devil's quadrangle is the possibility to compare changes in the performance over time as visually depicted in Fig. 1.

© Springer International Publishing AG 2017
I. Reinhartz-Berger et al. (Eds.): BPMDS/EMMSAD 2017, LNBIP 287, pp. 3–18, 2017.
DOI: 10.1007/978-3-319-59466-8_1

So far, process analysis has been a neglected field of process science and only a few suggestions have been made on how process performance could be measured according to those four dimensions, such as in the case of [8,10,11,20]. Furthermore, to the best of our knowledge, no metrics have been proposed for those dimensions that can be automatically measured over the log data of Business Process Management Systems (BPMSs). However, in the long run process analysis will be crucial for corporate success, thus demanding a framework that allows for a meaningful assessment of a process.

With a focus on the service sector, we propose a framework that suggests how metrics for the devil's quadrangle's dimensions can be derived by using log data generated by a process engine. Our final aim is to help the team involved in a BPM initiative to make informed decisions on the changes to apply to the processes under analysis, driven by factual knowledge stemming from real data. To increase the applicability of the suggested framework, we propose measurements based on values that are most com-

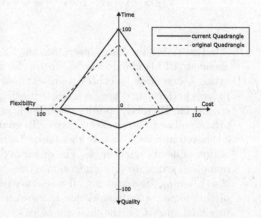

**Fig. 1.** Changes in process performance [4]

monly recorded by BPMSs, such as the time and resource allocation of activity executions & incident handling. In the spirit of the idea paper, we focus on the rationale behind the proposed metrics and exemplifications thereof, paving the path for formal and technical treatises. The presented framework is based upon the results of a dedicated investigation on the matter, conducted in the context of a research project in collaboration with PHACTUM Softwareentwicklung GmbH.

The remainder of the paper is structured as follows: Sect. 2 proposes a trailing example process and draws preliminary considerations on the analysis; Sect. 3 provides a framework on how the four dimensions of the devil's quadrangle can be measured by using log data generated by a process engine. Finally, Sect. 4 concludes the paper and draws some remarks for future research in the field.

## 2   Preliminaries

Figure 2 depicts an insurance claim process. The process starts with a claim that is received and forwarded (activity A) to a specialist by the secretary of the insurance company. The specialist then assesses the damage (activity B) and writes a damage report (activity C). Subsequently, it has to be decided whether the claim is approved or not. In case of approval, the money to cover the damage is transferred to the policyholder (activity D). If the claim is rejected, the insured party is informed (activity E).

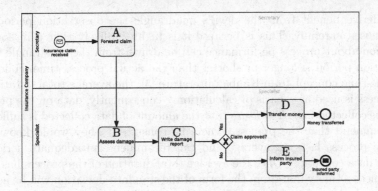

**Fig. 2.** Example process of an insurance claim

**Table 1.** Average duration of the insurance claim process

|  | A | B | C | D | E | Wait. time | Total |
|---|---|---|---|---|---|---|---|
| Avg. Duration | 10 | 300 | 150 | 20 | 20 | 460 | 940 |

As it can be seen in Table 1, the average duration of the process is 940 min, which is equivalent to 15.66 h. The total average duration consists of the average duration of every single activity (except for activities D and E who are counted as one, as one instance can only take one path, plus the time an instance had to wait for further processing, i.e., the wait time). To sum it up, the length of the observation period roughly corresponds to two working days, assuming that one working day amounts to 7.5 h. The reference period is by default also set to two working days, i.e. 940 min.

The example process and its log data will be exploited in the remainder of the paper to exemplify how the suggested metrics are measured. Before the derivation of the metrics for each dimension though, we draw some preliminary considerations about *(i)* the time span into which the process performance is assessed, and *(ii)* the comparability of the measurements.

For what the first point is concerned, we are interested in the notions of observation time and reference time. The observation time in terms of duration is equivalent to the lead time of a process, namely the time it takes to handle an entire case. To assess the performance of a process, it is crucial to know for how long data on a process needs to be collected in order to allow for a sound statement. Reference time, on the other hand, relates to the past performance of a process or, more precisely, to the period of time for which former process performance is observed. The setting of a reference time enables a comparison of current process performance and past process performance, thus making it possible to further enhance performance assessment. Therefore, the reference period is used to compare the metrics measured during the observation period with past process performance, so that conclusions about the development of the process can be drawn.

To derive benefit from the devil's quadrangle the observation period has to be chosen carefully. This is because it is highly unlikely that a reasonable conclusion about process performance can be drawn from the quadrangle if the observation period is longer or shorter than the actual process time. Following the cycle-time concept from Kanban literature [3], the average total duration of the process is used as a basis of calculation – consequently, data on the process has to be collected first. To ensure that the amount of data collected is sufficient, we recommend that the process owners be consulted. They would know how long the process lasts on average and can recommend an adequate period of time for data collection. Once the average total duration of the process has been determined, a safety margin in the form of the standard deviation will be added. Of course the time frame for the observation period can be modified by the user. The observation period calculated by the system is merely a default setting and has to be seen as a recommendation for the user. To calculate the duration of the observation period for the example process, the average total duration of the process has to be determined. According to Table 1 the average observation period should be set to 940 min. Please notice that for reasons of simplicity no safety margin was added.

In Fig. 1 the reference period is represented by a dashed line. The reference period depicts the past performance of a process for a predefined period of time. By default the reference period comprises the same time frame as the observation period. This setting can again be changed by the user according to the current evaluation needs. The reference period for the example process is equal to the observation period's duration and amounts for 940 min. Both the current quadrangle (i.e. observation period) and the original quadrangle (i.e. reference period) are put on top of each other in order to make comparison possible.

To guarantee the comparability of the devil's quadrangle's four dimensions their values should move within the same scale. In this paper it has been decided upon a scale ranging from 0 to 100%. The more the value of one dimension approaches 0, the worse the respective dimension performed.

# 3 Approach

Throughout this section, we define the metrics that we associate to each dimension of the devil's quadrangle: Sect. 3.1 deals with the time dimension, Sect. 3.2 is concerned with the cost dimension, Sect. 3.3 focuses on the quality dimension, and Sect. 3.4 discusses the flexibility dimension.

## 3.1 Time Dimension

When measuring the time dimension of a process, we are interested in how much time is dedicated to the carry-out of the tasks of a process instance. Consequently, we focus on the service time, i.e., the time the resources spend on actually handling a case [8]. The service time of a case is then compared with the case's lead time, thus indicating how much of the total time an instance takes to finish is spent on actual work. The higher the service time ratio, the better, as more time has been spent on actually handling a case and less time was lost due to a process instance being at a resting stage.

As it is very likely that more than one case is examined during the observation period, we once again calculate the service time ratio for each process instance, i.e., the comparison of a case's service time with its respective lead time, and calculate a median for all the single values. The resulting median is then transferred to the time axis of the quadrangle.

In order to generate data for the calculations regarding the insurance claim process, we ran an example of ten instances of a process (see Table 2). First, the lead time of the process, consisting of the duration of each activity and the wait time, i.e., the time an instance waited for further processing, was calculated. After that, the service time (i.e. the time a process instance was actually handled) was computed. These two steps were taken in order to be able to gather the service time ratio, which indicates how much time of the process was spent on actual work. In the end, the service time ratios for each run were sorted in descending order to calculate the median for the time dimension. The resulting median for our computation is 61.29%.

**Table 2.** Measurement of the time and cost dimensions

| | Activity | | | | | Wait. time | Lead. time | Service time | Service/time ratio |
|---|---|---|---|---|---|---|---|---|---|
| | A | B | C | D | E | | | | |
| Run 1 | 10 | 240 | 60 | 20 | | 360 | 690 | 330 | 47.83% |
| Run 2 | 5 | 300 | 120 | | 20 | 240 | 685 | 445 | 64.96% |
| Run 3 | 20 | 360 | 120 | 10 | | 240 | 750 | 510 | 68.00% |
| Run 4 | 10 | 240 | 120 | 10 | | 180 | 560 | 380 | 67.86% |
| Run 5 | 10 | 180 | 60 | | 20 | 360 | 630 | 270 | 42.86% |
| Run 6 | 25 | 300 | 240 | | 10 | 360 | 935 | 575 | 61.50% |
| Run 7 | 10 | 300 | 120 | 30 | | 300 | 760 | 460 | 60.51% |
| Run 8 | 10 | 240 | 60 | 10 | | 60 | 380 | 320 | 84.21% |
| Run 9 | 5 | 360 | 180 | 20 | | 360 | 925 | 565 | 61.08% |
| Run 10 | 5 | 360 | 180 | | 10 | 360 | 915 | 555 | 60.66% |
| Total runtime | 110 | 2.880 | 1.260 | 100 | 60 | | | | |

## 3.2 Cost Dimension

To calculate the process costs, personnel expenses for each process task are stored in a variable. Then the expenses for each task of the process are added up to a total value. A justification for the use of personnel cost for calculating a process' cost is seen in the importance of this type of cost for organisations. Personnel expenses normally represent the most relevant cost type of the service sector – in production industry they are the second most important cost type [6].

The personnel costs are most likely stored in a central database, which contains the salary of every employee. Through the integration of such an information in the database with the data logs of the BPMS, the current hourly payment of each employee can be calculated. It is important to notice that for cost calculation the actual personnel costs have to be used. The term *actual personnel costs* refers to direct payments to employees increased by continued payment of salaries (in case of holiday, sick leave and bank holidays), holiday pay, Christmas bonuses, the employer's social security contributions, overtime rates and other personnel costs [6].

As the event log stores information about how long an employee has been working on a task, a viable measurement of the process' cost can be achieved by multiplying the actual labour costs per hour by the processing time per task. The costs will then be determined for the selected observation period. The result is then compared with the total costs of the organisation for the same observation period resulting in a percentage value that can be transferred to the cost axis of the devil's quadrangle. The higher the value the worse the process performed with regard to the cost dimension (i.e. a high value means high personnel costs compared to total costs). However, it has already been mentioned in Sect. 2, we want all the axes to have a uniform meaning: The closer the value is to 100% the better process performance is rated. This is why the value received from the previous division has to be inverted before transferring it to the cost axis.

Considering the insurance claim process example, it is assumed that the costs for the secretary amount to $20 per hour and that the specialist is paid $40 per hour. Moreover, it is exactly known which activities are handled by whom. With this in mind, the total duration of activity A is multiplied by the hourly costs of the secretary, whereas the duration of the remaining activities is multiplied by the hourly rate of the specialist (the total duration can also be extracted from Table 2). The resulting sum is then compared with the total cost of the company, which we estimated with $4.000 per working day. The value for the cost dimension thus amounts to the inverted ratio: Its value, 27.42%, can be depicted on the quadrangle.

We remark here that we assume a complete knowledge of the work of resources, with information on the assigned task and duration of the carry-out thereof. This is a reasonable assumption in case a BPMS is supporting the process execution. Otherwise, the conduction of tasks in parallel, or the interruptions during task handling, holidays, weekends, etc., need a substantial amount of effort to be considered [1].

### 3.3   Quality Dimension

When measuring the quality of a process we want to consider two different aspects: First, we want to examine whether the process finished as planned. We will refer to this first aspect of quality as *outcome quality*, as it can help to judge the path a process instance took to finish the process. Second, it is to be checked whether any incidents (i.e., technical errors that can occur during process execution) were created. We will henceforth refer to it as *technical quality*.

**Table 3.** Process traces

| Run 1 | A | B | C | D |
|-------|---|---|---|---|
| Run 2 | A | B | C | E |
| Run 3 | A | B | C | D |
| Run 4 | A | B | C | D |
| Run 5 | A | B | C | E |
| Run 6 | A | B | C | E |
| Run 7 | A | B | C | D |
| Run 8 | A | B | C | D |
| Run 9 | A | B | C | D |
| Run 10 | A | B | C | E |

**Table 4.** Measurement of the technical quality

|        | Incidents | Elements | Incident rate |
|--------|-----------|----------|---------------|
| Run 1  | 0         | 8        | 0%            |
| Run 2  | 5         | 8        | 62.5%         |
| Run 3  | 0         | 8        | 0%            |
| Run 4  | 1         | 8        | 12.5%         |
| Run 5  | 1         | 8        | 12.5%         |
| Run 6  | 0         | 8        | 0%            |
| Run 7  | 2         | 8        | 25%           |
| Run 8  | 0         | 8        | 0%            |
| Run 9  | 0         | 8        | 0%            |
| Run 10 | 1         | 8        | 12.5%         |

After both subdivisions of quality have been evaluated they are combined and transferred to the quality axis of the devil's quadrangle.

**Outcome Quality.** The measurement of the outcome quality serves to assess the course a process instance takes to reach the end of a process. This implies the existence of one or more ideal paths through the process. Yet it would be very time-consuming to assess each process element's affiliation to the ideal path as in most of the times there are different ways through the process an instance can take. Moreover there could be various ideal paths.

Information on the termination of the process instance, typically depicted as end-events in executable process models, should be added. It should include the information whether the achieved outcome was positive or negative. Then, the number of end events that led to a positive outcome of the respective process instance are compared with the total number of process instances executed during the observation period, resulting in a percentage value that can be transferred to the quadrangle's axis. Within the scope of this paper, we assume that a process has at least two end elements, of which one has a positive and the other a negative outcome. The more end events a process has the higher the chance to make a fundamental statement about the process' ideal path(s). Other ways can indeed be adopted to mark the executions as reaching the expected process goal or not. For instance, a process does not necessarily have more than one end event. In this case there could be an exclusive or inclusive split at some point. Depending on the path the process instance takes after that split it is decided whether the decision had a positive or negative impact on the process.

Therefore, the approach to measure the outcome quality should be seen as a starting point for further research. Ideally, it will be possible in the future to identify a path quality, not just assessing the end elements of a process, but rather evaluating whether a specific process element belongs to the ideal path.

Table 3 shows all the paths that the simulated instances took through the insurance claim process. In order to calculate the outcome quality, the meaning for each end point of the process has to be defined. As an insurance company most likely prefers not to pay for a damage claimed by a policy holder, the end event *Money transferred* (subsequent to activity D) has a negative impact on process quality, whereas the end event *Insured party informed* (following activity E) has a positive impact. In Table 3 it can be observed that four out of ten runs ended with a rejection of the insurance claim, which has a positive meaning for the insurance company. At that stage, the number of positive end events is compared with the total number of process instances within the observation period. The four positive end events thus are divided by the total of ten, i.e., the number of process instances in the observation period. The result is an estimated outcome quality of 40%.

**Technical Quality.** To enable the assessment of a process' technical quality the number of incidents within a predefined observation period can be counted. The more incidents registered for a specific period of time, the worse the process performed in terms of technical quality. In the end, all incidents recorded in the observation period are compared with the total number of elements in a process.

The following example should help to better illustrate this procedure. It is assumed that a process instance records 20 events in the log. During the process execution five incidents are thrown. The technical quality given by the inverted ratio of incidents per process results in a value of 75% for that process instance. Afterwards, a median is calculated for all the values of the separate process instances. The resulting median is then transferred to the quadrangle's quality axis.

Table 4 summarises all the incidents that were registered during the run of one process instance of the example insurance claim process. The number of incidents is then compared with the number of elements that occurred within the same process instance, resulting in a percentage value. The higher this value, the higher the number of incidents within one process instance. To gather a value that represents the technical quality of the whole observation period, the median for all incident rates is calculated. Thus, the technical quality of the process equals 87.5% process performed. In contrast, a higher incident rate means lower technical quality, thus requiring for an inversion of the original result.

**Combining Outcome and Technical Quality.** To transfer a single value to the respective axis of the quadrangle, we combine the aforementioned quality measurements into a single one. This is achieved by assigning a weight, which can be chosen according to the interest of an organisation, to each of the two quality metrics, i.e., outcome quality and technical quality. Then the values resulting from the measurement of each dimension are multiplied with their respective weights in order to compute a single value that can be transferred to the quality axis of the devil's quadrangle.

For the example process, it was chosen to weigh both outcome and technical quality with 50% which results in a combined value of 66.88%, which can be transferred to the quadrangle's quality axis.

## 3.4   Flexibility Dimension

According to the Cambridge Dictionary, flexibility generally is "the quality of being able to change or be changed easily according to the situation". In BPM-related literature different specific ways of how to define flexibility can be found [5,9,12]. Accordingly, we adopt various definitions of flexibility, each contributing to a different aspect of the considered process.

In particular, we build upon the notion of run time flexibility as defined in [8]. Run time flexibility is the ability to react to changes while a workflow is executed. We identify two main components that contribute to it. We first focus on the concept of volume flexibility, namely the ability to handle changing volumes of input, rephrasing the definition of [9]. The paper discusses, among other things, a framework for IT-flexibility which can be divided into three dimensions. The first dimension, which is called "Flexibility in Functionality", is concerned with the reaction of a system to changing input conditions. The system is considered flexible if it can withstand varying input conditions. According to [17] flexibility is the maintenance of a stable structure in the face of change, where the structure is intended as what stands between the input and output. In the light of the above, we define the flexibility as follows: *Flexibility is the ability to keep the processing speed of the single instances at an approximately constant level even though the workload (i.e., the input) has increased (or decreased) significantly.* Even though our definition of flexibility slightly differs from the one of volume flexibility in [8] we will henceforth use this term to refer to the ability of a process to keep the instance's processing speed at a constant level when there has been an increase in work.

The other component of the run time flexibility concerns the ability to resolve system exceptions that are thrown during the execution of a process. By incident we mean a technical problem occurred during the BPMS-aided process execution. Such an aspect is of particular relevance in several scenarios where BPMSs are used in practice. This particular kind of flexibility will be thus referred to as *technical flexibility*.

The remainder of this section will be concerned with a more detailed description of the aforementioned components of the run time flexibility. Moreover it will be stated how metrics for the devil's quadrangle can be measured for each of the two.

**Volume Flexibility.** We define volume flexibility as the ability to guarantee a constant handling of process instances if there has been a change in the workload. To facilitate the understanding of this flexibility concept, we consider the case of the insurance company. In times of natural disasters, the number of insurance claims would increase significantly, resulting in a higher workload as well [2]. If the insurance company manages to adapt to the changed conditions it is considered flexible.

The measurement of volume flexibility is based upon the lead time of a process. Flexibility is examined from a holistic perspective here, which is highly suitable for the assessment of process performance at a glance. Within the scope of this paper the existence of a BPMS is assumed. Therefore each process instance is assigned an ID which allows for a proper estimation of when the process instance started and finished. Consequently, this knowledge enables us to make an exact statement of the process instance's lead time. From the measurements taken in the initial phase of the process analysis we know the planned average lead time of the process.

A first approach to the concept of flexibility is the calculation of an open-closed-ratio (OCR) for a previously defined observation period. This ratio is computed by comparing cases in progress (open cases) with completed cases (closed cases). When there has been an increase in the workload and the values for open and closed cases balance roughly, it can be presumed that there is a constant handling of cases. If, on the other hand, there is no balance between the two values, it can be concluded that the process lacks flexibility.

The only problem of measuring the flexibility dimension as suggested above is that the results could be corrupted. This is owing to the fact that the workload level is not taken into account. To put it differently, what would happen if the workload does not change, hence remains at a constant level, and the OCR indicates a constant handling of cases? It could be assumed that the organisation is highly flexible even though the workload remained stable. However, this does not correspond to the definition of flexibility, rooted in the ability to adapt to a changed or new situation. For this reason an additional factor has to be included in the measurement of flexibility: the workload itself.

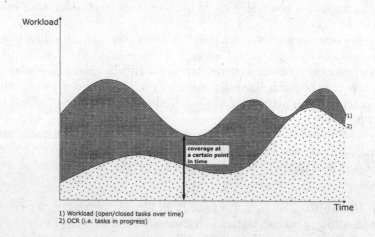

1) Workload (open/closed tasks over time)
2) OCR (i.e. tasks in progress)

**Fig. 3.** Measurement of the flexibility metrics

As it can be seen in Fig. 3, two factors are taken into consideration for the measurement of process flexibility: *(i)* the OCR, and *(ii)* the workload, i.e., the cases in progress. The OCR shows the open and closed cases of an observation period, i.e., the changing workload over time. If the workload increases (resp. decreases) over time, the OCR has to rise (fall) too in order to be able to speak of a highly flexible process. In contrast, if the OCR remains on the same level this is a sign of lacking flexibility, because the process is apparently not able to adapt to changing conditions.

To receive a percentage value for the volume flexibility, the coverages both of the workload and the OCR curve have to be compared. The higher the coverage, the more flexible the process is, as this indicates that the OCR is able to adapt to the changing workload conditions. However, we remark that the OCR will not rise immediately after an increase in the workload, because the cases take a certain time to finish – at least the average lead time. It still has to be considered that both the workload curve and the curve representing the OCR could exactly coincide, even though the number of open and closed cases over time did not increase recently, i.e., the backlog remained on the same level. Again we are confronted with a case where an organisation faces steady workload, which does not correspond to our definition of flexibility. Our understanding of flexibility is that an organisation is able to adapt to changing conditions. But where there is no change, there can be no reaction either. We thus integrate a warning signal that indicates an increased (decreased) amount of cases in progress (or congruent areas below the curves) but no significant rise (fall) of the backlog curve. The user should then be enabled to switch to a more detailed view where both curves are shown, as suggested in [14].

We report two examples showing different ways to measure the volume flexibility, both complying with the described rationale yet tackling the computation from two different perspectives: the first one measures volume flexibility in terms of the total duration per case, the second one adopts a more global perspective and focuses on the number of cases that were opened and closed within the observation period. Both examples refer to the example insurance claim process.

For what the first computation strategy is concerned, Table 5 shows the open cases within the observation period of 940 min. It is assumed that the usual number of open cases is ten. It can be then recognised that there are five additional cases to handle with respect to the expectations. This implies that the workload has increased and the measurement of the process' flexibility can be started. To consider the process flexible, each case has to finish within the average lead time of the process. In the "Lead time" column the actual lead time of the respective instance is reported. The average lead time, based on our calculation for the framework, is given in column "Target lead time". In another step, target lead time and actual lead time of every instance are compared, showing that in total the 15 instances took 225 min longer than planned to finish. Expressed as a percentage, the process took 1.60% longer than initially planned, thus reducing volume flexibility to 98.40%. The second strategy to measure the volume flexibility metric refers to open and closed cases in the observation period. In Table 6 the open cases in the observation period are reported. Under the assumption that the normal number of open cases is ten, it can be recognised that there are additional five cases to handle which signals a higher workload. In order to be considered flexible, all 15 cases have to be closed within the average lead time of the process. However, as can be gathered from Table 6, only five cases were

**Table 5.** Measurement of the process flexibility

| Open case | Lead time | Target lead time | Difference |
|-----------|-----------|------------------|------------|
| No. 1 | 690 | 940 | −250 |
| No. 2 | 685 | 940 | −255 |
| No. 3 | 750 | 940 | −190 |
| No. 4 | 560 | 940 | −380 |
| No. 5 | 630 | 940 | −310 |
| No. 6 | 950 | 940 | +10 |
| No. 7 | 940 | 940 | 0 |
| No. 8 | 960 | 940 | +20 |
| No. 9 | 1.000 | 940 | +60 |
| No. 10 | 960 | 940 | +20 |
| No. 11 | 1.200 | 940 | +260 |
| No. 12 | 1.500 | 940 | +560 |
| No. 13 | 1.300 | 940 | +360 |
| No. 14 | 1.000 | 940 | +60 |
| No. 15 | 1.200 | 940 | +260 |
| Total | 14.325 | 14.100 | +225 |

**Table 6.** Measurement of the volume flexibility

| Open cases | Closed cases | Ratio |
|------------|--------------|-------|
| 15 | 5 | 33,33% |

closed, meaning that 66.67% of the cases are still open for processing and thus reducing volume flexibility to 33.33%.

The purpose of the variation in the calculation of volume flexibility for the example process is to show how different viewpoints influence the outcome of metrics measurement. It can be recognised that the results for volume flexibility differ considerably when comparing the two versions. An organisation therefore has to decide how volume flexibility is measured according to the duration of the process or the number of processed cases, depending on the perspective that is to be emphasised.

**Technical Flexibility.** When it comes to the measurement of technical flexibility, the number of incidents thrown within a process over a predefined observation period has to be observed. As already stated before, incidents are technical errors which can occur during the execution of a process. To measure the technical flexibility we want to find out how long it takes to resolve one incident. In this case, we are interested in the reaction time. The reaction time for resolving an incident (or the sum of all the time intervals spent for each incident, in case more than one occurred within a process instance) is then compared with the lead time of the corresponding process instance. It is thus indicated how much time of the process execution is dedicated to the handling of technical issues. This way various ratios of the reaction time are received. In order to be able to transfer the ratios to the quadrangle's axis, we calculate a median for them. Before transferring the resulting value to the quadrangle, it is inverted. In practical real-world scenarios, the reaction time for resolving an incident is sometimes not accounted within the lead time. In such a case, the computed value would fall below zero, which is detrimental to our representation, because it aims at normalizing every measurement in the 0–100% range. To circumvent this problem, the incident reaction time can be added to the lead time in the computation.

We remark here that in our proposal the metrics for the technical flexibility deal with incidents as well as in the case of the technical quality. Nevertheless, we aim at representing with flexibility a perspective that mostly pertains the area of management within the organisation, whereas quality is intended to be perceived also outside the scope of the process owners [4], hence all the stakeholders. Owing to this, we look at the reaction time to handle incidents as a flexibility indicator, because it is an information mostly kept within the organisation. The time the delegated team spent on handling incidents is indeed an internal information that is usually not publicly shown. Ideally, the incident handling time is completely transparent to clients and partners. In contrast, we interpret the number of occurred incidents as an indicator that can be reverberated also outside the organisation, because of the possible disruptions caused thereby.

Table 7 depicts the ten instances of the provided example process, with the addition of the incidents thrown during the execution, and the time needed to resolve the incident in minutes. Subsequently a ratio for the reaction time is calculated, which in the end results in a median of 4.76%. After inverting the ratio, the value for technical flexibility is equal to 95.63%.

**Table 7.** Measurement of the technical flexibility

|        | Lead time | Incidents | Total reaction time | Reaction time ratio |
|--------|-----------|-----------|---------------------|---------------------|
| Run 1  | 690       | 0         | -                   | -                   |
| Run 2  | 685       | 5         | 60                  | 8.76%               |
| Run 3  | 750       | 0         | -                   | -                   |
| Run 4  | 560       | 1         | 10                  | 1.79%               |
| Run 5  | 630       | 1         | 30                  | 4.76%               |
| Run 6  | 935       | 0         | -                   | -                   |
| Run 7  | 760       | 2         | 10                  | 1.32%               |
| Run 8  | 380       | 0         | -                   | -                   |
| Run 9  | 925       | 0         | -                   | -                   |
| Run 10 | 915       | 1         | 40                  | 4.37%               |

**Combining Volume and Technical Flexibility.** So far we described two different metrics for the measurement of flexibility, namely volume and technical flexibility. In order to have a single metric accounting for both, our suggestion is again to assign a weight to each of the two flexibility components. An organisation, for example, may deem as very crucial to resolve incidents as quickly as possible. Therefore it would weigh the technical flexibility with 80% (out of 100%) and the remaining 20% would be assigned to volume flexibility. The values resulting from the measurement of each dimension would then be multiplied by their respective weights and summed up in order to form a single value that can be transferred to the flexibility axis of the devil's quadrangle.

If such a calculation is conducted for the example process with a weight of 50% each, the flexibility value would amount to 97,02%, in case the first measurement strategy for the volume flexibility is adopted, or to 64,49%, in case the second one was used.

## 4 Conclusion

Within this paper, suggestions for the measurement of metrics for the four dimensions of the devil's quadrangle have been made, exclusively based on the inspection of process data. All suggested calculations are made under the assumption that the data are extracted from a BPMS event log running the process. The log data used for metrics measurement has been chosen under the condition that it can be extracted from almost any BPMS. For the calculation of a value for the time dimension, the activity execution time is considered as reported in the log. The activity execution time is needed again in order to measure the cost metric. The additional piece of information needed in that case are the personnel expenses. Due to the amplitude of interpretations that can be given to the quality and flexibility dimensions in particular, we identified a combination of metrics, each singularly considering different aspects thereof. For the assessment of the outcome quality, a comparison between the positive and the negative terminations of the process instances is compared. For the measurement of the technical quality, the number of incidents within a process instance is considered. The quality dimension is ultimately assessed as a linear combination of the aforementioned ones. Process flexibility is also assessed as a weighted sum of two different components: the volume flexibility and the technical flexibility. The former is measured on the basis of a comparison between open and closed cases during the observation period. The latter is likewise based on the reaction time to incidents.

It is in our plans to extend the suggested framework towards further refinements and possibilities to customise the measurements. For instance, not only personnel costs but also total process costs should be considered for the cost dimensions, for instance by means of the activity-based costing model. For what the quality dimension is concerned, we would also consider alternative criteria beyond the final outcome or the registered technical incidents, e.g., an *enactment quality* based on the number of times exceptional paths were taken, compared to the expected course of the process unfolding. Furthermore, we are investigating how to better include the concept of dynamics in the flexibility dimension. The proposed metrics indeed average the ratio of values in the observation period (closed v. open cases, or incident reaction time v. lead time). However, the flexibility is arguably concerned with the responsiveness to *changes*, hence the suggestion for the analysis of trends. The exploitation of mathematical devices such as derivatives to be applied on the ratios demonstrate suitable and are in fact currently under investigation. In this paper, we described a theoretical framework for the measurement of the suggested metrics. Future work will be particularly concerned with its implementation supplemented by expert interviews, so as to conduct a thorough evaluation of the proposed approach on real-world use cases. From this perspective, the recent work of Nguyen et al. [14] for the staged process performance mining shows promising integration opportunities to automate the information extraction and processing needed by our framework. Moreover, it is in our plans to investigate the integration of existing approaches in literature such as SERVQUAL [15] to refine the definition and measurement of the quality dimension, and the SCOR metrics [18] to further investigate the interplay of internal and company-wide processes. Finally, we remark that due to the advanced globalisation, processes too will become more interconnected [7]. Consequently, there is the need to take process performance measurement to the next level and not only assess one single process but also to recognise the interplay of processes organisation-wide, if not beyond company boundaries.

# References

1. van der Aalst, W.M.P.: Business process simulation revisited. In: Barjis, J. (ed.) EOMAS 2010. LNBIP, vol. 63, pp. 1–14. Springer, Heidelberg (2010). doi:10.1007/978-3-642-15723-3_1
2. van der Aalst, W.M., Rosemann, M., Dumas, M.: Deadline-based escalation in process-aware information systems. Decis. Support Syst. 43(2), 492–511 (2007)
3. Dickmann, P.: Schlanker Materialfluss: mit Lean Production, Kanban und Innovationen, 3rd edn. Springer, Heidelberg (2015)
4. Dumas, M., La Rosa, M., Mendling, J., Reijers, H.A.: Fundamentals of Business Process Management. Springer, New York (2013)
5. Gong, Y., Janssen, M.: Measuring process flexibility and agility. In: ICEGOV, pp. 173–182. ACM (2010)
6. Horsch, J.: Kostenrechnung: Klassische und neue Methoden in der Unternehmenspraxis. Springer-Verlag (2015)
7. Houy, C., Fettke, P., Loos, P., van der Aalst, W.M.P., Krogstie, J.: BPM-in-the-large – towards a higher level of abstraction in business process management. In: Janssen, M., Lamersdorf, W., Pries-Heje, J., Rosemann, M. (eds.) EGES/GISP-2010. IAICT, vol. 334, pp. 233–244. Springer, Heidelberg (2010). doi:10.1007/978-3-642-15346-4_19
8. Jansen-Vullers, M., Loosschilder, M., Kleingeld, P., Reijers, H.: Performance measures to evaluate the impact of best practices. In: BPMDS Workshop, vol. 1, pp. 359–368. Tapir Academic Press Trondheim (2007)
9. Knoll, K., Jarvenpaa, S.L.: Information technology alignment or "fit" in highly turbulent environments: the concept of flexibility. In: SIGCPR, pp. 1–14. ACM (1994)
10. Kronz, A.: Managing of process key performance indicators as part of the aris methodology. In: Corporate Performance Management, pp. 31–44. Springer, Heidelberg (2006)
11. Kueng, P.: Process performance measurement system: a tool to support process-based organizations. Total Qual. Manag. 11(1), 67–85 (2000)

12. Kumar, R.L., Stylianou, A.C.: A process model for analyzing and managing flexibility in information systems. Eur. J. Inform. Syst. **23**(2), 151–184 (2014)
13. Müller, T.: Zukunftsthema Geschäftsprozessmanagement. Technical report, PricewaterhouseCoopers AG Wirtschaftsprüfungsgesellschaft (2011)
14. Nguyen, H., Dumas, M., ter Hofstede, A.H.M., La Rosa, M., Maggi, F.M.: Business process performance mining with staged process flows. In: Nurcan, S., Soffer, P., Bajec, M., Eder, J. (eds.) CAiSE 2016. LNCS, vol. 9694, pp. 167–185. Springer, Cham (2016). doi:10.1007/978-3-319-39696-5_11
15. Parasuraman, A., Zeithaml, V.A., Berry, L.L.: Servqual: a multiple-item scale for measuring consumer perc. J. Retail. **64**(1), 12 (1988)
16. Recker, J., Mendling, J.: The state of the art of business process management research as published in the BPM conference. Bus. Inform. Syst. Eng. **58**(1), 55–72 (2016)
17. Regev, G., Wegmann, A.: A regulation-based view on business process and supporting system flexibility. In: CAiSE, vol. 5, pp. 91–98. Springer (2005)
18. Stephens, S.: Supply chain operations reference model version 5.0: a new tool to improve supply chain efficiency and achieve best practice. Inform. Syst. Front. **3**(4), 471–476 (2001)
19. Van der Aalst, W.M.P.: Business process management: A comprehensive survey. ISRN Software Engineering 2013 (2013)
20. Venkatraman, N., Ramanujam, V.: Measurement of business performance in strategy research: a comparison of approaches. Acad. Manag. Rev. **11**(4), 801–814 (1986)

# Supporting Secure Business Process Design via Security Process Patterns

Nikolaos Argyropoulos$^{(\boxtimes)}$, Haralambos Mouratidis, and Andrew Fish

School of Computing, Engineering and Mathematics,
University of Brighton, Brighton, UK
{n.argyropoulos,h.mouratidis,andrew.fish}@brighton.ac.uk

**Abstract.** Security is an important non-functional characteristic of the business processes used by organisations for the coordination of their activities. Nevertheless, the implementation of security at the operational level can be challenging due to the limited security expertise of process designers and the delayed consideration of security during process development. To overcome such issues, expert knowledge and proven security solutions can be captured in the form of process patterns, which can easily be reused and integrated to business processes with minimal security-related knowledge required. In this work we introduce process-level security patterns, each of which contains the main activities required for the operationalisation of different security requirements. The introduced patterns are then used as a component of an existing framework for the creation of secure business process designs, the application of which, is illustrated through a working example. A preliminary evaluation of the proposed patterns is conducted via a workshop session.

**Keywords:** Security requirements · Business process modelling · Security process patterns · Business process security

## 1 Introduction

Business processes are essential instruments utilised by organisations for the coordination of their activities in order to produce value in the form of products and services [21]. During the design of business processes, in addition to their functional characteristics, a number of non-functional aspects also need to be taken into consideration. Security is one of the most important of such non-functional aspects due to the potential impact of its shortcomings for organisations in terms of finances, reputation and legal compliance [17]. Since the consideration of security during the early design stages of systems is considered highly beneficial [12], specialised security-oriented extensions have been developed for the majority of the established process modelling languages. Nevertheless, capturing the context and rationale behind general and security-related design choices made during process design, is outside of the scope of process modelling languages [5].

© Springer International Publishing AG 2017
I. Reinhartz-Berger et al. (Eds.): BPMDS/EMMSAD 2017, LNBIP 287, pp. 19–33, 2017.
DOI: 10.1007/978-3-319-59466-8_2

Aligning system requirements, as captured by goal models at the organisational level, with process activities at the operational level, augments the traceability between system models of different abstraction levels [6]. Additionally, it helps provide justification for design choices and leads to more robust and context-aware operationalisations of security [19]. Therefore, to enhance the alignment between an organisation's strategic goals and its operations, there needs to be a well-defined interconnection between a system's requirements and its process models.

Another obstacle in the design of secure business processes is the disconnect between security experts and the system developers [10]. Since the main concern of system developers is functionality, security is underprioritised and implemented in an ad-hoc manner during the later development stages. Security patterns are often utilised as a way to overcome such issues, as they are able to provide to non-experts standardised and proven solutions to common security-related issues [7]. Patterns can encapsulate security expertise and standardise proven solutions to recurring problems [10], which can facilitate a systematic and structured approach towards the operationalisation of security by non-experts [16].

In this work we introduce a number of reusable process fragments which can be integrated into business process models in order to operationalise different types of security requirements (e.g., confidentiality, integrity, availability). Each of the proposed fragments forms a business process level pattern, generic enough to be able to be instantiated by different types of security implementing technologies (e.g., the authentication pattern can be instantiated by user credentials, biometrics or smart card technologies). The introduced patterns are utilised as a component of an existing framework for the design of secure business processes. Moreover, an initial evaluation of their perceived usability and comparison to ad-hoc approaches is performed via a small-scale workshop session.

The rest of this paper is structured as follows; Sect. 2 introduces our security process patterns and then Sect. 3 presents, via a working example, a framework that utilises them for the creation of secure business process designs. Section 4 presents the evaluation of the proposed set of security process patterns, while Sect. 5 compares the contributions of our work to related literature. Finally, Sect. 6 concludes with a short discussion of this work and its future directions.

## 2    Security Process Patterns

A pattern, in the context of software development, is a reusable package which incorporates expert knowledge and represents a recurring structure, activity, behaviour or design [22]. A security pattern is a well-understood solution to a recurring information security problem and can be expressed either as a structural pattern, which incorporates designs that can be implemented in the final product or a procedural pattern, which represent high level directions for improving the process of developing security-critical software systems [10]. During the requirements and analysis phases of the system development lifecycle, the majority of the proposed design pattern focus on security attacks while patterns for implementing countermeasures are less represented [22]. Therefore, as part of this work we introduce a number of structural process design patterns aiming to model the implementation of countermeasures for the main types of security requirements at a business process model level of abstraction. Such patterns are generic enough to be implementation-agnostic but able to specify a basic sequence of activities and interactions between process participants which lead to the satisfaction of the system's security requirements.

The basic structure of each of the proposed patterns is captured using BPMN collaboration diagrams [18] and includes the activities required for the operationalisation of a security implementing technology, annotated with a padlock symbol at their top left corner to visually communicate their security-implementing nature. Corresponding activities exist at the user's lane describing any required interaction with the system's security implementing activities (e.g., username and password input). The security constraint activity or resource, which created the need for the implementation of security, is marked with a bold black border in order to be easily distinguishable. The activities contained within each pattern are not dependent on the implementation of a specific mechanism but rather on the type of the security requirement at hand. Therefore, the same pattern can be instantiated by a number of different mechanisms (e.g., smartcard, biometrics, username/password) which implement the same type of requirement (e.g., authentication). It is also the case that one pattern can be reused within another pattern depending on the security requirement it captures. For instance, the pattern for Authentication is reused within the Authorisation pattern since its functionality is required for the completion of the authorisation process. The patterns proposed by this work for each type of security requirement are the following:

**Authentication.** Authentication in the context of a business process requires a user to have a verified identity before performing a specific activity or accessing a resource. To realize the authentication requirement, as illustrated in Fig. 1, every time a user submits a request to the system for accessing an authentication-constraint resource or activity, the system should check that request and ask for the user's authentication data. Once the user submits the authentication data in the appropriate form (e.g., username/password, biometric data) the system should check its validity and if it is valid allow the user to access to the constraint resource or activity.

**Authorisation.** Authorisation, in terms of a business process model, requires that only users with the appropriate permissions can access a resource or perform an activity. As shown in Fig. 2, to realise the authorisation requirement, first a user requests access to authorisation-constraint activities or resources and the authentication process takes place in order for the user's identity to become known to the system. After the successful authentication, the role and/or the permissions attached to the user's account are checked and, if appropriate, the user gains access to the constraint activity or resource.

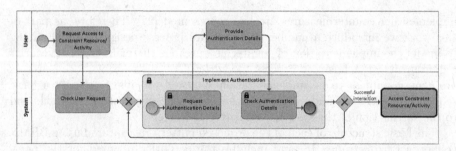

**Fig. 1.** Authentication pattern

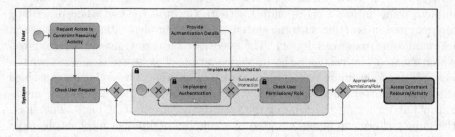

**Fig. 2.** Authorisation pattern

**Confidentiality.** Confidentiality ensures that any resource exchanged between the user and the system cannot be accessed by any unauthorised third party. As shown in Fig. 3, to achieve confidentiality in a business process, if the user is not already authorised, the authorisation process takes place as previously described. Next, a secure communication channel is created between the user and the system through which the confidentiality-constraint resource can be transferred.

**Integrity.** Integrity requires that resources exchanged between the user and the system cannot be modified during their transfer. As illustrated in Fig. 4, to achieve integrity, after an integrity-constraint resource has been transferred to the system, the system's copy of the resource needs to be compared to the original by data validation techniques.

**Availability.** Finally, the pattern for availability, presented in Fig. 5, is utilised to ensure that critical resources are always available to system users. To realise that requirement, when a requested resource is not available, the system has to maintain backups, using a number of available implementation technologies, from which the resource can be retrieved and be made available to the user.

## 3   Secure Business Process Design Framework

The process patterns introduced in the previous section are an important component of our ongoing work on the development of a secure business process

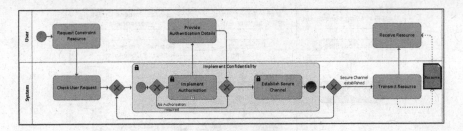

**Fig. 3.** Confidentiality pattern

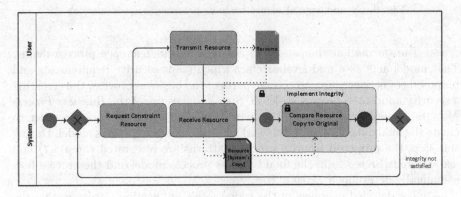

**Fig. 4.** Integrity pattern

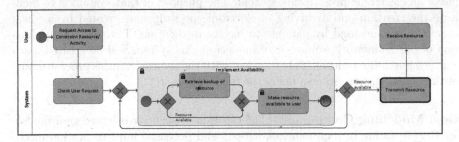

**Fig. 5.** Availability pattern

design framework [2–4]. The main objective of this framework is to create secure business process designs using as input the high-level security requirements of system stakeholders captured via organisational goal models. An illustration of the different components of the framework and their interconnections is provided in Fig. 6.

The steps for the application of our framework are described in Fig. 7. *Step 1* uses the *Goal Modelling component* to create a security-oriented goal model that captures a high abstraction view of the system to-be. Once such model has been created, a series of model transformation steps are applied in *Step 2* using the

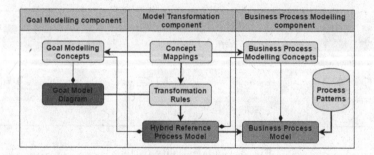

**Fig. 6.** Components of secure business process design framework

*Model Transformation component* to create a hybrid reference process model. That model acts as a mid-level artefact which maps security requirements and proposed countermeasures to specific parts of the business process, thus creating a security-annotated process skeleton. *Step 3* makes use of the *Business Process Modelling component* to refine the hybrid reference process model in order to create the final output of our framework, a secure business process model. During this step, the proposed security process patterns are integrated *(Step 3.1)* and instantiated *(Step 3.2)* in the final business process model and the process flow is manually determined *(Step 3.3)*.

A more detailed overview of the framework's application, incorporating the security patterns introduced in Sect. 2, will be demonstrated via a working example of an electronic prescription system. The purpose of that system is to facilitate the creation and archiving of electronic prescriptions created by medical practitioners and used by patients to receive medication. Through the application of our framework a number of models of this system will be created, each capturing a different level of abstraction, with the secure business process model of the e-prescription process being the final output.

**Goal Modelling Component.** The creation of security-oriented goal models for the elicitation of requirements, threats and potential implementation mechanisms for the system to-be is the starting point of our framework. The ability of Secure Tropos [14,15] to capture and analyse such concepts in an explicit and structured manner is the main reason for its selection as the modelling language of choice for performing the organisational level modelling.

An example of a Secure Tropos goal model diagram is presented in Fig. 8. The entities interacting within that system, namely the *"E-prescription system"*, the *"Medical Practitioner"* and the *"Patient"* are represented as actors. Each of them has a set of goals to achieve by interacting with each other. Their goals are decomposed into sub-goals and finally into plans which represent simple activities each actor has to perform (e.g., *"Create new prescription"*). Resources are also identified to represent documents created or required by plans or goals in order to be fulfilled (e.g., *"Prescription"*). Security constraints are connected to goals, plans or resources in order to restrict their functionality in favour of

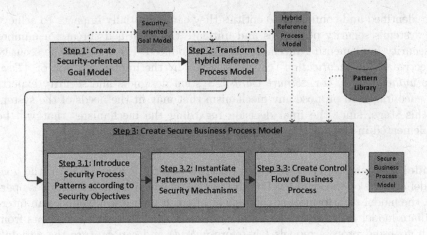

**Fig. 7.** Steps for the application of framework

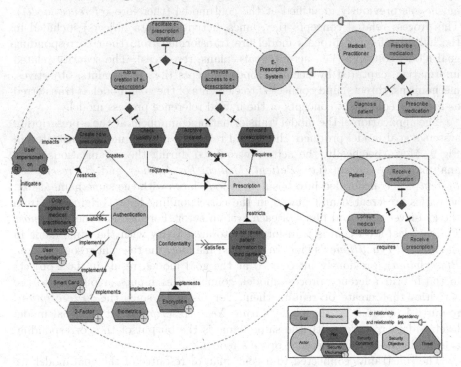

**Fig. 8.** Security Requirements view model of E-Prescription System

achieving a security objective. For instance, in the system modelled in Fig. 8, *"Only registered medical practitioners can access"* is an *"Authentication"* type constraint, while the *"Do not reveal patient information to third parties"* is a *"Confidentiality"* type of constraint. Threats (e.g., *"User Impersonation"*) are also identified and connected to entities they can potentially impact. To achieve the system's security objectives and mitigate the identified threats, a number of security implementing mechanisms are introduced. For example the security objective of *"Authentication"* can be satisfied by the implementation of *"Two-step authentication"* or *"Smart Cards"*. System designers and security experts are encouraged to propose any mechanism that may fit the needs of the system at this stage, since the final decision regarding the mechanisms that will be implemented in the final business process will take place at a later time.

**Model Transformation Component.** To achieve linkage between the goal model and the operational level of abstraction at which business processes operate, the model transformation component of our framework introduces an intermediate model called *hybrid reference process model*. It includes concepts from both goal and process models (therefore *hybrid*) and can capture the variability introduced by the different options regarding security implementing mechanisms, as previously identified at the goal model (therefore *reference model*). The process related concepts (i.e., lanes, activities, data objects) included in the hybrid reference process model are transformed from their corresponding goal model concepts (i.e., actors, goals, plans, resources). The security related information, captured by Secure Tropos concepts (i.e., constraints, objectives, mechanisms, threats) and connected to elements of the goal model, is transferred as-is to the equivalent concepts of the hybrid reference process model.

The application of the model transformation component at the e-prescription system's goal model produces the hybrid reference process model illustrated in Fig. 9. More specifically, the actors introduced during the organisational level analysis of the system (i.e., *Patient, Medical Practitioner* and *E-Prescription System*) are transformed into business process lanes with the same name. Next, activities are created and placed in the corresponding lanes, originating from the leaf-level goals and plans of each system actor. For instance the *"Diagnose Patient"* leaf-level goal is transformed into an activity with the same name in the *Medical Practitioner*'s lane. In a similar manner, the relevant resources (i.e., *Prescription*), previously introduced at the goal model, result in data objects in the hybrid reference process model, connected as inputs or outputs to the activities that create or require them. For instance, since the *"Prescription"* resource is created by the plan *"Create New Prescription"* at the goal model level, a data resource with the same name is the output of the corresponding activity in the hybrid reference process model.

The constraints connected to a goal, plan or resource of the goal model are now transferred at the hybrid reference process model and connected to the corresponding activity or data object (i.e., *"Only registered medical practitioners can access"* connected to the *"Create new prescription"* activity). The security constraints, which are now linked with specific process elements, are connected to security objectives, transferred from the goal model (i.e., *"Authentication"*). The security objectives categorise the identified security constraints and also help the process designers to select the appropriate process pattern which will

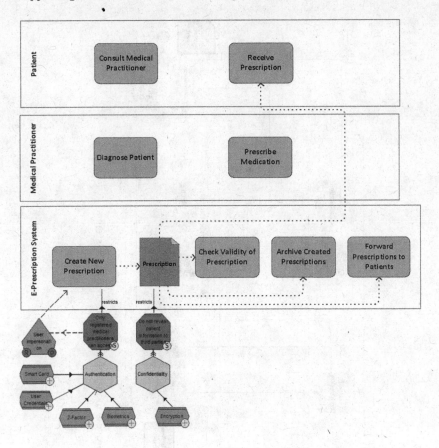

**Fig. 9.** Hybrid reference process model of the E-Prescription System

be integrated in the final business process model. The security mechanisms, proposed at the goal model for the implementation of each security objective, are also transferred in the hybrid reference process model to maintain the information regarding the range of potential configurations of security countermeasures at the process level. For instance, *Smart Cards, Biometrics* or *Usernames and Passwords* are amongst the security mechanisms that can be selected for the implementation of the *Authorisation* security objective, linked via the *"Only registered medical practitioners can access"* constraint to the *"Create new prescription"* activity.

**Business Process Modelling Component.** The business process modelling component uses the hybrid reference process model as input for creating secure business process designs. The security process patterns, introduced earlier in this work, are used at this point in order to guide the integration of the selected security mechanisms in the final business process model.

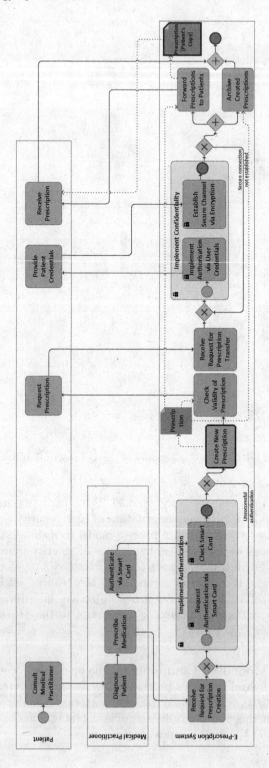

**Fig. 10.** Business process model of the E-Prescription System

Figure 10 presents the final business process model of the E-Prescription system. In the *"E-Prescription System"* lane of the business process model, the business process design pattern for the requirement of *"Authentication"* (c.f. Fig. 1), has been introduced before the security constraint activity *"Create new prescription"*, denoted with a bold-line border. The authentication pattern has been instantiated in order to implement the *"Smart Card"* security mechanism. Therefore, activities of the authentication pattern which were abstractly defined, such as *"Request Authentication Details"* are instantiated into more explicit declarations (i.e., *"Request Authentication via Smart Card"*) to reflect the implementation of the selected security mechanism. The same process was followed for the *"Confidentiality"* requirement connected to the "Prescription" resource, where the pattern for *"Confidentiality"* (c.f., Fig. 3) has been instantiated to implement the encryption security mechanism.

Other than the introduction of the instantiated process patterns, the control flow of the final business process has been manually created, including start and end events, gateways and flows indicating the order of execution of the included activities. The introduction of the control flow elements is a manual task since the goal model, which provided us with information regarding the basic structure of the intended system, is inherently not equipped to capture information regarding its temporal dimensions, such as the order of execution of its activities.

## 4   Evaluation

A small-scale experiment was conducted in order to (i) evaluate the perceived understandability and ease-of-use of the proposed security process patterns and (ii) compare their implementation to ad-hoc security integration in business process models. Twelve (12) postgraduate students (MSc and PhD level), in the areaS of information systems design and information security, completed the experiment.

The whole process was performed in a supervised workshop session with a total duration of thirty minutes. A brief overview of business process modelling concepts and diagrams was provided before the beginning of the experiment. After that, a fragment of the business process presented in Fig. 10 was presented to the participants without any security implementing activities. They were first asked to introduce any extra activities they considered necessary, in an ad-hoc manner, in order to satisfy the authentication objective for a specified element of the process. Only after that phase of the experiment was completed, the participants were presented with the authentication pattern. They were asked to apply it to the initial business process model fragment in order to accomplish the same security objective. After both phases were completed a short questionnaire was distributed in order to capture the opinions of the participants regarding their experience. The questionnaire entries were phrased as statements accompanied by a 5-point Likert scale, ranging from strongly disagree to strongly agree, from which the responders selected the option best reflecting their opinion. At the end of the questionnaire form there was also the option of providing free-form comments and remarks[1]. According to the participants' responses at the questionnaire:

- 83% either agreed or strongly agreed that the provided process pattern was easy to understand,
- 75% either agreed or strongly agreed that the provided process pattern was easy to integrate to the existing process model,
- 42% either agreed or strongly agreed that it was difficult to identify in an ad-hoc manner, the security related activities needed to be added in the process.
- 67% either agreed or strongly agreed that it easier to create a secure business process model using the provided process pattern compared to the ad-hoc security implementation.

The experiment allowed us to get an indication of the perceived usability and understandability of the proposed process patterns. It also indicated that such patterns are a preferable alternative to ad-hoc approaches as they provide more structure and guidance to process designers. A limitation of our experimental setup is its small sample size which limits the significance of its findings. The generalisability of the results is also limited since the participants only worked with a small subset of the proposed patterns. Nevertheless, the responses gathered through this small-scale experiment provide a valuable starting point for the further development and future evaluation of secure business process patterns.

## 5    Related Work

Kienzle et al. [10] have created a pattern repository including both structural and procedural patterns for web service security, expressed through a textual template. Mouratidis et al. [16] introduce security patterns to describe security implementing techniques (e.g., agent authenticator), expressed using Tropos, an agent-oriented software engineering approach, and a textual description template. Rosado et al. [19] link security requirements to architectural and design security patterns in order to guide the implementation of security in the area of web services. High-level architectural patterns and mid-level design patterns of security implementing mechanisms (e.g., secure message router, credential tokenizer) are matched to specific types of security requirements of web service applications. Ahmed et al. [1] identify potential risks and security requirements at the process level by matching process fragments with security-risk patterns used to capture common security requirements. A comprehensive survey of works in the area of security design patterns is provided by Laverdiére et al. [11], where a number of desirable properties of security design patterns and a template for pattern description are developed.

The above works [10,16,19] provide patterns which aim to capture specific types of security countermeasures or, in the case of [1], use process patterns to

---

[1] The questionnaire and a summary of the responses can be accessed in: http://www.sense-brighton.eu/process-patterns-questionnaire/.

identify where security-related violations can occur within the process. Each of the patterns presented in our work captures the operationalisation of one type of security requirement and can accommodate its implementation by any suitable security implementing technology. Therefore, their implementation-independent nature, allows a higher degree of generalisability and flexibility compared to countermeasure-specific patterns.

Salnitri et al. [20] introduce SecBPMN which extends BPMN 2.0 in order to perform security-related annotation of business processes. The security requirements captured via such annotations are formalised by a series of predicates which, similar to security process patterns, encapsulate security-related information. Li et al. [13] introduce a method for constructing goal models which are able to capture and analyse attack patterns depending on the contextual environment of the system. Kalloniatis et al. [8,9] introduce the PriS framework for the design of privacy-aware processes, starting from goal models. A set of privacy process patterns are used by PriS for the incorporation of privacy requirements into business processes, which are refined and expressed in BPMN 2.0 in [3].

Similar to the works above, our framework also uses of goal models but it provides explicit steps for transitioning from them to the operational level of abstraction. Additionally, it allows the mapping of both security requirements and security countermeasures, captured at a high abstraction level, to specific business process elements. Therefore, via the use of security process patterns, it facilitates the alignment between security requirements at the organisational level and the operationalisation of security countermeasures at the process level.

# 6    Conclusion

Designing secure business processes can be a challenging endeavour since system developers often have limited knowledge regarding the analysis and implementation of security. Process patterns, encapsulating expert knowledge and proven solutions, can be a way to overcome the lack of security expertise during a system's development process. Identifying security process patterns of the appropriate abstraction level and granularity is another challenge, since over-specified patterns may be not flexible enough to fit the specific context of the system at hand, while high-level architectural patterns may be too generic.

The work presented in this paper proposes a series of reusable security-oriented process fragments which can be utilised as process patterns for the integration of security in business process models. This collection of patterns is used as a component of a broader framework for the design of secure business process models, the application of which has been illustrated through an example. The most important characteristic of the proposed process patterns is the level of abstraction at which they are expressed, as it allows them to capture the steps required for the operationalisation of security requirements in a generic but expressive and implementation-agnostic manner.

The perceived usability and understandability of the proposed patterns was positively evaluated during a small-scale workshop session. The participants of the same workshop session also indicated that designing secure processes via the proposed set of patterns was preferable to ad-hoc approaches to security.

Our future work in this area will focus on the further refinement and extension of the proposed pattern library. In addition to that, the privacy process patterns, introduced by our previous work [3], will be added to the pattern library of our framework so it will be able to cover the analysis and operationalisation of both security and privacy countermeasures in business process models. Finally, a large-scale evaluation of the overall framework via a case study of an existing system will allow us to extract valuable conclusions regarding its applicability.

**Acknowledgement.** This research received funding from the Visual Privacy Management in User Centric Open Environments (VisiOn) project, supported by the EU Horizon 2020 programme, Grant agreement No 653642.

# References

1. Ahmed, N., Matulevičius, R.: Securing business processes using security risk-oriented patterns. Comput. Stand. Interfaces **36**(4), 723–733 (2014)
2. Argyropoulos, N., Márquez Alcañiz, L., Mouratidis, H., Fish, A., Rosado, D.G., Guzmán, I.G.-R., Fernández-Medina, E.: Eliciting security requirements for business processes of legacy systems. In: Ralyté, J., España, S., Pastor, Ó. (eds.) PoEM 2015. LNBIP, vol. 235, pp. 91–107. Springer, Cham (2015). doi:10.1007/978-3-319-25897-3_7
3. Argyropoulos, N., Kalloniatis, C., Mouratidis, H., Fish, A.: Incorporating privacy patterns into semi-automatic business process derivation. In: IEEE 10th International Conference on Research Challenges in Information Science (RCIS), pp. 1–12. IEEE (2016)
4. Argyropoulos, N., Mouratidis, H., Fish, A.: Towards the derivation of secure business process designs. In: Jeusfeld, M.A., Karlapalem, K. (eds.) ER 2015. LNCS, vol. 9382, pp. 248–258. Springer, Cham (2015). doi:10.1007/978-3-319-25747-1_25
5. Decreus, K., Poels, G.: A goal-oriented requirements engineering method for business processes. In: Soffer, P., Proper, E. (eds.) CAiSE Forum 2010. LNBIP, vol. 72, pp. 29–43. Springer, Heidelberg (2011). doi:10.1007/978-3-642-17722-4_3
6. Decreus, K., Poels, G., Kharbili, M.E., Pulvermueller, E.: Policy-enabled goal-oriented requirements engineering for semantic business process management. Int. J. Intell. Syst. **25**(8), 784–812 (2010)
7. Fernandez, E.B., Pan, R.: A pattern language for security models. In: Proceedings of PLoP. vol. 1 (2001)
8. Kalloniatis, C., Kavakli, E., Gritzalis, S.: Using privacy process patterns for incorporating privacy requirements into the system design process. In: 2nd International Conference on Availability, Reliability and Security (ARES 2007), pp. 1009–1017. IEEE (2007)
9. Kalloniatis, C., Kavakli, E., Gritzalis, S.: Addressing privacy requirements in system design: the PriS method. Requirements Eng. **13**(3), 241–255 (2008)
10. Kienzle, D.M., Elder, M.C.: Security patterns for web application development. University of Virginia Technical report (2002)
11. Lavérdiere, M., Mourad, A., Hanna, A., Debbabi, M.: Security design patterns: Survey and evaluation. In: 2006 Canadian Conference on Electrical and Computer Engineering, pp. 1605–1608. IEEE (2006)

12. Leitner, M., Miller, M., Rinderle-Ma, S.: An analysis and evaluation of security aspects in the business process model and notation. In: 8th International Conference on Availability, Reliability and Security (ARES 2013), pp. 262–267. IEEE (2013)
13. Li, T., Paja, E., Mylopoulos, J., Horkoff, J., Beckers, K.: Security attack analysis using attack patterns. In: IEEE 10th International Conference on Research Challenges in Information Science (RCIS), pp. 1–13. IEEE (2016)
14. Mouratidis, H., Argyropoulos, N., Shei, S.: Security requirements engineering for cloud computing: the Secure Tropos approach. In: Karagiannis, D., Mayr, H.C., Mylopoulos, J. (eds.) Domain-Specific Conceptual Modeling, Concepts, Methods and Tools, pp. 357–380. Springer, Cham (2016)
15. Mouratidis, H., Giorgini, P.: Secure tropos: a security-oriented extension of the tropos methodology. Int. J. Softw. Eng. Knowl. Eng. **17**(2), 285–309 (2007)
16. Mouratidis, H., Weiss, M., Giorgini, P.: Modeling secure systems using an agent-oriented approach and security patterns. Int. J. Softw. Eng. Knowl. Eng. **16**(03), 471–498 (2006)
17. Neubauer, T., Klemen, M., Biffl, S.: Secure business process management: a roadmap. In: 1st International Conference on Availability, Reliability and Security (ARES 2006), p. 8. IEEE (2006)
18. Object Management Group: Business Process Model Notation (BPMN) Version 2.0. Technical report (2011)
19. Rosado, D.G., Gutiérrez, C., Fernández-Medina, E., Piattini, M.: Security patterns and requirements for internet-based applications. Internet Res. **16**(5), 519–536 (2006)
20. Salnitri, M., Dalpiaz, F., Giorgini, P.: Designing secure business processes with SecBPMN. Softw. Syst. Model., 1–21 (2016)
21. Weske, M.: Business Process Management: Concepts, Languages, Architectures. Springer, Heidelberg (2010)
22. Yoshioka, N., Washizaki, H., Maruyama, K.: A survey on security patterns. Prog. Inform. **5**(5), 35–47 (2008)

# NFC-Based Task Enactment for Automatic Documentation of Treatment Processes

Florian Stertz[(⊠)], Juergen Mangler, and Stefanie Rinderle-Ma

Faculty of Computer Science, University of Vienna, Vienna, Austria
{florian.stertz,juergen.mangler,stefanie.rinderle-Ma}@univie.ac.at

**Abstract.** In nursing homes documentation is a mandatory yet time consuming task: typically, nurses document their work after performing the treatments at the end of their shifts which might lead to a decline in the quality of the documentation. The utilization of process-oriented technology in the care domain has already been shown to have high potential in support for documentation of treatment tasks. We want to further this idea, by transforming physical objects into smart objects through equipping them with NFC tags. They can then be used to automatically register their usage with NFC readers specific to care residents. Our analysis shows that many treatment tasks are using care utilities and are candidates for automatic task documentation. We present three scenarios for automatic documentation in nursing homes, an implementation through a proof-of-concept prototype, and an evaluation through expert interviews in the care domain. The interviews indicate an average decrease in documentation time per shift of more than 60%.

**Keywords:** Business process ecosystem · Transformative technologies · NFC · Automation · Care domain

## 1 Introduction

High quality documentation is not only a requirement by legislators, but also a much discussed topic for nurses in general [12]. Documenting every interaction with a patient, from administering drugs to cleaning patients to hydrating them, is very time-consuming and decreases the time spent with a patient. Additionally, the documentation is often conducted at the end of shifts, which leads to missing entries and even wrong entries as documentation is created from memory. Thus enhancing the documentation process is a top priority for nurses and care homes:

1. Continuous documentation: documentation steps should be conducted when a care activity is done, to not miss any details. This can include reminding the nurse that she should take audio notes.
2. Automatic documentation: for many steps, especially when a detailed care process is available for every patient, only its completion has to be documented, no further details are needed.

© Springer International Publishing AG 2017
I. Reinhartz-Berger et al. (Eds.): BPMDS/EMMSAD 2017, LNBIP 287, pp. 34–48, 2017.
DOI: 10.1007/978-3-319-59466-8_3

This paper elaborates the second aspect, the automatic documentation through monitoring physical objects. Automating the documentation of steps that require physical interaction leads to both (1) a reduction of time and effort for care takers, and (2) an improvement in documentation quality (as automatic documentation is always consistent and complete), without any downsides.

In order to understand the idea of automatic documentation support a typical care process is described in the following. Figure 1 depicts the morning routine of nurses (as delineated by international nursing guidelines [1] and national laws) and modeled in a process-oriented way (cf. [22]). It was interesting to learn that for each of the morning routine tasks a physical object was utilized such as a comb.

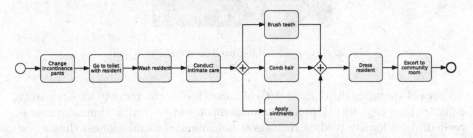

**Fig. 1.** Daily morning care routine (BPMN notation using signavio)

The following physical objects (denoted as *care utilities*) are used during morning routine:

- Change incontinence pants: Pants
- Go to toilet with resident: Toilet paper
- Wash resident: Washing cloth
- Conduct intimate care: Washing cloth
- Brush teeth: Toothbrush
- Comb hair: Hair brush
- Apply ointments: Ointment package

For task *Change incontinence pants*, e.g. *pants* are employed as care utility. Moreover, all these tasks are manual tasks conducted by the nurse and do not require extensive data input. Consequently, the documentation of these steps includes merely a confirmation that the task has been done, equipped with information on the patient, the actor (nurse), time when it was conducted, and possibly some limited data (e.g., dosage of a drug).

To accomplish a reduction of time committed for tasks involving the documentation of care activities, this paper outlines a way to document steps connected to physical objects automatically, without disturbing nurses or residents. In order to achieve this, each physical object has to provide information about it's existence (and potentially its state).

Several technologies were compared and it was decided to use *Near Field Communication (NFC)* due to reasons such as availability and security[1]. In detail, care utilities are equipped with NFC tags storing precise information about the care utility. Figure 2 shows a resident bed equipped with NFC reader in the lab at the Research Group Workflow Systems and Technology.

**Fig. 2.** NFC reader integrated into resident's bed

For not changing the daily routine of nurses too much, a way to unobtrusively register these tags with a process management system during care activities is needed. Additionally reading the tags is not intended to take longer than a few seconds and should happen right at the moment the care task is finished.

To realize this, we decided to build tag readers into the nursing home residents' beds. Every tag reader is connected to one specific resident. Every time the reader detects a tag, it tries[2] to find a matching active task in the residents treatment process, marks it as finished and documents the occurrence with a timestamp and the care utility. This can effectively reduce the time a nurse needs for the documentation of a resident and improve the quality of the documentation at the same time.

In order to achieve the results presented in this paper, we used the design science research methodology [24]. This paper is structured as follows: we start by presenting the scenarios for the solution design derived from literature in Sect. 2. Section 2 also presents the solution design itself. The evaluation of the solution is two-fold: Sect. 3 presents the implementation of the solution and explains technical design choices such as using NFC. In Sect. 4, the solution is evaluated with nurses from two nursing homes by analyzing their working processes, i.e., morning, lunch, and afternoon/evening routines. The initial solution has been designed and realized for the care domain, however, as discussed in Sect. 5 can be transferred to other application domains such as manufacturing and logistics. Related work is discussed in Sect. 6. Section 7 provides a summary and outlook to future work.

Overall, the results are promising. The evaluation indicates that automatic task enactment and documentation can be widely applied in the care domain.

---

[1] E.g. no accidental triggering due to low range.

[2] If no task is found, the activity for the resident is logged with a note that it was either an emergency or an error.

Moreover, based on the assessment of the experts, the documentation time per nurse can be decreased by more than 60% on average.

## 2  Solution Design

The solution design covers nine scenarios that are relevant for sensor-supported enactment in treatment processes. These scenarios are derived from interviews with experts in the care domain and IT experts and created following the guidelines of [20] and aim for an easy to integrate system. Particular focus is on the automation of documenting the tasks. Due to space restrictions, in the following, a selection of three scenarios will be presented. The entire set of scenarios can be found on http://cs.univie.ac.at/project/ants. Note that the scenarios are described for treatment processes, but can be easily adapted for other domains (see Sect. 5).

In order to connect a physical object to our system, we have to write information to a NFC tag connected to the object. Two types of objects are possible: *simple* and *complex*.

**Simple** care utilities just have function (like hair brushes, tissues) thus only their application or hand over is relevant. Thus only the ID of the care utility is relevant.

For **Complex** care utilities the NFC tag holds additional information, e.g., the dosage for utility drug (for example see Table 1). An example is the painkiller Parkemed which can be administered in dosages 250 mg and 500 mg. Dosage is a critical parameter in the context of care utilities due to the prevention of misuse. Table 1 can be generalized to other parameters. Nested information can be stored on a NFC tag as well, i.e., using containers. Containers also enable to store the information of more than one care utility on the NFC tag. The NFC tag writing of a container, can be done via a NFC tablet in the nurses room for example.

**Table 1.** Write utility information

| | |
|---|---|
| *primary actor* | care staff |
| *stakeholders and interests* | staff member (stakeholder 1) wants to connect a care utility to a specific NFC tag; resident (stakeholder 2) wants care with high quality |
| *preconditions* | utility type is complex; dosage needs to be specified (see *realization*) |
| *postconditions* | dosage is written on NFC tag with ID of care utility (see *realization*) |
| *realization* | 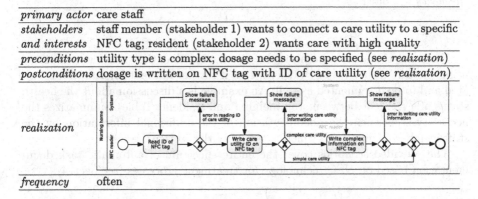 |
| *frequency* | often |

Table 2, *Give Utility to Resident* realizes the automatic documentation of a care task. The care utility carries a NFC tag which is placed on the NFC reading device of the resident. Doing so the connection between resident (specifying the treatment process instances) and care utility (specifying the care task) is made. The NFC reader decodes the information read from the NFC tag. The system automatically documents that the care task has been completed for the resident with all necessary information such as timestamp and possibly dosage. Looking at the morning care shown in Fig. 1 together with care utilities, the automatic documentation would be conducted, e.g., when the staff member hands the toothbrush to resident *Smith*. The system would then automatically document that task *Brush teeth* has been completed for process instance *Smith*.

**Table 2.** Give utility to resident

| | |
|---|---|
| *primary actor* | care staff |
| *stakeholders and interests* | staff member (stakeholder 1) wants automatic documentation of care utility given to resident; resident (stakeholder 2) wants care with high quality |
| *preconditions* | resident is ready to receive care utility; NFC reading device for resident is registered; NFC tag of care utility is registered and has necessary information stored (e.g., dosage) |
| *postconditions* | resident successfully receives care utility; this is documented automatically in the system (see *realization*) |
| *realization* | |
| *frequency* | often |

For some tasks the automatic documentation that the task was completed using the care utility is not sufficient, e.g., if further relevant information is created and to be documented as well. An example is a discussion about the health status of a resident between staff member and resident. Table 3 summarizes the necessary steps, i.e., the documentation of the additional information by the staff member using a form which is stored in the system.

The provided scenarios cover the entire spectrum of automatic task documentation based on NFC technology for treatment processes (see Sect. 4).

**Table 3.** Document further information

| | |
|---|---|
| *primary actor* | care staff |
| *stakeholders and interests* | staff member (stakeholder 1) wants to document further information, e.g., the health status of a resident; resident (stakeholder 2) wants care with high quality |
| *preconditions* | additional information cannot be stored on NFC tag |
| *postconditions* | additional information is (correctly) stored in database (see *realization*) |
| *realization* | 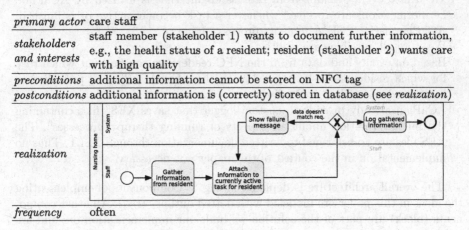 |
| *frequency* | often |

## 3  Implementation

In order to prove the viability of the solution design, a prototype implementation supporting the scenarios above was conducted. As mentioned above the implementation uses NFC as means to connect care utilities to the system (see rationale below). The implementation has the following properties:

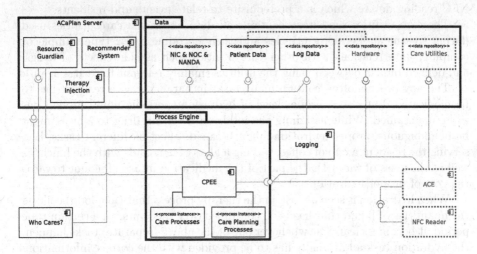

**Fig. 3.** System architecture, taken from [22]. The red dotted components are new components, developed in this work. (Color figure online)

- We extended an existing solution called Adaptive Care Planning (ACaPlan) [13] that realizes therapy processes for nursing homes. I.e. based on the list of residents stored in the system we store NFC readers for each residents.

- We utilize event streams from process engine that is utilized by ACaPlan: i.e. notifications are received whenever a task becomes active or is finished. ACaPlan uses CPEE[3] [16] as its process engine.
- We store all possible care utilities.
- Based on events and data from the NFC readers we can find out which task for which residents can be marked as finished. For ACaPlan all tasks had to be marked as finished manually.
- ACaPlan already provides a custom logger that saves XES[4] files containing the full information about all aspects of running therapy processes[5]. The XES files are transformed to written documentation through XSLT. Thus no implementation in the context of this paper was necessary.

The overall architecture is depicted in Fig. 3. Components or implementing the ideas in this paper are modeled with dotted outlines (red). All other components (black) are part of the solution we built our implementation on, and are explained in [13].

In the remainder of this section we will detail the components specific to them implementation in this paper. Furthermore we show how the components interact during the enactment of one of the above scenarios.

### 3.1   Contribution - Data Repositories: Hardware and Care Utilities

In the hardware repository, all residents are stored with the ID of the related NFC reading device which is a prerequisite to relate events and residents.

The care utilities repository contains all data about the care utilities used during treatment, i.e., care utilities and their encoding, their type (simple or complex), interrelations with other care utilities such as side effects of drugs, and defined breaks between using the utilities (mainly relevant for drugs again).

Therapy process often contain many tasks in parallel. E.g. a resident has to be medicated, but also a proper level of hydration (periodic liquid intake) has to be maintained. While assigning the intake of a certain drug to a task might be unambiguous, proper hydration might be a side effect of different tasks. E.g. serving the resident a cup of coffee, serving a glass of lemonade with the lunch, as well as the glass of water that is part of the medication intake all count towards the goal of proper hydration.

When hydration is seen as task in the therapy process that (in a loop) collects the quantities of liquid that has been consumed over the course of a certain time period, it becomes clear that whenever one of the above (separate) tasks happen, the hydration task additionally has to be provided with the correct information.

Thus the care utility repository does not merely contain a list of data, but a flexible ontology that contains all facts connected to a certain care utility. Thus

---

[3] http://cpee.org.

[4] http://www.xes-standard.org.

[5] Extensions to the format are utilized to store all information available in certain tasks.

it becomes possible to identify the correct hydration task from a multitude of care utility applications. All facts in the ontology are described as turtle triplets and can be queried through SPARQL [19].

## 3.2  Contribution: NFC Reader

Whenever a NFC reader sends information about a care utility, with the help of the repositories above the following information can be deducted:

- Which patient is affected and thus: which therapy process is affected?
- What additional information about this care utility is available?

## 3.3  Contribution: Automatic Care Enhancement (ACE)

ACE as the main component has the following functionalities:

- Collection of events from the process engine implementing the therapy processes. It knows all currently active tasks for all residents.
- Collection of events from the NFC readers. It knows all care utilities and the properties that have been used for each patient.
- Enactment on active tasks. ACE selects all tasks that are potentially affected by a care utility and supplies it with information found on the NFC tag and allows the process engine to finish this task. Alternatively it notifies the care taker that additional (manual) input is necessary. We envision that in future revisions of the system, care takers are prompted to record voice messages which are automatically assigned to the correct task.

## 3.4  Implementation of Scenario: Give Care Utility to Resident

As an example the implementation of Table 2 is provided[6]. In order to register the usage of a care utility, the NFC tag attached to the utility has to be moved near the NFC reader. Using a care utility can inhibit other utilities or suggest alternative ones. Inhibiting other utilities can become necessary in order to, for example, prevent undesired side effects between drugs. Suggesting other care utilities can be also important in the context of drugs, for example, if a gastric protection drug is suggested for accompanying another drug that is aggressive to the stomach. Finally, for complex care utilities information such as dosage and time interval (e.g., for administering drugs) have to be stored.

When the NFC tag is put close to the NFC reader of the resident, the NFC reader automatically scans the data of the NFC tag. The data of the NFC tag is then sent to a connected computer, running ACE. A local copy of the event will be stored and a matching active activity in the resident's process is searched. If the search is successful, the data of the NFC tag will be sent to the process

---

[6] A detailed description of further scenarios and more technical details can be found in [22].

engine, and the open event will be locally deleted on the ACE system. The activity is then marked finished in the process engine and the next task will be marked as active and the ACE system stores the new activity for future searches. The documentation is stored in XML files, containing timestamps of the events, the ID of a care utility with the described details, like inhibitors, suggestions and dosage. If the search fails, the event will be stored and put into the documentation with a warning. Note that for this prototype XML was used, because of the readability. For a real care home, a standard database approach is recommended, since XML parsing is usually slow.

### 3.5    Implementation Choice: NFC

NFC is one of the technologies for sending and receiving data wireless in close range. Alternative technologies would be Barcodes or RFID.

*Barcodes:* 1D barcodes store rather little information (13 digits) since usually additional information is then looked up in the database [14]. 2D barcodes, e.g., QR-Codes, can hold more information which can be decoded without accessing a database. Limitations of using barcodes are restricted usage ("line of sight" is needed), lack of reusability (barcodes are printed on the object), and that they cannot be edited. *Radio-frequency identification technology, RFID* [23] supports active and passive devices. Another advantage is that no "line of sight" is required. Moreover, RFID devices are cheap to produce, hence can be used at a large scale from an expenses point of view. *Near Field Communication, NFC* [2] is used in many applications and devices such as Smartphones, Debit cards, and tickets for public transportation. NFC builds upon the RFID technology [2] and communicates on a very short range below 10 cm. NFC can work with an active device, the NFC reader, and a passive object, like a tag or card. The reader can write and read information of the object. A big difference to RFID is the range. A RFID reader can create a larger electromagnetic field to automatically detect different objects going through it. Since the communication range of the NFC reader is quite low in comparison, there will not be any unwanted detection of different tags entering a room, which would create a flawed documentation. NFC tags are cheap to produce, very thin, and can be attached to any surface, like stickers. In conclusion, NFC was chosen because of three advantages:

1. *Ubiquitous availability:* NFC capable devices can be found everywhere nowadays. Smartphones, Toys, table computers and even watches. This allows for an approach which is feasible to acquire and relatively easy to learn, since the devices are used in everyday lives.
2. *Better security:* Since the distance to communicate is only about a few centimeters, it is safer to use than RFID. The short range does increase the level of difficulty to create unwanted detections and or malfunctioned detections.
3. *No unwanted detection:* Another advantage of the close communication range of the NFC technology is the elimination of unwanted tag detection. In a room of a resident are many care utilities. RFID creates a large field, where every

tag will be detected. This is very useful for warehouses, but in the nursing home we only want to detect the right NFC tag at the right time. The short communication range allows only one tag to be detected if it is right in front of the NFC reading device, thus allowing for a correct documentation.

For communicating with the NFC reader[7], a binary communication protocol is available, which was utilized in a C library, and made available in a high level language as open source[8].

# 4  Evaluation

The evaluation is based on two expert interviews with nurses from two different nursing homes. The nurses where asked, for each shift and for each task, how much time could be saved with the solution presented in this paper, taking into account that some tasks need additional information (i.e. comments by the nurses) that can not be automatically acquired. Thus the nurses, for each shift and each task, provided the following information:

- Potential physical objects and how practical it would be to use them for automatic logging.
- Current documentation effort, and estimated savings with the solution presented in this paper.

The overall savings (Table 4), as expected by the experts are rather encouraging: the total **expected saving** are about 60%.

**Table 4.** Possible improvements through automatic documentation

| Task | Morning | | Evening & Night | | |
|------|---------|---|-----------------|---|---|
| Residents | 14 | | 70 | | |
| Tasks per resident | 12 | | 3–6 (4.5 avg.) | | |
| Tasks total | 168 | | 370 | | |
| Worktime (nurses) | 540 min | | 420 min | | |
| Worktime per task | 03:12 min | | 01:06 min | | |
| Nurses | 2 | | 1 | | |
| Documentation | Manual | Automatic | Manual | Automatic | Improvement |
| Per resident | 07:30 min | 02:00 min | 03:00 min | 01:10 min | 68.00% |
| Per nurse | 52:30 min | 14:00 min | 210:00 min | 90:50 min | 64.87% |
| Average per task | 00:38 min | 00:10 min | 00:40 min | 00:10 min | 74.34% |

The daily routines can be divided in morning routine, lunch, and afternoon & evening routine. Lunch mainly consists of two tasks, i.e., assist residents with

---

[7] http://www.kronegger.com/.
[8] https://rubygems.org/gems/nfclib.

intake and give drugs. For the intake a form has to be filled manually for documentation. Support for this documentation task has been outside the scope of this work so far. Giving drugs is supported by the system.

The time for using an physical care object is determined by three aspects:

- How long is the physical object used for the care purpose?
- How long does it take to bring the physical object next to a NFC reader (integrated into the bed)?
- How long has the physical object to remain next to a NFC reader, in order for the data to be read out?

While the duration of the first aspect is fixed, the two other aspects replace the manual documentation. They are assumed to take about 10 s in total per task[9].

## 4.1   Morning Routine

The process model for the morning routine is depicted in Fig. 1 together with the assigned care utilities. One nurse is typically responsible for 14 residents. The morning shift for a nurse starts at 7:30 am and he/she has to conduct the morning routine all by himself/herself within 2 h. Afterwards a second nurse joins. The tasks for the residents are split evenly. The residents have different levels of care, i.e., are able to conduct a varying number of tasks in the morning routine themselves. Even though the independence of the residents is to be preserved as much as possible, each of the tasks has to be documented by the nurse. This results in a higher amount of time for residents with a low level of care. As there is a substantial time pressure to finish the morning routine for all residents before breakfast, often the documentation of the morning routine is postponed to the end of the shift from noon to 13:00 pm. This constitutes a risk of lowering the documentation quality (e.g., by forgetting tasks).

*Assessment:* 12 tasks have to be performed for 14 residents resulting in 168 tasks altogether. The average time per task is 03:12 min. The manual documentation time has been estimated as 07:30 min per resident, 52:30 min per nurse, and 00:38 min per task.

## 4.2   Evening and Night Routine

Figure 4 depicts the evening and night routine. For this shift a nurse is typically responsible for about 70 residents. During the night, additionally, a graduate nurse is present for emergency cases. The night shift runs from 8 pm to 7:30 am the next day. After handover of shift the general health status and clothes are checked. Repeating tasks of the night routine are changing incontinence pants and bed positions of the residents in order to avoid bedsore, typically performed

---

[9] It took about 2 s in tests with nurses, but we conservatively estimated 10 s to account for delays due to sloppy usage.

every 2 to 3 h. In quieter periods in between documentation is performed. In case of emergencies the nurse prepares the associated documents and calls the ambulance if necessary.

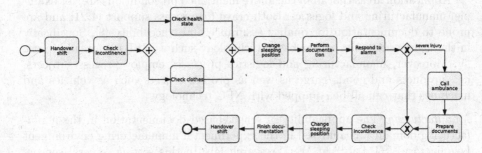

**Fig. 4.** Process model for afternoon/evening routine

Though the nurse is responsible for more residents the tasks are less intense and frequent. The shift handover takes about 30 min. On average, 370 tasks are performed by one nurse per night, taking 420 min of the shift. 210 min. are left for documentation, resulting in an average documentation time of approx. 40 s per tasks. The experts were positive, that except for the health status check, all tasks contained in the process model in Fig. 4 can be documented automatically. Again tests revealed a time of 10 s per task for automatic documentation under pessimistic assumptions. The documentation time per nurse will be reduced from 210 min to 90:50 min.

This means a reduction of 74.34% of time per documentation task, 68% per resident and 64.87% per nurse on average for both shifts. It should also be noted, that in this approach, the identity of the nurse fulfilling a task gets drawn out of the shift schedule. An adaption could be NFC tags placed on the clothes of a nurse as identifier.

## 5 Transferability to Other Domains

The evaluation indicates a high potential for sensor-based automatic task documentation for treatment processes. What are the preconditions for an application to benefit from automatic sensor-based task enactment and documentation?

1. Process-oriented solution
2. Need for documentation
3. Process subjects and/or objects can be equipped with NFC tags and connected to NFC reading devices. Process subject [9] denotes the person or item that denominates the process instance, e.g., the resident or the product. Process objects describe in a broader sense data that is processed during process execution as well as physical objects that are utilized for conducting process tasks such as a vehicle, a comb, or an employee card.

4. Currently, only a restricted amount of data input can be processed through NFC technology, e.g., dosage. For future applications., extended solutions connecting automatic documentation with data input are conceivable as well.

Application areas that fulfil the above mentioned preconditions are, for example, manufacturing and logistics. Both crave for process support [4, 21] and are prone to documentation for quality assurance and traceability [8]. Specifically in the logistics domain, sensor-based technology such as RFID is already in use [5]. Moreover, manufacturing and logistics processes employ process subjects, i.e., products and goods/cargo as well as process objects such as vehicles and machines that can all be equipped with NFC technology.

*Manufacturing:* The applicability of sensor-based documentation in the manufacturing domain was analysed in the experimental manufacturing environment LegoFactoryWST Lab[10] at WST research lab. In this setting, several sensors are integrated and utilized anyway. Here the product is the driving factor for the process execution, i.e., the product is to be equipped with a NFC tag and the different machines with readers in order to document automatically that a product has passed a certain machine.

*Logistics:* Similar to the manufacturing domain, the goods are the process subjects are drive the process execution. Hence, for logistics as already done in practice, goods can be equipped with NFC tags and the utilities for transportation, e.g., the truck, equipped with the readers. This would not only facilitate documentation, but also foster the traceability of the goods on the transport. An interesting question is whether single goods are equipped with NFC tags each or cargo, i.e., bundles of goods. This becomes particularly important for bundling and unbundling of cargo.

## 6   Related Work

AdaptFlow [7] enables the dynamic adaptation of medical processes, specifically to deal with exceptional situations. AGENTWORK [17] is similar in that it provides adaptive process technology equipped with reactive and predictive strategies for exceptional situations based on planning. OzCare [15] also deals with flexible support of treatment processes based on a declarative description of the processes. AdaptFlow, AGENTWORK, and OzCare do not support sensor-based task enactment and documentation.

Poulymenopoulou et al. [18] also focuses on emergency care, in particular on supporting the interaction between emergency services and hospitals. The standard exchange format used is CDA [6] employing a RESTful service orchestration. The latter is similar to ACAPLAN and ACE, however, no attention is paid to the automatic task enactment and documentation.

The approach presented by Anju et al. [3] aims at improving the medical documentation. The main application focus in on intensive care units (ICU)

---

[10] http://gruppe.wst.univie.ac.at/projects/LegoIndustry/index.php?t=project.

where time management is crucial. Hence, this approach assumes manual data input and provides information management on PCs and tables used in the ICU based on apps. These are two major differences to the work at hand, i.e., automatic versus manual data input and web services versus apps.

Horsky [11] deals with computerized assistance for emergency facilities based on recommendations for process models. Specifically, it enables the usage of RFID tags in order to update patient records automatically. The work at hand advocates to use NFC instead of RFID due to reasons such as security and minimal invasiveness furthering the acceptance of end users. Gunter [10] also employs Bluetooth and WiFi as well as RFID for identifying patients and updating patient data, more precisely their electronic health records (EHR). The distinction to the work at hand is that this work does not only enable updates of measures for the patient, but documentation of entire tasks as well as opting for NFC instead of RFID for the above stated reasons.

# 7   Conclusion and Outlook

The sensor-based enactment and documentation of care process tasks constitutes a crucial edge for nursing homes by relieving the staff and providing a constant quality of the documentation. The paper has shown the potential of automatic documentation for a large share of routine tasks. The solution has been presented in its design and implementation. The results are very promising, i.e., more than 60% of documentation time per task could be saved as indicated by interviews with nurses. Moreover, the potential of automatic task enactment and documentation is interesting for other domains as well. The transferability has been discussed for manufacturing and logistics.

In future work, sensor-based task enactment and documentation will be applied to the manufacturing test lab setting for investigating and furthering the application in another domain. It will be also investigated how the sensor-based documentation can be utilized for purposes such as compliance checks.

# References

1. Implementation of NANDA nursing diagnose... [Comput. nurs. 1998 Nov-Dec] - PubMed - NCBI. http://www.ncbi.nlm.nih.gov/pubmed/9844258
2. Agrawal, P., Bhuraria, S.: Near field communication. SETLabs Bridfings **10**(1), 67–74 (2012)
3. Anju, K., Mathew, A., Antony, J., Joy, S., Vijayan, B., Santhoshkumar, G.: Business process reengineering of the workflows in intensive care unit supported with a tablet pc based automation system. In: Advances in Computing and Communications, pp. 265–268 (2013)
4. Baumgrass, A., Cabanillas, C., Di Ciccio, C.: A conceptual architecture for an event-based information aggregation engine in smart logistics. In: Enterprise Modelling and Information Systems Architectures, pp. 109–123 (2015)
5. Chow, H.K., Choy, K., Lee, W.: A dynamic logistics process knowledge-based system an RFID multi-agent approach. Knowl.-Based Syst. **20**(4), 357–372 (2007)

6. Dolin, R.H., Alschuler, L., Beebe, C., Biron, P.V., Boyer, S.L., Essin, D., Kimber, E., Lincoln, T., Mattison, J.E.: The hl7 clinical document architecture. J. Am. Med. Inform. Assoc. **8**(6), 552–569 (2001)
7. Greiner, U., Ramsch, J., Heller, B., Loffler, M., Muller, R., Rahm, E.: Adaptive guideline-based treatment workflows with AdaptFlow. Studies in health technology and informatics, pp. 113–117 (2004)
8. Grob, K., Stocker, J., Colwell, R.: Assurance of compliance within the production chain of food contact materials by good manufacturing practice and documentation part 1: legal background in Europe and compliance challenges. Food Control **20**(5), 476–482 (2009)
9. Grossmann, W., Rinderle-Ma, S.: Fundamentals of Business Intelligence. Data-Centric Systems and Applications. Springer, Heidelberg (2015)
10. Gunter, E.L., Yasmeen, A., Gunter, C., Nguyen, A., et al.: Specifying and analyzing workflows for automated identification and data capture. In: Hawaii International Conference on System Sciences, pp. 1–11 (2009)
11. Horsky, J., Gutnik, L., Patel, V.L.: Technology for emergency care: cognitive and workflow considerations. In: AMIA Annual Symposium Proceedings, vol. 2006, p. 344 (2006)
12. Jefferies, D., Johnson, M., Griffiths, R.: A meta-study of the essentials of quality nursing documentation. Int. J. Nurs. Pract. **16**, 112–124 (2010)
13. Kaes, G., Mangler, J., Stertz, F., Vigne, R., Rinderle-Ma, S.: ACaPlan - adaptive care planning. In: BPM Demo, pp. 11–15 (2015)
14. Kato, H., Tan, K.: 2D barcodes for mobile phones. In: 2nd International Conference on Mobile Technology, Applications and Systems, p. 8 (2005)
15. Lee, W., Kaiser, G.E., Clayton, P.D., Sherman, E.H.: OzCare: a workflow automation system for care plans. In: AMIA Annual Fall Symposium, p. 577 (1996)
16. Mangler, J., Rinderle-Ma, S.: CPEE - cloud process execution engine. In: International Conference on Business Process Management (2014). CEUR-WS.org
17. Müller, R., Greiner, U., Rahm, E.: AgentWork: a workflow system supporting rule-based workflow adaptation. Data Knowl. Eng. **51**(2), 223–256 (2004)
18. Poulymenopoulou, M., Malamateniou, F., Vassilacopoulos, G.: Emergency healthcare process automation using mobile computing and cloud services. J. Med. Syst. **36**(5), 3233–3241 (2012)
19. Prud'Hommeaux, E., Seaborne, A., et al.: SPARQL query language for RDF. W3C recommendation 15 (2008)
20. Robertson, S., Robertson, J.: Mastering the requirements process: getting requirements right. Addison-wesley (2012)
21. Schulte, S., Schuller, D., Steinmetz, R., Abels, S.: Plug-and-play virtual factories. IEEE Internet Comput. **16**(5), 78–82 (2012)
22. Stertz, F.: Sensor supported automatic workflow enactment for treatment processes. Master's thesis, Medical University of Vienna (2016)
23. Want, R.: An introduction to RFID technology. Pervasive Comput. **5**, 25–33 (2006)
24. Wieringa, R.: Design Science Methodology for Information Systems and Software Engineering. Springer, Heidelberg (2015)

# New Challenges in Business Process Modeling and Support

# Discovering Social Networks Instantly: Moving Process Mining Computations to the Database and Data Entry Time

Alifah Syamsiyah[✉], Boudewijn F. van Dongen, and Wil M.P. van der Aalst

Eindhoven University of Technology, Eindhoven, Netherlands
{A.Syamsiyah,B.F.v.Dongen,W.M.P.v.d.Aalst}@tue.nl

**Abstract.** Process mining aims to turn event data into insights and actions in order to improve processes. To improve process performance it is crucial to get insights into the way people work and collaborate. In this paper, we focus on discovering social networks from event data. To be able to deal with large data sets or with an environment which requires repetitive discoveries during the analysis, and still provide results instantly, we use an approach where most of the computation is moved to the database and things are precomputed at data entry time. Differently from traditional process mining where event data is stored in file-based system, we store event data in relational databases. Moreover, the database also has a role as an engine to compute the intermediate structure of social network during insertion data. By moving computation both in location (to database) and time (to recording time), the discovery of social networks in a process context becomes truly scalable. The approach has been implemented using the open source process mining toolkit ProM. The experiments reported in this paper demonstrate scalability while providing results instantly.

**Keywords:** Social network · Process mining · Relational database · Repetitive discovery

## 1 Introduction

Consider the following example: a production process in a company is conducted by several branches. Each branch has a dedicated group of responsible resources, and a resource may collaborate with other resources from the other branch. Based on the report from company's business analysts, some branches are well-performing, but in some other branches there may be performance problems. In order to solve this problem, the production manager needs information about resource performance in problematic batches; how each resource collaborates with others, how they maintain collaboration with good branches, whether there are under-utilized resources, etc. These questions can be addressed by social network analysis in a process mining context.

Suppose that the production manager instructs the company's business analysts to give a report in each month for checking the progress since the beginning

© Springer International Publishing AG 2017
I. Reinhartz-Berger et al. (Eds.): BPMDS/EMMSAD 2017, LNBIP 287, pp. 51–67, 2017.
DOI: 10.1007/978-3-319-59466-8_4

of the year. In this case, the business analysts need to repeatedly look at results based on event logs that grow over time. For the report in January, they look at results based on logs recorded in January. For the report in February, they analyze results based on logs in January plus February, and so on.

Process mining is a research discipline where the aim is to improve organization's process given the information from the so called *event logs*. The application of social network analysis in process mining was firstly studied in [16,17]. The combination of these two research disciplines has proven to be valuable: novel insights in business processes performance can be obtained by combining both.

In traditional process mining, we import an event log when we want to perform an analysis and need to do an end-to-end computation at analysis time. This approach suffers from two main problems. First of all, we need to load all event data into main memory to do the computation. For larger event logs the data needs to be partitioned to perform the computation. Second, the computation may be very time consuming. Hence, it may take some time to get results if all of this is done on-demand. Third, in an environment where some repetitive discoveries are required, as illustrated in the example, unnecessary reloading and mining the prior data must be performed.

In this paper, we propose a solution to tackle these problems using mature and established relational database technology. We first move event data to a relational database, define a notion of *intermediate structures* in social networks, pre-compute the intermediate structure inside the database, and set up a connection between the database and process mining tools. By this technique, we easily pass the intermediate structures to existing social network algorithms. The algorithms will run normally and not be aware that the intermediate structures are retrieved from the database. They run even faster because some computations have been already done inside the database. Furthermore, the intermediate structures are always kept alive, i.e., they are always updated when a new data is inserted, hence this technique is well-applied for the needs of repetitive discovery for event data that grows over time.

While many discovery techniques can be identified, this paper focuses on the social network analysis particularly the *handover of work network*. In handover of work network, we analyze how a task is passed over from one resource to the other in the context of a process instance. From the handover of work metric we can get insights into how job allocation is done, whether a resource is always busy compared to others, or whether unnecessary handovers of work happen. In spite of that, the work trivially extends to other types of social networks as long as we can identify an intermediate structure used by the technique which can be updated when inserting new events into the database.

This paper is organized as follows. In Sect. 2, we present some related work. In Sect. 3, we give general overview of process mining and the computation of handover of work network. Then, in Sect. 4, we explain how to enable social network discovery in database. In Sect. 5 we introduce the step-by-step to mine social networks instantly. We explain the implementation and experimental results in Sects. 6 and 7 respectively. Finally, Sect. 8 concludes the paper.

## 2   Related Work

How social network analysis and process mining can be combined was first shown in [17]. This work gave a foundation of social network metrics in the context of process mining. Based on a log data consisting resource information, one can mine organizational perspective using notions such as handover of work, working together, and subcontracting. As an extension of this work, the authors presented concrete metrics and demonstrated them using a case study in [16].

Visualizing social networks, especially with huge volume of data, is a challenging task. The work in [9] supports social network analysis using chord diagram where nodes are represented by arcs and chords represent interactions among nodes. Each element is defined formally and the results showed that this approach can support investigation of new insights from the social network better than the traditional approach.

To deal with large event logs, the work in [19] presented a streaming-based framework that defines online cooperative network discovery in a generic way. It considers the organizational perspective using real time, online, and, infinite event streams. Stream representation of event logs has also been adapted in [1]. The method uses time-based window model in a finite streams of events. It first transforms the event log into a finite stream of events, then it divides the stream into windows.

Differently from streaming-based technique, the work in [5] employed a hierarchical clustering to deal with large event logs. By clustering the users and considering the working together metric, it discovers a community structure in social networks.

A study in [10] examined multiple online social network at a big data scale. It studied the structural perspective of social network. The data showed that social networks are structurally different from the web network. Social networks have a much higher fraction of symmetric links and also exhibit much higher levels of local clustering.

Social network analysis based on Hadoop was investigated in [20]. This work introduced a framework called big cloud-parallel data mining but only focused on huge scale telecom data. Moreover, social network analysis based on the MapReduce framework was investigated in [14]. However, this work only discussed about social influences in social network analysis.

The use of relational databases in process mining has been investigated earlier. For example, the ontology-based approach in [4] provides on-demand access to the data in the database using query unfolding and rewriting techniques in Ontology-based Data Access [3,11]. Furthermore, RXES presented in [18] introduced the relational representation of XES.

Building on top of RXES, the work in [12] introduced an approach to discover resource assignment constraints by means of SQL queries. The queries can be customized in order to analyze the interplay of different perspectives, specifically to discover the influence of resources on the control flow of the process. However, this technique does not handle live event data, the focus is on static data that has been imported in a database.

As an improved version of RXES, DB-XES was introduced in [13]. DB-XES defined a basic schema which resembles the standard structure of event data, i.e., the XES standard [8]. To enable a specific family of discovery techniques, this basic schema was extended with directly follows relations (DFR). Moreover it introduced a technique to precompute the DFR inside DB-XES. Using experiments on real-life data, it was shown that storing event data and DFR in DB-XES not only leads to a significant reduction in memory use of the process mining tool, but can even speed up the analysis of process discovery. However, this technique is limited to the control flow perspective only.

To the best of our knowledge, this is the first work that considers the organizational perspective in process mining while moving computation to the database and recording time such that it is able to discover social networks instantly.

## 3 Preliminaries

### 3.1 Process Mining

Process mining is a research discipline that sits between machine learning and data mining on the one hand and process modeling and analysis on the other hand. The goal of process mining is to turn event data into insights and actions in order to improve processes. Three main tasks in process mining are *process discovery, conformance checking,* and *enhancement* [15].

Process mining requires an *event log*, i.e., a set of *traces* of *events*, as the input. Each event has properties called *event attributes*, such as *timestamp* when the event is executed, *activity name* which represents the task name, and *resource* who conduct the event. In this paper, we focus on two particular relations between events, namely the *Directly Follows Relation (DFR)* and the *Causality Relation (CR)*. DFR is a pair of two consecutive events happened in a trace, and CR is a pair of events $(x, y)$ where $x$ is sometimes directly followed by $y$ but $y$ is never followed by $x$. Formally, they are defined as follows.

**Definition 1 (Event Log).** *Let $E$ be a set of events. An event log $L \subseteq E^*$ is a set of event sequences (called traces) such that each event appears precisely once in precisely one trace.*

**Definition 2 (Event Attributes).** *Let $E$ be a set of events and let $X$ be a set of attribute names. For any event $e \in E$ and name $x \in X$: $\#_x(e)$ is the value of attribute $x$ for event $e$, $\#_x(e) = \bot$ if there is no value. {activity, resource, timestamp} $\in X$ are standard event attributes, such that:*

- *$\#_{activity}(e)$ is the activity name of event $e$.*
- *$\#_{resource}(e)$ is the resource who executes event $e$.*
- *$\#_{timestamp}(e)$ is the timestamp when event $e$ is executed.*

Note that each event is unique and appears only once in the event log. There may be many event sequences that follow the same sequence of activities. However, these are all distinguishable and events in these sequences may have different timestamps, resources, etc.

**Definition 3 (Directly Follows Relation).** *Let $L \subseteq E^*$ be an event log. $x$ is directly followed by $y$, denoted $x >_L y$, if and only if there is a trace $\sigma = \langle e_1, e_2, ..., e_n \rangle \in L$ and $1 \le i < n$ such that $\#_{activity}(e_i) = x$ and $\#_{activity}(e_{i+1}) = y$.*

**Definition 4 (Causality Relation).** *$x$ is in causality relation with $y$, denoted $x \to_L y$, if and only if $y$ sometimes directly follows $x$ but never the other way around, i.e., $x >_L y$ and $y \not>_L x$.*

## 3.2   Social Network Analysis

Social network analysis is an approach for investigating social structures where the context of the social actor, or the relationships between actors are considered [6]. Social networks are applicable to a wide range of substantive domains, ranging from the analysis of concepts within mental models to the study of war between nations. Network methods can also be applied to intrapersonal networks, as well as developmental phenomena such as the structure of individual life histories [2].

In process mining context, social network analysis is harnessed to mine organizational relation. Resource utilization, performance issues, and hierarchical structure within an organization are some examples of the social network usage in process mining. In this context, we derive social networks from the information in the event log. In the following we list some examples of social network analysis in process mining [16]:

- *Subcontracting.* The main idea is to count the number of times individual $r_2$ executed an activity in-between two activities executed by individual $r_1$. This may indicate that work was subcontracted from $r_1$ to $r_2$.
- *Working-together.* Working-together metric counts how often two resources are working together in the same case. For example, resource $r_1$ and $r_2$ work together in twenty cases, while $r_1$ and $r_3$ only work together in two cases. In this example, the relation between $r_1$ and $r_2$ is stronger than $r_1$ with $r_3$.
- *Reassignment.* Reassignment metric measures how often a resource $r_1$ reassigns the work to another resource $r_2$. This arises if there is reassign status in the lifecycle extension (one of the standard extension in [8]) stated in the log. This metric provides insight about hierarchical relation of an organization. If $r_1$ frequently delegates work to $r_2$ but not vice versa, it is likely that $r_1$ is in a higher hierarchy than $r_2$.

## 3.3   Handover of Work

Handover of work is one of the social network analysis. Within a trace (i.e., process instance), there is handover of work from individual $r_1$ to individual $r_2$ if there are two subsequent activities where the first is completed by $r_1$ and the second by $r_2$. In [16], there are three kinds of refinement applied to handover of work metrics. First of all, one can differentiate with respect to the degree of causality, e.g., the length of handover. It means that we can consider not only direct succession but also indirect succession. Second, we can ignore multiple transfers within one process instance or not. Third, we can consider arbitrary transfers of work or only consider those where there is a causal dependency.

In this paper we focus on causality relations with degree one, i.e., the directly follows relation. We differentiate the metrics into four categories: (1) *absolute handover of work*, is the basic metric where arbitrary transfers of work with length one are considered, (2) *boolean handover of work*, is the metric for arbitrary transfers of work and ignores multiple transfers within one trace, (3) *absolute causal handover of work*, is similar to (1) but takes into account the causality relation, and (4) *boolean causal handover of work*, is similar to (2) but plus causality.

Suppose we have log $L = \{\langle a_{Alif},\ b_{Berli},\ c_{Charlie},\ d_{Dania},\ e_{Eliaz}\rangle, \langle a_{Alif},$ $b_{Berli},\ d_{Dania},\ c_{Charlie},\ e_{Eliaz}\rangle\}$, with $x_y$ denotes that an activity $x$ is executed by a resource $y$. Based on this log, we mine four types of handover of work as depicted in Fig. 1. The figure shows that the structure of absolute and boolean handover of work is the same, however later we will see that the handover values in the two networks are different. Moreover, the difference between non-causal (Fig. 1a) and causal (Fig. 1b) handover of work is in the edges between *Charlie* and *Dania*. Handover of work which takes into account the causality relation does not have those edges since activity $c$ and $d$ are not in causality relation.

(a) Absolute/boolean handover of work     (b) Absolute/boolean causal handover of work

**Fig. 1.** Handover of work networks for log $L$

Formally, the four categories of handover of work are formalized as follows [16].

**Definition 5** ($\triangleright, \trianglerighteq$)**.** *Let $L \subseteq E^*$ be a log, $A$ be a set of attributes and $R = \{r \mid \exists_{\sigma \in L}\ \exists_{e \in \sigma}\ r = \#_{resource}(e)\}$ be a set of resources. For $a_1, a_2 \in A, r_1, r_2 \in R,$ and $\sigma = \langle e_1, e_2, ..., e_n\rangle \in L$:*

- $r_1 \triangleright_\sigma r_2 = \exists_{1 \leq i < |\sigma|}\ \#_{resource}(e_i) = r_1 \wedge \#_{resource}(e_{i+1}) = r_2$

- $|r_1 \triangleright_\sigma r_2| = \sum_{1 \leq i < |\sigma|} \begin{cases} 1, & if \#_{resource}(e_i) = r_1 \wedge \#_{resource}(e_{i+1}) = r_2 \\ 0, & otherwise \end{cases}$

- $r_1 \trianglerighteq_\sigma r_2 = \exists_{1 \leq i < |\sigma|}\ \#_{resource}(e_i) = r_1 \wedge \#_{resource}(e_{i+1}) = r_2 \wedge$
  $\qquad\qquad \#_{activity}(e_i) \rightarrow_L \#_{activity}(e_{i+1})$

- $|r_1 \trianglerighteq_\sigma r_2| = \sum_{1 \leq i < |\sigma|} \begin{cases} 1, & if \#_{resource}(e_i) = r_1 \wedge \#_{resource}(e_{i+1}) = r_2 \wedge \\ & \#_{activity}(e_i) \rightarrow_L \#_{activity}(e_{i+1}) \\ 0, & otherwise \end{cases}$

**Definition 6 (Handover of Work Metrics).** *Let $L$ be a log and $R$ be a set of resources. For $r_1, r_2 \in R$, we define:*

- $r_1 \triangleright_L r_2 = \left( \sum_{\sigma \in L} |r_1 \triangleright_\sigma r_2| \right) \Big/ \left( \sum_{\sigma \in L} (|\sigma| - 1) \right)$
  *as Absolute Handover of Work.*
- $r_1 \triangleright'_L r_2 = \left( \sum_{\sigma \in L \,\wedge\, r_1 \triangleright_\sigma r_2} 1 \right) \Big/ \left( \sum_{\sigma \in L} 1 \right)$
  *as Boolean Handover of Work.*
- $r_1 \trianglerighteq_L r_2 = \left( \sum_{\sigma \in L} |r_1 \trianglerighteq_\sigma r_2| \right) \Big/ \left( \sum_{\sigma \in L} (|\sigma| - 1) \right)$
  *as Absolute Causal Handover of Work.*
- $r_1 \trianglerighteq'_L r_2 = \left( \sum_{\sigma \in L \,\wedge\, r_1 \trianglerighteq_\sigma r_2} 1 \right) \Big/ \left( \sum_{\sigma \in L} 1 \right)$
  *as Boolean Causal Handover of Work.*

If we apply log $L$ from the previous example to the metrics above, we get the following handover values: *Charlie* $\triangleright_L$ *Dania* $= \frac{1}{8}$, *Charlie* $\triangleright'_L$ *Dania* $= \frac{1}{2}$, *Charlie* $\trianglerighteq_L$ *Dania* $= 0$, and *Charlie* $\trianglerighteq'_L$ *Dania* $= 0$.

## 4 Enabling Social Network Discovery in Database

As mentioned before, process mining needs the so-called input *event log*. This log is a file-based system and imported to process mining tools every time we do process mining analysis. Existing process mining techniques can handle event log that fits into computer's memory fast. However, the process becomes slower when the log size exceeds the memory since swapping to disk needs to be performed. It becomes more challenging for repetitive discovery where we need to repeatedly mine event data that grows over time.

In this paper, we utilize relational database technology to enable social network discovery. The database is used both for storing event data and computing social network metrics. We choose database technology as the data storage since it is persistent and we can always retrieve back the data when needed. Furthermore, the metrics computed inside the database are designed to be aware of new addition in data, hence there is no need to reload the data as in the case of traditional repetitive discovery. Aside from database, any other persistent storages such as Hadoop and Google File System could also be exploited.

We use a database schema called *DB-XES* as presented in [13]. On top of this schema, we add handover of work tables for each type of the metrics introduced in Definition 6, namely tables *Absolute_HoW*, *Boolean_HoW*, *Absolute_Causal_HoW*, and *Boolean_Causal_HoW*. With these tables, we enable social network discovery through DB-XES. Formally, the handover of work tables are defined as follows.

**Definition 7 (Handover of Work Tables).** *Let $L \subseteq E^*$ be an event log, $N = \{n \mid \exists_{\sigma \in L} \, \exists_{e \in \sigma} \, n = \#_{activity}(e)\}$ is the set of activity names, and $R = \{r \mid \exists_{\sigma \in L} \, \exists_{e \in \sigma} \, r = \#_{resource}(e)\}$ is the set of resources. We define:*

- $\#_{activity}(e) >_L \#_{activity}(e')$ *if and only if*
  $\exists_{\langle e_1,...,e_n \rangle \in L} \exists_{1 \leq i < n}\ e = e_i \ \wedge\ e' = e_{i+1}$
- $f(r_1, r_2, e_1, e_2) := r_1 = \#_{resource}(e_1) \ \wedge\ r_2 = \#_{resource}(e_2) \ \wedge$
  $\#_{activity}(e_1) >_L \#_{activity}(e_2)$
- $g(n_1, n_2, r_1, r_2, e_1, e_2) := n_1 = \#_{activity}(e_1) \ \wedge\ n_2 = \#_{activity}(e_2) \ \wedge$
  $r_1 = \#_{resource}(e_1) \ \wedge\ r_2 = \#_{resource}(e_2) \ \wedge$
  $\#_{activity}(e_1) >_L \#_{activity}(e_2)$
- Absolute_HoW $\in R \times R \nrightarrow \mathbb{N}$ *where:*
  - $dom(\text{Absolute\_HoW}) = \{(r_1, r_2) \in R \times R \mid \exists_{e_1, e_2}\ f(r_1, r_2, e_1, e_2)\}$
  - Absolute_HoW$(r_1, r_2) =$
    $\sum_{\langle e_1,...,e_n \rangle \in L} |\{i \in \{1, ..., n-1\} \mid f(r_1, r_2, e_i, e_{i+1})\}|$
- Boolean_HoW $\in R \times R \nrightarrow \mathbb{N}$ *where:*
  - $dom(\text{Boolean\_HoW}) = \{(r_1, r_2) \in R \times R \mid \exists_{e_1, e_2}\ f(r_1, r_2, e_1, e_2)\}$
  - Boolean_HoW$(r_1, r_2) = |\{\langle e_1, ..., e_n \rangle \in L \mid \exists_{1 \leq i < n}\ f(r_1, r_2, e_i, e_{i+1})\}|$
- Absolute_Causal_HoW $\in N \times N \times R \times R \nrightarrow \mathbb{N}$ *where:*
  - $dom(\text{Absolute\_Causal\_HoW}) =$
    $\{(n_1, n_2, r_1, r_2) \in N \times N \times R \times R \mid \exists_{e_1, e_2}\ g(n_1, n_2, r_1, r_2, e_1, e_2)\}$
  - Absolute_Causal_HoW$(n_1, n_2, r_1, r_2) =$
    $\sum_{\langle e_1,...,e_n \rangle \in L} |\{i \in \{1, ..., n-1\} \mid g(n_1, n_2, r_1, r_2, e_i, e_{i+1})\}|$
- Boolean_Causal_HoW $\in N \times N \times R \times R \nrightarrow \mathbb{N}$ *where:*
  - $dom(\text{Boolean\_Causal\_HoW}) =$
    $\{(n_1, n_2, r_1, r_2) \in N \times N \times R \times R \mid \exists_{e_1, e_2}\ g(n_1, n_2, r_1, r_2, e_1, e_2)\}$
  - Boolean_Causal_HoW$(n_1, n_2, r_1, r_2) =$
    $|\{\langle e_1, ..., e_n \rangle \in L \mid \exists_{1 \leq i < n}\ g(n_1, n_2, r_1, r_2, e_i, e_{i+1})\}|$

There are some differences between the handover of work metrics (Definition 6) and the handover of work tables (Definition 7). First, the handover of work tables only store the numerator of the handover of work metrics. Second, the handover of work tables only incorporate the directly follows relations, while the handover of work metrics incorporate causality relations. This design choice is preferred because of the nature of intermediate structures which is explained in the next section.

## 5   Mining Social Networks Instantly

To analyze event data, process mining algorithms typically create an *intermediate structure*, which is an abstraction of event data in a structured way, e.g., the directly follows relation, a prefix-automaton, etc. [13]. In the context of handover of work, the four tables mentioned in Definition 7 are such intermediate structures.

Defining an intermediate structure is not trivial. We have to consider which operation is more suitable to be handled by executing SQL queries over relational databases, which operation can be executed on the fly during analysis. Such design choices heavily influence the performance. Since the intermediate structure reflects the abstraction of *event* data, it should cover operations related to *events*, e.g., a new insertion of event, the order of events, events removal, etc. In other words, the intermediate structure should accommodate all changes in the event data.

In the handover of work case, operations related to events are captured in the numerator of the metrics. Moreover, the causality relations can be derived from the directly follows relations. Therefore, the handover of work tables only store the numerator values and count based on the directly follows relations. As defined in Definition 7, the intermediate structure in handover of work is *a pair of resources* $(r_1, r_2)$ *(possibly with the corresponding activity names) where* $r_1$ *directly handed over the work to* $r_2$, *followed by the frequency of how often this pair appears in the log.*

In this paper, the computation of the intermediate structures is done inside DB-XES, unlike traditional process mining which compute these intermediate structures only when a social network is constructed. This migration obviously will accelerate the analysis time since the intermediate structures are now available beforehand. Besides, this approach is well-suited for analysis in increasing data since new insertions in data are automatically captured by the intermediate structures. Figure 2 describes four main steps to mine social networks instantly: (a) *initialization*, (b) *update*, (c) *retrieving the intermediate structure*, and (d) *mining the social network*.

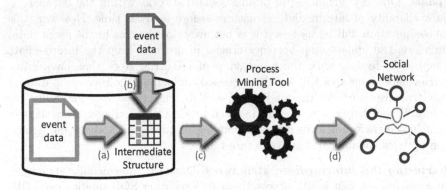

**Fig. 2.** The steps for mining social networks instantly

*Initialization.* The initialization step is done before process mining analysis. During this step, we create intermediate structures from the last snapshot of DB-XES, i.e., we incorporate all elements that are currently stored in DB-XES. For each type of handover of work, we create a SQL query and execute it against DB-XES. For example, to obtain the intermediate structure for *absolute handover of work*, the SQL query extracts all pairs of resources whose events happened one after another, and then counts how often it takes place in a particular log (as pointed in the SQL query below; we omit some parts in < ... > for readability). Note that in order to create the intermediate structure for *boolean (causal) handover of work*, we need a temporary intermediate structure. These types of handover of work ignore multiple transfers within one trace, hence we need a temporary intermediate structure to keep track whether a pair of resources has been observed in the same trace. After the initialization step is done, the intermediate structures for four handover of work metrics are ready to be accessed by process mining tools at any time for further analysis.

```
1   SELECT id, resource1, resource2, count(*) as freq
2   FROM (    /* get pairs of consecutive events */
3           SELECT <...>
4           FROM trace_has_event as t1
5           INNER JOIN trace_has_event as t2
6           ON t1.trace_id = t2.trace_id
7           WHERE t1.sequence = t2.sequence - 1
8       ) as pairs_of_events,
9       attribute as a1, attribute as a2,
10      event as event1, event as event2, log_has_trace
11  /* join condition to take resource values
12  (resource1 of event1 and resource2 of event2)*/
13  WHERE <...>
14  GROUP BY id, resource1, resource2
```

**Update.** One key advantage of mining social networks within the database is the availability of intermediate structures before analysis time. However, this pre-computation will be useless if it is not aware of changes in the event data. Therefore, the update step becomes crucial in order to keep the intermediate structure up-to-date with the latest view of DB-XES. Note that having live intermediate structures will avoid unnecessary reloading the increasing data in repetitive discovery. To this end, we use SQL trigger features for doing the update. When there is a new event inserted to a trace, the trigger takes the last event in the trace, retrieves its corresponding resource and activity name, and then updates the intermediate structure tables.

**Retrieving the intermediate structures.** Once the intermediate structures are available, we can easily access them by executing SQL queries over DB-XES. In general, this operation is relatively fast since the size of intermediate structures is far less than the log size. In the worst case, the size of intermediate structures is as big as the log size, when each resource only executes one event. However, this would be a very atypical scenario where it would not be worthwhile to create a social network.

**Mining the social network.** The next step is to compute the handover of work values between pairs of resources. As explained before, the intermediate structure only captures the metric's numerator, hence we need to compute the denominator in order to get the handover values. Computing the denominator (i.e., counting the number of events and traces in the log) is a constant operation, hence it can be done during the analysis time. Moreover, we have to deal with causality relation since the intermediate structure only captures the directly follows relation. Given the directly follows graph and causal handover of work tuples $(n_1, n_2, r_1, r_2, f)$ with $n_1, n_2$ are the activity names, $r_1, r_2$ are the resources, and $f$ is the frequency number, we select the pair of resources $(r_1, r_2)$ such that the causality relation $n_1 \rightarrow_L n_2$ is preserved in log $L$. Checking causality relation is a linear operation to the size of intermediate structures. Due to this simplicity, we can compute it on the fly during the analysis and still provide instant mining time.

For the visualization of the network, users can set a threshold value to show the most important relation between two resources. In the node representation, users can select to show the name of resource, the name of event, or combination of both of them.

# 6  Implementation

We implement this work as a ProM plug-in called *Database Social Network* and it is distributed within the *DatabaseSocialNetwork* package (https://svn.win.tue. nl/repos/prom/Packages/DatabaseSocialNetwork/Trunk/).

The *DatabaseSocialNetwork* plug-in requires a database configuration of DB-XES as the input, which includes username and password, database name, server, and a log identifier which the handover of work will be built upon. After the plug-in establishes a connection to DB-XES, it retrieves all necessary rows from the handover of work tables in DB-XES. Based on these row values, it constructs the network representations using Java objects. To visualize the network, it uses the GraphViz library [7] and the current implementation provides support for four types of handover of work: *Absolute Handover of Work*, *Boolean Handover of Work*, *Absolute Causal Handover of Work*, and *Boolean Causal Handover of Work*. To incorporate causality relations, the plug-in gives options to display the activity names executed by the resources. In addition, the plug-in provides a feature to filter infrequent handover values. If the threshold is set to 0.8, for instance, it keeps handover values which are greater or equal than 80% of the maximum value.

Figure 3 shows handover of work mining from a real dataset of a company which contains 154 resources and 846 handovers between resources. The process pertains to the data entry operations of insurance claim forms. These forms are sent by insurance companies; they are sorted, classified, scanned, and some automated OCR (Optical Character Recognition) are done. They are then sent for manual data entry which could happen at different locations based on the type of form. Once the manual data entry is done, the entries are checked for quality and then archived.

Figure 3 shows handover of work before applying any filtering. This spaghetti-like network is not readable hence it is difficult to grasp any insights. Therefore, we set the threshold value to remove some infrequent edges and nodes as depicted in Fig. 4a. The network in this figure is simpler and easier for getting the insights. For example, the network shows that there are handovers of work in both directions between Mr. Auto and Mr. CorrAck. Moreover, the self loop in Mr. Auto

**Fig. 3.** Social network based on handover of work before applying any filtering

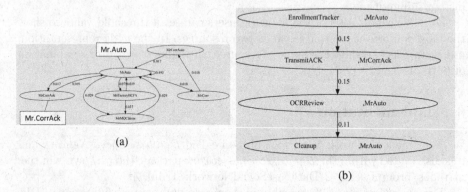

**Fig. 4.** (a) Social network based on handover of work after setting the threshold value, (b) Social network based on handover of work with activity name information

indicates that there are some activities which are executed consecutively by the same resource.

In order to see the activity name executed by these resources, the plug-in provides a feature to display nodes with resources and activity names information. In Fig. 4b, we see that after Mr. Auto did "Enrollment Tracker", he handed over the work to Mr. CorrAck to do the "Transmit ACK". Then, Mr. CorrAck handed back the work to Mr. Auto for doing "OCR Review", and finally Mr. Auto himself who "Clean up" the process.

## 7   Experimental Result

This section discusses the experimental result. We conducted two different experiments: (1) an experiment to show that the time spent in handover of work analysis based on DB-XES is less than the traditional approach, ignoring the in-database computations, and (2) an experiment to show the running time of each step in mining a handover of work from DB-XES and the feasibility of the approach for repetitive discovery.

In the first experiment, we used a real dataset from a company with some extensions in the number of traces, events and attributes. We extend the dataset by inserting copies of the original dataset with some modifications in the identifier, activity name, and timestamp. More precisely, we extend the dataset to be two, three, four, six, and eight times bigger than the original dataset.

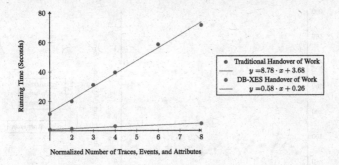

**Fig. 5.** Comparison between mining handover of work using traditional approach and DB-XES (Color figure online)

The result from the first experiment is shown in Fig. 5. Here we compare two different approaches for mining absolute handover of work. The first approach (shown as a red line in the figure) used DB-XES for storing the event data and computing the intermediate structure. The second approach (shown as a blue line in the figure) used the traditional way where the event data is stored in XES file and imported to ProM. In this figure, the x-axis represents the normalized number of traces, events, and attributes. For example, "2" in x-axis means that the number of traces, events, and attributes is twice bigger than the original dataset. The y-axis represents the running time for mining the network in seconds scale.

As shown in Fig. 5, both approaches present a linear trendline. However, the gradient of the traditional approach is higher than the DB-XES approach. This is due to the fact that the handover of work algorithm passes through the log and counts how many times a handover happens between two resources. Therefore, the increasing log size gives linear impact to the running time of the algorithm. In contrast, the increasing log size does not give significant influence to DB-XES since the number of resources does not necessarily increase linearly too. Note that during the mining time, the DB-XES approach only retrieves pre-computed values from the database and computes a handover network based on these. Most of the computation has been already done before the mining time. This experiment proves that the total time needed by users to mine a handover of work from DB-XES is less than the current existing approach when intermediate structures are present in the database.

In the second experiment (as depicted in Fig. 6), we use a real dataset which includes 460 different resources, around one million traces, and fifteen million events spanning one month. The goal of this experiment is to analyze the end-to-end steps of mining handover of work in DB-XES and to show that the technique is well-suited for repetitive discovery.

At the first step we imported one hundred thousand traces into the database. Then we *initialized* the intermediate structures. In this step we created the intermediate structures from scratch and the running time is shown by the green triangle in the figure. Then we *updated* the database by inserting ten thousand traces. In each insertion, a trigger function is automatically called to update

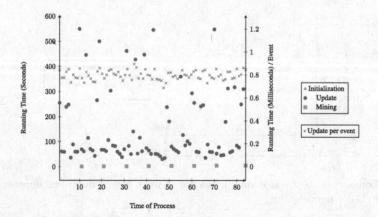

**Fig. 6.** Running time of each step in mining handover of work from DB-XES: initialization, update, and mining are plotted to the left y-axis; update per event is plotted to the right y-axis (Color figure online)

the intermediate structure. The running time to insert ten thousand traces and call the triggers is depicted by the blue dots in the figure. The total number of inserted events in each update is variable, hence we also count the average time to insert a single event. In other words, the average time is the total time to update ten thousand traces divided by the number of events. This average time is depicted by the red cross in the figure. After ten times doing update, i.e., after one hundred thousand new traces were added to the database, we *mined* the handover of work. The running time for mining the network is shown by the orange square. In each mining, the network size was increasing since we added traces every time we did the update (typical scenario in repetitive discovery).

Figure 6 shows four types of marks. The green triangle, blue circles, and orange squares are plotted according to the first y-axis on the left hand side, while the red crosses are plotted according to the secondary y-axis on the right hand side. The x-axis represents time of process where each unit of work is undertaken, the left y-axis represents the running time in seconds scale, while the right y-axis represents the running time for an event update in milliseconds scale.

From Fig. 6 we see that the average time needed to insert an event and call the trigger to update the intermediate result (red crosses) is relatively fast, i.e., 0.8 milliseconds. The update time for a set of traces (blue dots) are variable since the number of imported events in each trace is diverse as well. The mining time (orange squares) are always close to 0, and this shows the increase of log size does not really influence the mining time as the number of resources does not increase dramatically. This also shows that the time in each mining does not really change and quite stable, hence it matches with the needs in repetitive discovery. Moreover, the mining time is always faster than the initialization and update time, which generally can be ignored since these steps can be done offline and run automatically. Our approach always provides immediate answers because there is no need to traverse the event log and reload the prior data.

# 8    Conclusion

This paper focuses on scalability in social network discovery. We use DB-XES [13] as the relational representation of event log to store event data and shift the work from analysis time to insertion time. On top of the core DB-XES schema, we add specific intermediate structures for social network mining. We define the intermediate structure for handover of work metrics by determining which part should be computed in the database and be kept up-to-date when inserting new events into the database, and which part should be computed on the fly during the analysis time.

The paper explains the approach step-by-step and shows that the time required for mining the result is less than the time required for initialization and update which can be done offline and automatic. Moreover, using experiments on real-life data, the paper shows that the time spent in handover of work analysis based on DB-XES is far less than the existing techniques (thereby ignoring the in-database computations done at insertion). The experiment also shows the compatibility of applying the technique for repetitive discovery where we repeatedly do mining to the data that grows over time.

This paper uses handover of work as the social network. However, the work trivially extends to other types of social networks as long as we can identify an intermediate structure used by the technique which can be updated when inserting new events into the database. For example, in working-together network, a new inserted event will trigger an update in the intermediate structure by looking into all preceding events in the trace. Not only for organizational mining, it is also feasible to apply the approach into others discovery techniques, such as control flow discovery. In fact, the approach has been successfully implemented to do process discovery using Inductive Miner algorithm [13]. Finally, as a concrete research product, this work has been implemented in ProM.

For future work, we plan to implement more social network metrics, such as working together and subcontracting. We also plan to encompass other process discovery paradigms, e.g., declarative process discovery. Besides, we aim to improve the updating process of the intermediate structures by looking at a batch of new inserted events. Hence we reduce the updating time of the intermediate structures which now is always triggered every time a new event comes. Furthermore, we plan to implement also the removal of events such that the intermediate structures remain consistent under both insertion and deletion of events.

# References

1. Appice, A., Pietro, M., Greco, C., Malerba, D.: Discovering and tracking organizational structures in event logs. In: Ceci, M., Loglisci, C., Manco, G., Masciari, E., Ras, Z.W. (eds.) NFMCP 2015. LNCS, vol. 9607, pp. 46–60. Springer, Cham (2016). doi:10.1007/978-3-319-39315-5_4
2. Butts, C.T.: Social network analysis: a methodological introduction. Asian J. Soc. Psychol. 11, 13 (2008)

3. Calvanese, D., De Giacomo, G., Lembo, D., Lenzerini, M., Poggi, A., Rodriguez-Muro, M., Rosati, R.: Ontologies and databases: the DL-lite approach. In: Tessaris, S., Franconi, E., Eiter, T., Gutierrez, C., Handschuh, S., Rousset, M.-C., Schmidt, R.A. (eds.) Reasoning Web. Semantic Technologies for Information Systems. LNCS, vol. 5689, pp. 255–356. Springer, Heidelberg (2009). doi:10.1007/978-3-642-03754-2_7

4. Calvanese, D., Montali, M., Syamsiyah, A., Aalst, W.M.P.: Ontology-driven extraction of event logs from relational databases. In: Reichert, M., Reijers, H.A. (eds.) BPM 2015. LNBIP, vol. 256, pp. 140–153. Springer, Cham (2016). doi:10.1007/978-3-319-42887-1_12

5. Ferreira, D.R., Alves, C.: Discovering user communities in large event logs. In: Daniel, F., Barkaoui, K., Dustdar, S. (eds.) BPM 2011. LNBIP, vol. 99, pp. 123–134. Springer, Heidelberg (2012). doi:10.1007/978-3-642-28108-2_11

6. Furht, B.: Handbook of Social Network Technologies and Applications, 1st edn. Springer, New York (2010)

7. Gansner, E.R.: Using Graphviz as a library (2014)

8. Günther, C.W.: XES standard definition (2014). http://www.xes-standard.org

9. Jalali, A.: Supporting social network analysis using chord diagram in process mining. In: Řepa, V., Bruckner, T. (eds.) BIR 2016. LNBIP, vol. 261, pp. 16–32. Springer, Cham (2016). doi:10.1007/978-3-319-45321-7_2

10. Mislove, A., Marcon, M., Gummadi, K.P., Druschel, P., Bhattacharjee, B.: Measurement and analysis of online social networks. In: IMC 2007, pp. 29–42, New York, USA (2007)

11. Poggi, A., Lembo, D., Calvanese, D., Giacomo, G., Lenzerini, M., Rosati, R.: Linking data to ontologies. In: Spaccapietra, S. (ed.) Journal on Data Semantics X. LNCS, vol. 4900, pp. 133–173. Springer, Heidelberg (2008). doi:10.1007/978-3-540-77688-8_5

12. Schönig, S., Rogge-Solti, A., Cabanillas, C., Jablonski, S., Mendling, J.: Efficient and customisable declarative process mining with SQL. In: Nurcan, S., Soffer, P., Bajec, M., Eder, J. (eds.) CAiSE 2016. LNCS, vol. 9694, pp. 290–305. Springer, Cham (2016). doi:10.1007/978-3-319-39696-5_18

13. Syamsiyah, A., van Dongen, B.F., van der Aalst, W.M.P.: DB-XES: enabling process mining in the large. In: SIMPDA 2016, pp. 63–77 (2016)

14. Tang, J., Sun, J., Wang, C., Yang, Z.: Social influence analysis in large-scale networks. In: KDD 2009, pp. 807–816, New York, USA (2009)

15. van der Aalst, W.M.P.: Process Mining: Data Science in Action. Springer, Heidelberg (2016)

16. van der Aalst, W.M.P., Reijers, H.A., Song, M.: Discovering social networks from event logs. CSCW **14**(6), 549–593 (2005)

17. Aalst, W.M.P., Song, M.: Mining social networks: uncovering interaction patterns in business processes. In: Desel, J., Pernici, B., Weske, M. (eds.) BPM 2004. LNCS, vol. 3080, pp. 244–260. Springer, Heidelberg (2004). doi:10.1007/978-3-540-25970-1_16

18. van Dongen, B.F., Shabani, S.: Relational XES: data management for process mining. In: CAiSE 2015, pp. 169–176 (2015)

19. van Zelst, S.J., van Dongen, B.F., van der Aalst, W.M.P.: Online discovery of cooperative structures in business processes. In: Christophe, D., Hervé, P., Robert, M., Tharam, D., Eva, K., Declan, O., Agostino, A.C. (eds.) OTM 2016. LNCS, vol. 10033. Springer, Heidelberg (2016). doi:10.1007/978-3-319-48472-3_12

20. Yu, L., Zheng, J., Shen, W.C., Wu, B., Wang, B., Qian, L., Zhang, B.R.: BC-PDM: data mining, social network analysis and text mining system based on cloud computing. In: KDD 2012, pp. 1496–1499. ACM (2012)

# Re-evaluation of Decisions Based on Events

Luise Pufahl, Sankalita Mandal$^{(\boxtimes)}$, Kimon Batoulis, and Mathias Weske

Hasso Plattner Institute at the University of Potsdam, Potsdam, Germany
{luise.pufahl,sankalita.mandal,
kimon.batoulis,mathias.weske}@hpi.uni-potsdam.de

**Abstract.** Business operations include decisions having impact on their success and performance. The digital world provides access to massive amount of data being relevant in decision making. After a decision, often succeeding activities are not immediately started or preparation activities are conducted. Meanwhile new information could be received which lead to a different decision output. Considering this can save organizations process cost or flow time. In this paper, we provide a concept to realize the re-evaluation of decisions based on event processing. We integrated a re-evaluation scope in business processes in which change of decision is still accepted and which dynamically subscribes to those events leading to new decision output. The concept is evaluated by a proof-of concept implementation and a single-case experiment on a logistic use case. There, re-evaluation was relevant for almost a quarter of the transports reducing the traveling time.

**Keywords:** BPMN · DMN · Re-evaluation · Event processing

## 1 Introduction

The effective and efficient design and execution of business processes is a key driver for organizations. Therefore, organizations capture their business processes in form of process models, e.g., with the industry-standard BPMN (Business Process Model and Notation) [14] serving as guidance for the implementation of information systems [21]. Recently, the importance of decision in business processes and structurally capturing them has been revived by the new Decision Model and Notation (DMN) standard [15]. Decisions have a direct influence on the quality and performance of business processes, because they determine the course of the processes. Decision models describe the needed inputs for a decision, the decision logic, and the generated output.

Usually, when a decision is taken, a specific path is chosen immediately based on that or the output is used by the process later on. However, in the digital world, organizations have the possibility to access an abundance of data in real-time. This offers the possibility to re-evaluate decision: if updated and relevant data arrives within a certain time frame, then changing the decision would be possible and more beneficial. In situations where activities after a decision are not immediately started or preparation activities are needed to be conducted (e.g.,

© Springer International Publishing AG 2017
I. Reinhartz-Berger et al. (Eds.): BPMDS/EMMSAD 2017, LNBIP 287, pp. 68–84, 2017.
DOI: 10.1007/978-3-319-59466-8_5

in retail); if the decision about the price of an offer depends on the exchange rate, then as long as the offer is not approved the decision might be re-evaluated in case of an immense change of the exchange rate.

To realize the concept of re-evaluation, the following aspects should be considered: (1) Decisions can be re-evaluated only until a certain point. We need to detect till which point the actions following a certain decision can be canceled or rolled back without severe consequences. (2) Relevant data has to be selected. Only updates that lead to a different decision output should be considered.

In this paper, a re-evaluation concept for decisions is presented using event processing techniques. Due to recent development of digital systems and sensors generating a lot of data, event processing systems are an already established platform to produce, consume and analyze data in form of events [8]. We can receive relevant information from events, take decisions based on them and react according to our decisions.

This paper introduces a re-evaluation scope which is formalized by using the BPMN semantics, describing the set of activities where re-evaluation is still allowed. The re-evaluation scope can be interrupted by an event. For the event subscription, we introduce a concept to generate queries dynamically at run-time based on the actual decision output and the decision logic to consider only those events which trigger a different decision output. We call this context-sensitive event queries.

The remainder of this paper is structured as follows. In Sect. 2, a real-world motivating example is introduced. After introducing the background of our work in Sect. 3, we present our decision re-evaluation technique – the *re-evaluation scope* in Sect. 4. The approach is validated in Sect. 5 by proof-of-concept implementation with the existing open-source process engine Camunda [5] and the open-source event platform Unicorn [3]. Further the approach is applied to a real-world use case from the logistic domain in a single-case mechanism experiment to observe the effect of our approach. Section 6 is dedicated to related work. The paper is concluded with Sect. 7.

## 2 Motivating Example

In this section, we present an use case from the logistic domain which we retrieved as project partner from *Green European Transportation* project[1]. The use case is represented in Fig. 1 and includes a decision for determining the transportation mode (Euro tunnel vs. ferry) for crossing Strait of Dover.

The process starts when the transport plan is received. According to the plan the truck drives to the pick-up center where the goods are loaded. Then, the truck receives the current status (e.g., waiting and journey time) of Euro tunnel which is used as input to the **Determine Route** decision. The receipt of an external event is here represented by a catching message event. The **Determine Route** business rule task references a DMN decision model which is shown in Fig. 2.

---

[1] getservice-project.eu.

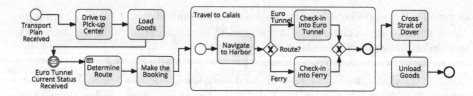

**Fig. 1.** The motivating example from logistic domain: transportation process to UK

The model consists of a decision requirements diagram (DRD) and the decision logic as described by the DMN standard. As shown by the DRD in Fig. 2a, the decision needs two inputs: the waiting time and the journey time. The decision logic is represented by a decision table consisting of a set of rows (Fig. 2b). Each row represents a rule that defines for which input values which output value is selected. In the given use case, the waiting time and journey time are added. If the sum is lower then 120 min, then Euro tunnel will be chosen. But if due to congestion or technical difficulties the sum is higher than 120 min, then the ferry is selected.

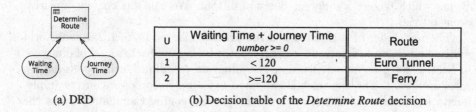

| (a) DRD | (b) Decision table of the *Determine Route* decision |

**Fig. 2.** The decision model for determining the transportion route

Payment for the journey is possible directly at check-in, but an early booking can be done at a reduced price until 30 min prior to the truck's arrival at check-in. Therefore, the logistics company already books the ticket at this point. After the booking, the sub-process `Travel to Calais` is entered. Calais is the port from where Euro tunnel or ferry can be taken. In the sub-process, the navigation guides the truck to the harbor where the truck checks in either for Euro tunnel or ferry. After crossing the Strait of Dover, the goods are unloaded for further transportation in UK and the process ends.

In the above process flow, the logistics company decides on the route (Euro tunnel or ferry) after loading goods and follows it throughout the process. However, the status of the Euro tunnel may change during navigation to the harbor. Loads of traffic or an accident might create an unusual delay which could be not taken into consideration during the business rule task. Although, the ferry might be now the faster option, following the prescribed process in Fig. 1 the truck will still use the Euro tunnel, because the updated information is not anymore considered in this process state. Usually the re-evaluation of the decision might be done by the drivers if they are listening to traffic news etc., but it is not covered in the model.

The advantage of the logistics company by integrating the re-evaluation of decision in the process model is that it provides an automatic support for the drivers to opt for the best suitable decision. Therefore, it can be assumed that the re-evaluation can be used in each case and that rules are explicitly given in the process and decision model. When integrating the re-evaluation, few aspects have to be considered. For example, once check-in is initiated for the Euro tunnel or ferry, it can not be canceled any more. Thereby, the last point of re-evaluating the decision, i.e., till which point the current decision can be rolled back without any major consequences, need to be specified. Another example, if the decision was already made for the ferry and another update is published providing the information that the delay at Euro tunnel has further increased, this update should not trigger a re-evaluation. It means, only information should be considered for the re-evaluation which trigger a change of the decision output.

Summarized, our concept considers: (1) decisions can only be re-evaluated until certain process state and (2) only events influencing the decision output are included.

## 3   Background

This section presents a brief introduction to the main domains addressed in this paper, namely, process and decision modeling and event processing.

**Process and Decision Modeling.** A process model consists of nodes and edges [21]. Nodes can be activities, gateways and events. A process model is a blue print for a set of process instances which are the executions of this process. Each process instance consists of several activity instances which traverse through different life cycle states as shown in Fig. 3. With start of a process instance, each activity is initialized and the instance is in *init* state. As soon as the incoming flow of an activity is triggered, the instance gets *enabled* and is in state *ready*. When the task performer *begins* to execute it, the state changes to *running* and finally the activity instance is *terminated*. In some situations, the activity instance is *not started* and the process execution chooses a different path, then it transfers into the *skipped* state. Due to the occurrence of an attached boundary event, a running activity instance can be *canceled*. During one process instance execution, an activity can be re-instantiated after it is terminated or canceled.

There exist different type of activities: user tasks, system tasks or business rule tasks. Each business rule task references a decision model as specified by the DMN standard. DMN defines two levels for modeling, the decision requirements level and the decision logic level. The decision requirements

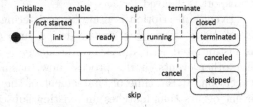

**Fig. 3.** Activity instance life cycle states transition

diagram represents how decisions depend on each other and what input data is needed for the decisions. A decision may additionally refer to the decision logic level which describes how to take the decision. This can be represented differently, e.g., by an analytic model or a decision table. We focus on decision tables as they are standardized in DMN [15]. A decision table describes the relation between a set of input values and a set of output values. Each input has a domain over which logical expressions can specify conditions. Given a value for each input, if the conjunction of logical expressions of all inputs evaluates to true, the corresponding output values can be determined, taken from the domains of the outputs. The possibilities of relating different inputs to outputs are represented in a tabular manner such that each row of the table corresponds to a rule.

It is possible to define overlapping rules, i.e., rules that match for the same set of input values but do not necessarily map to the same output values. Thus, DMN defines several hit policies that determine a unique output in case more than one rule is matched, like *unique, any, priority, first*. There are also multi-hit policies such as *output order* and *rule order* that return a list (or sequence) of outputs, namely the outputs of each matching rule, in a particular order. More detailed information about these policies is provided in the DMN standard [15].

**Event Processing.** An event is something that has happened in a particular system or context [8]. A set of temporally totally ordered associated events form an event stream. Events can be represented in various forms, e.g., as an email, XML, CSV, JSON. Different event sources generate events in different formats.

Process engines or other event consumers can subscribe directly to event sources, e.g., an weather API. However, setting up a central event processing platform has the advantage that it can connect to an event source that can be relevant for many business processes. These processes then can subscribe to the platform without dealing with different formats of the event sources [10]. Further, EPPs can connect to events generated in a distributed fashion and perform operations such as reading, creating, transforming and deleting events. These operations can be done on a single event (Simple Event Processing), multiple events in a single stream (Event Stream Processing) or multiple events in multiple streams (Complex Event Processing). For example, the truck's onboard unit can send the current location during transportation process and a traffic API can send news about an accident, both to the platform. The platform then aggregates these events and sends an alert to the logistic company that the transport is delayed.

Event subscription is done by registering an event query to the EPP. This event query is specified at the design time of the process model. If a process is instantiated with an event, the query is registered at process deployment. For other events in the process flow, a subscription is made during process execution: at the time of enablement of the catching message event. When an event occurs that matches an existing subscription, the EPP notifies the subscriber(s) about it. Event queries can perform various operations (e.g., filtering) on event streams to receive only relevant ones according to the need. The Euro tunnel source provides latest travel information including the departures per hour, waiting time before check-in and journey time. For the motivating example, the intermediate message event should receive information only on the waiting and journey time as these are the inputs to the decision table. An example query (written in Esper event processing language [7]) for subscribing to the event may look like following: SELECT waitingTime, journeyTime FROM LatestTravelInformation. Unlike relational databases, this query is activated by the occurrence of an event of type LatestTravelInformation.

## 4    Re-evaluation Scope for Business Processes

In this section, we present the notion of 'Re-evaluation Scope' for enabling re-evaluation of decisions in business processes (Sect. 4.1). Our approach extends event subscription with context-sensitive queries such that the queries are dynamically created during runtime including decision information (Sect. 4.2). Finally the concept of *point of no return* is discussed which allows to explicitly specify the moment when re-evaluation cannot be considered anymore (Sect. 4.3).

### 4.1    Basic Idea

The basic idea of our approach centers around the re-evaluation scope which is shown in Fig. 4. We used BPMN and DMN to formalize our ideas, but it can be applied to other settings also. Let us have a closer look on the single elements.

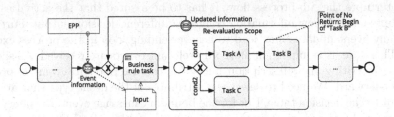

**Fig. 4.** Concept of the re-evaluation scope

*Catching message event:* The intermediate catching message event is used to receive events in real time from an EPP. The information carried by this event is used as input to the business rule task. The event is extended at design with an event query. At runtime, the event query is registered in the EPP with a subscription as soon as the event node is enabled. The EPP filters the event stream to select only those events that satisfy existing subscription and notifies the process engine if a matching event occurs. In this case, the process flow continues and the event subscription is deleted.

*Business rule task:* The business rule task is associated with a decision model in which the decision logic is represented by decision tables. We assume that at least one of the inputs to the decision is based on a real-time event caught by the previous message event node. Process data might also be used as decision inputs. The business rule task can be re-triggered by the re-evaluation scope.

*Re-evaluation scope:* A re-evaluation scope is a new type of BPMN sub-process that references a message event and a business rule task. The re-evaluation sub-process describes the set of activities where re-evaluation of the decision is still accepted. It has an attached interrupting boundary message event to receive the updates. At each enablement of the re-evaluation scope, an event query is generated to make sure that only updates having an influence on the decision output are received. The re-evaluation scope uses the query of the intermediate catching message event and extends it with decision information of the business rule task. The details on this will be discussed in next sub-section. After generating the context-sensitive query, the re-evaluation scope sends a subscription with the query to the EPP. If a matching event occurs, the process engine gets notification and the attached boundary event is fired. With this, the subscription for the event is deleted, all currently active activities in the re-evaluation scope are canceled, and the outgoing flow of the boundary event is activated. Finally, this path leads to the respective business rule task where the decision is taken again with the updated event information as input. On this path compensation activities could also be added.

## 4.2   Context-Sensitive Event Queries

As described, the boundary message event receives the updated information and interrupts the sub-process flow. It has to be assured that the activities are interrupted only if new information triggers a different decision output. Further, too many event updates may lead to a never-ending loop in the process execution. Therefore, it is important that only relevant events are received. As shown in Sect. 3, writing the subscription query for the intermediate event is pretty straight-forward. We need to select the attributes of the event type that are fed as input to the decision table. But for the boundary message event, the query has to be created using runtime information at each enablement of the sub-process. So we call it context-sensitive event query.

For the query, we have to identify those rules which lead to the previous output. These are then used to exclude events which would fulfill one of these rules. In the following, query generation for different cases is discussed: (1) tables with no overlapping output and in which no two rules with the same output exist, (2) tables with overlapping rules, (3) tables with rules leading to the same output, and (4) nested decisions.

For (1) unique decision tables always only one rule is triggered. If such a table has no two rules with the same output, then the event query simply has to make sure that all events triggering the last matching rule are excluded. Let us take the table of Fig. 2b and assume that last rule fired was <120 with *Euro Tunnel* as output. The resulting event query looks as following: SELECT waitingTime, journeyTime FROM LatestTravelInformation WHERE NOT (waitingTime

+ journeyTime $< 120$). To generalize the approach, the event query for the intermediate message event is taken and the WHERE-part is extended by the negation of the input condition of the last triggered rule (i.e., AND NOT ≪input condition≫ resp. WHERE NOT ≪input condition≫ if no where-clause exists). Thereby, only the part of the input condition is selected which focuses on event attributes. Here we assume that the event inputs to the table are labeled in the same way as the event attributes.

| F | input<br>Number | output<br>{x,y,z} |
|---|---|---|
| 1 | ∈[4,6] | x |
| 2 | ∈[1,4] | y |
| 3 | ∈[2,7] | z |

(a) First-hit table with overlapping rules

| F | input<br>Number | output<br>{x,y,z} |
|---|---|---|
| 1 | ∈[4,6] | x |
| 2 | ∈[1,4] | y |
| 3 | ∈[2,7] | y |

(b) Table with rules with the same output

| F | input<br>Number | output |
|---|---|---|
| 1 | ∈[4,6] | x |
| 2 | ∈[1,4] ∨ ∈[2,7] | y |

(c) Table combining them disjunctively

**Fig. 5.** Comparison of different styles of representing decision logic using DMN decision tables

If we relax our assumption to (2) tables with overlapping rules solved by non-default hit policy (any, first, priority, rule, output order, or rule order), then we still have to exclude those inputs which trigger the same result, but include those inputs which would trigger another rule. For example, the table in Fig. 5a has overlapping rules and specifies the *first* hit policy. Given that *input* = 5 rules 1 and 3 are matched, but because of the 'first' hit policy only rule 1 is triggered leading to *output* = x. We define the following algorithm to exclude from the overlapping inputs of the triggered rules all the inputs of the non-matching rules in order to define the set of inputs for which the decision should not be evaluated again:

o Let $R$ be the set of rules of the decision table.
o Let $MR$ be the set of rules that were matched in the previous decision.
o Let $TR \subseteq MR$ be the set of rules that were triggered in the previous decision.
o Let $NTR = MR \backslash TR$ be the set of rules that were matched but not triggered in the previous decision. In case of single-hit policies, $TR$ consists of one element and in case of multi-hit policies $TR = MR$ and $NTR = \emptyset$.
o Let $NR = R \backslash MR$ be the set of rules that were *not* matched in the previous decision.
o Let $UNR = Input_{Union}(NR)$ be the set of inputs for which at least one of the rules in $NR$ matches.
o Let $ITR = Input_{Intersect}(TR)$ be the set of inputs for which all of the rules in $TR$ match; this intersection of inputs is needed for multi-hit tables selecting only those inputs which have triggered all rules and ignores those which trigger a subset of them leading to a different output.
o Let $INTR = Input_{Intersect}(NTR)$ be the set of inputs for which all of the rules in $NTR$ match.

○ Then, $(ITR\backslash(UNR\backslash INTR))$ is the set of inputs which are excluded from the event query such that SELECT ≪input attributes≫ FROM e WHERE NOT $(ITR\backslash(UNR\backslash INTR))$.

In our example decision table, the set of rules are $\{1, 2, 3\}$. For $input = 5$, the set of matching rules is $MR = \{1, 3\}$ and the set of triggered rules is $TR = \{1\}$, then the set of non-triggered rules is $NTR = \{3\}$ and the set of non-matched rules is $NR = \{2\}$. The input union is $UNR = [1..4]$ and the input intersections are $ITR = [4..6]$ and $INTR = [2..7]$. Thus, the query should filter only values that match $\neg([4..6]\backslash([1..4]\backslash[2..7])) = \neg[4..6]$ in this example.

Since the described algorithm is based only on set of operations on the set of rules of the decision table, its complexity is linear with the number of rules of that table. This algorithm is executed each time after the decision was evaluated, in order to determine the query that would trigger a re-evaluation of the decision.

In cases where (3) different rules with the same output exist, the table needs to be preprocessed a single time. Let us, for example, consider the table in Fig. 5b in which rules 2 and 3 have the same output. Thus, cases exist in which two different inputs trigger two different rules, but still lead to the same output. For example, $input = 1$ triggers rules 2 leading to $output = y$. The same output also results from $input = 7$, triggering rule 3. For identifying all inputs leading to the same output, the table needs to be transformed into a table which disjunctively combines the input conditions of those rules as shown in Fig. 5c. For this table, we can now generate queries as described above. In case of a multi-hit table, it needs additionally for all overlapping rules having the same output the conjunction of the inputs of these rules. For instance, if we imagine that the table given in Fig. 5b has a rule-order hit policy, then the conjunction of the inputs of rules 2 and 3 would look as follows: $\in [1..4] \wedge \in [2..7]$. This allows, for example, that for $input = 4$ the correct $output = [x, y, y]$ is returned.

So far, we have only considered the case in which the (updated) event is input to the top level decision of the decision model. However, there can also be situations where (4) the decision which takes the event as an input is not the top level decision, but a sub-decision. In such cases, we traverse the decision requirements diagram starting from the top level decision along the path that leads to the input data element representing the event. Then we combine all the decision tables on this path as a single decision table (according to DMN semantics [15]); thereby deleting all sub-decision on the path and providing their inputs (including the event) directly to the top level decision table. Combining a decision table and a sub-decision table into one has complexity $O(1)$. Therefore, the complexity of combining all tables on the path from the top decision to the decision with the event input is linear with the length of this path.

Since our approach for re-evaluating decisions based on context-sensitive event queries has only linear runtime complexity we consider it superior and more efficient than the simpler alternative of continually polling events and "simulating" the decision to determine if it would generate a different output than the previous one. This is especially true in situations where decision is made based on events with high frequency.

### 4.3    Point of No Return

In a re-evaluation scope, we can often find different execution paths as visualized in Fig. 4 because outputs of decisions are used to determine which path of a process should be taken. In principle, the re-evaluation scope is till the end of any of these paths. But for certain path(s) the rollback might not be possible after a specific point in execution, even if that is earlier than the end of original re-evaluation scope. In Fig. 4, this situation is reflected by the XOR gateway inside the re-evaluation scope. Let us assume that re-evaluation is allowed for all activities in the scope, except that if a task performer starts with executing Task B (i.e., transfers from the *ready* into the *running* state by the *begin* event), then a re-evaluation should be not anymore possible. Just like in case of our motivating example, once we begin the check-in activity, the decision can not be changed anymore. Therefore, even if the sub-process is not terminated, re-evaluation should not be anymore considered.

To accommodate the problem mentioned above, we introduce the concept of *Point of No Return (PNR)*. It signifies the point after which an unsubscription has to be made for the boundary message so that the process is not interrupted anymore. With the PNR, the process designers are enabled to chose between two alternative points for unsubscription. It can be the termination of the sub-process as well as a specific activity life cycle state transition (as introduced in Sect. 3). For example the *enable*, *begin*, or *termination* transition of any activity within the re-evaluation scope can be a Point of No Return. In other words, the PNR is an attribute which extends the BPMN activity and references one of its state transition. When this transition is fired during execution, the activity sends a request to the EPP for deleting the subscription. In Fig. 4, if the process instance takes the upper brunch, then the re-evaluation can be done till the beginning of Activity B since this is specified as PNR. However, if the instance follows the lower brunch, then the re-evaluation will be possible till the end of the sub-process.

## 5    Evaluation

In this section we evaluate our approach in a two-fold manner. First, we present a proof-of-concept implementation, which shows the feasibility of the described concepts. Secondly, we conduct a single case mechanism experiment [22] to evaluate the impact of our approach using a simulated environment. The application to the real-world use case describes the influence of re-evaluation, both at design and execution level.

### 5.1    Proof-of-Concept Implementation

For proof-of-concept implementation, we used the open-source Business Process Management (BPM) platform Camunda [5], because it supports BPMN models as well as DMN tables. We connect the Camunda engine to the event processing

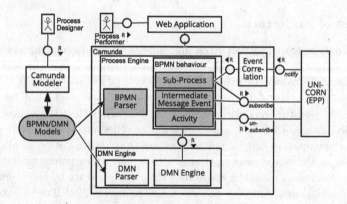

**Fig. 6.** Implementation architecture

platform (EPP) UNICORN [3] for receiving external events. Figure 6 shows the main components of Camunda with our extensions in grey and their interactions as FMC block diagram [11].

BPMN models and DMN tables can be deployed to the Camunda Engine with the help of the respective parsers. With the start of a process instance, the Process Engine leads the execution and triggers the needed BPMN behavior for each specified process node. In case of a business rule task, the DMN Engine is called by the respective BPMN behavior indicated by a request $R \blacktriangleright$ in the diagram.

In our approach, intermediate message events are used to receive events. We extend the *execute*-method of message event to send a subscription consisting of a query and a notification path to UNICORN. As response UNICORN sends a UUID which is stored in Camunda. This is later used by the Event Correlation service to correlate the received event to corresponding process instance. After the event occurs, UNICORN uses the notification path along with the UUID to notify the Camunda engine. Then, an unsubscription is performed and the process flow continues.

The properties of the re-evaluation scope, e.g., reference to a business rule task, are captured by extension elements of the sub-process supported by BPMN [14]. The BPMN Parser was adapted to capture them. For the re-evaluation scope, we extended (1) the Sub-Process behavior to create context sensitive-queries and (2) the general Activity behavior to perform unsubscription in case of reaching a PNR. As a boundary event has no own behavior, the subscription was added to the *execute*-method of the sub-process. For the creation of a context-sensitive query, the sub-process accesses a process variable in which all input conditions of previously triggered rules were stored by the business rule task and adds its value negated to the WHERE-clause of the referenced event query. The PNR is enabled by adding an *unsubscription*-method to the general activity behavior. Depending on the PNR definition, this is triggered with start or termination of an activity. If in case of user tasks the *begin*-transition was selected, it is triggered when a user opens it in the web application for the first time.

The prototypical implementation shows if a BPM platform already supports BPMN and DMN, the process engine only needs to be connected to an EPP and then with a few extensions the re-evaluation can be enabled.

## 5.2 Application to Use Case

The concepts presented so far are now applied to the motivating logistic use case from our project partner. Enabling the re-evaluation scope impacts both the design and execution of the process as described in the following.

**Impact on Design.** In Fig. 7, an extract of the transportation process depicted in Fig. 1 and extended by the re-evaluation scope is shown. Few model level changes were detected to incorporate the re-evaluation concepts. First, the `Determine Route` business rule task is now triggered from the intermediate event receiving the current status and the boundary event on the new re-evaluation scope receiving updates. We join both paths in a XOR gateway before this task. Secondly, the booking activity now becomes optional, because as mentioned in Sect. 2, early booking can be done only until 30 min before the truck reaches the check-in. The truck would pay the normal price at check-in if an early booking is not possible anymore. After the booking activity, the re-evaluation scope is added which is basically the sub-process described earlier. Since there is possibility of rollback due to re-evaluation, the model should be updated to accommodate the change of decision, if necessary. In our case, if the decision changes from Euro tunnel to ferry or vice versa, then we need to cancel the previously made booking. Therefore the activity `Cancel Booking` is added which can be executed optionally. According to the domain experts, there can be a gap between the enablement of the check-in activities and the actual begin of them, e.g., it is very probable that the driver takes a short break after reaching the check-in point. So, we included the check-in activities in the re-evaluation scope, but once one of them is started, the decision cannot be changed further. Thus, we specify a PNR for each branch which references the *begin* of the respective check-in activity. As soon as a PNR is reached, the corresponding check-in activity performs the unsubcription for the Euro tunnel updates. We can also put the

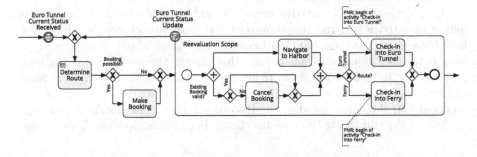

**Fig. 7.** The motivating example adopted with re-evaluation scope

check-in activities outside of the scope as an alternative design decision. Then, the unsubcription would take place at the end of the sub-process when navigation and the canceling of the booking are terminated. The application shows that apart from the re-evaluation scope additional process elements might have to be added and/or removed to enable the re-evaluation. Also, the PNR offers the flexibility to add activities to the re-evaluation scope for which re-evaluation should be stopped as soon as their execution reaches a specific state change.

**Impact on Execution.** For evaluating the impact on process execution, we simulated the logistic use case from start until the arrival at the harbor and connected the simulated process log data with real-world events. The Euro tunnel provides its status publicly in an RSS feed[2]. This, we fetched in a regular interval of 15 min and parsed the natural language description to detect the waiting time before check-in and the journey time to UK. If no waiting or journey time is mentioned, then we take waiting time = 0 and journey time = 38 minutes (i.e., the average time to cross the channel in normal situation). For the simulation, parameters were extracted from the use case description collected from domain experts which are shown in Fig. 8. We assumed that 50 transports are executed per day with an inter-arrival time of average 20 min. A normal distribution was deduced

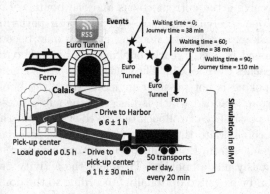

**Fig. 8.** Set up for the evaluation

for the driving activities (see Fig. 8) and an exponential distribution for the loading activity which is very stable and hardly longer. We simulated the process with BIMP[3] which also returns an event log. The simulation and the event data was collected for four consecutive days. We wanted to check the advantages of using re-evaluation in different traffic situations and therefore included data of the weekdays and also weekend.

After generating the activity event log, we mapped the start and termination of activities to the timestamps of the Euro tunnel updates. First the initial decision based on the decision logic of Fig. 2b about Euro tunnel or ferry is taken. Then, the event updates that change the previous decision output and are received within the re-evaluation scope are analyzed. The findings over 180 transports (20 were excluded as their arrival ended after the observed four days) are listed in the following Table 1. The results depict that for 23% of the transports the updates changed the initial decision. This change

---

[2] eurotunnelfreight.com/uk/contact-us/travel-information.
[3] bimp.cs.ut.ee/.

**Table 1.** Impact of re-evaluation on process execution

|  | Number of transports | Average saved time | Maximum saved time |
|---|---|---|---|
| **Total of adapted transports** | **42 (23%)** | **1:26 h** | **3:00 h** |
| Ferry → Euro tunnel | 32 (18%) | 1:18 h | 1:22 h |
| Euro tunnel → Ferry | 10 (5%) | 1:51 h | 3:00 h |

led to a saving of average 1:26 h and at maximum 3:00 h of the travel time. Thereby, 18% of the transports changed from the ferry to Euro tunnel and 5% vice versa. Figure 9 details how many transports saved how much time. In 30 of the cases, 1:22 h could be saved as the journey time at Euro tunnel in normal situation is 38 min and the ferry takes 2 h. On the other hand, if the decision changed from Euro tunnel to ferry, time savings could be more than 2 h, i.e., our approach could avoid long delays in Euro tunnel. Only in very few occasions, in 11 of 180 transports, the decision changed twice such that the initial and final decision coincide. To mitigate the cost of canceling the activities but still getting advantage by

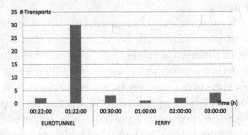

**Fig. 9.** Number of transports per saved time

implementing re-evaluation, the logistics company may analyze the trend and define the decision rules according to their need. E.g., taking the ferry if delay is greater than 150 min decreases the frequency coinciding changes to only once, but the other results remain very similar.

## 6   Related Work

Our work spans over three research areas of BPM, namely flexibility, decision modeling, and integration of event processing. By considering real-world events for the re-evaluation of decisions, we want to increase the flexibility of business processes. Reichert and Weber [17] distinguishes between four needs of flexibility: *variability*, *looseness*, *adaptation*, and *evolution*. Our approach targets process adaptation by reacting on changing environment as long as the decision still can be re-evaluated. BPMN [14] offers *event-based sub-processes* to conduct certain activities in reaction to an event whereby the main process can be interrupted or not. We did not apply it because, though event occurrence may interrupt the current process flow and execute certain steps, in our work, steps are interrupted to repeat the business rule task and the succeeding activities. Thus we opted for a normal sub-process.

DMN [15] supports looseness as it decouples decision logic from process models to allow more flexibility in combining those two. The existence of decision models is a prerequisite of our approach. They are usually identified based on expert knowledge, extracted from business process models [1], or discovered based on execution logs [2]. Further, the DMN decision tables need to be consistent and complete; a recent work [4] on the verification of them allows to identify missing and overlapping rules. Re-evaluation of decision is also done in operations research for reacting on events, e.g., to reroute vehicles [13] in case of congestion or to reschedule manufacturing jobs [19] in case of machine break-down. But it is conducted based on each received or pulled event. In our approach, a subscription is only made to those events which would lead to a different decision. Currently executed activities are only interrupted in case of a relevant event. By capturing this using an interrupting boundary event enhanced with a dynamic subscription query makes our approach more aligned to BPMN semantics.

Krumeich et al. gives in [12] an overview on approaches which integrate event processing with BPM. It shows that it is mainly used for process monitoring in different settings, e.g., general, cross-organizational, compliance. In order to detect conformance issues, Weidlich et al. developed in [20] an approach to generate event queries based on process models. In our approach, we use decision models to optimize event queries for adapting the process execution. With regards to process adaptation, in [9,16], event processing is used to detect exceptions and anomalies based on which the process is then adapted (activities are added or skipped). These are in comparison to our approach more general by allowing all kinds of process adaptations. However in these works, event queries have to be created manually or by a goal-definition [18] whereby our approach reuses decision models and execution data for dynamic event query generation. Further, our re-evaluation scope provides guidance on how to use and integrate event-triggered process adaptation for decisions in the process. In [6], Doehring et al. propose an architecture on how a BPM system, a rule engine and an EPP can be integrated. Our prototypical implementation represents a possible instance of this, although we have no direct connection between the event cloud and rule engine yet.

## 7   Conclusion

In this work, we connected process and decision modeling with event processing techniques to enable re-evaluation of decisions. We introduced a re-evaluation scope which defines the start and end point between which a decision can be re-evaluated. This can be interrupted by an attached boundary event which receives the updated information based on which the decision might change. The event query for the boundary event follows a dynamic approach such that the queries can be generated automatically at run-time by reusing decision information: all inputs of the last triggered decision rule is filtered by the event query. We have implemented the simple decision logic, but also presented discussions for almost all type of exceptions, i.e., for overlapping rules, for rules with the same output and nested decisions. The collective hit policy is currently not considered by our approach to which can be a future direction to extend.

The prototypical implementation shows that it is feasible to integrate our approach into an existing BPM system by setting up a connection to an event processing platform. The application to a real-world use case at design level shows that there are changes required on the process model; apart from adding the re-evaluation scope, there might be additional activities needed. However, the execution evaluation shows that a significant number of executions can profit from the re-evaluation.

In future, it should be evaluated on further cases, e.g., on cases from retail domain which are highly influenced by external changes. Further, this approach can be extended to a general process adaptation technique which reuses both model and execution information for subscribing to specific events automatically.

**Acknowledgments.** We thank Heiko Beck for the helpful input and implementation.

# References

1. Batoulis, K., Meyer, A., Bazhenova, E., Decker, G., Weske, M.: Extracting decision logic from process models. In: Zdravkovic, J., Kirikova, M., Johannesson, P. (eds.) CAiSE 2015. LNCS, vol. 9097, pp. 349–366. Springer, Cham (2015). doi:10.1007/978-3-319-19069-3_22
2. Bazhenova, E., Buelow, S., Weske, M.: Discovering decision models from event logs. In: Abramowicz, W., Alt, R., Franczyk, B. (eds.) BIS 2016. LNBIP, vol. 255, pp. 237–251. Springer, Cham (2016). doi:10.1007/978-3-319-39426-8_19
3. Bülow, S., Backmann, M., Herzberg, N., Hille, T., Meyer, A., Ulm, B., Wong, T.Y., Weske, M.: Monitoring of business processes with complex event processing. In: Lohmann, N., Song, M., Wohed, P. (eds.) BPM 2013. LNBIP, vol. 171, pp. 277–290. Springer, Cham (2014). doi:10.1007/978-3-319-06257-0_22
4. Calvanese, D., Dumas, M., Laurson, Ü., Maggi, F.M., Montali, M., Teinemaa, I.: Semantics and analysis of dmn decision tables. arXiv preprint (2016). arXiv:1603.07466
5. Camunda: camunda BPM Platform. https://www.camunda.org/
6. Döhring, M., Karg, L., Godehardt, E., Zimmermann, B.: The convergence of workflows, business rules and complex events. In: 12th International Conference on Enterprise Information Systems, pp. 338–343 (2010)
7. EsperTech: Esper Event Processing Language EPL. http://www.espertech.com/esper/release-5.4.0/esper-reference/html/
8. Etzion, O., Niblett, P.: Event Processing in Action. Manning Publications Co., Greenwich (2010)
9. Hermosillo, G., Seinturier, L., Duchien, L.: Creating context-adaptive business processes. In: Maglio, P.P., Weske, M., Yang, J., Fantinato, M. (eds.) ICSOC 2010. LNCS, vol. 6470, pp. 228–242. Springer, Heidelberg (2010). doi:10.1007/978-3-642-17358-5_16
10. Herzberg, N., Meyer, A., Weske, M.: An event processing platform for business process management. In: EDOC. IEEE (2013)

11. Knöpfel, A., Gröne, B., Tabeling, P.: Fundamental Modeling Concepts: Effective Communication of IT Systems. Wiley, San Francisco (2005)
12. Krumeich, J., Weis, B., Werth, D., Loos, P.: Event-driven business process management: where are we now? Bus. Process Manage. J. **20**(4), 615–633 (2014)
13. Li, J., Mirchandani, P.B., Borenstein, D.: The vehicle rescheduling problem: model and algorithms. Networks **50**(3), 211–229 (2007)
14. OMG: Business Process Model and Notation (BPMN), Version 2.0., January 2011
15. OMG: Decision Model and Notation (DMN), Version 1.1., June 2016
16. Patiniotakis, I., Papageorgiou, N., Verginadis, Y., Apostolou, D., Mentzas, G.: An aspect oriented approach for implementing situational driven adaptation of BPMN2.0 workflows. In: Rosa, M., Soffer, P. (eds.) BPM 2012. LNBIP, vol. 132, pp. 414–425. Springer, Heidelberg (2013). doi:10.1007/978-3-642-36285-9_44
17. Reichert, M., Weber, B.: Enabling Flexibility in Process-Aware Information Systems: Challenges, Methods, Technologies. Springer, Heidelberg (2012)
18. Verginadis, Y., Papageorgiou, N., Patiniotakis, I., Apostolou, D., Mentzas, G.: A goal driven dynamic event subscription approach. In: Proceedings of the 6th ACM International Conference on Distributed Event-Based Systems, pp. 81–84. ACM (2012)
19. Vieira, G.E., Herrmann, J.W., Lin, E.: Rescheduling manufacturing systems: a framework of strategies, policies, and methods. J. Sched. **6**(1), 39–62 (2003)
20. Weidlich, M., Ziekow, H., Mendling, J., Günther, O., Weske, M., Desai, N.: Event-based monitoring of process execution violations. In: Rinderle-Ma, S., Toumani, F., Wolf, K. (eds.) BPM 2011. LNCS, vol. 6896, pp. 182–198. Springer, Heidelberg (2011). doi:10.1007/978-3-642-23059-2_16
21. Weske, M.: Business Process Management: Concepts, Languages, Architectures, 2nd edn. Springer, Heidelberg (2012)
22. Wieringa, R.J.: Design Science Methodology for Information Systems and Software Engineering. Springer, Heidelberg (2014)

# Requirements Framework for Batch Processing in Business Processes

Luise Pufahl[(✉)] and Mathias Weske

Hasso Plattner Institute, University of Potsdam, Potsdam, Germany
{luise.pufahl,mathias.weske}@hpi.de

**Abstract.** Business process automation improves organizations' efficiency. In existing systems for business process automation, process instances run independently from each other. However, synchronizing instances for particular activities in a business process can reduce process execution costs. Only a few works exist to enable the so-called *batch processing* in business processes, which also lack a complete understanding of requirements. This paper provides a requirements analysis based on a literature review and real-world scenarios, taken from different domains. The resulting requirements framework gives an overview of aspects which need to be considered when developing a concept to integrate batch processing into business processes. Further, it fosters the comparison of existing solutions. The application of the framework shows that current approaches could be extended in terms of flexibility, user involvement, and multi-process support.

**Keywords:** BPM · Batch processing · Requirements analysis

## 1 Introduction

The effective and efficient design of business processes is a success factor for organizations. Many of them use Business Process Management Systems (BPMS) to automate processes, especially those with a high degree of repetition [28]. For example, an online retailer handling orders from customers implements this process to cope with many orders per day automatically. After documenting a process with a process modeling language, e.g., the industry-standard BPMN (Business Process Model and Notation) [12], the obtained process diagram serves as a blueprint for several process instances whereby one instance represents the execution of one business case [28]. As Russell et al. [20] observed, "each of these is assumed to have an independent existence and they typically execute without reference to each other".

However, in practice, we can observe settings where the synchronized execution of several instances is beneficial and can improve process performance. For instance, in healthcare, it is more time-efficient to first collect a set of blood samples taken from different patients and deliver them at once to the laboratory instead of bringing them individually. This approach called *batch processing* [7]

© Springer International Publishing AG 2017
I. Reinhartz-Berger et al. (Eds.): BPMDS/EMMSAD 2017, LNBIP 287, pp. 85–100, 2017.
DOI: 10.1007/978-3-319-59466-8_6

allows business processes which usually act on a single item, to bundle the execution of a group of process instances for particular activities in order to improve performance.

Existing process modeling notations do not support the explicit design and configuration of batch processing on the process model-level. In practice, batching of instances is either enacted manually or hard-coded in a software. Some BPMS providers, e.g., the *Process Maker*[1], allow to manually create batches in the user interface. Since no support exists to configure the batch processing, it is mainly driven by the users. When organized manually, the rules of a batch execution might be unclear, or the batching may just be forgotten which results in lower process performance. Conversely, when controlled by a specific software, batch configurations are not traceable by the process stakeholders. In addition, adaptations result in high efforts. Existing contributions [7,10,17,21] on integrating batch processing in business processes explicitly show it on the model level, rather than hide it in the system implementation. However, they are limited to certain scenarios and do not provide a complete overview of requirements.

In this paper, we propose a requirements framework which captures aspects to be considered while designing a batch processing approach for business processes. Additionally, it should allow a comparison of existing and future solutions. To this end, the paper provides a literature review of batch processing in general and specifically in the business process management (BPM) domain. Further, it presents a set of real-world scenarios discussed with experts taken from different domains. Finally, the resulting framework is used to identify open gaps in existing solutions.

The remainder of this paper is structured as follows; after discussing related work in Sect. 2, a framework collecting requirements for making batch processing efforts explicit in business processes is presented in Sect. 3. Thereby, also requirements of real-world scenarios are discussed. An application of the framework to structurally compare existing approaches as well as the requirements of the scenarios is provided in Sect. 4, whilst a conclusion is outlined in Sect. 5.

## 2    Literature Review

For this literature review, we first look into other domains such as computer science, manufacturing, and queuing research where batch processing originates from and identify which kind of approaches are useful for business processes. Afterward, batch processing works from the business process management (BPM) domain are discussed.

### 2.1    Batch Processing in Other Domains

Batch processing is a common term used in computer science for programs processing a series of jobs one after another without any user interaction [23]. It

---

[1] http://wiki.processmaker.com/3.0/Batch_Routing.

originates from the days of punch cards when it was time-consuming to provide input to mainframes [24]. General aim was to schedule batch jobs when system utilization was low, and it is not needed by any user, typically at night. Business processes are different in this regard as usually, there can also be a user interaction with the batch. In the manufacturing domain, batch processing has the goal to schedule available jobs on a single or on multiple machines in order to reduce the set-up times and the job times in the system. Potts and Kovalyov [15] provide a survey in this regard. Thereby, they distinguish between two types of scheduling models, namely the family scheduling model (i.e., similar jobs are scheduled together to save setup costs being still executed in sequence) and the batching machine model (i.e., batches of jobs which can be executed at the same time). We name them sequential batch processing and parallel batch processing, respectively. In contrast to the approaches from computer science and manufacturing domain, in many cases no optimal schedules can be predisposed in business processes, because process instances are started randomly. Pre-scheduling would reduce the flexibility of most business processes and could lead to longer waiting times.

In queuing research, several works, e.g., [9,11,13], can be found regarding the batch service problem being described as follows [2]: "Customers arrive at random, form a single queue in order of arrival and are served in batches." The more customers can be served in a batch, the lower are the execution costs per customer, but the longer is the waiting time for a single client because it requires certain time to fill the batch. Waiting times are also associated to certain costs, e.g., loss in future sales [3]. The primary objective of this investigation is to find the optimal point in time to start a batch which is discussed for different settings [13]. The described problem statement can be suitably applied to most business processes where process instances are randomly initiated. Batch processing can also be used to lower the average execution costs. Nevertheless, cycle time is an important performance indicator in business processes [4]. On the one hand, the cycle time of an instance can increase by waiting for other instances to be batched with them. On the other hand, batching can also decrease processing times by handling a set of instances at once. Summarized, an approach for batch processing in business processes needs to ensure an optimal trade-off between time and costs.

## 2.2   Batch Processing in Business Process Management

In the BPM domain, existing activity-oriented process modeling notations (e.g., BPMN, UML, EPC, or YAWL) as well as the workflow patterns [1] do not support the explicit representation of batch processing needs in business processes, although the need for it is identified. For instance, Fdhila et al. [5] present a classification and formalization of instance-spanning constraints, among which the execution of instances in batches is mentioned as an important constraint. A common assumption is that batch requirements can be solved with multi-instance patterns [1], which provide a means to trigger multiple instances of an activity in the scope of a process instance and synchronize their termination; these instances are still independently handled. As batch processing aims at collectively executing a set of instances, batch requirements need to be differently incorporated. The resource patterns *Piled Execution* and *Simultaneous Execution* in [20] cover some aspects of batch processing: While *Piled Execution* pipelines and allocates similar tasks to one resource whereby the execution is still done in sequence, *Simultaneous Execution* allows users to work on several tasks simultaneously while switching among them is possible, but a collective execution of several work items is not.

Currently, only few research works, e.g., [6,7,10,14,17,21,26] exist in BPM on the integration of batch processing which are discussed in the following. The process fragment-oriented approaches *Proclets* by Van der Aalst et al. [26] and *Philharmonic Flow* by Künzle and Reichert [6] highlight the need for batch-oriented activities to handle a set of data entities (e.g., a set of reviews for a paper) in an activity. In non-fragment-oriented process modeling languages as BPMN, this is solved by a read or write association between an activity and a data object list. This means, here batch-oriented activities are simply used to handle a set of multiple data objects created within the context of one process instance, but not to synchronize the execution of several process instances.

The approaches presented in [7,10,17,21] propose to integrate a new type of activity – the batch activity (resp. compound activity) which collects sets of activity instances for a synchronized execution which are afterward handled individually again. Sadiq et al. highlight in their work [21] a "contradiction between the preferred work practice and some fundamental principles behind workflow systems" and they identify the need in different scenarios to group several activity instances for specific tasks, in order to work on them in parallel and split them again at activity completion. The authors differentiate between an auto-invoked assignment of activity instances to batches with a predefined number of required instances and a user-invoked batch assignment, creating a batch with user-selected instances. Also the requirement for specific grouping of instances regarding their data characteristics is observed, whereby the authors state that this should be mainly user-driven. The batch activity approach by Liu et al. [7] aims at integrating the batch service problem from operational research into business processes. Hence, they request instances arriving at a batch activity to be collected in a queue and, then, to be assigned to batches based on an algorithm. Thereby, the activity instances should be also grouped according their data characteristics. Further, it is assumed that a resource has only a limited capacity. The batch assignment and the scheduling of a batch on a resource should be conducted at an optimal point in time. For this, they follow the threshold rule given in [11] according to which the batch assignment and scheduling is activated when the resource is free and a certain time resp. instance size threshold is reached. Pufahl et al. [17] have identified similar requirements, but they assume that multiple task performers might be available. According to the authors, instances should be assigned to batches which get activated based on user-defined rules. With batch activation, a batch is provided to the respective task performer(s) regarding different resource allocation patterns [20]. Here, the task performer is also enabled to decide in which order to execute her/his assigned batches. Additionally, the authors observe that a batch processing operation can also span over several connected activities. Natschläger et al. propose in [10] a combined-instance approach to process several instances in parallel for an activity. They highlight that constraints such as resource capacities and the type of instances that can be processed together should be considered. According to them, an optimal batch, if it exists, should be identified based on different batch candidates. This means that batch processing is optionally conducted when matching instances exist. The optimal batch should also include instance which might arrive in future at the batch activity. As the authors are focused on production and logistic domains, a batch should be scheduled on a resource and should be activated if all future instances have arrived at the batch activity or a certain due date is reached.

Van der Aalst et al. defined in [25] that "batch processing is when an employee is able to perform a number of work items of the same type ... without switching back to the worklist handler", similar to the piled execution resource pattern. Based on this idea, Pflug et al. [14] provide a dynamic queuing approach for activities with long waiting queues. Here, instances need to be collected and if the resource is free, they are dynamically clustered into groups, which are then allocated for sequential execution.

Beside time, cost, and quality, flexibility is one important performance dimension and multiple research efforts focus on enabling flexibility in business processes. Reichert and Weber distinguish four major flexibility needs, namely support for variability, looseness, adaptation, and evolution [19]. Research work exists to increase the flexibility and, in particular, the adaptation ability of existing batch processing approaches is targeted, respectively run-time adaptation of the batch configuration [16] and of the batch execution due to exceptions [29].

Summarized, presented works for the integration of batch processing focus on one or two use cases and lack therefore on a complete understanding of requirements. A first effort in this direction is made in [18] which we want to extend further.

## 3    Requirement Analysis for Batch Processing in Business Processes

This section presents the requirement analysis for batch processing in business processes. First, we start in Sect. 3.1 with a collection of scenarios from different domains requiring batch processing and study their needs to complement existing research work. These, together with the discussed literature, provide the basis for our requirements framework presented in Sect. 3.2. The section closes with a discussion on the completeness of the framework in Sect. 3.3.

## 3.1  Scenarios Requiring Batch Processing

Scenarios from the business world and their requirements were collected by interviewing domain experts and scanning the forums of existing Business Process Management System (BPMS) providers (e.g., Camunda, Bizagi, ProcessMaker) focusing mainly on the execution of processes. The interviews were conducted with internal process analysts of the organization. They were asked open questions regarding details on the batch processing use case, its current implementation and challenges. Table 1 presents eight identified scenarios from five different domains, such as health care, retail, manufacturing, business administration, and finance. For each scenario, its origin, a short description and the problem context are introduced.

From the table, we can observe that batch processing is needed in different domains. In the given scenarios, batch processing is often manually organized where an automated approach could increase efficiency. From the forums, it becomes apparent that stakeholder already try to support batch processing by applying existing process modeling concepts, but these workarounds are highly complex. Further, it can be observed that most of the candidates for batching are routine activities with a high processing rate, such as transportation tasks or fully automated tasks on machines. Some candidates, like the leave application or the invoice processing, involve also a decision by a user, but they are still highly repetitive activities. Based on this, it can be assumed that batch processing is useful for routine activities processing a high number of cases which can be executed automatically, but as well with user-involvement. These types of processes have a higher rate of created batches which have in turn an higher influence on the overall process performance. The outlined characteristics of batch activities will be considered in the following requirements analysis.

## 3.2  Requirements Framework

The requirements framework presented in this section gives an overview on the requirements which have to be considered when developing a batch processing approach for business process models. Besides, the framework can help comparing the capabilities of existing and future solutions.

For the framework, we first deduced all mentioned requirements from examining related work and summarized them. The result was compared with external scenarios and extended where necessary. Then, the collected requirements were classified. The classification will be further explained in the next paragraph. The resulting framework was then discussed and improved with a group of six BPM experts. The final result will be presented in the following.

First of all, the requirements classification is introduced. Figure 1 visualizes regular activity execution in comparison to an activity execution with batch processing behavior - a batch activity execution. Based on this, Fig. 1 shows the four requirement classes: *R1 Process Model*, *R2 Batch Creation*, *R3 Batch Execution*, and *R4 Context*. Unlike the regular activity execution, an activity instance in the batch execution is not directly offered by the process engine

**Table 1.** Scenarios requiring batch processing and their requirements

| Scenario | Origin | Description | Problem context |
|---|---|---|---|
| *Health care* | | | |
| SC-1 Blood sample test process | Expert interview with a Dutch Hospital | If a blood test is needed, it is taken and brought by a nurse to the laboratory where the test is conducted. Usually a nurse delivers several samples to save transportation time. In the laboratory, several blood samples from different wards are collected to save machine costs. | - Batch activities are currently manually organized; automation can help to fill batches more optimally and to consider the expiration of blood samples<br>- Machine and nurse have an upper limit in the number of blood samples which they can handle simultaneously<br>- Blood samples are ordered based on their expiration time at the laboratory<br>- In case of emergencies, blood samples have to be immediately transported to the laboratory |
| *Retail* | | | |
| SC-2 Order process | Expert interview with a German Retailing Company; Entry in Camunda Forum[a] | Customers place orders on the online retailer website. For each accepted order, the articles are taken out of stock. Then, they are packed in a parcel and shipped. Often, no transportation costs are charged with the effect that customers place multiple orders in short time frames. In such situation, orders of the same customer could be packed and shipped together to save shipment costs. | - Expert interview → batch processing rules are hard-coded, cannot be easily accessed by stakeholders<br>- Camunda Forum → tries to implement it with existing BPMN elements leading to a complex workaround where activation rules cannot be specified<br>- Grouping of cases in specific batches by customer is needed<br>- Batch processing spans over several activities<br>- Need for batching is optional, only if other orders of a customer exist batch processing should take place |
| SC-3 Process of shipping orders abroad | Expert interview with a German Retailing Company | Shipments to another country are first collected. The collected orders of one day are then transported to the respective country where they are handed over to a local shipment company. | - Manual rule that activates a batch of orders for one country once a day → efficiency could be increased by using a batch activation rule balancing the cost savings with the waiting times of the customers<br>- Grouping of cases in specific batches by country is needed |
| SC-4 Return handling process | Expert interview with a German Retailing Company | Customers can return some or all ordered items in a defined time frame. In case of advanced payment, they are reimbursed. Every financial transaction is associated with costs such that the retailer waits some time in case that another return is received to bundle them. In case that all items are returned or the time frame is closed, reimbursement is done immediately. | - Batch processing rules are hard-coded, cannot be easily accessed by stakeholders, the activation considers whether the return is complete and whether the return time frame is still open<br>- Need for batching is optional, only if returns are still open and the return time frame is not closed<br>- Grouping of cases in specific batches by customer is needed |
| *Manufacturing* | | | |
| SC-5 Manufacturing process | Expert interview with a Britain Manufacturer of Glasses | Some activities are conducted on a production line where work orders are processed as batch. Employees manually release batches to the line when it is ready. Further, all work orders with a manufacturing fault are collected and batches of them are sent back for reprocessing. | - Batch activities are currently manually organized → automation would help to fill batches efficiently and to consider maximum processing time<br>- Production line has a upper bound in the number of work orders which it can handle simultaneously<br>- Batch processing spans over several activities |
| *Business administration* | | | |
| SC-6 Leave application process | Entry in Camunda Forum[b] | If an employee wants to take vacation, the request needs a manager's approval. In case of many requests, manager prefer to work on the bulk of cases in one user view and decide each case. | - Batch is manually created and activated by the manager<br>- User processes the instances here in sequence, despite the visualization should be in one user view<br>- Grouping of cases in specific batches by responsible manager is needed |
| SC-7 Invoice processing process | Entry in Bizagi Forum[c] | If an invoice is received, it is forwarded to the responsible individual for approval. A common practice is not to approve each incoming invoice immediately, but to check regularly the set of received invoices to minimize the time to get familiar. | - Stakeholders tried to implement use case with existing BPMN elements leading to a complex workaround<br>- Batch should be activated after a certain time<br>- User processes the instances of a batch here in sequence<br>- Grouping of cases in specific batches by responsible person is needed |
| *Finance* | | | |
| SC-8 Send customer notification | Expert interview with a German Online Bank | Certain events, e.g., the opening of a bank account, trigger several processes which all send out a customer notification (e.g., welcome letter, credit card, ATM card). Although those notifications are created by different processes, they can be batched for sending only one letter to save shipment costs and increase the customer experience. | - Batch processing of customer notification created by multiple processes is considered as important, but not realized today<br>- Grouping of cases in specific batches by customer is needed<br>- Need for batch processing is optional, only if other notifications for a customer should be sent out, batch processing should take place |

[a] http://forum.camunda.org/t/building-a-batch-through-a-process/1722.
[b] https://groups.google.com/d/msg/camunda-bpm-users/nJoPZg7dLo4/0Q-OpHVHFQAJ.
[c] http://feedback.bizagi.com/suite/en/topic/add-existing-entities-to-a-collection.

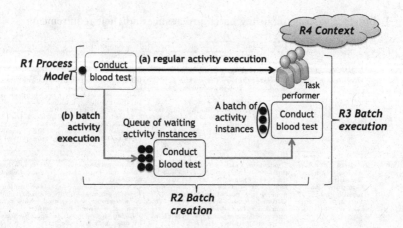

**Fig. 1.** Classification of requirements on batch processing in business processes.

to a task performer since its execution is paused to allow the instance being grouped with others. A task performer can be either a human or a non-human resource (e.g., a machine, a software service). Since batched activity instances can originate from one or several connected activities in one process model as well as in different process models, a *Process Model* class is defined. From the queue of activity instances, batches are created and then provided to the task performer where the batch execution takes place. Therefore, a *Batch creation* phase can be distinguished from a *Batch execution* phase. Each one is represented as a class in the framework. Changes in the execution context of a process instance can influence both, regular and batch activity execution. These can require certain reactions on them, e.g. handling of exceptions during the batch creation or execution, which are reflected by the *Context* class.

Figure 2 shows the complete requirements framework for batch processing in business processes with the classified requirements. After each requirement's name, its origin – the related work in brackets and the scenarios in parenthesis – are shown. Next, the requirements of each class will be presented in detail.

*R1 Process Model.* A batch operation in a business process can involve one or several activities being part of one or several processes. Thus, aspects which have to be consider during setting up batch processing in business processes are the involved activities and involved process models.

**(R1.1) Involved activities:** In several scenarios, e.g., SC2 and SC5, we observed that batch processing operations can span not only over one activity but also over several connected ones, which still can be executed by different actors. In the scenarios, batch operations were not interrupted. Therefore, the activities have to be connected. A single-instance activity between two batch activities would lead to two different batch operations [18].

**(R1.2) Involved process models:** Batch processing can be conducted for process instances of one process model, but as well for process instances of

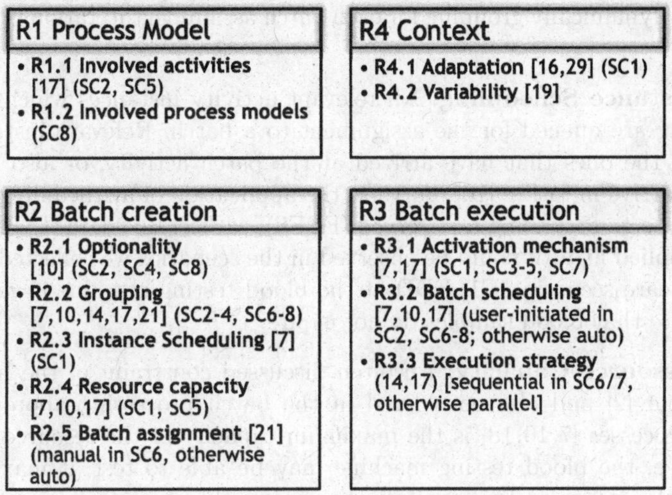

**R1 Process Model**
- **R1.1 Involved activities** [17] (SC2, SC5)
- **R1.2 Involved process models** (SC8)

**R4 Context**
- **R4.1 Adaptation** [16,29] (SC1)
- **R4.2 Variability** [19]

**R2 Batch creation**
- **R2.1 Optionality** [10] (SC2, SC4, SC8)
- **R2.2 Grouping** [7,10,14,17,21] (SC2-4, SC6-8)
- **R2.3 Instance Scheduling** [7] (SC1)
- **R2.4 Resource capacity** [7,10,17] (SC1, SC5)
- **R2.5 Batch assignment** [21] (manual in SC6, otherwise auto)

**R3 Batch execution**
- **R3.1 Activation mechanism** [7,17] (SC1, SC3-5, SC7)
- **R3.2 Batch scheduling** [7,10,17] (user-initiated in SC2, SC6-8; otherwise auto)
- **R3.3 Execution strategy** (14,17) [sequential in SC6/7, otherwise parallel]

**Fig. 2.** Requirements framework for batch processing in business processes.

various process models. In most of our given scenarios, batch processing is bound to one process, but in SC8 the activity `Send out notification` is used by several processes such that several created notifications to one customer can be collected and sent together. Organizations being active in BPM often manage large collections of processes where also similar activities or process fragments can be found in different processes [27]. Repetitive activities or process fragments offer the chance to use batch processing benefits and reduce costs over instances of multiple process models.

*R2 Batch Creation.* In the batch creation phase, activity instances are assigned to batches. *Batch assignment* requires several aspects to be considered.

**(R2.1) Optionality:** First of all, it musts be taken into account whether batch processing is an *optionality*. Either each process instance of a batch activity is used for batching (i.e., (1) batching is required) or only the ones which can form a batch (i.e., (2) batching is optional), whereas all other instances are processed as single instance. For optional batch processing, the decision can be based on all enabled instances of a batch activity, as well as on instances which will arrive this activity in future [10].

**(R2.2) Grouping:** In studies from queuing research, it is discussed that customers may be homogeneous or heterogeneous in their demand [13]. If they are heterogeneous, different types of batches have to be formed. Also in several scenarios, a grouping of cases in specific batches by customer (SC2, SC4, SC8), by country (SC3), or by responsible employee (SC6–7) is necessary. In [21], grouping is driven by the user, whereas in [7,10,17] grouping is conducted based on context data of process instances, whereby the grouping specification is given at runtime. A dynamically grouping for each batch assignment iteration is proposed in [14].

**(R2.3) Instance Scheduling:** All relevant activity instances which are used for batching are queued for the assignment to a batch. Relevant instances are either only the ones that have arrived at the batch activity, or also instances which will arrive in future [10]. Further, the application of a scheduling strategy is necessary, e.g., first-come-first-served (FCFS), earliest due date (EDD). Often, FCFS is applied [9] as it could be observed in the scenarios we collected. Only in the health care scenario SC1, EDD at the blood testing machine is very useful to make sure that blood samples do not expire.

**(R2.4) Resource Capacity:** An often discussed constraint of the batch service problem [2] and also considered in the batch processing approaches for business processes [7,10,18] is the maximum capacity of the resources needed. For instance, the blood testing machine may be able to test at maximum 50 blood samples in a run. This capacity determines the maximum size of a batch.

**(R2.5) Batch Assignment:** The process instances collected by the process engine have then to be assigned to a batch. Sadiq et al. [21] distinguish between a user-invoked batch assignment, creating a batch with user-selected instances, or auto-invoked one, where the system assigns the process instances to batches based on a specific mechanism. The user-invoked batch assignment is a manual approach where rules are not explicit and benefits of batch processing might not be fully usable. However, in certain use cases, it might be required. If execution data is captured, then it is possible after a while to identify the rules for the auto-invoked mechanism with process mining techniques [8]. The auto-invoked mechanism has to consider the grouping, order of the instances queue(s) and the resource capacity. It can be further sub-divided in *continuous* assignment, where each arriving instance is assigned, e.g., in [10,17], or *resource-dependent* assignment, where the assignment is conducted as soon as the resource is free, e.g., in [7,14].

*R3 Batch Execution.* In the batch execution phase, the batch operation have to be first activated by an *activation mechanism* and then be provided to the task performer.

**(R3.1) Activation Mechanism:** Batch processing is used to save execution costs. Pausing instances in their execution can increase flow times. Hence, time and cost appear to be in conflict, and the trade-off between them has to be managed. This is the responsibility of the activation mechanism [7,18] that determines when batch operations can be started. The resource availability is always the prerequisite for the execution of a batch such that an activation mechanism usually describes the earliest possible moment when the execution of a batch can be started. We can distinguish between (1) user-invoked activation (i.e., starting self- or system-created batches) and (2) system-based activation. User-invocation has the similar disadvantages as discussed for Requirement R2.5. For system-based activation, one often considered rule is the threshold rule which states that a batch is started, when the length of the waiting queue with customers is equal or greater than a given threshold (i.e., a value between one and the maximum server capacity) and the server is free [11]. This rule can be extended by a maximum waiting time, such that a group smaller than the set threshold is also served.

**(R3.2) Batch Scheduling:** After activation, enabled batches need to be queued and scheduled for execution. In some use cases, often where machines are involved, an automatic scheduling (regarding a scheduling policy) as proposed in [7,14] is needed. In use cases where humans are often involved (e.g., SC2, SC6–8), user-initiated scheduling (i.e., the system shows a possible schedule, but the user can decide which batch to execute as proposed in [17]) should be used, as done for work items in [20]. For the latter, batch processing approaches should consider that batches are not always immediately executed by the task performer.

**(R3.3) Execution Strategy:** Batch processing occurs in two versions: (1) parallel and (2) sequential execution [15]. In parallel batch execution, the activity instances of a batch are processed by the task performer simultaneously [17]. In sequential batch execution, the task performer enacts the activity instances one after another. They are processed as batch because they share the same setup, e.g., a familiarization phase [14]. In the latter case, the order of the batch might have an influence. Scheduling strategy, e.g., FCFS, EDD might be relevant here as well [25].

*R4 Context.* Context information reflects changing circumstances during process execution [22] and can support the design of a flexible batch processing approach. Flexibility is defined as the ability to react on changes [4]. Current work and scenarios reveal mainly requirements targeting adaptability of batch processing.

**(R4.1) Adaptation:** Thereby, (1) Exception and (2) special cases can have influence and might require adaptations during (a) batch creation and (b) batch execution [16,29]. For example, if the blood testing machine has to be maintained, expectation handling is triggered, such that all batches are finished before the start of maintenance. Special cases often require a special treatment. In case of batch processing, special cases are the process instances which cannot follow the normal batch procedure. For instance, if a customer has selected the fast delivery option, her/his order has to be sent out as soon as possible. For these cases, the option of fast handling should be provided.

**(R4.2) Variability:** Additional to process adaptation three other major flexibility needs are differentiated [19]. Whereas looseness and evolution are needs targeting the modeling paradigm respectively the BPMS, variability is also relevant for batch processing in business processes. Several customer groups, several product types etc. which are handled by one process model can require different batch configuration variants, e.g. different activation mechanisms. For instance, a

premium customer group can require that its members are only handled optionally as batch, whereas in all other customer groups the batch processing mechanism is always applied.

### 3.3  Discussion on Completeness of the Framework

The requirements framework consists mainly of aspects which were elicited based
a structured state-of-art review. Due to this methodological choice, it includes
mainly requirements which are already supported. Since only a limited number of
contributions enabling batch processing in business processes exists, we included
in the requirements analysis also real-world use cases. Thereby, we interviewed
interested domain experts and scanned the forums of existing BPMS providers.
Nevertheless, the interviewees have currently no approach in place with which
they can explicitly represent batch processing configurations in process models.
Hence, they might not yet be able to think about every aspects which is needed.
This can lead to further requirements in the future. We think that especially the
requirements targeting flexibility in *Context* group will be get more detailed in
future. With the elicited requirements from literature and scenarios, the given
grouping of requirements was proposed which was discussed and validated with
a group of BPM experts. In future, it should be further validated with BPMS
providers and domain experts. We are confident that the framework covers the
most important aspects, but we can not guarantee its completeness.

## 4    Application of the Framework

In this section, we will apply the framework to structurally compare, first, the
requirements of the given scenarios in Sect. 3.1 and secondly, the existing batch
processing solutions in the BPM domain to discuss future research directions.

| | SC1 - Blood Sample Test | SC2 - Order process | SC3 - Shipping Abroad | SC4 - Return Handling | SC5 - Manu-facturing | SC6 - Leave Application | SC7 - Invoice | SC8 - Customer notifications |
|---|---|---|---|---|---|---|---|---|
| **Process Model** | | | | | | | | |
| R1.1  Involved activities | single | multiple | single | single | multiple | single | single | single |
| R1.2  Involved processes | single | single | single | single | single | single | single | multiple |
| **Batch Creation** | | | | | | | | |
| R2.1  Optionality | no | yes | no | no | no | yes | no | yes |
| R2.2  Grouping | no | yes | yes | yes | no | yes | yes | yes |
| R2.3  Instance scheduling | EDD | FIFO | FIFO | FIFO | FIFO | FIFO | FIFO | FIFO |
| R2.4  Resouce capacity | limited | unlimited | unlimited | unlimited | limited | unlimited | unlimited | unlimited |
| R2.5  Batch assignment | auto-invoked | auto-invoked | auto-invoked | auto-invoked | auto-invoked | user-invoked | auto-invoked | user-/auto-invoked |
| **Batch Execution** | | | | | | | | |
| R3.1  Activation mechanism | auto-invoked based on costs and due date | user-/auto-invoked based on cost and | auto-invoked based on costs and time | auto-invoked based on return completed | auto-invoked based on costs and time | user-invoked | auto-invoked based on time | user-/auto-invoked |
| R3.2  Batch scheduling | automatic | user-initiated | automatic | automatic | automatic | user-initiated | user-initiated | user-initiated |
| R3.3  Execution strategy | parallel | parallel | parallel | parallel | parallel | sequential | sequential | parallel |
| **Context** | | | | | | | | |
| R4.1  Adoption | needed | - | - | - | - | - | - | - |
| R4.2  Variability | - | - | - | - | - | - | - | - |

**Fig. 3.** Comparison of the eight scenarios based on the requirements framework resulting in two types of batch activities: automated (in white) and user-involved (in grey)

In Fig. 3, all scenarios are listed with their needed configuration for each aspect of the requirements framework. For example for the blood sample test in SC1, we can observe that the batch processing is required for a single activity and a single process, instances have to be always executed in a batch (i.e., no optionality allowed), no grouping is necessary, etc. From the table, we can identify two preliminary types of batch activities: (1) automated batch activities and (2) user-involved batch activities.

*Automated batch activities* (e.g., in SC1, SC3–5) are either executed by machines which have a capacity greater than one, or by information technology (e.g., the automatic triggering of a financial transaction in the return handling scenario). Batch processing can span over a single or multiple activities. Batching is here required (i.e., no optionality allowed) and the instances are executed in parallel. For full-automation, instances need to be automatically assigned to batches, an activation mechanism is necessary and the batches should be automatically scheduled on the resources. Thereby, different instance scheduling approaches may be relevant to be considered, such as FIFO and EDD. In case of machine-support, the capacity is usually limited.

*User-involved batch activities* (e.g., in SC2, SC6–8) can consist of multiple activities and, in scenario SC8, we see an example of batching over several processes. However, this might be also possible for automated batch activities, as *process model* aspects are independent from the types. Specific for user-involved batch activities is that batching is, in most cases, optional and more user involvement is desired, for instance, in the batch assignment (cf. SC6 and SC8), in the batch activation (cf. SC2, SC6 and SC8), or in the batch scheduling (cf. SC2, SC6–SC8). This means that user-involved batch activities are user tasks which can be executed more efficiently by introducing additional batching, if possible. Depending on the use case, it has to be decided to which degree the user-involvement is desired: process performers might simply get auto-generated batches on which they can decide when to work or they might be also able to activate or create batches on their own. In contrast to manual batch processing, the degree of user-involvement can be adjusted here. Additionally, user-involved activities may be executed in parallel or in sequence by the users. For the latter, it is important that a decision can be made for each individual case. From a user interface perspective, two options are possible; cases could be individually represented, or a comprehensive user view can be chosen, where individual data for each case can be entered.

Currently, information on the flexibility needs is limited. A reason is that since many scenarios are currently manually executed, flexibility is always possible, and, thus, practitioners do not foresee which flexibility needs they might have. This needs to be further investigated.

Figure 4 presents a comparison of the currently existing solutions. We have focused on the works presented in [7,10,14,17,21] which aimed at improving the process performance by extending it with batch processing. It can be observed that the approaches get more and more elaborated. Starting with a very basic approach in [21] for assigning activity instances to batches by users or by a

| | Sadiq et al. 2013 [21] | Liu et al. 2013 [7] | Pufahl et al. 2014 [17] | Natschläger et al. 2015 [10] | Pflug et al. 2013 [14] |
|---|---|---|---|---|---|
| **Process Model** | | | | | |
| R1.1 Involved activities | single | single | multiple | single | single |
| R1.2 Involved processes | single | single | single | single | single |
| **Batch Creation** | | | | | |
| R2.1 Optionality | - | - | - | + | - |
| R2.2 Grouping | - | + | + | + | + |
| R2.3 Instance scheduling | not defined | enabled instances, FIFO | enabled instances, FIFO | future instances, FIFO | enabled instances, FIFO |
| R2.4 Resouce capacity | - | + | + | + | - |
| R2.5 Batch assignment | user-/auto-invoked | auto-invoked | auto-invoked | auto-invoked | auto-invoked |
| **Batch Execution** | | | | | |
| R3.1 Activation mechanism | - | auto-invoked | auto-invoked | auto-invoked | - |
| R3.2 Batch scheduling | user-initiated | auto-initiated | user-/auto-initiated | auto-initiated | auto-initated |
| R3.3 Execution strategy | parallel | parallel | parallel/sequential | parallel | sequential |
| **Context** | | | | | |
| R4.1 Adoption | - | - | Extension in [19] for flexible configuration | - | - |
| R4.2 Variability | - | - | - | - | - |

**Fig. 4.** Comparison of the batch processing solutions based on the requirements framework

system to work on them in parallel, it got extended in [7] with an automated grouping and activation mechanism to balance cost and time. In addition to that, Pufahl et al. [17] focus on supporting multiple activities, a batch configuration, where aspects like grouping, resource capacity, and execution strategy can be specified, and on allowing batches being allocated according to different resource allocation patterns [20]. Natschläger et al. [10] follow a fully-automated approach with no user-involvement and parallel execution, but consider additionally future instance and optionality. Pflug et al. [14] focus on the sequential execution, thus, not considering any capacity limit, and target a fully automated approach.

The presented approaches focus mainly on automated batch activities where users do not have the possibility to adapt the batch assignment, the activation of batches or the batch scheduling – the latter is only considered by [17]. The BPMS *Process Maker* is an example of very high user-involvement: users have to assign activity instances to batches, and have to activate as well as start them on their own. Still, the *Process Maker* provides no possibility to adjust the user-involvement that, for example, systems-generated batches are provided to the task performers. Hence, we categorize this as a manual batch processing approach, only driven by users. Further, only one of the given approaches considers flexibility aspects [16]. Finally, all approaches are currently bound to single processes, but batching over multiple processes might allow additional performance improvements.

Based on this, we can summarize that future research options are the increase of user involvement and flexibility in the approaches, as well as the extension to multi-process batch processing.

# 5    Conclusion

This paper provides a requirements framework for integrating batch processing into business processes which resulted from a set of real-world use cases and analysis of literature. The framework consists of aspects regarding *process models*, *batch assignment*, *batch execution*, and *context*. By applying the framework to structurally compare the requirements of the real-world use cases and existing batch processing approaches, two type of batch activities – *automated batch activities* and *user-involved batch activities* – were identified. In future more use cases should be investigated to validate these types. Additionally, future research directions were detected, such that (1) the involvement of users is enabled at different stages, (2) flexibility aspects are strengthened, or (3) batch processing is extended to multiple-processes. Currently, none of the existing batch processing approaches is actively used in practice. Hence, we think that with application of the approaches in future, the framework might get more detailed or extended some requirements. So far, the requirements framework was validated with BPM experts, but we plan to also validate it with BPMS providers and domain experts.

# References

1. van der Aalst, W.M.P., ter Hofstede, A.H.M., Kiepuszewski, B., Barros, A.P.: Workflow patterns. Distrib. Parallel Databases **14**(1), 5–51 (2003)
2. Bailey, N.: On queueing processes with bulk service. J. Royal Stat. Soc. Ser. B (Methodological) **16**(1), 80–87 (1954)
3. Davis, M.M.: How long should a customer wait for service? Decis. Sci. **22**(2), 421–434 (1991)
4. Dumas, M., La Rosa, M., Mendling, J., Reijers, H.A., et al.: Fundamentals of Business Process Management, vol. 1. Springer, Heidelberg (2013)
5. Fdhila, W., Gall, M., Rinderle-Ma, S., Mangler, J., Indiono, C.: Classification and formalization of instance-spanning constraints in process-driven applications. In: La Rosa, M., Loos, P., Pastor, O. (eds.) BPM 2016. LNCS, vol. 9850, pp. 348–364. Springer, Cham (2016). doi:10.1007/978-3-319-45348-4_20
6. Künzle, V., Reichert, M.: PHILharmonicFlows: towards a framework for object-aware process management. J. Softw. Maintenance Evol. Res. Pract. **23**(4), 205–244 (2011)
7. Liu, J., Hu, J.: Dynamic batch processing in workflows: model and implementation. Future Gener. Comput. Syst. **23**(3), 338–347 (2007)
8. Martin, N., Swennen, M., Depaire, B., Jans, M., Caris, A., Vanhoof, K.: Retrieving batch organisation of work insights from event logs. Decis. Support Syst. (2017)
9. Medhi, J.: Stochastic Models in Queueing Theory. Academic Press, San Diego (2002)
10. Natschläger, C., Bögl, A., Geist, V., Biró, M.: Optimizing resource utilization by combining activities across process instances. EuroSPI. CCIS, vol. 543, pp. 155–167. Springer, Cham (2015). doi:10.1007/978-3-319-24647-5_13
11. Neuts, M.: A general class of bulk queues with poisson input. Ann. Math. Stat. **38**(3), 759–770 (1967)
12. OMG: Business Process Model and Notation (BPMN), V. 2.0 (2011)

13. Papadaki, K., Powell, W.: Exploiting structure in adaptive dynamic programming algorithms for a stochastic batch service problem. Eur. J. Oper. Res. **142**(1), 108–127 (2002)
14. Pflug, J., Rinderle-Ma, S.: Dynamic instance queuing in process-aware information systems. In: Proceedings of the 28th Annual ACM Symposium on Applied Computing, pp. 1426–1433. ACM (2013)
15. Potts, C.N., Kovalyov, M.Y.: Scheduling with batching: a review. Eur. J. Oper. Res. **120**(2), 228–249 (2000)
16. Pufahl, L., Herzberg, N., Meyer, A., Weske, M.: Flexible batch configuration in business processes based on events. In: Franch, X., Ghose, A.K., Lewis, G.A., Bhiri, S. (eds.) ICSOC 2014. LNCS, vol. 8831, pp. 63–78. Springer, Heidelberg (2014). doi:10.1007/978-3-662-45391-9_5
17. Pufahl, L., Meyer, A., Weske, M.: Batch regions: process instance synchronization based on data. In: EDOC, pp. 150–159. IEEE (2014)
18. Pufahl, L., Weske, M.: Batch activities in process modeling and execution. In: Basu, S., Pautasso, C., Zhang, L., Fu, X. (eds.) ICSOC 2013. LNCS, vol. 8274, pp. 283–297. Springer, Heidelberg (2013). doi:10.1007/978-3-642-45005-1_20
19. Reichert, M., Weber, B.: Enabling Flexibility in Process-Aware Information Systems: Challenges, Methods, Technologies. Springer, Heidelberg (2012)
20. Russell, N., Aalst, W.M.P., Hofstede, A.H.M., Edmond, D.: Workflow resource patterns: identification, representation and tool support. In: Pastor, O., Falcão e Cunha, J. (eds.) CAiSE 2005. LNCS, vol. 3520, pp. 216–232. Springer, Heidelberg (2005). doi:10.1007/11431855_16
21. Sadiq, S., Orlowska, M., Sadiq, W., Schulz, K.: When workflows will not deliver: the case of contradicting work practice. In: Abramowicz, W. (ed.) BIS, vol. 1, pp. 69–84. Springer, Heidelberg (2005)
22. Saidani, O., Nurcan, S.: Towards context aware business process modelling. In: BPMDS, CAiSE, p. 1 (2007)
23. Silberschatz, A., Galvin, P.B., Gagne, G.: Operating System Concepts, vol. 8. Addison-Wesley, Reading (2009)
24. Tanenbaum, A.: Modern Operating Systems, 4th edn. Pearson Education Inc., Hoboken (2014)
25. Van Der Aalst, W., Van Hee, K.M.: Workflow Management: Models, Methods, and Systems. MIT press, Cambridge (2004)
26. Van Der Aalst, W.M., Barthelmess, P., Ellis, C.A., Wainer, J.: Proclets: a framework for lightweight interacting workflow processes. Int. J. Coop. Inf. Syst. **10**(04), 443–481 (2001)
27. Weber, B., Reichert, M., Mendling, J., Reijers, H.A.: Refactoring large process model repositories. Comput. Ind. **62**(5), 467–486 (2011)
28. Weske, M.: Business Process Management: Concepts, Languages, Architectures, 2nd edn. Springer, Heidelberg (2012)
29. Wong, T.Y., Bülow, S., Weske, M.: Monitoring batch regions in business processes. In: Persson, A., Stirna, J. (eds.) CAiSE 2015. LNBIP, vol. 215, pp. 317–323. Springer, Cham (2015). doi:10.1007/978-3-319-19243-7_30

# Testing Business Processes

# Performance Comparison Between BPMN 2.0 Workflow Management Systems Versions

Vincenzo Ferme[1]([⊠]), Marigianna Skouradaki[2], Ana Ivanchikj[1],
Cesare Pautasso[1], and Frank Leymann[2]

[1] Faculty of Informatics, USI Lugano, Lugano, Switzerland
vincenzo.ferme@usi.ch
[2] Institute of Architecture of Application Systems (IAAS),
University of Stuttgart, Stuttgart, Germany

**Abstract.** Software has become a rapidly evolving artifact and Workflow Management Systems (WfMSs) are not an exception. WfMSs' changes may impact key performance indicators or resource consumption levels may change among different versions. Thus, users considering a WfMS upgrade need to evaluate the extent of such changes for frequently issued workload. Deriving such information requires running performance experiments with appropriate workloads. In this paper, we propose a novel method for deriving a structurally representative workload from a given business process collection, which we later use to evaluate the performance and resource consumption over four versions of two open-source WfMSs, for different numbers of simulated users. In our case study scenario the results reveal relevant variations in the WfMSs' performance and resource consumption, indicating a decrease in performance for newer versions.

**Keywords:** Performance testing · Performance regression · BPMN · Workflow management systems · Workflow engine

## 1 Introduction

In the era of rapidly evolving software, semantic versioning has introduced a standardized meaning for version numbers. While this versioning style conveys the extent of changes introduced with the new version, in terms of backward compatibility, new features or bug fixes; it fails to provide information regarding changes in system's performance. This holds for Workflow Management Systems (WfMSs) as for any other software. As the number of proprietary and open-source WfMSs increases, measuring and comparing their performance between different versions becomes imperative for continuously improving them [18]. Information on the performance and/or resource consumption differences between versions is not only relevant for the developers, but is also important for the decision-making regarding the upgrade or selection of a WfMS by the end users. Especially, when the WfMS is running in the Cloud.

© Springer International Publishing AG 2017
I. Reinhartz-Berger et al. (Eds.): BPMDS/EMMSAD 2017, LNBIP 287, pp. 103–118, 2017.
DOI: 10.1007/978-3-319-59466-8_7

However, WfMSs' performance does not only depend on its version, but also on the workload (i.e., the workload mix, load function and test data) applied to the System Under Test (SUT). The end user requires performance information related to a given workload mix, i.e., the mix of Business Process (BP) models, which is structurally representative of a possibly large BP collection and related to a representative load function, which describes how the workload mix is issued to the WfMS. To address this challenge, we define and follow a novel method for deriving a synthetic workload mix from a given BP models collection. We focus on the Business Process Model and Notation (BPMN 2.0) [8] as a common modeling and execution language, since it allows to use a uniform standard representation for the workload mix.

As a case study, we apply the proposed method to derive a structurally representative workload mix from a real-world collection, which we then use to execute performance tests on the process navigator of two different popular open-source WfMSs. The process navigator is a core component of the WfMSs, that is responsible for navigating through the control flow of the BP models [7]. For each of the WfMSs, we test and compare the last four minor versions using the reliable BenchFlow environment [4]. Hence, the scientific contributions of this work are: (1) a method for deriving a structurally representative workload mix, and (2) an extensive analysis of the results from applying the proposed method on a case study scenario, providing insights on the evolution of two WfMSs in terms of performance and resource consumption.

The rest of this paper is structured as follows: Sect. 2 presents the method for generating a representative workload model; Sect. 3 refers to the configuration of the performance testing environment and the WfMSs; Sect. 4 presents and discusses the results from the case study; threats to validity are addressed in Sect. 5 and related work in Sect. 6. We conclude the paper and present plans for future work in Sect. 7.

## 2   Defining a Representative Workload Model

In previous work [5], we have identified the WfMS workload model components and their interactions. Failing to derive a workload model which is representative of a given initial BP model collection might produce misleading results and hence inappropriate decisions [3]. Therefore, in this section we present a parametric method for generating such workload model. Consequently, instead of using arbitrary BP models in performance tests, companies may generate synthetic BP models that reflect the essence of their BP models collection. The advantage of applying a parametric method for the workload mix generation, is that it enables a future re-application on diverse BP collections and/or domain-specific requirements. Then, we also discuss the parametric definition of the load functions.

## 2.1   Workload Mix Generation Method

For deriving BPs with representative structures we propose the following four phased *workload mix generation method*: (Phase 1) Analyze the initial BP model collection; (Phase 2) Discover the reoccurring structural patterns; (Phase 3) Synthesize the BPs of the workload mix with respect to user defined parameters; and (Phase 4) Partition the BPs into workload classes. The *workload mix generation method* takes as an input a collection of real-world BPs. In Phase 1 we apply statistical analysis on that collection to identify its main structural characteristics. Moreover, we execute clustering analysis based on the BPs' static metrics (e.g., number of activities, number of gateways) to obtain additional insight on the collection's characteristics. Clustering analysis is a grouping method that places similar objects in the same group (i.e., cluster). In Phase 2 we proceed to the detection and extraction of the most frequently reoccurring structural patterns in the BPs of the collection via the RoSE algorithm [16]. The detected patterns are extracted and annotated with their frequency of appearance in the original collection, as well as other metadata regarding their structure. The extracted structures and their metadata are then used in Phase 3 for recognizing and synthesizing [14] representative BPs, in accordance with user-defined parameters, such as the size and the control flow characteristics of the synthesized BPs, which can be derived from the statistical and clustering analysis. Graph synthesizing has been previously used (e.g., by Gupta [6]). However, this is the first time that parametric generation of representative BPs out of reoccurring structures is used for performance testing. Finally, in Phase 4 we divide the BPs into workload classes. A *workload class* is the pair of BP and intensity with which each BP participates in the workload mix. Thus, the workload mix is comprised of the different workload classes used as input to the SUT [5]. Each class participates in the workload mix with a different intensity, which corresponds to the degree of the model's representativeness of the collection.

Let us assume a set $C = \{c_1, c_2, ..., c_k\}, k \in \mathbb{N}$ of BP models that we include in the classes of the workload mix. In our case the set $C$ maps to the BP models shown in Figs. 1, 2, 3, 4 and 5. For calculating the representativeness *repr* of a BP model ($c_k \in C$) to the collection we define the following formula:

$$ repr(c_k) = \frac{1}{2\,|S_k|} \sum_{s_i \in S_k} \left( \frac{t(s_i)}{|Sc|} + \frac{m(s_i)}{|M|} \right) \tag{1} $$

where:

$M = \{m_1, m_2, ..., m_j\}$ is the set of BP models in the original collection.

$Sc = \{s_1, s_2, ..., s_n\}$ is the collection of all the reoccurring structures $s_i$ detected in the original BP models collection $M$. A given structure $s_i$ can reoccur multiple times within the same $m_i \in M$, and/or in different models in $M$, and thus multiple times in the collection $Sc$.

$S_k \subset Sc$ is the set of reoccurring structures participating in the BP model $c_k$.

$t\colon Sc \to \mathbb{N}$ is a function counting how many times a structural pattern $s_i \in Sc$ is present in all $m_i \in M$, counting each time $s_i$ is found in the same $m_i$.

**Fig. 1.** Class 1: $s_1$, Cluster 1            **Fig. 2.** Class 2: $s_2$, Cluster 1

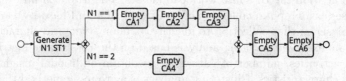

**Fig. 3.** Class 3: $s_3$, Cluster 2

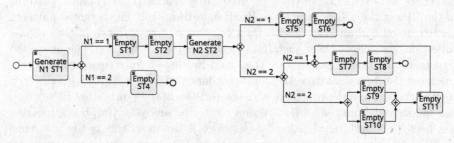

**Fig. 4.** Class 4: $s_3 + s_4$, Cluster 3

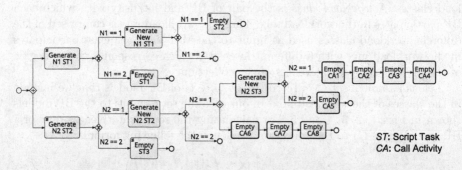

ST: Script Task
CA: Call Activity

**Fig. 5.** Class 5: $s_5 + s_6$, Cluster 4

$m: Sc \rightarrow \mathbb{N}$ is a function returning the number of BPs in the set $M$, in which the structural pattern $s_i \in Sc$ is present at least once.

The *intensity* is then computed as the normalized representativeness ($repr(c_k)$, Eq. (1)) with respect to the whole collection.

## 2.2   Applying the Workload Mix Generation Method

*Phase 1:* To create a case study scenario, we use a collection of 3'247 valid and complete real-world BPMN 2.0 BPs originating from: (i) IBM Industry Process and Service Models[1], (ii) sample models provided by the BPMN 2.0 standard, (iii) the research by Pietsch et al. [12], (iv) the BPM Academic Initiative[2] (invalid and incomplete BP models were removed) and (v) other research and industrial partners. The diversity of our collection reflects companies with a big portfolio of different processes and results in a more "general" synthetic workload. Since event logs or real data to simulate the BP execution were not shared with us, a behavioral analysis of the example collection was not possible at this point. In the collection, the BP size ranges from 3 to 120 nodes. Models with size $5 \leqslant size \leqslant 32$ represent 82% of the collection. Despite BPMN 2.0's expressiveness, the detected reoccurring structures contain only a small subset of the BPMN 2.0 constructs. More than 95% of the elements are one of the following: Call Activity, Exclusive/Parallel/Inclusive Gateway, Task (Script, User, Receive, Send), or Start and End Event. This confirms the findings of earlier literature studies [11]. The performed clustering analysis resulted in six clusters of gradual complexity. This result is important to better characterize the collection, and in our use case it is used as input parameter for Phase 3. The first four clusters represent 94% of the collection, while the last two the remaining 6%. Therefore, we consider the first four clusters to be the most representative of the collection's structure:

**Cluster 1:** 1 Start, 2 End Events, 4 Activities, 1 Ex. Gateway
**Cluster 2:** 1 Start, 2 End Events, 6 Activities, 2 Ex. Gateways
**Cluster 3:** 1 Start, 3 End Events, 11 Activities, 4 Ex. Gateways, 1 Par. Gateway
**Cluster 4:** 1 Start, 3 End Events, 16 Activities, 5 Ex. Gateways, 1 Par. Gateway

*Phase 2:* The RoSE algorithm [16] is a novel algorithm that applies techniques of sub-graph isomorphism to detect reoccurring structural patterns in a collection of BP models. For the aforementioned collection of BP models it detected 143 structural patterns appearing more than once in the collection.

*Phase 3:* The clusters indicate the structural attributes a BP should have, while the detected recurring structural patterns indicate their control flow. The combination of these results helps us to parametrize the workload mix generation by controlling the structural characteristics of the produced synthetic BP model (e.g., the number of constructs per type of construct). Namely, the parameters are formed with respect to the results of the clustering analysis. After the synthesis we obtain the representative BPs shown in Figs. 1, 2, 3, 4 and 5. The times $(t(s_i))$ and BPs $(m(s_i))$ of occurrence of the participating structures are shown in Table 1. To obtain fully automated executable models, we implement all tasks as *script tasks* or *call activities*. We omit external interactions (i.e., human

---

[1] http://www-01.ibm.com/software/data/industry-models/.
[2] http://bpmai.org/.

tasks and web service invocations) in order to focus on the observation of the performance of one of WfMS's critical components, i.e., the process navigator. Additionally, the original collection had low ratio of intermediate and boundary events (i.e., at most 5 occurrences in the whole collection), thus they are not included in the synthesised BPs. Empty *script tasks* are used, except when they precede an exclusive gateway, in which case the script task generates random numbers producing a uniform probability of taking any outgoing control flow branch of the exclusive gateway. Call activities call an empty BP (*Start event - Empty Script Task - End Event*).

*Phase 4:* Finally, we divide the derived BPs into classes ($c_k$) and compute their corresponding *intensity* (cf. Table 1).

**Table 1.** Occurrences of appearance ($t$ within the structures, $m$ within the BPs) of the reoccurring structures and their intensity (c.f., Eq. (1))

|           | Class 1 | Class 2 | Class 3 | Class 4 |       | Class 5 |       |
|-----------|---------|---------|---------|---------|-------|---------|-------|
| $s_i$     | $s_1$   | $s_2$   | $s_3$   | $s_3$   | $s_4$ | $s_5$   | $s_6$ |
| $t(s_i)$  | 1'602   | 953     | 640     | 640     | 309   | 130     | 30    |
| $m(s_i)$  | 1'731   | 2'303   | 1'710   | 1'710   | 635   | 157     | 30    |
| *Intensity* | 39%   | 27%     | 19%     | 13%     |       | 2%      |       |

## 2.3   Load Function

The interactions with the WfMS needed to start new BP instances follow the load function defined by different parameters: the set of workload classes to be started with the given *intensity*; a ramp-up period (30 s) during which the number of instantiated BP instances is gradually increased, followed by a steady state (10 min), where the number of instantiated BP instances remains stable, and a ramp-down period (30 s), during which the number of instantiated BP instances is gradually decreased; a variable number of simulated users; and a think time [9] of 1 s. Such short think time leads to a load function that stresses the WfMSs depending on the number of concurrent users. To reflect realistic number of users interacting with a WfMS in differently sized companies[3], we parametrize and issue the defined load function by setting 50, 500 and 1'000 simulated users in three different experiments. All parameters of the load function, are configurable by the designer of the performance test.

## 3   Case Study Settings

The WfMSs' configuration and the setup of the performance testing environment aim at reducing, as much as possible, the noise in the measurements. To that

---

[3] http://www.gartner.com/it-glossary/smbs-small-and-midsize-businesses/.

end we isolate the individual testing components through containers [5] and control the testing environment to ensure the absence of interferences in the measurement. For the tests, we used the same methodology as in [15] and run the experiments with the BenchFlow environment [4], an end-to-end framework for WfMSs' performance testing relying on Docker[4]. BenchFlow aims at ensuring reliable and reproducible results, that can be verified by means of dedicated statistics, reported in Sect. 4.2.

The WfMSs we tested are two widely used open source engines[5]. They are widely used in industry and have a large user community as per vendors' websites. We cover their last two years of development (2014–2016), i.e., versions 7.2.0, 7.3.0, 7.4.0, 7.5.0 for WfMS A and versions 5.18.0, 5.19.0.2, 5.20.0, 5.21.0 for WfMS B. Comparing versions provides insights on how system's evolution impacts its performance. For WfMS A we used the official Docker images and vendor suggested configurations. WfMS B's default configuration has been reported as insufficient for the deployment of realistic loads, thus we used the one suggested at the vendor's website. We deployed it using the most popular Docker image, since no official Docker image is currently available. The configurations of WfMS A and WfMS B are comparable in terms of the connection pool, the Java Virtual Machine and the Application server settings they rely on, as well as, in terms of the BP execution logging level, which we set to log the full history. Both WfMSs utilize MySQL Community Server 5.7.15 as Database Management System (DBMS), installed in a Docker container[6].

The WfMS and the DBMS run on two exclusively dedicated servers connected via a dedicated 10 Gbit/s network, without relying on the Docker network bridge (i.e., we use the Docker's *host* network option). The WfMS dedicated server has 64 Cores (2 threads) and a clock speed of 1'400 MHz mounting 128 GB of RAM and a magnetic disk with 15'000 rpm. The DB dedicated server has 64 Cores (2 threads) and a clock speed of 2'300 MHz mounting 128 GB of RAM and a SSD SATA disk. The aim of such resource allocation is to avoid the DBMS becoming a performance bottleneck. Different machines, interacting with the WfMS on a second dedicated 10 Gbit/s network, are allocated for the simulation of the users, thus ensuring sufficient resources for simulating the defined load.

## 4 Evaluation

### 4.1 Performance Metrics

We characterize WfMSs' performance, using metrics that represent the performance from different points of view: (1) the client (i.e., representing the users starting BP instances), (2) the BP execution behavior, and (3) the system's resource consumption. To ensure results' reliability, given the non-determinism

---

[4] https://www.docker.com.

[5] We do not have an explicit vendors' consent to publish WfMSs' names.

[6] https://hub.docker.com/_/mysql/.

in WfMS's performance, we perform three rounds of executions for each experiment. Out of these multiple rounds, we compute aggregated metrics representing WfMS's observed behavior and the performance variability across different rounds.

On the client-side we include the *number of requests per second - #REQ/s* issued by the simulated users. The maximum expected $\#REQ/s$ equals the number of simulated users defined in the load function. The actual obtained value is impacted by the WfMS's response time. We report the $\#REQ/s$ metric aggregated using the average $(avg)$ of the metric across the different rounds, as well as the 95% T-based confidence interval $(ci)$ [10, Chap. 8]. The $ci$ sets up a range of values for the analyzed metric in which we can be 95% confident.

A second set of metrics are computed starting from the server-side performance data logged by the WfMSs. In this work we include the *BP instance ($bp_i$) duration in milliseconds - D [ms]* and the *throughput - T [#$bp_i$/s]*. The duration $D$ is defined as the time interval between the start and the completion of a BP instance. We report the weighted average $(wavg(D))$ of $D$ aggregated among all the executed BP instances and for each single BP in the workload mix, where we compute the weights based on the number of executed BP instances in each round. As throughput $T$ we define the number of executed BP instances per second. We report its average $(avg(T))$ along with the corresponding $ci$.

We also compute resource consumption metrics, based on data with a sampling interval of 1 s. In this work, we include the *weighted average of CPU, RAM consumption - wavg(CPU) [%]*, $wavg(RAM)$ [$MB$] among different rounds. The weights are based on the number of CPU and RAM data points in each experiment round. Given the logged execution data, when necessary other metrics can be defined by the performance test designer depending on its goal.

## 4.2   Reliability of Results

To ensure reliable results, we use *Little's Law* to verify that the BenchFlow environment was able to simulate the number of defined users. It compares the number of defined users versus the number of actually simulated users. Bench-Flow was able to simulate the number of users defined in the load functions, with an acceptable small variation of less than 1% (at maximum).

Every software system experiences a warm-up time during which its transient behaviour differs from the one in the steady-state [9]. To account for it, we identify the outlier BP three instances during the ramp-up phase of the load function, and remove them from the analyzed data set. To verify that the three rounds obtain similar, and reliable results, we compute the *coefficient of variation - cv [%]*. The $cv$ is the ratio between the standard deviation of the means of the rounds and the mean of all the rounds, expressed as a percentage. The $cv$ resulted always below 3.5%. This indicates a stable behavior across the different rounds.

**Table 2.** Performance and resource consumption metrics - WfMS A

| | | Load | WfMS A | | | |
|---|---|---|---|---|---|---|
| | | | 7.2.0 | 7.3.0 | 7.4.0 | 7.5.0 |
| Client-side | $avg(\#REQ/s) \pm ci$ | 50 | 49.13±0.04 | 49.17±0.03 | 49.16±0.02 | 49.09±0.01 |
| | | 500 | 484.87±0.39 | 486.44±0.10 | 484.84±0.82 | 482.91±2.20 |
| | | 1'000 | 890.84±4.82 | 879.15±9.94 | 859.81±3.42 | 763.46±2.17 |
| Server-side | $avg(T) \pm ci$ [#$bp_i$/s] | 50 | 118.23±0.21 | 119.72±0.17 | 120.08±0.79 | 120.05±0.42 |
| | | 500 | 1'185.12±0.45 | 1'185.56±0.33 | 1'180.80±4.34 | 1'175.10±0.58 |
| | | 1'000 | 2'121.35±6.23 | 2'130.90±9.50 | 2'087.26±2.72 | 1'849.88±5.17 |
| | $wavg(D)$ [ms] | 50 | 1.03 | 1.08 | 1.12 | 1.24 |
| | | 500 | 0.87 | 0.91 | 1.07 | 1.14 |
| | | 1'000 | 0.93 | 0.99 | 1.05 | 1.15 |
| Resource Consumption | $wavg(CPU)$ [%] | 50 | 1.66 | 1.33 | 1.33 | 1.35 |
| | | 500 | 8.07 | 6.26 | 7.03 | 6.95 |
| | | 1'000 | 11.39 | 8.33 | 8.81 | 8.79 |
| | $wavg(RAM)$ [MB] | 50 | 637.28 | 590.82 | 634.79 | 648.67 |
| | | 500 | 885.10 | 860.70 | 886.53 | 866.37 |
| | | 1'000 | 970.61 | 957.47 | 978.97 | 971.43 |

| | | $bp_i$ | | | | |
|---|---|---|---|---|---|---|
| Server-side | $wavg(D)$ [ms] | Class 1 | 1.09 | 1.14 | 1.24 | 1.35 |
| | | Class 2 | 1.34 | 1.41 | 1.54 | 1.67 |
| | | Class 3 | 2.31 | 2.43 | 2.64 | 2.88 |
| | | Class 4 | 1.13 | 1.20 | 1.30 | 1.42 |
| | | Class 5 | 1.93 | 2.03 | 2.21 | 2.40 |

## 4.3   Results

The performance metrics (cf. Sect. 4.1) for all tested versions of WfMS A and WfMS B, with different number of users are reported in Tables 2 and 3 respectively.

**WfMS A's** ability to handle incoming requests, depicted by the average requests per second, is close to the expected for 50 and 500 simulated users, with actual numbers of over 49 and over 482 requests per second respectively. With 1'000 users the client-side performance drops from 890.84 $REQ/s$ in v7.2.0 to 763.46 $REQ/s$ in v7.5.0. There is a slight increase in throughput from 118.23 $bp_i/s$ to 120.05 $bp_i/s$ from the oldest to the newest version analyzed for 50 users. For 500 and 1'000 users the best throughput of 1'185.56 $bp_i/s$ and 2'130.90 $bp_i/s$ respectively is achieved with v7.3.0. There is a reduction to 1'175.10 $bp_i/s$ and 1'849.88 $bp_i/s$ respectively in v7.5.0, the newest version. Given that most of the BPs used in the workload mix contain *call activities* which instantiate a globally defined BP, the throughput is much higher than the actual number of requests per second sent by the users, because it considers the instantiated BP instances as well. The average duration of the execution of one BP instance is the lowest in v7.2.0 for 500 users with 0.87 ms execution time, and the highest in v7.5.0 for 50 users with 1.24 ms execution time as it increases with newer versions of the WfMS. The same applies to the average duration at BP level (rolled-up by the number of users), with lowest duration of 1.09 ms for Class 1 in v7.2.0, and highest of 2.88 ms for Class 3 in v7.5.0. The duration of the empty BP instantiated by the *call activities*, omitted in the table, is on average 0.31 ms. A lower number of started and completed BP instances require less CPU (from an average of 1.42% across all versions for 50 users, to 9.33% with

**Table 3.** Performance and resource consumption metrics - WfMS B

| | | Load | WfMS B | | | |
|---|---|---|---|---|---|---|
| | | | **5.18.0** | **5.19.0.2** | **5.20.0** | **5.21.0** |
| Client-side | $avg(\#REQ/s) \pm ci$ | 50 | 48.84±0.02 | 48.72±0.05 | 48.66±0.03 | 48.65±0.04 |
| | | 500 | 488.61±0.12 | 487.72±0.13 | 487.34±0.15 | 487.71±0.55 |
| | | 1'000 | 906.10±3.81 | 900.14±4.09 | 891.62±1.76 | 885.80±2.97 |
| Server-side | $avg(T) \pm ci\ [\#bp_i/s]$ | 50 | 119.87±0.07 | 119.82±0.09 | 119.99±0.09 | 119.82±0.14 |
| | | 500 | 1'161.88±0.98 | 1'160.46±1.13 | 1'160.96±1.67 | 1'132.92±2.43 |
| | | 1'000 | 2'182.78±8.25 | 2'202.37±6.37 | 2'189.36±4.83 | 1'974.01±10.59 |
| | $wavg(D)$ [ms] | 50 | 6.53 | 6.75 | 6.90 | 7.19 |
| | | 500 | 5.08 | 5.27 | 5.56 | 5.65 |
| | | 1'000 | 5.18 | 5.34 | 5.39 | 5.43 |
| Resource Consumption | $wavg(CPU)$ [%] | 50 | 3.01 | 1.59 | 1.63 | 1.66 |
| | | 500 | 8.82 | 7.55 | 9.59 | 9.50 |
| | | 1'000 | 12.05 | 12.74 | 12.78 | 11.84 |
| | $wavg(RAM)$ [MB] | 50 | 1'764.83 | 2'430.69 | 2'620.57 | 2'455.11 |
| | | 500 | 8'686.66 | 8'653.84 | 8'633.66 | 8'583.11 |
| | | 1'000 | 9'549.54 | 9'749.74 | 9'509.81 | 9'350.82 |

| | | $bp_i$ | | | | |
|---|---|---|---|---|---|---|
| Server-side | $wavg(D)$ [ms] | Class 1 | 9.28 | 9.52 | 9.79 | 10.02 |
| | | Class 2 | 6.09 | 6.24 | 6.42 | 6.57 |
| | | Class 3 | 16.73 | 17.16 | 17.64 | 18.06 |
| | | Class 4 | 3.53 | 3.62 | 3.73 | 3.81 |
| | | Class 5 | 22.49 | 23.07 | 23.72 | 24.28 |

1'000 users) and less RAM (from an average of 627.89 MB across all versions for 50 users to 969.62 MB with 1'000 users).

Comparable tendencies are noticeable for **WfMS B** which handles over 48 and over 487 requests per second for 50 and 500 users respectively. Greater variation among versions is present when 1'000 users are simulated with actual number varying from 906.10 in v5.18.0 down to 885.80 requests in v5.21.0. Similar trends are evident in the throughput, which is relatively stable for 50 users and amounts to an average of 119 completed BP instances per second and an average of 1'160 for 500 users, except for v5.21.0 where the throughput drops to 1'132.92 $bp_i/s$. As with the number of requests per second, the throughput also decreases from 2'182.78 in v5.18.0 to 1'974.01 $bp_i/s$ in v5.21.0 for 1'000 users. The average duration of a single BP instance follows the same trends as in WfMS A, but with much higher absolute values of 5.08 ms in v5.18.0 for 500 users as the lowest duration, to a value of 7.19 ms in v5.21.0 for 50 users as the highest duration. When analyzed at BP level, the lowest average duration of 3.53 ms is observed for Class 4 in v5.18.0, while the highest of 24.28 ms for Class 5 in v5.21.0. The duration of the empty BP instantiated by the *call activities*, omitted in the table, is on average 1.17 ms. Usage of CPU is comparable to WfMS A, with an average of 1.97% across versions for 50 users increasing to 12.35% for 1'000 users. RAM usage, on the other hand, is much higher than in WfMS A with an average of 2'317.80 MB across versions for 50 users and 9'539.98 MB for 1'000 users.

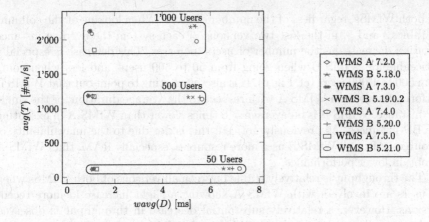

**Fig. 6.** Instance duration $(D)$ vs. Throughput $(T)$

## 4.4   Discussion

In Tables 2 and 3 we can see the detected differences in performance and resource consumption between the two WfMSs, as well as among different versions of the same WfMS. Some of these differences only become obvious when a higher number of users is interacting with the system, making it relevant to have para-metrized load functions representing both small and large companies.

The number of client requests per second shows the average performance of the system from the user point of view. It is relatively stable between all versions of both WfMSs when tested with 50 and 500 users. However, there is a more substantial decrease when tested with 1'000 expected users, especially in WfMS A. The expected maximum is the number of simulated users. The actual value depends mainly on the WfMS's response time and it gets more distant from the expected value as the number of simulated users increases (cf. Tables 2 and 3). The resource consumption metrics in Tables 2 and 3 verify that this behavior does not emerge due to unavailability of resources. The actual resource consumption in all versions is far from the theoretical maximum of the servers (see Sect. 3). The DBMS resource consumption data did not point to any bottlenecks in the communication with the DBMS. They showed that the DBMS had enough resources to handle the issued load. While WfMS A slightly outperforms WfMS B in this metric with a load of 50 users, it falls behind with a load of 500 and 1'000 users. WfMS B experiences 5.65% better $\#REQ/s$ on average than WfMS A, mainly due to the last version of WfMS A being c.a. 15% slower than the last version of WfMS B in starting new BP instances with 1'000 users. If one expects performance improvements with new system releases, these results could be surprising given that, with respect to these metrics, older versions show better performance than newer versions.

The performance decrease with newer versions is made even more evident by the BP instance duration metric $(D)$. As we can see from Tables 2, 3 and Fig. 6, the average duration of a BP instance increases as new versions are introduced for both WfMSs, regardless of the number of users. When looking at the columns of Tables 2 and 3, in the last two versions of each system the average instance duration decreases as the number of users increases. This decrease is especially noticeable for WfMS B when going from 50 to 500 users, and less when going from 500 to 1'000 users (cf. Fig. 6). It is also interesting to point out that WfMS B performs worse than WfMS A with respect to the average duration for the single BP instance. WfMS B is on average 5–6 times slower than WfMS A in executing the BP instances. As previously noticed, this is not due to the unavailability of resources. After all WfMS B uses more resources, especially RAM, than WfMS A to obtain lower performance.

The throughput is relatively stable between all versions of both WfMSs when 50 users are involved, with WfMS A showing a slight increase in more recent versions. However, a relatively substantial decrease in throughput is observed in the newest version of both WfMS A and WfMS B when the load is raised to 1'000 users (cf. Fig. 6). When looking at both systems, their throughput is comparable with 50 users. Then WfMS A outperforms WfMS B by 2% to 4% in newer versions with 500 users, but WfMS B takes the lead when there are 1'000 users by 3% to 6% in newer versions. This might be unexpected given that WfMS B's average BP instance duration is 5 times greater than WfMS A's. It might be due to the fact that WfMS B accepts 15% more instances per second with 1'000 users by exploiting parallelism when executing the instances, thus balancing the longer instance duration.

We also show the average BP instance duration for each model class among all loads in Tables 2 and 3 (bottom). When looking at the data, care needs to be taken as the averages for the different BPs are calculated using different numbers of data points. This is due to the different intensities in the execution of the different models as presented in Table 1. Tables 2 and 3 show that the mentioned increase in average BP instance duration in newer WfMS versions is not caused from one particular BP, but is noticeable in all BPs. However, different models perform differently for the two WfMSs. While Class 1 (cf. Fig. 1) is the fastest in WfMS A with an average duration of 1.21 ms across all loads and versions, in WfMS B Class 4 (cf. Fig. 4) is the fastest with an average of 3.67 ms. And while Class 5, the model with the greatest size (cf. Fig. 5), has the longest duration in WfMS B (avg. 23.39 ms), this is not the case with WfMS A, where Class 3 (cf. Fig. 3) is the slowest one (avg. 2.56 ms). Having noticed such differences, we examined the execution data at construct level. While WfMS B is on average 7 times slower than WfMS A in executing the *call activities* (avg. 5.06 ms vs. 0.70 ms respectively), it actually performs better in executing parallel gateways (avg. 0.01 ms vs. 0.11 ms). WfMS B executes parallel gateways faster than exclusive gateways (avg. 0.01 ms vs. 0.04 ms) which might explain the faster execution of Class 2 vs. Class 1. The slower execution of instances in WfMS B also partially results from its slow instance start-up, with an average duration of the start event of 0.56 ms vs. 0.04 ms in WfMS A. When analyzing the execution duration of individual constructs at model level, stable behaviour is noticed for start and end events, while the greatest variation between models is observable for the *call activity* and *script task* in WfMS B and for the gateways in WfMS A.

Last, but not least, the resource consumption metrics verify that the WfMSs' performance behavior is not caused by lack of resources. Average CPU and RAM consumption is relatively stable between versions for both systems. In fact, the average CPU consumption is at most 12.78% across the different experiments, while the maximum (not reported in the table) is 85% for WfMS B, and 82% for WfMS A. The average RAM consumption is at most 9'749.74 MB, out of the maximum available of 128 GB. These metrics are also a powerful indication of the required resources for obtaining the results produced by the other performance metrics. The CPU consumption is comparable between the two systems, with slightly higher values for WfMS B especially for 1'000 users for all versions. Regarding the RAM consumption, WfMS B always needs more RAM than WfMS A, up to $10x$ times more for certain experiments.

## 5   Threats to Validity

The complexity of running performance experiments on WfMSs, contributes to the following threats to validity.

Construct validity is threatened from the fact that the extracted workload mix depends on the collection used as an input to the analysis of recurring structures. We mitigate the resulting generalization limitations by using a large and heterogeneous collection. Moreover, we provide a parametric method to derive the workload mix, so that it can be applied to other collections (e.g., domain-specific or customer-specific). Another threat to the construct validity is the unavailability of log data, which has resulted with a randomly generated artificial data for evaluating the path to follow in conditional path decisions. Moreover, all the scripts not used for data generation are empty, thus limiting the evaluation of the performance impact of data stored by tasks in the BP instances. The workload mix has not been experimentally compared to any similar baseline approach, leaving a degree of uncertainty regarding the level of accuracy. Finally, the generated workload mix remains unchanged between the experiments, thus hindering a profound comparison between the WfMSs and their versions with regard to the characteristics of the workload mix. We mitigate this by a short discussion about the performance differences between the classes of models used in the workload mix.

A threat to the external and construct validity is that specific settings of our load functions (e.g., the number of users and their think time) could be more realistic. However, the parametric method can still be applied upon availability of additional real-world data and execution logs. Nonetheless, the load functions used were sufficient to stress the system and obtain initial performance insights.

The use of different servers for the WfMS and the DBMS connected through a dedicated 10 Gbit/s network is also a potential threat to external and construct validity, because of the network latency that might impact the communication between the WfMS and the DBMS. However, we are confident that our set-up mitigates the impact of network latency and congestion on the attained measurements. Related to this, results may differ when using a system with different (e.g., higher) hardware specifications than the ones used in our experiments or, for example, when using another DBMS. Additional threat is the use of a single configuration per WfMS. Performance differences may be noticed when changing the configuration.

# 6 Related Work

**Parametric Workload Generation.** Graph-based workloads have been applied for performance testing applications that model data as graphs. In addition to size, Duan et al. [2] introduce the metric of "structuredeness" of RDF datasets generated for performance testing purposes. Vicknair et al. [17] compare the performance of a graph DB and a relational DB. The defined workload is divided into structural and data queries. The structural queries address the storage of data provenance information as Directed Acyclic Graphs. The data queries use payload data, with artificial provenance information. Similar to both, for the definition of our representative workload mix, we combined structural characteristics of the BPs by considering size and other statistical information. Gupta [6] stresses the need for a parametric method to allow the user to dynamically generate workload with respect to structural parameters. Our method offers generation and parametrization of the workload mix, when the original collection or the performance goals vary. The importance of the graph's structure is most of the times ignored [2], and the structural information is represented by empirical and/or artificial data [17]. In our case, the structural information of the workload is defined by extracting the reoccurring structural patterns in a collection. The same method can be applied to any BPMN 2.0 collection, due to its parametric nature. By combining the derived information with other statistical data, such as descriptive statistics, clustering and popularity metrics [3], we are able to define different classes in the workload mix [14]. Overall, in the area of big and linked data, the generation of realistic graphs for performance testing purposes is well established. However, to the extent of our knowledge, this is the first time that an approach for BP synthesis is proposed for WfMSs performance testing. To this end, the experimental comparison of the proposed approach to a less advanced approach is currently not possible.

**WfMSs Performance Testing.** In the literature we can find work on characterizing WfMSs' performance. As reported by Röck et al. [13], who conducted a systematic review on approaches that test the performance of WS-BPEL WfMSs, all performance tests are custom or micro-benchmarks. The most prominent one is SOABench [1], which uses a simple workload mix composed by basic BPEL structures. SOABench is used to compare the response time of three open-source WfMSs (ActiveVOS, jBPM, and Apache ODE) using a different number of clients with variable think times and has identified some scalability limitations of the tested systems. To the best of our knowledge, our existing work on micro-benchmarking [15], is the first effort to propose a performance testing method for BPMN 2.0 WfMSs. The results in [15] showed bottlenecks in architectural design decisions and resource consumption, as well as limits on the load the WfMS can sustain. The results presented in this paper extend our earlier observations with experiments based on a more complex, structurally representative, parametric workload and by comparing different WfMSs versions.

## 7 Conclusion and Future Work

In this paper we presented a novel parametric method for deriving a structurally representative workload mix from a potentially large BPMN 2.0 collection, to respond to the need of evaluating the performance of different WfMSs versions with an appropriate workload. We illustrated how to obtain the BP models of a workload mix, using the proposed method for distilling the most prominent control-flow characteristics of the given collection. We also proposed a method for using such collection to determine the proportion of instantiated BPs in the workload mix. We then parametrized the load function for different numbers of simulated users (50, 500, and 1'000) representing differently sized companies. We issued the derived workload model to four different versions of two widely used open-source BPMN 2.0 WfMSs. After validating the reliability of the obtained results we computed diverse performance metrics. While WfMS A demonstrated significantly lower average duration of a single BP instance and lower RAM usage, WfMS B had the lead in throughput. Furthermore, over both system releases within the past two years, it appears that priority was given to adding new features as opposed to improving the performance. The obtained results justify the need for performance testing of different WfMSs versions using a workload mix representative of user's needs and BP collections.

As future work we plan to apply the proposed method to domain-specific model collections. In such settings we also plan to extend our method to support events, human tasks, and WfMS interaction with external systems, such as Web Service APIs. We also aim at the experimental comparison of the synthetic workload mixes to real-world process models, in order to identify the accuracy of our workload mix generation method. Moreover, we have started analyzing execution logs of real world BP instances to define even more realistic load functions. We plan to add more WfMSs and run the experiments with different configuration settings.

**Acknowledgements.** This work is partially funded by the Swiss National Science Foundation and the German Research Foundation through the BenchFlow: A Benchmark for Workflow Management Systems (DACH Grant Nr. 200021E-145062/1) project.

## References

1. Bianculli, D., et al.: Automated performance assessment for service-oriented middleware: a case study on BPEL engines. In: Proceedings of WWW, pp. 141–150 (2010)

2. Duan, S., et al.: Apples and oranges: a comparison of RDF benchmarks and real RDF datasets. In: Proceedings of SIGMOD. Association for Computing Machinery (2011)
3. Feitelson, D.G.: Workload Modeling for Computer Systems Performance Evaluation. Cambridge University Press, New York (2015)
4. Ferme, V., Ivanchikj, A., Pautasso, C.: A framework for benchmarking BPMN 2.0 workflow management systems. In: Motahari-Nezhad, H.R., Recker, J., Weidlich, M. (eds.) BPM 2015. LNCS, vol. 9253, pp. 251–259. Springer, Cham (2015). doi:10.1007/978-3-319-23063-4_18
5. Ferme, V., Ivanchikj, A., Pautasso, C., Skouradaki, M., Leymann, F.: A Container-centric methodology for benchmarking workflow management systems. In: CLOSER 2016 - Proceedings of the 6th International Conference on Cloud Computing and Services Science, vol. 2, Rome, Italy, April 23-25, pp. 74–84 (2016). doi:10.5220/0005908400740084
6. Gupta, A.: Generating large-scale heterogeneous graphs for benchmarking. In: Rabl, T., Poess, M., Baru, C., Jacobsen, H.-A. (eds.) WBDB -2012. LNCS, vol. 8163, pp. 113–128. Springer, Heidelberg (2014). doi:10.1007/978-3-642-53974-9_11
7. Hollingsworth, D.: The workflow reference model. WfMC 68 (1995)
8. Jordan, D., et al.: Business process model and notation (BPMN) version 2.0. Object Management Group, Inc. (2011). http://www.omg.org/spec/BPMN/2.0/
9. Molyneaux, I.: The Art of Application Performance Testing: From Strategy to Tools, 2nd edn. O'Reilly Media, Sebastopol (2014)
10. Montgomery, D.C., Runger, G.C.: Applied Statistics and Probability for Engineers. Wiley, New York (2003)
11. Muehlen, M., Recker, J.: How much language is enough? Theoretical and practical use of the business process modeling notation. In: Bellahsène, Z., Léonard, M. (eds.) CAiSE 2008. LNCS, vol. 5074, pp. 465–479. Springer, Heidelberg (2008). doi:10.1007/978-3-540-69534-9_35
12. Pietsch, P., Wenzel, S.: Comparison of BPMN2 diagrams. In: Mendling, J., Weidlich, M. (eds.) BPMN 2012. LNBIP, vol. 125, pp. 83–97. Springer, Heidelberg (2012). doi:10.1007/978-3-642-33155-8_7
13. Röck, C., et al.: Performance benchmarking of BPEL engines: a comparison framework, status quo evaluation and challenges. In: Proceedings of SEKE, pp. 31–34 (2014)
14. Skouradaki, M., Andrikopoulos, V., Leymann, F.: Representative BPMN 2.0 process model generation from recurring structures. In: Proceedings of ICWS 2016 (2016)
15. Skouradaki, M., Ferme, V., Pautasso, C., Leymann, F., Hoorn, A.: Micro-benchmarking BPMN 2.0 workflow management systems with workflow patterns. In: Nurcan, S., Soffer, P., Bajec, M., Eder, J. (eds.) CAiSE 2016. LNCS, vol. 9694, pp. 67–82. Springer, Cham (2016). doi:10.1007/978-3-319-39696-5_5
16. Skouradaki, M., Andrikopoulos, V., Kopp, O., Leymann, F.: RoSE: reoccurring structures detection in bpmn 2.0 process model collections. In: Debruyne, C. et al. (eds) On the Move to Meaningful Internet Systems: OTM 2016 Conferences. OTM 2016. LNCS, vol 10033. Springer, Cham (2016). doi:10.1007/978-3-319-48472-3_15
17. Vicknair, C., et al.: A comparison of a graph database and a relational database. In: Proceedings of ACM SE 2010. Association for Computing Machinery (ACM) (2010)
18. Wetzstein, B., et al.: Monitoring and analyzing influential factors of business process performance. In: Proceedings of EDOC 2009, pp. 141–150 (2009)

# BPMN-Based Model-Driven Testing of Service-Based Processes

Daniel Lübke[1,2(✉)] and Tammo van Lessen[3]

[1] FG Software Engineering, Leibniz Universität Hannover, Hannover, Germany
daniel.luebke@inf.uni-hannover.de
[2] innoQ Schweiz GmbH, Cham, Switzerland
[3] innoQ Deutschland GmbH, Monheim am Rhein, Germany
tammo.van-lessen@innoq.com

**Abstract.** Executable Business Processes realized in WS-BPEL and BPMN2 are used more and more for automating digitalized core processes in organizations. Due to their critical nature for the organization, these processes need to be developed with high quality standards. Existing literature concentrates on testing such processes, but do not offer integration into the development lifecycle and validation with other stakeholders. Our approach is based on Test Models that allow both the easier definition of automated test cases as well as discussion with non-technical stakeholders and, thus, can be used for business process validation and process modeling support. We define a meta-model for the BPMN-based Test Models that has been validated in a case study in an industrial project.

**Keywords:** BPMN · Model-driven testing · Business process · Service composition · Process validation

## 1 Introduction

Executable Business Processes are becoming more and more common to implement the flow of business activities in business software systems. These languages, like WS-BPEL [5] and BPMN2 [19], are allow the visual modeling of process flow, data-flow and service invocations. The standards mandate parallel execution, business transactions by compensation management, and message correlation, which are implemented in the middleware and need not be written manually by developers.

Executable Business Processes are also software artifacts and offer high expressiveness. They can carry complex process logic and data transformation logic that is critical from an availability point of view: Business-critical processes need to be available to the organization and software failures or unwanted behavior may cause huge losses. The more business processes are automated in an organization and the more complex they get over time, the more important quality assurance of such executable business processes gets.

One important part of quality assurance for executable business processes is the development of automated tests. In development projects, different project

© Springer International Publishing AG 2017
I. Reinhartz-Berger et al. (Eds.): BPMDS/EMMSAD 2017, LNBIP 287, pp. 119–133, 2017.
DOI: 10.1007/978-3-319-59466-8_8

members develop tests for finding defects on different levels (unit tests, integration tests and system tests [9]). These tests aim to discover different error sources of the system. All tests need to be maintained alongside the business processes, which can take considerable effort in complex systems. Especially changes to service contracts lead to large maintenance efforts for migration of test definitions and test data.

Complexity adds another challenge for project teams: They need to validate the process models with the business side. Depending on the business side's ability to understand and work with large business process models, this task can represent a challenge in itself. However, it is essential to agree on the functionality and necessary acceptance tests for the executable business processes. This can only be achieved, if the testing approach is combined with a review of the business processes – and even better the test cases are validated by the business side.

This paper builds upon an experience report published by the authors in [11]. This paper presents the meta-model, integration options into the development process and a case study. The goal is to make the approach applicable for others and provides initial empirical validation. This paper is therefore structured as follows: In the following section, existing approaches for testing executable business processes are presented. In Sect. 3, the model-driven testing approach is presented with describing the underlying requirements (Sect. 3.1), the underlying meta-model (Sect. 3.2), a short description of the generator (Sect. 3.3) and a discussion on how the requirements are fulfilled (Sect. 4.2.) This main section is followed by Sect. 5 which discusses how the approach can be integrated into software development processes. An empirical evaluation of the presented approach in the form of a case study is described in Sect. 6 before the paper concludes in Sect. 7.

## 2   Related Work

Testing service compositions implemented in BPEL and BPMN is an active research area. Rusli et al. [17] conducted a mapping study and found that 58% of the test publications concentrate on Test Generation, but they did not list profiles nor meta-models as research objectives. The only approach the authors identified to use profiles was by Rauf et al. [16], which used UML profiles to help with test case generation.

For their testing approach, Kaschner and Lohmann [6] informally introduced their specification models and public view models as examples. They used black-box pools for participating parties/services and described the behavior of processes by giving abstracted process descriptions.

Many tools for automating test execution against BPEL service compositions have been developed. At least two of those (Li et al. [8] and Mayer and Lübke [13]) provided a test framework that was capable of sending and receiving SOAP messages independently of BPEL. Due to this ability, they can also be used to test BPMN service orchestrations that utilize SOAP services and provide the technical infrastructure for running tests defined with our approach.

Dong et al. [7] presented a testing approach for BPEL based on Petri Nets. The approach analyzes an existing BPEL process and deducts test cases from it. Maâlej et al. [12] used model-based testing for checking conformance with times autonoma. Ji et al. [4] used data-flow analysis techniques to deduct regression tests from existing BPEL processes. Yuan et al. [20] proposed the use of UML Activity Diagrams in conjunction with the BPEL specification.

All these approaches have in common that the test models are not to be understood by business stakeholders and are often even derived from the BPEL model itself. Thus, no validation of the test cases by business stakeholders can occur and the tests can only be defined after the creation of the BPEL process has been finished.

## 3   Model-Driven Test Approach

### 3.1   Requirements

In order to enable a development project to define, implement, and maintain executable test cases for executable business processes efficiently, we identified the following requirements when discussing testing challenges in an industrial project. Those were later amended during the case study (those requirements are marked with an *):

**R01:** Test Cases must be reviewable by business stakeholders, business analysts, business process modelers, and developers. Because at least business stakeholders are often not familiar with technical notations, test cases must be defined in an easy and intuitive way.

**R02:** Test Cases must be deterministic, i.e. they must be defined so precisely that the same process flow will be executed every time the test case is executed in order to replicate error scenarios and re-run test cases for determining whether a defect has been fixed.

**R03*:** Test Cases must express timing dependencies between different services (e.g. sub-processes or different participants) for expressing scenarios which are timing sensitive.

**R04:** Test Cases must be easy to maintain. Especially changes to the environment like new versions of service contracts must be achieved with as low effort as possible.

**R05:** Effort invested into the definition of test cases should not be lost, but the business-friendly description should be the basis for test case automation.

**R06:** Test Cases definitions should be "living" documents: Their usage should be for practical reasons mandatory or so useful that they are updated in the normal development activities.

**R07:** Test Cases should be derivable from the business process ("test-later" approach) or should be the basis for the business process model implementation ("test-first" approach [1]).

**R08:** Test Cases should ideally serve as process documentation allowing stakeholders to find specified behavior easily in a given context.

**R09:** Test Cases need to serve as a manual for testers for conducting the tests manually. Besides automation, it is initially still necessary to test those functions manually that have user interactions to check for usability and formatting issues.

**R10:** Test Cases need to define a way to store values generated by the process, e.g. correlation tokens, in order to provide all information necessary for producing an executable test case.

**R11\*:** Test Cases must allow the hiding of technical information, especially of empty acknowledgement messages (relates to R01).

### 3.2   Meta-Model for Test Models and Test Case Models

In order to satisfy the requirements, our approach defines two sets of artifacts: Those defined from a business point of view and those defined from a technical point of view. This separation allows us to fulfill technical requirements and still have artifacts that business stakeholders can discuss and comprehend.

A simplified version of the meta-model is shown in Fig. 1. The gray colored classes are part of the BPMN standard. The meta-models main class is the *Test Model* that contains a set of *Test Case Models* that are modeled in BPMN. The control-flow restrictions of these models are explained in further detail below and

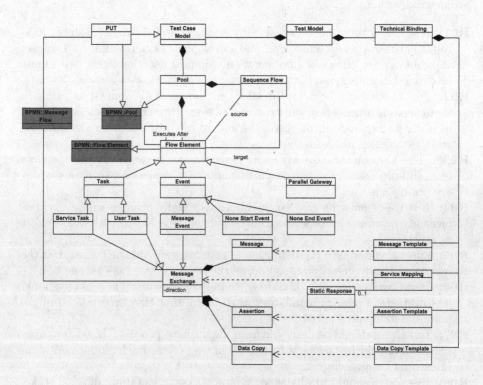

**Fig. 1.** A simplified meta-model of the BPMN test profile

are enforced by only allowing a sub-set of BPMN to be used. Every BPMN Test Case Model has one BPMN Pool that represents the process/system under test (PUT). All other *Pools* represent process participants that should be mocked during the test.

Pools contain *Flow Elements* that are derived from *BPMN Flow Elements*. The allowed Flow Elements contain only the control-flow structures (*Tasks*, selected *Events* and selected *Gateways*) that are necessary to organize *Message Exchanges* between the PUT and another Pool. Every Message Exchange can have multiple *Assertions* for data that is sent to a participant and can define a *Message* that is sent back to the PUT. The cardinalities of assertions and messages are dependent on the service contract: In case of incoming (i.e. received by the participant) one-way operations, no returning message must be defined. In case of outgoing one-way operations, no assertions must be defined. For two-way operations, a message must be defined that is sent to the process.

Messages and Assertions are not defined absolutely but are references to *Templates* with parameters. Like Behavior-Driven Development (BDD) [15], this is done with a structured text form that looks like normal language to readers but must conform to a template. This allows the reuse of information by referencing it from different Test Case Models. Templates are implementation specific, e.g. SOAP messages and XPath assertions might be defined for testing SOAP Web services. In addition to the Templates, there are technology-dependent *Service Mappings* that map message exchanges in the Test Case Model to physical operations, e.g. as defined in a WSDL. By doing this, all technical information is extracted from the Test Case Model itself and can be replaced by a different one. This allows the same set of Test Cases to be used for testing different service versions as long as the process stays the same: Templates and Service Mappings can be provided for both service versions.

The Test Case Models as illustrated as an example in Fig. 3 are BPMN models that are required to use a subset of BPMN with one extension taken from [3]. The restrictions make the process flow deterministic in order to satisfy Requirement R02: The control-flow in BPMN is controlled by the use of gateways that can be defined explicitly with their own diamond-shaped symbol or implicitly by having multiple sequence flows ("arcs") from a single activity. All implicitly defined control-flows are forbidden in our profile and only parallel gateways, i.e. those that trigger all paths after them, are allowed. Originally, no gateways were allowed but when testing our approach in an industry project we encountered situations that required parallel activities by process participants. We also found that process participants need to be synchronized (Requirement R03): An activity in one participant must only be executed if another participant completed another activity. Such cross-participant dependencies cannot be expressed in BPMN. When testing, such synchronization must occur, e.g. when the process has manual parts and the software takes over after some manual activities are completed. Also in order to test compensation in parallel processes, test cases needed to be able to express such dependencies in order to eliminate uncontrolled execution orders in parallel branches.

### 3.3   Generator Implementation

In order to roll out our approach in the case study project, we needed to provide a working tool. Thus, we developed a generator that reads BPMN models in the official OMG XML format and generates BPELUnit [13] test suites. By using the official XML format, our generator can be used with all BPMN-compliant tools. BPELUnit was already used by the project and, thus, the new test cases could be integrated well into the development tool chain, e.g. the nightly build. It provides the infrastructure for testing and mocking arbitrary SOAP services – not only those implemented in BPEL – because it operates by sending predefined SOAP messages and evaluating incoming messages by the use of XPath assertions. In addition it supports run-time templating of both messages and assertions. However, our metamodel is technology-agnostic and a generator could be developed that e.g. generates JUnit tests that use REST.

While setting up the case study, the project faced one problem: The test profile requires the use of an academic timing extension to BPMN, which is not available in the modeling tool used by the project nor in any commercially supported tool that we know of. As a consequence, we replicated the dependency by replacing it with a textual annotation, e.g. *Depends-On: Flight Booked.*

The generator reads a spreadsheet that contains various sheets for configuration purposes. A shortened version of the BPELUnit technical binding metamodel is shown in Fig. 2 that defines the contents of the different sheets. The gray-colored classes are technology-specific to WSDL and SOAP:

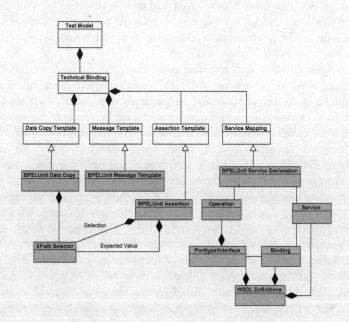

**Fig. 2.** Technical binding to BPELUnit elements

- Services in the Test Model are mapped to services, bindings and operations of WSDL service descriptions.
- Assertions are mapped to two XPath expressions: The first selects the value in the received message to be compared (e.g. `//customerNo`) and the second defines the expected value (e.g. `'123-A-B'`).
- Message Templates are implemented by using XSLT transformations. The parameters from the templated text are passed into an XSLT templates, which returns an XML document that will be sent in the SOAP message.
- For Data Copies, an XPath expression is defined that selects the value to be stored from a SOAP message. This value will be placed in a variable that can be managed by BPELUnit and injected into outgoing SOAP messages. Data Copies are used to extract correlation values (e.g. the process id) and make it accessible for messages sent later in the test case.

## 4  Example

### 4.1  Process and Test Case Models

In order to illustrate the usage of our approach, we define test cases for a very simple example travel process: A travel is booked that consists of a flight and a hotel. If either booking fails, compensation for already booked items will be triggered, i.e. the bookings will be canceled.

For illustrating the testing of this process, we define two Test Case Models (see Fig. 3): One that successfully books a hotel and a flight, and another one that successfully books the hotel but fails to book the flight. Because the bookings for the flight and the hotel are done in parallel, we need a synchronization for

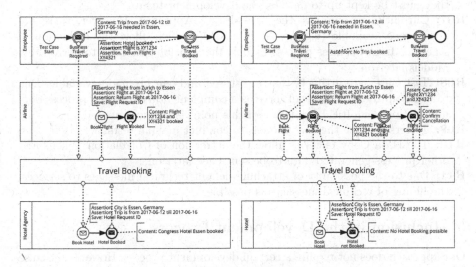

**Fig. 3.** Example test cases

the error cases in order to guarantee that one item is already booked and, thus, needs to be compensated.

The example diagrams contain all information as BPMN comments for illustrative purposes; in real models, assertions and messages are stored in the BPMN documentation elements that can be exported but are not shown in the diagram itself. While initially we used BPMN comments, it became clear during the case study (see Sect. 6) that diagrams became too hard to read and cluttered.

## 4.2 Mapping to Initial Requirements

Within this section we map the different model elements and generator features to the requirements initially outlined in order to show that our approach satisfies all requirements in general.

**R01:** The Test Cases are defined as a simple BPMN subset that is understandable by business stakeholders and does not contain any complex constructs.

**R02:** Because the control-flow in the Test Models is sequential except for parallel flow where necessary, and additional cross-participant constraints can be enforced, test designers and process modelers can model completely deterministic test cases.

**R03:** This requirement was a special case to R02 and is satisfied by the introduction of cross-participant dependencies.

**R04:** New Service Contracts only require a new set of technical bindings that are centralized. No changes to the Test Models are necessary.

**R05:** The BPMN test cases are easy to understand and also work as scenarios for discussing complex business processes and special corner cases.

**R06:** Because test cases are integrated into the development process and are the source of generation, they need to be current and maintained. As such they must be kept up-to-date by the development team.

**R07:** Currently, we support the "Test-First" Approach. However, there are approaches available (e.g. by Ni et al. [14]) which allow the deduction of scenarios from business process models that can be enhanced to derive Test Models later on.

**R08:** Test Cases are artifacts that are stored and can be made available. Due to being up-to-date they can serve as a complementary business process documentation. Empirical validation of this point is however needed.

**R09:** Testers can use the Test Models to conduct manual tests.

**R10:** The Data Copy facilities allow the extraction of Correlation Tokens and other process-generated data to be sent back later on.

**R11:** Due to the possibility of attaching default technical messages to services, the hiding of technical messages is possible.

## 5    Inclusion in the Development Process

Our approach does not require a certain development process. However, because the two domains of business process modeling and software engineering (especially the fields of requirements engineering and testing) are concerned and must

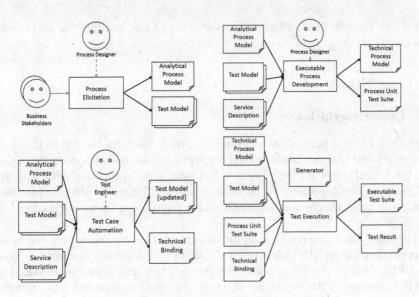

**Fig. 4.** Development Process Building Blocks

be interlinked, we define four Development Process Building Blocks that are shown as information flows using the FLOW notation [18] in Fig. 4:

**Process Elicitation:** The goal of this development activity is to create and document an understanding of the project's underlying business process(es). Within this activity at least an analytical process model and the test models as per our approach are created. The elicitated Test Models are used in all other Development Process Building Blocks.

**Executable Process Development:** This Building Block uses the Test Case Models that provide smaller grained units that can be used for developing stories or smaller project tasks and help the Process Designer in understanding the overall model. Deliverables of this building block is the executable business process model as well as the unit tests covering it.

**Test Case Automation:** The Test Engineer role is responsible for adding the necessary technical bindings to the Test Models. This might require refinements of the test cases and the standardization of the messages and assertions.

**Test Case Execution:** This Development Process Building Block is fully automated and uses the generator to create a test suite out of the provided artifacts and executes it in order to create a test result.

This Development Process Buildings Blocks can be used in different arrangements to be used with different project methodologies, e.g. more waterfall-based approaches (strictly following the order of Process Elicitation, Executable Process Development, Test Case Automation, Test Case Execution) or agile ones (in which these four phases are repeated and done iteratively.) The project in the case study already used different arrangements of the building blocks in order to achieve certain project goals.

## 6    Case Study

### 6.1    Case Description

Terravis [2,11] is a large-scale process integration platform for conducting land registry-related business between land registries, banks, notaries, geometers, pension funds and other parties. Terravis has been developed since 2011 with the first services going productive in 2012. It offers 15 core end-to-end processes with many sub-variants and 12 administrative processes for managing mortage depots.

The analytical process models for documentation purposes and discussion are created using BPMN2 and the executable process models are realized using WS-BPEL. All service interactions between parties and Terravis are based on SOAP Messages. With increasing success, Terravis functionality was extended by both new processes as well as new variants in existing processes, which led to more process models and more complex process models [10].

Because Terravis is in the center of many parties that have different software lifecycles for their systems, it needs to offer multi-version support: Different service versions have to be offered in parallel to give all parties a chance to migrate to the newest version within their lifecycle model. Also a multi-channel approach for using a portal and integrated systems in parallel was added. These developments made manual testing overly complicated because of many new test cases and required more test automation to keep the desired quality level.

The research questions to be answered in this case study mainly focus on the requirements of our approach. These are:

**RQ1:** Is the test profile expressive enough to test real-world processes/services?
**RQ2:** Does the generator approach save testing effort by increasing reuse?
**RQ3:** Can the model-based approach improve the communication and the understanding within the development team by utilizing BPMN scenarios?

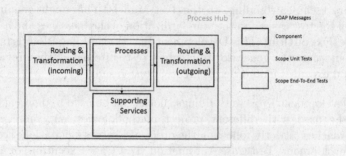

**Fig. 5.** Test scope of the model-driven tests

**RQ4:** Can the same Test Models be reused for testing different service versions of the same executable business process?

The Architecture of the Process Hub of Terravis is shown in Fig. 5: The Process Hub is a backend component that consists of business processes run on a BPMS that are calling supporting service, e.g. for generating documents. The BPMS is accompanied by two routing and transformation chains that shield it from changes in the environment, e.g. service version changes.

The already existing unit test cases cover only the executable processes directly and in isolation. The goal for creating the new test cases was to cover the message flow end-to-end, i.e. call a process via the same infrastructure components like external parties do. This tests the integration of the routing and transformation chains with the processes as well as the supporting services. Because the new test cases only cover the externally visible interfaces they are smaller in size compared to the unit tests which mock all services regardless of their external visibility.

For creating the needed automated regression tests, an analysis of process instance frequency was conducted, the 12 most frequent process variants were selected, and one Test Case Model was created for each. The Development Process Buildings Blocks "Test Case Automation" and "Test Execution" were used to implement regression tests for already specified and implemented processes.

## 6.2    RQ1: Expressiveness of the Test Model

While implementing the set of regression tests, the testers needed a mechanism for synchronizing the timings of different Process Participants (pools). As a result, requirement R03 was added and both the meta-model as well as the generator were extended. With this expressiveness all test cases could be modeled and executed. This means that for this case study, the answer to RQ1 is that all processes could be successfully tested with the extended expressiveness of this profile.

## 6.3    RQ2: Effort of the Generation Approach

For answering RQ2, we analyzed the Test Case Models and technical bindings in order to compute the metrics presented in Table 1: All elements of the technical binding are – on average – referenced multiple times from the test case models. For example, on average every message template is used 2.25 times, every assertion template 6.42 times, and every data copy template 7.5 times in the case study project. By reusing these elements multiple times from the set of test case models, developers and testers should be able to better handle changes to the service because only the templates need to be changed and not all occurrences. All in all, the answer to RQ2 is that all element types are highly reused.

**Table 1.** Static metrics for the test suites

| Element | Static count | Usage | Avg. usage |
|---|---|---|---|
| Test cases | 12 | – – | – |
| Message template | 20 | 45 | 2.25 |
| Assertion template | 21 | 135 | 6.42 |
| Data copy template | 2 | 13 | 7.50 |
| Service mapping | 35 | 91 | 2.60 |

### 6.4    RQ3: Improvement of Communication

The metrics also show that the introduced facility for returning static XML content in case of empty messages was frequently used. Although 91 services were used (the same as the number of service mapping usages), only 45 message templates were used. This means that nearly the half of all (response) messages contained no business-viable content but were empty acknowledgement messages.

The project had to develop one new end-to-end process, which is comparably small compared to the other end-to-end processes. Also a change to a sub-process used by 7 end-to-end processes was required. Besides the full process models, Test Case Models conforming to our meta-model were created prior as part of the process and requirements analysis. Both the new end-to-end process and the sub-process required 8 new test case models. However, the sub-process development and definition has not yet been completed as the time of writing: The sub-process test cases need to be integrated into the test cases of the 7 end-to-end processes yet.

The project team concerned with the development of the new process and the extension of the existing processes used all four Development Process Building Blocks and was asked whether the scenarios were helping in the discussion and with the understanding of the process and its variants. All team members answered with yes. Thus, RQ3 can be cautiously answered that the approach improves communication and understanding of business process requirements in a development team.

### 6.5    RQ4: Effort with Service Version Changes

After introducing the initial regression test suite, a new version of the bank-side interfaces was rolled out and required a transformation component in the outer layers of the process solution. The Test Case Models could be kept and only a new set of technical bindings including the SOAP messages and assertions with the new schema was defined. This set of automated tests was run against the process solution and early defects could be spotted easily and be verified by the developers because the whole test generation and execution process was automated and made available on the Build Server. This reduced the time for testing the transformations compared to previous transformations for prior service version changes. Unfortunately, we could not measure the testing and integration effort required for the already existing mapping components but developers said that the new test cases saved time. Having made the service version transition without changes to the Test Models, we can answer RQ4 with yes. However, we unfortunately lack the data to estimate the saved effort.

### 6.6 Improvements to the Original Approach

As part of the case study we could identify practical shortcomings together with the development team. These led to the following enhancements:

**Usage of Documentation Elements:** Our initial approach used BPMN comments for storing the message content and assertion text. However, these grew too large when used on real messages because in services much business payload is transferred. As a countermeasure we moved the contents into the non-visible BPMN Documentation elements during our case study.

**Cross-Participant Synchronization:** We encountered the need for synchronizing two participants in the Test Model because information is exchanged via paper in the real-world imposing a certain order of service calls. To support this constellation we added requirement R03.

**Participant Propagation for Templates:** SOAP messages contain technical fields, especially information about which participant sends or receives a message. Because messages might contain the same business information but are sent by different participants, the associated participant name is passed as a parameter to the message templates reducing the number of necessary templates.

**Static Response:** The project used many two-way operations with empty responses for indicating the successful transmission of the request. The empty responses contain no business information and as such testers and business stakeholders do not want to see them in the Test Case Models. Also technical stakeholders did not like to declare empty message contents repeatedly. In order to address this issue, we added requirement R11 and allowed service bindings to specify a default message. This default message is used when no other message content is specified on the test activity.

Because this case study was only conducted within one project, its findings cannot be generalized easily before further empirical validation has been conducted, e.g. by further case studies or experiments. Also the case study was conducted in the project that had the need for improve its testing, which can result in confirmation bias. However, the case study shows that the application of our approach is likely to positively influence stakeholder communication and reduce the effort for test creation and maintenance.

## 7    Conclusions and Outlook

Within this paper we presented a model-driven testing approach utilizing BPMN. The approach allows development projects of executable business processes to define test cases and validate both the test cases and the overall process as a set of scenarios with various stakeholders. It basically transfers the idea of Behavior-Driven Development to the area of Executable Business Process Development combined with Model-Driven Testing. In contrast to "traditional" BDD projects, customized BPMN is used. This allows the usage of BPMN as the "lingua franca" for all project participants and the reuse of already existing editors and repositories. Using the same modeling language lowers the entry barrier for the different stakeholders and allows the same tooling to be used.

Consequently, the required test case generator can be implemented based on the official BPMN XML Schema. We implemented a generator that creates BPELUnit test suites for testing SOAP-based business processes, although our approach is independent of the underlying test execution infrastructure.

Our approach builds a bridge between the two domains of Business Process Modeling and Software Engineering. Both domains are highly related in business process execution projects that will be more common as part of further digitalization of organisations. In order to support the cooperation of roles from these domains, we specified Development Process Building Blocks that can be used to add the presented approach to software development processes. We hope to see more inter-domain research for building improved and demonstratedly better solution development methodologies.

The validation in a case study showed positive effects on communication, test creation, and test maintenance. However, future research will need to provide further and stronger validation of these results in order to demonstrate advantages in a more generalizable manner. During the conduction of the case study we have already seen the need for small improvements that greatly improved the practical applicability both to the meta-model as well as to the tooling.

# References

1. Beck, K.: Test-Driven Development by Example. Addison-Wesley, Boston (2003)
2. Berli, W., Lübke, D., Möckli, W.: Terravis - large scale business process integration between public and private partners. In: Plödereder, E., Grunske, L., Schneider, E., Ull, D. (eds.) Proceedings INFORMATIK 2014. Lecture Notes in Informatics, pp. 1075–1090. Gesellschaft für Informatik e.V., Bonn (2014)
3. Cheikhrouhou, S., Kallel, S., Guermouche, N., Jmaiel, M.: Toward a time-centric modeling of business processes in BPMN 2.0. In: Proceedings of International Conference on Information Integration and Web-Based Applications & Services (IIWAS 2013), pp. 154:154–154:163. ACM, New York (2013)
4. Ji, S., Li, B., Zhang, P.: Test case selection for data flow based regression testing of BPEL composite services. In: 2016 IEEE International Conference on Services Computing (SCC), pp. 547–554. IEEE (2016)
5. Jordan, D., Evdemon, J., Alves, A., Arkin, A., Askary, S., Barreto, C., Bloch, B., Curbera, F., Ford, M., Goland, Y., Guízar, A., Kartha, N., Liu, C.K., Khalaf, R., König, D., Marin, M., Mehta, V., Thatte, S., van der Rijn, D., Yendluri, P., Yiu, A.: Web Services Business Process Execution Language Version 2.0. OASIS, April 2007

6. Kaschner, K., Lohmann, N.: Automatic test case generation for interacting services. In: Feuerlicht, G., Lamersdorf, W. (eds.) ICSOC 2008. LNCS, vol. 5472, pp. 66–78. Springer, Heidelberg (2009). doi:10.1007/978-3-642-01247-1_7

7. Dong, W.l., Yu, H., Zhang, Y.B.: Testing BPEL-based web service composition using high-level petri nets. In: 2006 10th IEEE International Enterprise Distributed Object Computing Conference (EDOC 2006), pp. 441–444, October 2006

8. Li, Z., Sun, W., Jiang, Z.B., Zhang, X.: BPEL4WS unit testing: framework and implementation. In: Proceedings of the IEEE International Conference on Web Services (ICWS 2005), pp. 103–110, Washington, DC. IEEE Computer Society (2005)

9. Lübke, D.: Test and analysis of service-oriented systems. In: Baresi, L., Di Nitto, E. (eds.) Unit Testing BPEL Compositions. Springer, Heidelberg (2007)

10. Lübke, D.: Using metric time lines for identifying architecture shortcomings in process execution architectures. In: 2015 IEEE/ACM 2nd International Workshop on Software Architecture and Metrics (SAM), pp. 55–58. IEEE (2015)

11. Lübke, D., van Lessen, T.: Modeling test cases in BPMN for behavior-driven development. IEEE Software, 17–23 September/October 2016

12. Maâlej, A.J., Krichen, M., Jmaiel, M.: Model-based conformance testing of WS-BPEL compositions. In: 2012 IEEE 36th Annual Computer Software and Applications Conference Workshops, pp. 452–457, July 2012

13. Mayer, P., Lübke, D.: Towards a BPEL unit testing framework. In: Proceedings of the 2006 Workshop on Testing, Analysis, and Verification of Web Services and Applications (TAV-WEB 2006), Portland, pp. 33–42. ACM Press, New York (2006)

14. Ni, Y., Hou, S.-S., Zhang, L., Zhu, J., Li, Z.J., Lan, Q., Mei, H., Sun, J.-S.: Effective message-sequence generation for testing BPEL programs. IEEE Trans. Serv. Comput. **6**(1), 7–19 (2013)

15. North, D.: Introducing BDD (2006). http://dannorth.net/introducing-bdd

16. Rauf, I., Iqbal, M.Z.Z., Malik, Z.I.: Model based testing of web service composition using UML profile. In: Proceedings of the 2nd Workshop on Model-Based Testing in Practice (2009)

17. Rusli, H.M., Ibrahim, S., Puteh, M.: Testing web services composition: a mapping study (2011)

18. Schneider, K.: Software process improvement from a FLOW perspective. In: Birk, A. (ed.) Workshop on Learning Software Organizations (LSO 2005) (2005)

19. Silver, B., Richard, B.: BPMN Method and Style, vol. 2. Cody-Cassidy Press, Aptos (2009)

20. Yuan, Q., Ji, W., Liu, C., Zhang, L.: A model driven approach toward business process test case generation. In: 2008 10th International Symposium on Web Site Evolution, pp. 41–44, October 2008

# Business Process Model Comprehension

# Cognitive Insights into Business Process Model Comprehension: Preliminary Results for Experienced and Inexperienced Individuals

Michael Zimoch[1]([✉]), Rüdiger Pryss[1], Thomas Probst[1], Winfried Schlee[2], and Manfred Reichert[1]

[1] Institute of Databases and Information Systems, Ulm University, Ulm, Germany
{michael.zimoch,ruediger.pryss,thomas.probst,manfred.reichert}@uni-ulm.de
[2] Department of Psychiatry and Psychotherapy,
Regensburg University, Regensburg, Germany
winfried.schlee@googlemail.com

**Abstract.** Process modeling constitutes a fundamental task in the context of process-aware information systems. Besides process model creation, the reading and understanding of process models is of utmost importance. To better understand the latter, we have developed a conceptual framework focusing on the comprehension of business process models. By adopting concepts from cognitive neuroscience and psychology, the paper presents initial results from a series of eye tracking experiments on process model comprehension. The results indicate that experiences with process modeling have an influence on overall model comprehension. In turn, with increasing process model complexity, individuals with either no or advanced expertise in process modeling do not significantly differ with respect to process model comprehension. The results further indicate that both groups face similar challenges in reading and comprehending process models. The conceptual framework takes these results into account and provides the basis for the further experiments.

**Keywords:** Business process model comprehension · Eye tracking · Cognition

## 1 Introduction

*Process models* document the tasks, decisions, and actors of business processes following a specific goal. In practice, the latter is specified in terms of textual or graphical artifacts. Regarding graphical process models, a variety of visual shapes like oblongs, rhombuses, and circles, together with other symbols, are used. Besides syntactical rules, process models express pertinent aspects of the respective business process. In general, the use of graphical process representations yields advantages compared to textual ones [1].

Regarding graphical process modeling, there exists a plethora of different modeling languages including *Flow Chart* [2], *BPMN* [3], *EPC* [4], or *Gantt Chart* [5].

© Springer International Publishing AG 2017
I. Reinhartz-Berger et al. (Eds.): BPMDS/EMMSAD 2017, LNBIP 287, pp. 137–152, 2017.
DOI: 10.1007/978-3-319-59466-8_9

Each modeling language, in turn, provides different graphical elements for documenting the business processes. Research on process model comprehension has shown that appropriate symbols and visual elements foster the reading as well as the comprehension of process models [6]. It is further known that individuals perceive graphical representations differently, resulting in modeling preferences based on a variety of personal factors [7]. Despite existing research in this field, there exist open issues on how these factors might influence process model comprehension. *Cognitive neuroscience* and *psychology*, in turn, can provide valuable insights into process model comprehension. We are therefore developing a *conceptual framework* that incorporates methods and theories from these two disciplines, with a particular focus on the

- improvement of statistical and empirical evaluations existing in this context,
- identification of rules on how to foster process model comprehension,
- categorization (e.g., level of complexity or construct-related similarities) of process models based on experimental data, and
- provision of directives towards creating better readable process models.

This paper discusses the results of a pilot eye tracking experiment that was conducted using the conceptual framework. The experiment evaluates process model comprehension based on measured eye movements of the subjects. In detail, the latter were tracked while comprehending different process models. By applying the conceptual framework, the experiment revealed preliminary but promising results with respect to process model comprehension.

The remainder of this paper is organized as follows: Sect. 2 presents theoretical backgrounds and introduces the proposed conceptual framework. Section 3 discusses the experimental setting. Section 4 deals with the preparation and execution of the experiment. Obtained results from the experiment are presented and analyzed in Sect. 5. Finally, Sect. 6 discusses related work and Sect. 7 summarizes the paper.

## 2  Theoretical Backgrounds

This section introduces fundamentals required for understanding our work. Section 2.1 discusses relevant work on process modeling, whereas Sect. 2.2 deals with process modeling from the viewpoint of cognitive neuroscience and psychology. Finally, Sect. 2.3 presents the conceptual framework in detail.

### 2.1  Process Modeling

The documentation of business processes using a graphical representation has its origins back in the 19th century. Since the creation of Gantt Charts in 1899, many graphical process modeling languages (e.g., Flow Charts, Event-Driven Process Chains (EPC)) emerged as alternatives for a graphical documentation. With its visual elements representing tasks, events, control flow, and actors, process modeling has become increasingly important [8]. In this context, high process model quality is crucial to increase the comprehensibility of business processes [9].

Note that the concrete scenario, in which business processes shall be used, is relevant with respect to the appropriation of a particular modeling language. Which process modeling language fits best in a particular scenario, however, constitutes a challenging task.

## 2.2 Cognitive Neuroscience and Psychology

Cognitive neuroscience is dealing with biological as well as underlying processes (e.g., neural response to a stimulus). The rapid progression in this field let to new findings on cognitive processes and neural mechanisms (e.g., *perception*) [10]. Using specific measurement methods, along with useful technology from the research field of cognitive neuroscience (e.g., electrodermal activity), our understanding on how sensory information is processed by the human brain has significantly improved. Cognitive neuroscience overlaps with the field of cognitive psychology, with a stronger emphasis on the neural function of the brain. In turn, cognitive psychology is the scientific investigation of mental processes concerned with the observations in human functions such as attention, memory, information processes, and thinking [11]. Compared to cognitive neuroscience, emphasis is put on the use of methodological theories (e.g., *Cognitive Load Theory (CLT)*). In the context of business process modeling, this offers promising opportunities providing, for example, insights into the cognitive processes of individuals when reading and comprehending process models.

## 2.3 Conceptual Framework

The emphasis of the conceptual framework we developed is put on process modeling and on the influence personal factors have on process model comprehension. Figure 1 illustrates the conceptual framework and its components:

**(1) Reference process models in different notations.** With the increasing adoption of *process-aware information systems (PAIS)*, more and more enterprise repositories comprise large collections of business process models created by process modeling experts [12]. For graphically documenting business processes, there exists a variety of process modeling languages (e.g., *BPMN*, *EPC*). Often, the chosen language for representing process models lacks consistency and, therefore, the graphical representation varies significantly. In turn, the heterogeneous process model representations might affect process model comprehensibility [13]. In particular, non-experts are frequently confronted with challenges regarding how to properly read process models.

**(2) Process model characteristics.** There are factors related to process modeling that influence an individual's capability to comprehend process models.

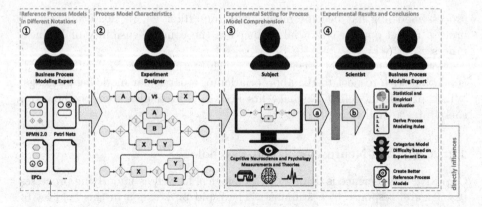

**Fig. 1.** Conceptual framework for process model comprehension

For example, the chosen graphical representation, level of complexity, or activity labeling are such factors that must be carefully considered when designing experiments.

**(3) Experimental setting for process model comprehension.** Individuals perceive graphical representations differently, depending on personal factors. For example, expertise in process modeling is an important factor in this context. What is easy to learn for a particular individual, might be more difficult for another one. Cognitive neuroscience and cognitive psychology are promising fields that might provide new means for research and observations. Throughout a series of experiments, which make use of concepts from cognitive neuroscience and psychology (e.g., *eye tracking, event-related potential*), the identification of stumbling blocks and obstacles will be addressed by the conceptual framework.

**(4) Experimental results and conclusions.** The aggregated findings obtained from conducted experiments are analyzed by scientists using different methods (e.g., *clustering, similarity matching*). The results are used to rate and classify individuals with respect to process model comprehension ⓐ (cf. Fig. 1). This classification reflects the perceived difficulty of an individual regarding process model comprehension and the importance of personal factors in this context. Taking the results into account, further steps and activities can be derived. For example, process modeling languages and visual constructs may be categorized into groups of different levels of complexity ⓑ (cf. Fig. 1). Finally, all outcomes serve as additional indicators on how to create better process models.

## 3   Experimental Setting

This section introduces the definition and planning of the experiment for measuring process model comprehension. Section 3.1 illustrates the context of the experiment and defines its goals. Section 3.2 introduces the hypotheses considered for testing, whereas Sect. 3.3 presents the experimental setup. Finally, Sect. 3.4 discusses the design of the experiment.

## 3.1 Context Selection and Goal Definition

A potentially relevant factor for process model comprehension is the expertise in process research question:

> **Research Question**
>
> *Does expertise in the domain of process modeling has a positive effect on reading and comprehending business process models?*

To address this research question, the conceptual framework is used for an eye tracking experiment. *Eye tracking* constitutes a technique measuring eye movements in response to a visual stimulus (e.g., picture) [14]. Moreover, it is a cost-effective and unobtrusive method to gain deeper insights into human cognitive processes. Most common types of evaluated eye movements are *fixations, saccades,* and *gaze paths* [15]. Fixations constitute eye movements of very low velocity at a specific point in the stimulus, while saccades constitute quick changes of eye movement. Note that during saccadic eye movements, no visual information is perceived. A gaze path, in turn, represents the path (i.e., chronological order of fixations and saccades) the eyes take while analyzing a stimulus. Based on a controlled eye tracking experiment, participating subjects needed to comprehend three process models and were asked to answer a set of comprehension questions related to these models, while their eye movements were recorded.

## 3.2 Hypothesis Formulation

Based on the research question, five hypotheses were derived that shall investigate whether intermediates (i.e., individuals with expertise in the field of process modeling) are more effective than novices (i.e., individuals with no expertise in the field of process modeling) in respect to process model comprehension:

$H_{0,1}$: Intermediates need not less duration time for process model comprehension compared to novices.

$H_{1,1}$: Intermediates need significantly less duration time for process model comprehension compared to novices.

$H_{0,2}$: Intermediates do not achieve a better score for answering the questions compared to novices.

$H_{1,2}$: Intermediates achieve a significantly better score for answering the questions compared to novices.

$H_{0,3}$: Intermediates do not have a better response time for answering the questions compared to novices.

$H_{1,3}$: Intermediates have a significantly better response time for answering the questions compared to novices.

$H_{0,4}$: Intermediates do not have less fixations in process model comprehension compared to novices.

$H_{1,4}$: Intermediates have significantly less fixations in process model comprehension compared to novices.

$H_{0,5}$: Intermediates do not have a shorter gaze path in process model comprehension compared to novices.

$H_{1,5}$: Intermediates have a significantly shorter gaze path in process model comprehension compared to novices.

## 3.3 Experimental Setup

This section describes subjects and objects as well as independent and dependent variables of the experiment.

**Subjects.** There were no prerequisites for participating in the experiment. For the specification of groups (i.e., novices and intermediates), a median split (i.e., based on time spent on process modeling) was performed after experimental execution as done in other scientific fields (cf. Sect. 4.3).

**Objects.** In the experiment, subjects needed to comprehend three process models reflecting different levels of difficulty, i.e., level of complexity. The created process models were expressed in terms of the *Business Process Model and Notation (BPMN)* and were divided up into three levels of difficulty (i.e., easy, medium, and hard) [3]. To be more precise, the easy process model contains only basic modeling elements (e.g., activities) of BPMN. With rising level of difficulty, the total number of elements was increased and new BPMN elements, previously not contained in the process model, were added. Throughout process model comprehension, the eye movements of the participating subjects were tracked and recorded. After analyzing a process model, the subjects had to answer four *true-or-false* comprehension questions. The questions solely referred to the scenario semantics of the process models and were created to evaluate whether or not the subjects interpreted the models correctly.[1]

**Independent variables.** In the experiment, two independent variables were considered: the ① *level of difficulty* for each considered process model and the ② *expertise level* in process modeling from participating subjects.

**Dependent variables.** For each level of difficulty, the considered dependent variables are the ① *duration* required for comprehending a process model, the ② *achieved score* regarding the comprehension questions, and the ③ needed *response time* for answering the questions. In the context of eye tracking, we recorded the ④ *number of fixations* and the ⑤ *length of the gaze path* taken in the process model. Figure 2 summarizes the research model of the experiment.

## 3.4 Experimental Design

For the experimental setting, we apply the guidelines described in [16]. The procedure used for the experiment is as follows (cf. Fig. 3): First, participating subjects received an introduction and had to sign a consent form. Then, demographic data was collected. Following this, the eye tracker was calibrated and subjects completed a tutorial. To eliminate the linguistic barrier and ambiguities, the experiment could be done in either English or German. After completing these mandatory steps, subjects were asked to read and comprehend the provided process models. Starting with the process model reflecting an easy level of

---

[1] Material downloadable from: www.dropbox.com/sh/peecwj4dyqwz9ew/AAAi4tew WOR7jJmPbz6gPsHpa?dl=0.

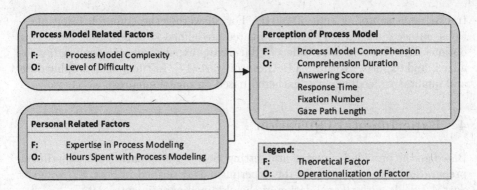

**Fig. 2.** Research model

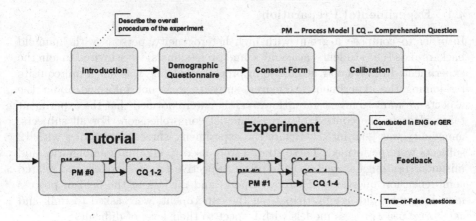

**Fig. 3.** Experimental design

difficulty, followed by the medium, and, finally, the hard one had to be accomplished. After each process model had been analyzed by the subjects, they had to answer four questions related to the previously evaluated process model. The process models were not visible while answering their related questions. The comprehension questions could be answered with 'true', 'false', or 'uncertain'. We are aware of the fact that the pure comprehension of process models without any guidance (e.g., purpose) is uncommon. However, for the first experiment, we wanted to deliberately disclose the approaches for the pure comprehension of process models. Finally, subjects could provide feedback (i.e., textual or oral).

**Instrumentation and data collection procedure.** For eye tracking, we used the SMI iView X Hi-Speed system[2], which allows for accurate orbital eye tracking even over a longer time of recording. The tracking appliance was placed in front of a monitor that provides the process models to subjects. Eye movements were

---

[2] http://www.smivision.com/en/gaze-and-eye-tracking-systems/products/ iview-x-hi-speed.html.

tracked at a sampling rate of 240 Hz. For answering the comprehension questions, subjects used a keyboard with three predefined keys providing answering options. Eye tracking data collected during the experiment was analyzed, visualized, and exported with SMI BeGaze software [17]. In turn, demographic data and qualitative feedback was gathered based on questionnaires.

## 4    Experimental Operation

Based on the provided experimental setting, Sect. 4.1 summarizes the experiment preparation. The execution of the experiment is described in Sect. 4.2, whereas Sect. 4.3 deals with the validation of the obtained experimental data.

### 4.1    Experimental Preparation

In order to compose a group with high heterogeneity, persons with manifold backgrounds (i.e., students, academics, and professionals) were invited to join the experiment. In particular, expertise in process modeling was not a prerequisite for joining the experiment. Moreover, subjects were not informed about the aspects we want to investigate. However, they were notified that the experiment takes place in the context of process model comprehension. For all subjects, anonymity was guaranteed. Before the experiment, three pilot studies with 12 subjects were performed. These studies were used to eliminate ambiguities and misunderstandings as well as to improve respective process models and related comprehension questions. Thereby, experts and novices in the field of process modeling, who did not participate in the experiment, were asked to rank and categorize used process models with respect to their level of difficulty.

### 4.2    Experimental Execution

The experiment was executed in a lab at Ulm University. Altogether, 36 subjects participated. Each experiment session lasted about 15 min and was operated as follows: ① The procedure of the experiment was explained, ② subjects signed a consent form, and ③ a questionnaire, capturing different personal factors (i.e., work status and expertise in process modeling), was handed out. Then, ④ subjects were motioned to the front of the eye tracker and the appliance was individually calibrated. Following this, ⑤ a brief tutorial was presented to the subjects in order to familiarize them with the functionality of the eye tracker. After completing the tutorial and before starting the actual experiment, ⑥ subjects got the additional instruction that they should perform the experiment as fast as possible but, at the same time, as careful as possible. Following Sect. 3.3, ⑦ subjects needed to evaluate three BPMN process models with different levels of difficulty (i.e., easy, medium, and hard). After subjects finished with the reading of a process model, they were asked to answer four questions related to the model. These questions could be answered with 'true', 'false' or 'uncertain'.

## 4.3   Data Validation

In total, data from 36 subjects were collected. 20 subjects were students, 12 were academics, and 4 were professionals. Furthermore, 19 were computer scientist, 4 were economist, 4 were psychologists, 4 were social workers, and 5 provided no precise statements. Moreover, 13 of them were female and 23 were male. Prior to the experiment, the median of the total hours spent by the subjects on process modeling was 20.5 h. Based on their expertise in process modeling, we categorized subjects into two groups, i.e., novices and intermediates. After a median split, subjects who have spent less than 20.5 h on process modeling were characterized as novices. All other subjects were characterized as intermediates. In the experiment, the group of novices then consisted of 15 subjects, whereas 21 subjects were in the group of intermediates. Moreover, results related to novices are of particular interest as some of them (i.e., 5) have never been facing BPMN and, hence, it is particularly interesting how they perform in the experiment. For evaluating the comprehension questions, all data sets were used. Regarding eye tracking data, six data sets were excluded due to invalidity, i.e., eye movements were not captured properly due to incorrect calibrations. In the end, eye tracking data from 30 subjects was used for the subsequent evaluation and analysis. Considering the excluded subjects, the group of novices composed 14 subjects and the one of intermediates consisted of 16 subjects.

## 5   Data Analysis and Interpretation

Section 5.1 presents descriptive statistics of the data gathered during the experiment and Sect. 5.2 tests the hypotheses. Factors threatening the validity of the results are discussed in Sect. 5.3. Finally, Sect. 5.4 discusses the results of the conducted experiment along the conceptual framework.

### 5.1   Empirical Evaluation and Descriptive Statistics

Table 1 presents mean and standard deviation (i.e., STD) for novices and intermediates. It shows the time needed (in ms) to comprehend the respective process models (i.e., process model comprehension duration) and the achieved answering scores. For analyzing the answers provided to the respective questions, a specific value was assigned to each option, i.e., 'true' = 1, 'false' = −1, and 'uncertain' = 0. The response time for answering the questions (in ms), total fixation number, and total gaze path length (in px) are shown in Table 1 (i.e., theoretical factor and operationalization of factor).[3]

Regarding the easy process model, results indicate that intermediates tend to be more effective in terms of process model comprehension compared to novices. Comprehension duration is shorter and the answers given to the questions are more precise. Furthermore, intermediates needed less fixations and the gaze path

---

[3] Sample images downloadable from: www.dropbox.com/sh/peecwj4dyqwz9ew/AAAi4tewWOR7jJmPbz6gPsHpa?dl=0.

through the process model reflects a smaller distance, i.e., fewer eye movements through the respective process model.

For the process model with a medium level of difficulty, the experiment revealed results similar to the above ones. Overall, the score achieved for the given answers is decreasing; however, the answering score of novices is surpassing the one of intermediates.

For the process model with the highest level of difficulty, novices perform slightly better and faster regarding their answering score. In general, no significant differences could be observed.

**Table 1.** Obtained experimental results

| | | Theoretical Factor | Operation. of Factor | Both | | Novices | | Intermediates | |
|---|---|---|---|---|---|---|---|---|---|
| | | | | Mean | STD. | Mean | STD. | Mean | STD. |
| Difficulty | Easy | Comprehension | Duration | 34968 | 14728 | 39334 | 17744 | 31850 | 11606 |
| | | | Score | 0.40 | 0.86 | 0.3 | 0.91 | 0.5 | 0.81 |
| | | | Resp. Time | 6448 | 4352 | 6252 | 4432 | 6644 | 4298 |
| | | Eye Tracking | Fixations | 112 | 38 | 123 | 43 | 98 | 25 |
| | | | Gaze Path | 19901 | 7388 | 21682 | 8091 | 17570 | 5852 |
| Difficulty | Medium | Comprehension | Duration | 54106 | 21957 | 63685 | 25062 | 47264 | 16912 |
| | | | Score | 0.32 | 0.91 | 0.33 | 0.93 | 0.3 | 0.90 |
| | | | Resp. Time | 8029 | 4083 | 7685 | 3330 | 8373 | 4647 |
| | | Eye Tracking | Fixations | 191 | 59 | 207 | 66 | 171 | 43 |
| | | | Gaze Path | 35649 | 11997 | 38284 | 12083 | 32203 | 11423 |
| Difficulty | Hard | Comprehension | Duration | 69740 | 29027 | 75406 | 34803 | 65693 | 24193 |
| | | | Score | -0.24 | 0.88 | -0.17 | 0.92 | -0.32 | 0.85 |
| | | | Resp. Time | 9388 | 5126 | 8842 | 4675 | 9934 | 5450 |
| | | Eye Tracking | Fixations | 230 | 81 | 231 | 97 | 228 | 56 |
| | | | Gaze Path | 41438 | 15140 | 41904 | 17979 | 40829 | 11058 |

Figures 4, 5, 6 and 7 show selected results of the experiment. Figure 4 indicates that with rising level of difficulty the time needed for process model comprehension increases as well. While the response time for giving a correct or wrong answer is roughly the same, the frequency for giving 'uncertain' answers increases over time (cf. Fig. 5). Figure 6 illustrates that the achieved answering scores are decreasing with rising level of difficulty. The fixation number for novices is greater, but aligns with the number for intermediates in the final process model (cf. Fig. 7).

With increasing level of difficulty, the overall performance of comprehending a process model and correctly answering the related comprehension questions is decreasing for both novices and intermediates. Furthermore, the number of fixations and the length of gaze paths are increasing according to the level of difficulty. Concerning the easy process model, it appears that novices show a

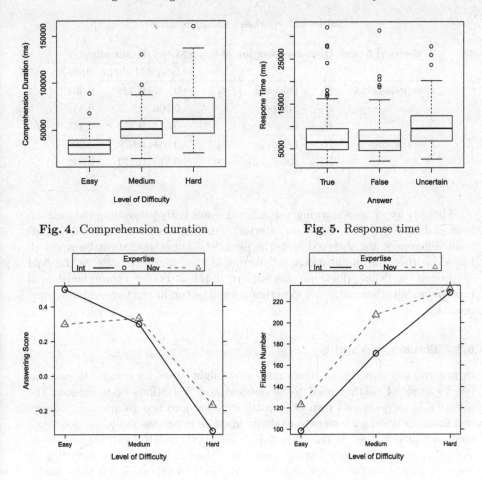

**Fig. 4.** Comprehension duration          **Fig. 5.** Response time

**Fig. 6.** Answering score          **Fig. 7.** Fixation number

weaker performance compared to intermediates. In turn, the performance of novices is approaching the same level as the one of intermediates with rising level of difficulty. It is remarkable, however, that the results do not differ significantly considering the fact that few novices (i.e., 5) have no experience in BPMN at all. Overall, it seems that BPMN process models can be intuitively comprehended. These observations are based on descriptive statistics. For a more rigid investigation, the hypotheses are tested for statistical significance in Sect. 5.2.

## 5.2 Hypotheses Testing

Section 5.1 indicates differences regarding novices and intermediates. In the following, we test whether the observed differences are statistically significant (cf. Table 2). We test the dependent variables with the *Student's t-test*. A successful t-test (with $p < p_0$ at risk level $\alpha = 0,05$) will reject a null hypothesis [18].

**Table 2.** Hypotheses testing results

| Theoretical factor | Operationalization of factor | Level of difficulty | | |
|---|---|---|---|---|
| | | Easy | Medium | Hard |
| Comprehension | $H_{1,1}$ - Duration | 0.167 | 0.038* | 0.361 |
| | $H_{1,2}$ - Score | 0.206 | 0.842 | 0.352 |
| | $H_{1,3}$ - Resp. time | 0.624 | 0.359 | 0.245 |
| Eye tracking | $H_{1,4}$ - Fixations | 0.061 | 0.079 | 0.906 |
| | $H_{1,5}$ - Gaze path | 0.117 | 0.170 | 0.842 |

The only hypothesis showing a significant result is $H_{1,1}$ regarding the medium level of difficulty (indicated by an asterisk). Furthermore, no statistically significant differences are observed and, therefore, the hypotheses must be rejected. Based on this, the implications will be raised that high expertise in the field of process modeling does not necessarily imply a better comprehension of process models. However, more experiments will be conducted to reevaluate these results.

### 5.3   Threats to Validity

In general, any experiment bears risks that might affect its results. In particular, its levels of validity need to be checked and limitations be discussed. The selection of subjects and respective categorization into two groups (i.e., novices and intermediates) with respect to their expertise in process modeling done by a median split is a possible risk. It is debatable whether an individual can be considered as an intermediate having spent more than 21 h on process modeling. A broader distribution with novices, intermediates, and experts needs to be evaluated as well. The considered scenarios constitute an additional risk. A familiar or recurring scenario might affect process model comprehension positively. Therefore, additional research on the influence of the considered scenarios on process model comprehension is needed. Further, the missing option to see the process model, while answering related questions, constitutes another threat to validity. The process models must be memorized and, hence, there is a growing risk that given answers were guessed due to wrong or incomplete memorization. Another risk concerns the reflected level of difficulty from respective process models. The number of elements as well as the structures of these models might be imbalanced between the different levels of difficulty. First results are promising, but their generalization needs to be confirmed by additional experiments.

### 5.4   Experimental Results and Conceptual Framework

The conducted experiment focused on BPMN process models. The considered factor related to process modeling was the *level of difficulty*. Subjects were divided into two groups (i.e., novices and intermediates). Furthermore, we used eye tracking to evaluate how subjects read and comprehend process models with varying levels of difficulty. The obtained results indicate that an increase in model difficulty might affect process model comprehension. Upon these findings, we make the first decisive step towards the intended conceptual framework (i.e., statistical and empirical evaluation as well as categorization of process models based on their difficulty). In general, the reasons for this outcome might be manifold, ranging from *modeling* to *personal factors*. On one hand, familiarity of an individual with a process scenario and their following confrontation thereof as well as resulting impact on respective cognitive load may be a reason. On the other hand, the use of flattened (i.e., non-modular) or ramified process models might be another reason. Currently, we are conducting experiments measuring the *heart rate variability* and *electrodermal activity* of subjects as well as making use of the *Construal Level Theory* aiming on further objectives of the conceptual framework (i.e., identification of modeling rules) [19].

# 6 Related Work

In [20], various process modeling languages are assessed. In turn, [21] gives insights into the factors influencing the comprehension of process models. The influence of complexity on process model comprehensibility is investigated in [22], whereas [23] analyzes the effect of modularity on process understanding. A discussion of the factors influencing process model comprehension is presented in [24]. Regarding process modeling, only little work exists taking cognitive aspects into account as well. [25] discusses how a reduced cognitive load influences end user understanding of conceptual models, whereas [26] describes the cognitive difficulty of understanding different relations between process model elements. Issues related to visual notations are discussed in [27], which defines a set of principles for designing cognitively effective visual notations. Based on the *Physics of Notations*, [28] provides an approach that aims at operationalizing perceptual properties of notations. Furthermore, [7] explores which kind of process representation individuals prefer depending on their cognitive style.

Eye tracking is an emerging technique and related research is conducted in various application domains [29,30]. In line with this trend, eye tracking is increasingly used in process modeling research. In [31], it is shown that task-based process models result in a change of pupil dilation as an evidence for higher mental effort. Findings how eye tracking can contribute to a more fine-grained understanding and evaluation of business process models by a subject's perspective can be found in [32]. Furthermore, in [33] the research on the factors influencing process model comprehension tasks is addressed using eye tracking.

Common to the discussed approaches is their focus on the resulting process model. However, [34] evaluates the process of process modeling itself, whereas [35] identified fixation patterns with eye tracking for acquiring a better understanding of factors impacting process model comprehension. Moreover, the research question on how process models are created by individuals is addressed.

Altogether, none of the discussed works deal with process model comprehension as proposed by the presented conceptual framework.

# 7    Summary and Outlook

The paper presented a conceptual framework for the comprehension of business process models. From the perspective of cognitive neuroscience and psychology, the goal is to identify factors fostering the comprehension of process models with an emphasis put on process modeling and on the influence of personal factors. First results from an eye tracking experiment were presented. We hypothesized that individuals with expertise in process modeling are more efficient regarding process model comprehension. In the end, the stated hypotheses need further research using the conceptual framework. The results indicate that novices are not struggling more than intermediates regarding process model comprehension. The next step will be the consideration of other process modeling languages and recording methods as well as the use of theories originating from cognitive psychology. Additionally, we strive for an extensive examination considering the specific visual symbol sets of respective modeling languages. The overall goal with the conceptual framework is to provide rules for a better comprehension of process models as well as directives for creating better process models.

# References

1. Ottensooser, A., Fekete, A., Reijers, H.A., Mendling, J., Meicstas, C.: Making sense of business process descriptions: an experimental comparison of graphical and textual notations. J. Syst. Softw. **85**, 596–606 (2012)
2. Schultheiss, L.A., Heiliger, E.: Techniques of flow-charting. In: Proceedings of the 1963 Clinic on Library Applications of Data Processeing, pp. 62–78 (1963)
3. OMG: Business Process Management and Notation 2.0 (2017). www.bpmn.org. Accessed 27 Feb 2017
4. van der Aalst, W.M.P.: Formalization and verification of event-driven process chains. Inf. Softw. Technol. **41**, 639–650 (1999)
5. Wilson, J.A.: Gantt charts: a centenary appreciation. Eur. J. Oper. Res. **149**, 430–437 (2003)
6. Johansson, L.O., Wärja, M., Carlsson, S.: An evaluation of business process model techniques, using moody' quality criterion for a good diagram. In: CEUR Workshop Proceedings, vol. 963 (2012)
7. Figl, K., Recker, J.: Exploring cognitive style and task-specific preferences for process representations. Requirements Eng. **21**, 63–85 (2014)
8. Indulska, M., Green, P., Recker, J., Rosemann, M.: Business process modeling: perceived benefits. In: Laender, A.H.F., Castano, S., Dayal, U., Casati, F., Oliveira, J.P.M. (eds.) ER 2009. LNCS, vol. 5829, pp. 458–471. Springer, Heidelberg (2009). doi:10.1007/978-3-642-04840-1_34
9. Mendling, J., Reijers, H.A., van der Aalst, W.M.: Seven process modeling guidelines (7PMG). Inf. Softw. Technol. **52**, 127–136 (2010)
10. Baars, B.J., Gage, N.M.: Cognition, Brain, and Consciousness: Introduction to Cognitive Neuroscience. Academic Press, London (2010)
11. Anderson, J.R.: Cognitive Psychology and its Implications. WH Freeman/Times Books/Henry Holt & Co, San Francisco (1990)
12. Weber, B., Reichert, M., Mendling, J., Reijers, H.A.: Refactoring large process model repositories. Comput. Ind. **62**, 467–486 (2011)

13. Mendling, J.: Metrics for Process Models: Empirical Foundations of Verifiation, Error Prediction, and Guidelines for Correctness. Springer, Heidelberg (2008)
14. Majaranta, P.: Gaze Interaction and Applications of Eye Tracking: Advances in Assistive Technologies. IGI Global, Hershey (2011)
15. Salvucci, D.D., Goldberg, J.H.: Identifying fixations and saccades in eye-tracking protocols. In: Proceedings of the 2000 Symposium on Eye Tracking Research and Application, pp. 71–78 (2000)
16. Wohlin, C., Runeson, P., Höst, M., Ohlsson, M.C., Regnell, B., Wesslen, A.: Experimentation in Software Engineering - An Introduction. Kluwer, Norwell (2000)
17. SMI: iView X Hi-Speed (2016). http://www.smivision.com/en/gaze-and-eye-tracking-systems/products/iview-x-hi-speed.html. Accessed 27 Feb 2017
18. Sirkin, M.: Statistics for the Social Sciences. vol. 3. Sage, Beverly Hills (2005)
19. Zimoch, M., Kolb, J., Reichert, M.: Considering social distance as an influence factor in the process of process modeling. In: Schmidt, R., Guédria, W., Bider, I., Guerreiro, S. (eds.) BPMDS/EMMSAD -2016. LNBIP, vol. 248, pp. 97–112. Springer, Cham (2016). doi:10.1007/978-3-319-39429-9_7
20. Kiepuszewski, B., Hofstede, A.H.M., Bussler, C.J.: On structured workflow modelling. In: Wangler, B., Bergman, L. (eds.) CAiSE 2000. LNCS, vol. 1789, pp. 431–445. Springer, Heidelberg (2000). doi:10.1007/3-540-45140-4_29
21. Melcher, J., Mendling, J., Reijers, H.A., Seese, D.: On measuring the understandability of process models. In: Rinderle-Ma, S., Sadiq, S., Leymann, F. (eds.) BPM 2009. LNBIP, vol. 43, pp. 465–476. Springer, Heidelberg (2010). doi:10.1007/978-3-642-12186-9_44
22. Mendling, J., Reijers, H.A., Cardoso, J.: What makes process models understandable? In: Alonso, G., Dadam, P., Rosemann, M. (eds.) BPM 2007. LNCS, vol. 4714, pp. 48–63. Springer, Heidelberg (2007). doi:10.1007/978-3-540-75183-0_4
23. Reijers, H.A., Mendling, J.: Modularity in process models: review and effects. In: Proceedings of the 5th International Conference on Business Process Management, pp. 20–35 (2008)
24. Mendling, J., Strembeck, M., Recker, J.: Factors of process model comprehension-findings from a series of experiments. Decis. Support Syst. 53, 195–206 (2012)
25. Moody, D.L.: Cognitive load effects on end user understanding of conceptual models: an experimental analysis. In: Benczúr, A., Demetrovics, J., Gottlob, G. (eds.) ADBIS 2004. LNCS, vol. 3255, pp. 129–143. Springer, Heidelberg (2004). doi:10.1007/978-3-540-30204-9_9
26. Figl, K., Laue, R.: Cognitive complexity in business process modeling. In: Mouratidis, H., Rolland, C. (eds.) CAiSE 2011. LNCS, vol. 6741, pp. 452–466. Springer, Heidelberg (2011). doi:10.1007/978-3-642-21640-4_34
27. Moody, D.: The "Physics" of notations: toward a scientific basis for constructing visual notations in software engineering. Trans. Softw. Eng. 35, 756–779 (2009)
28. Linden, D., Zamansky, A., Hadar, I.: How cognitively effective is a visual notation? On the inherent difficulty of operationalizing the physics of notations. In: Schmidt, R., Guédria, W., Bider, I., Guerreiro, S. (eds.) BPMDS/EMMSAD -2016. LNBIP, vol. 248, pp. 448–462. Springer, Cham (2016). doi:10.1007/978-3-319-39429-9_28
29. Mele, M.L., Federici, S.: Gaze and eye-tracking solutions for psychological research. Cogn. Process. 13, 261–265 (2012)
30. Jacob, R.J.K., Karn, K.S.: Eye tracking in human-computer interaction and usability research: ready to deliver the promises. In: Mind, vol. 2 (2003)

31. Dobesova, Z., Malcik, M.: Workflow diagrams and pupil dilatation in eye tracking testing. In: Proceedings of 13th International Conference on EMER eLearning Technology and Application, pp. 59–64 (2015)

32. Hogrebe, F., Gehrke, N., Nüttgens, M.: Eye tracking experiments in business process modeling: agenda setting and proof of concept. In: Proceedings of 4th International Workshop on Enterprise Modelling and Information Systems Architectures, pp. 183–188 (2011)

33. Petrusel, R., Mendling, J.: Eye-tracking the factors of process model comprehension tasks. In: Proceedings of 25th International Conference on Advance Information System Engineering, pp. 224–239 (2013)

34. Martini, M., Pinggera, J., Neurauter, M., Sachse, P., Furtner, M., Weber, B.: The impact of working memory and the process of process modelling on model quality: investigating experienced versus inexperienced modellers. In: Scientific Reports, vol. 6 (2016)

35. Weber, B., Pinggera, J., Neurauter, M., Zugal, S., Martini, M., Furtner, M., Sachse, P., Schnitzer, D.: Fixation patterns during process model creation: initial steps toward neuro-adaptive process modeling environments. In: Proceedings 49th International Conference on System Sciences, pp. 600–609 (2016)

# Eye Tracking Experiments
# on Process Model Comprehension:
# Lessons Learned

Michael Zimoch[(✉)], Rüdiger Pryss, Johannes Schobel, and Manfred Reichert

Institute of Databases and Information Systems, Ulm University, Ulm, Germany
{michael.zimoch,ruediger.pryss,
johannes.schobel,manfred.reichert}@uni-ulm.de

**Abstract.** For documenting business processes, there exists a plethora
of process modeling languages. In this context, graphical process models
are used to enhance the process comprehensibility of the stakeholders
involved. The large number of available modeling languages, however,
aggravates process model comprehension and increases the knowledge
gap between domain and modeling experts. Upon this, one major challenge is to identify factors fostering the comprehension of process models. This paper discusses the experiences we gathered with the use of eye
tracking in experiments on process model comprehension and the lessons
learned in this context. The objective of the experiments was to study
the comprehension of process models expressed in terms of four different modeling languages (i.e., BPMN, eGantt, EPC, and Petri Net). This
paper further provides recommendations along nine identified categories
that can foster related experiments on process model comprehension.

**Keywords:** Process model comprehension · Eye tracking · Experiment

## 1 Introduction

During the last years, a lot of research was conducted to enhance our understanding of working with process models. Besides their creation, particular
emphasis has been put on their reading and understanding, i.e., on *process
model comprehension*. Despite extensive research in this field [4,17,45], there still
exists a knowledge gap between inexperienced process stakeholders and modeling experts. Usually, process models are not fully understood by all involved
stakeholders, who neither have experiences with process modeling nor deeper
knowledge of any specific process modeling language. This raises the challenging
question to identify the factors fostering the comprehension of process models.
One promising approach for coping with this challenge is to perform experiments.

This paper contributes to the field of business process model comprehension
through experimental research. It discusses the experiences we gathered and the
lessons we learned when performing a series of experiments on process model
comprehension relying on eye tracking. In detail, the experiments conducted

I. Reinhartz-Berger et al. (Eds.): BPMDS/EMMSAD 2017, LNBIP 287, pp. 153–168, 2017.
DOI: 10.1007/978-3-319-59466-8_10

dealt with process model comprehension in connection with four process modeling languages (i.e., *BPMN*, *eGantt*, *EPC*, and *Petri Net*). In these experiments, we measured the eye movements of subjects in order to assess their approaches of comprehending process models. On one hand, we want to enable a comparison between different process modeling languages. On the other hand, the perceived pros and cons of respective modeling languages shall be unraveled. To the best of our knowledge, only few approaches have considered eye tracking for such comparison in the context of business process model comprehension so far. Notably, during the preparation, execution, and analysis of the experiments, several difficulties have been encountered and various issues emerged. They constitute valuable lessons learned that will allow for optimizations of future experiments on process model comprehension.

As another valuable insight for researchers performing experiments on process model comprehension, this paper introduces nine categories C1–C9 of the lessons learned. Process models are related to specific scenarios and, hence, familiarity of individuals with the considered process scenario varies (C1). Following this, the understanding (C2) and creation (C3) of process models can be juxtaposed. Afterwards, a discussion on the structuring and layouting (C4) of the respective process models is provided, followed by the presentation of the used process modeling languages (C5) and their specific characteristics (i.e., basic modeling elements (e.g., activities) (C6) and modeling constructs (e.g., gateways (C7)). Finally, individuals (C8) as well as measurement methods (C9) are addressed.

The remainder of this paper is organized as follows: Sect. 2 presents the experimental setting. The gathered experiences and the lessons learned from the experiments are presented in Sect. 3. Related work is discussed in Sect. 4, whereas Sect. 5 concludes the paper with a summary and an outlook.

## 2    Experimental Setting

The lessons learned refer to experiments on process model comprehension that use *eye tracking* as measuring technique. Moreover, eye tracking constitutes a cost-effective and unobtrusive method to gain deeper insights into human cognitive processes [34]. Thereby, it measures eye movements in response to a visual stimulus (e.g., picture). Most common types of evaluated eye movements are *fixations*, *saccades*, and *gaze paths* [37]. Fixations constitute eye movements of very low velocity at a specific point during a stimulus. Saccades, in turn, constitute quick eye movements. Note that during saccadic eye movements, no visual information is perceived. In turn, a *gaze path* represents the chronological order of fixations and saccades the eyes take while analyzing a stimulus. Furthermore, an *area of interest (AOI)* constitutes a manually defined subregion in the presented stimulus. Generally, it can be used to extract metrics, specifically for these defined regions. For tracking and recording the eye movements in our experiments, the SMI iView X Hi-Speed system[1] was used, which allows for accurate

---

[1] http://www.smivision.com/en/gaze-and-eye-tracking-systems/products/
iview-x-hi-speed.html.

eye tracking, even over a longer time of recording. The tracking appliance was placed in front of a monitor that presents the stimuli (i.e., process models) to the subjects; eye movements were tracked at a sampling rate of 240 Hz. The eye tracking data collected during the experiments were analyzed, visualized, and exported with SMI BeGaze software. The latter enables behavioral and gaze analyses [33].

In the controlled eye tracking experiments, the subjects had to comprehend 12 different process models and were asked to answer several comprehension questions related to these process models. At the same time, their eye movements were tracked and recorded. In more detail, the process models were expressed in terms of *BPMN* [38], *eGantt* [41], *EPC* [39], and *Petri Net* [40], respectively. Subjects, in turn, needed to comprehend three process models for each modeling language reflecting different levels of difficulty. More precisely, the process models were subdivided into three levels of model difficulty (i.e., easy, medium, and hard). The simple process models solely contain basic elements (e.g., activities, start event) of the respective modeling language. Furthermore, with rising level of difficulty, the total number of elements was increased and new elements provided by the respective modeling language, not introduced before, were added. After each process model had been analyzed by the subjects, the latter had to answer four *true-or-false* comprehension questions (cf. Fig. 1). The questions solely referred to the semantic content of the process models and were used to evaluate whether or not subjects interpret the process models correctly. Thereby, correct answers have been stored with '1' and incorrect answers with '−1', whereas '0' corresponds to 'I am uncertain' answers. We are aware of the fact that the comprehension of process models without any guidance (e.g., purpose) is uncommon. However, in the first experiments we wanted to investigate the approaches for the pure comprehension of process models. In general, one of the objectives was to evaluate the overall performance of subjects, when being confronted with different modeling languages in the context of process model comprehension. The results obtained may serve as contributions allowing a meaningful comparison between various process modeling languages in the future.

Concerning the overall procedure of the experiments (cf. Fig. 1), at the beginning of the experiment, for one second, a fixation cross was displayed on the center of the monitor. The cross was used to fixate the gaze of the subjects on a defined point on the monitor. Afterwards, the process model was presented to subjects, who could take as much time as they wanted for model comprehension. Moreover,

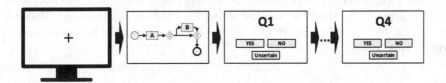

**Fig. 1.** Overall procedure of the experiments

**Table 1.** Obtained experimental results

| | | Category | Item | Modeling Languages | | | |
|---|---|---|---|---|---|---|---|
| | | | | BPMN | eGantt | EPC | Petri Net |
| Difficulty Easy | | Subjects | Number of Subjects | 29 | 30 | 30 | 30 |
| | | Comprehension | Comprehension Duration | 35270 | 31840 | 36120 | 36930 |
| | | | Response Time | 6210 | 5710 | 4890 | 6580 |
| | | | Answering Score | 0.66 | 0.58 | 0.92 | 0.78 |
| | | Eye Tracking | Number of Fixations | 112 | 105 | 103.93 | 110 |
| | | | Number of Saccades | 101 | 94 | 89 | 95 |
| | | | Gaze Path Length | 19958 | 14858 | 15169 | 19128 |
| Difficulty Medium | | Subjects | Number of Subjects | 29 | 30 | 28 | 28 |
| | | Comprehension | Comprehension Duration | 53910 | 34860 | 53100 | 49170 |
| | | | Response Time | 7640 | 6160 | 7790 | 8290 |
| | | | Answering Score | 0.62 | 0.74 | 0.75 | 0.63 |
| | | Eye Tracking | Number of Fixations | 191 | 119 | 171 | 151 |
| | | | Number of Saccades | 180 | 108 | 153 | 133 |
| | | | Gaze Path Length | 35682 | 19653 | 26442 | 21562 |
| Difficulty Hard | | Subjects | Number of Subjects | 28 | 29 | 27 | 28 |
| | | Comprehension | Comprehension Duration | 68940 | 58270 | 86520 | 76860 |
| | | | Response Time | 9170 | 8360 | 8240 | 8230 |
| | | | Answering Score | 0.27 | 0.53 | 0.54 | 0.23 |
| | | Eye Tracking | Number of Fixations | 230 | 169 | 278.93 | 282 |
| | | | Number of Saccades | 215 | 146 | 252 | 254 |
| | | | Gaze Path Length | 41503 | 20556 | 40602 | 52377 |

subjects were told that they should perform the experiments as fast as possible, but at the same time as careful as possible. Following the model comprehension task, four related questions were presented of which only one was shown on the monitor at the same time. While answering the questions, it was not possible to reinspect the studied process model. The experimental procedure was repeated for all considered process models.[2]

Regarding the considered process models and their level of difficulty, Table 1 presents the number of subjects that studied the respective process models as well as the results (i.e., means) they delivered by showing the required time to comprehend the models (i.e., duration time in ms). Furthermore, the response times for answering the comprehension questions (in ms) as well as corresponding answering scores (i.e., absolute frequency of correct answers) are illustrated. Finally, the total number of fixations, saccades, and total gaze path lengths (in px) are presented.

The results indicate that, with rising level of model difficulty, overall comprehension performance is decreasing. In particular, the duration time needed for model comprehension increases, in this context. Furthermore, the response times for answering comprehension questions increase as well with rising level of model difficulty, whereas the corresponding answering scores decrease with rising level of difficulty. Finally, the total number of fixations and saccades increase, depending on the level of difficulty. Hence, the lengths of gaze paths are increasing as well in this context.

---

[2] Sample material downloadable from: www.dropbox.com/sh/our1qp7vkpv020i/AABr3a24DwCKjWAU_2DDCIWMa?dl=0.

Figure 2 presents selected evaluation screenshots of the used SMI BeGaze software. The evaluation provides information about fixations and saccades of the *difficult* eGantt process model. Thereby, circles represent subjects fixations. The size of a circle, in turn, corresponds to the subjects dwell time. Finally, the concatenation of fixations and saccades generates the gaze path.

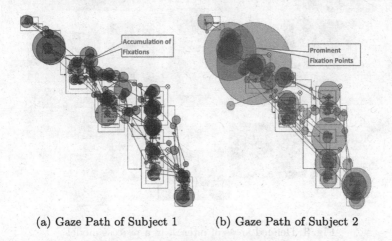

(a) Gaze Path of Subject 1          (b) Gaze Path of Subject 2

**Fig. 2.** Examples of subjects gaze path

In Fig. 2(a), several accumulations of fixations on specific areas of the process model become visible. In Fig. 2(b), in turn, prominent fixation points can be identified. To be more precise, the corresponding subject spent much time at these points. Furthermore, Fig. 3 presents the results we obtained when analyzing specific areas of interests of a process model. It further indicates the complexity of analyzing eye tracking data. In particular, such analysis allows for an extensive evaluation of eye movements. For example, the number of fixations is higher in areas of interests comprising XOR gateways compared to areas with AND gateways. Moreover, the XOR represented by the area of interest XOR_2 contains more fixations and highest average dwell time.

## 3  Lessons Learned

This section discusses the lessons learned during the eye tracking experiments in which we compared different process modeling languages. In particular, these lessons are grouped into nine categories C1–C9 (cf. Fig. 4).

### C1 - Familiarity with Process Scenarios

The kind of scenario considered in the context of an experiment might influence experimental outcomes as it might be easier for individuals to deal with scenarios from an application domain they are familiar with (e.g., pizza delivery

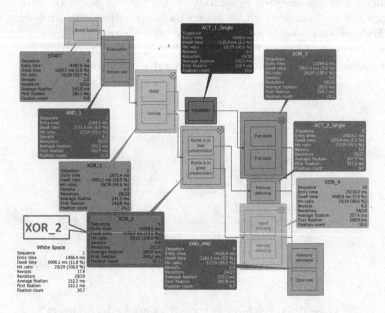

**Fig. 3.** Defined areas of interest in a process model

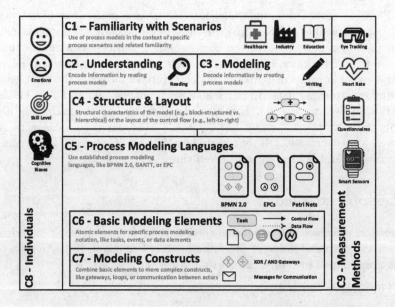

**Fig. 4.** Categories describing the experimental setting

vs. bomb defusing). Accordingly, with increasing familiarity with the scenario, the cognitive load in the working memory might become lower. By contrast, if individuals are unfamiliar with a process scenario, they first need to get an overview of the scenario they are confronted with. Consequently, comprehending process models related to a scenario an individual is unfamiliar with requires a higher cognitive load. To reduce this *familiarity bias* in the experiments we conducted, the subjects were confronted with process models representing different scenarios. For example, subjects needed about the same time for comprehending a process model describing a shopping process (cf. Table 1; BPMN - Medium) and a process dealing with the editing of a wikipedia article (cf. Table 1; EPC - Medium); i.e., for these two scenarios, no differences could be observed. However, if the process models are exceeding a certain level of model difficulty, in turn, the working memory of individuals might be confronted with an information overload resulting in a reduction of overall understanding. For example, the more complex BPMN model describes a pizza delivery process, i.e., a process which can be considered as well-known. However, the subjects were facing difficulties regarding the comprehension of respective model that might be owed to the level of model difficulty.

## C2 - Understanding of Process Models

In general, the understanding of process models (i.e., *process model comprehension*) is a complex matter as the information contained in these models need to be decoded and captured by an individual. Consequently, comprehension constitutes a cognitive process trying to establish relations between available information on objects and events in the long term memory, together with information perceived at the moment from the sensory, working, or short term memory. Concerning process model comprehension, individuals must handle the complexities of parsing the relevant syntactic, semantic, and pragmatic information of a process model expressed in terms of a particular language. The easier and clearer this information is presented, the more positive will be the impact on process model comprehension (e.g., Cognitive Load Theory (CLT)). In our experiments, several policies for comprehending a process model could be identified. Independent from the experience a subject has with process modeling, all policies are similar in the first comprehension iteration (i.e., after having a first glance at the process model). More precisely, subjects visually discover all elements of a process model in an element-to-element procedure. Usually, this procedure begins with the start element of a process model. During the second comprehension iteration, subjects follow different policies (e.g., jumping back and forth between specific modeling constructs or elements). For this reason, the comprehension questions might serve as an indicator to evaluate the efficiency of the comprehension policies. The identification of concrete patterns for process model comprehension will be addressed in future work.

## C3 - Modeling of Process Models

The modeling of processes deals with the encoding of information of a process model. This activity, in turn, involves various factors as well as specific cognitive processes that can be neglected in process model comprehension. The conducted experiments so far, focused on the comprehension of process models. However, the lessons learned in this context might apply to process modeling as well.

## C4 - Structure and Layout

The processes were presented as flat (i.e., non-modularized) models to the subjects; i.e., no sub-processes were used. Additionally, all models were block- structured [35], which fits well with one of the seven process modeling guidelines [14]. In general, one needs to investigate to what extent a particular structuring of a process model influences its comprehensibility. Furthermore, all process models were created in a way to be either read from left-to-right or top-to-bottom. However, one of the process models (i.e., Petri Net - Hard) was designed using a very ramified structure (i.e., sequence flows running in all directions). Regarding the results depicted in Table 1, it is unclear whether or not ramified structures affect the comprehension of process models.

## C5 - Process Modeling Languages

Table 2 presents the answering scores (i.e., means) for all considered process models and their respective levels of difficulty.

**Table 2.** Answering scores obtained in the experiments

|  |  | Modeling Languages | | | |
|---|---|---|---|---|---|
|  |  | BPMN | eGantt | EPC | Petri Net |
| Difficulty | Easy | 0.66 | 0.58 | 0.92 | 0.78 |
|  | Medium | 0.62 | 0.74 | 0.75 | 0.63 |
|  | Hard | 0.27 | 0.53 | 0.54 | 0.23 |

The results indicate that the comparison of process modeling languages with respect to model comprehension allows for interesting insights. For example, one might expect that the answering scores are decreasing with rising level of model difficulty. Interestingly, in this context, the results related to eGantts constitute a counterexample, i.e., an increase of the answering scores for the process models with an easy and medium level of difficulty can be observed. Moreover, one might expect that for all process modeling languages a comparable decrease can be observed with rising level of difficulty. However, regarding the BPMN answering scores obtained from the process models reflecting an easy and medium level of difficulty, the results are different in orders of magnitude compared to EPC and Petri Net.

## C6 - Basic Modeling Elements

During the experiments it turned out that process models with an explicit start and an end symbol foster process model comprehension. Initially, subjects are trying to locate a start symbol in the process model. Usually, the start symbol is assumed to be on the left or upper left side of the process model. However, if subjects are unable to identify a start symbol on the assumed positions in the process model, their gaze paths become directionless, due to the search of the start symbol. The same effect can be observed with respect to end symbols.

## C7 - Modeling Constructs

As opposed to basic elements, more complex modeling constructs (e.g., gateways) seem to be difficult for individuals. In the experiments, the main challenge subjects were facing concerns the identification of the semantic meaning of the presented modeling constructs (e.g., AND gateways). A common approach was to identify the meaning of a construct by considering the described process scenario in detail. Furthermore, split-and-join gateways (i.e., XOR) appear to be particular challenging for subjects. Referring back to Figs. 3 and 5 presents a binning chart showing the proportion of fixations over the duration needed for process model comprehension. Figure 5 indicates that subjects spend more time with studying the first gateway (i.e., the first gateway along the reading direction) compared to the subsequent other. The same effect can be observed in the binning charts of other process models. In this context, it makes no differences whether an AND or an XOR gateways appears first. As a next step, we want to provide an extensive and direct comparison between the specific modeling constructs (i.e., AND vs. XOR) of the respective languages as well as their effect on model perception and interpretation of individuals.

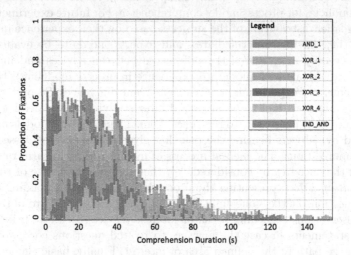

**Fig. 5.** Binning chart for gateways in a process model

## C8 - Individuals

The experiment revealed that the used process models, which were expressed in different process modeling languages, can be intuitively understood by subjects, independent from their modeling experience. In particular, the performance of the subjects regarding the comprehension of easy process models is satisfactory (cf. Table 1). However, with increasing level of model difficulty, the performances of the subjects are decreasing to the same extent. Moreover, we assumed that subjects being experienced with process modeling are more efficient regarding process model comprehension. Finally, subjects without any modeling experience are facing the same challenges than experienced ones regarding process model comprehension. The reasons for this might be manifold, ranging from *personal factors* (e.g., familiarity with the provided scenario) to *modeling factors* (e.g., process model quality). The identification of those factors that might positively or negatively influence the individuals regarding process model comprehension will be subject of future experiments. So far, a decrease of the performance can be observed with rising level of model difficulty (cf. Table 1). Future experiments will particularly focus on the cognitive processes of individuals. For example, considering *cognitive psychology* (e.g., Split Attention Effect), *cognitive biases* (e.g., Framing), or specific *emotional states* (e.g., Alexithymia).

## C9 - Measurement Methods

The use of eye tracking in the context of research on process model comprehension has led to tangible results. In the experiments, we obtained valuable insights into how subjects understand process models that are expressed with different modeling languages. The evaluation of fixations and saccades as well as the gaze paths observed during process model comprehension reveal interesting facts on particular policies for process model comprehension. For future experiments, first of all, a broader distribution of the subjects based on their experience in process modeling (i.e., novices, intermediates, and experts) needs to be evaluated. So far, we have only investigated the differences between novices and intermediates (i.e., individuals with moderate experience in process modeling). However, the involvement of experts might reveal significant differences. Second, the comprehension questions had to be answered after studying the respective process model without the possibility to reinspect them. Therefore, the models had to be memorized by subjects bearing the risk that given answers were guessed due to wrong memorizations. The mental process of memorization, in turn, raises various issues that need to be considered. We therefore will make use of the visual *Split Attention Effect*, presenting the process model and corresponding comprehension questions at the same time. This approach will allow us to obtain more precise observations regarding areas of interest (cf. Fig. 3). In addition, it will allow for statements in case the answers to related questions correlate with a subjects' gaze path in the defined area of interest. Finally, basic elements (e.g., activities) and constructs (e.g., AND) should be comparable across all modeling languages. Therefore, future experiments will focus on measurement methods other than eye tracking, as known from *cognitive neuroscience* (e.g., smart sensors) and *psychology* (e.g., Construal Level Theory).

# 4   Related Work

This section discusses related work along the presented categories (cf. Fig. 4).

**C1 - Familiarity with Process Scenarios.** In a study dealing with various process model representations (i.e., flattened vs. modularized), [5] found no evidence that domain knowledge influences process model comprehension. Despite different cognitive abilities, learning styles and motives as well as policies of individuals, [6] could not confirm an influence of domain knowledge on process model comprehension. Assessing the use of a particular process modeling language, [7] shows that domain-specific modeling experience and knowledge have no significant effect on the understanding of process models.

**C2 - Understanding of Process Models.** Regarding process model comprehension, considerable research was conducted in the last decade. Comparing BPMN models with a textual notation (i.e., a written use-case), [12] presents a significant increase regarding model comprehension. More precisely, when reading the textual models, all individuals show an increase, whereas for BPMN models, solely the experienced individuals show an increase. [15] investigates whether there are significant differences in terms of understanding, depending on the process model representation (i.e., text vs. graphical model). An extensive discussion of a series of experiments related to process model comprehension is presented in [29]. Finally, the SEQUAL framework provides various aspects of process model quality fostering the comprehension of suchlike [31].

**C3 - Modeling of Process Models.** Common to the work related to category C3 is its focus on the resulting process model, i.e., the product of process modeling. [2] evaluates the process of process modeling itself. Furthermore, [13] focuses on how process models are created. The different steps a process modeler accomplishes during the creation of process models are discussed in [48].

**C4 - Structure and Layout.** [42] identifies visual features and metrics fostering the creation of understandable process models. A set of propositions on the effects of the notational aspects on the improvement of process model comprehension is presented in [43]. In turn, [44,46] discuss how modularity enhances process model expressiveness. Taking end user preferences into account, [47] demonstrates the importance of structuring process models.

**C5 - Process Modeling Languages.** Several frameworks exist dealing with the quality issues of different kinds of conceptual models (e.g., process models). In this context, [3] presents frameworks for evaluating the quality of conceptual models. In turn, [30] investigates how different representations affect model comprehension. In this context, it is shown that modeling languages, which allow for concurrent activities (i.e., parallel branches) are difficult to understand. In an empirical investigation, [32] elaborated UML Activity Diagrams as the most versatile modeling language in the context of process model comprehension. To be more precise, the latter outperformed the comprehension of models expressed in terms of EPC or BPMN.

**C6 - Basic Modeling Elements.** [23] conducted an experiment comparing the effects different flow directions have on model comprehension. In particular, it was shown that readers adapt well to uncommon reading directions. In turn, [24] investigates human understanding of process models, trying to identify influence factors with respect to "local" comprehensibility (e.g., activities, sequences) in process models. A comparison of the understanding of imperative and declarative process models is presented in [26].

**C7 - Modeling Constructs.** [18] demonstrates in an experiment that the interpretation of process models benefits from gateway constructs (i.e., AND), due to the perceptual discriminability effect of the latter. Especially, this effect is evident for complex process models. Specific thresholds for gateway complexity metrics can be found in [19]. These metrics serve as guidelines for novices to classify process models in specific level of understandability. In turn, [20] provides a structural equation model, depicting the relationships between flow orientation in a process model, quality of process models, and business process redesign success. The equation model shows that flow orientation constitutes a key factor. Finally, [21] investigates basic symbol sets of various process modeling languages, showing that notational deficiencies concerning perceptual discriminability and semiotic clarity have a negative impact on process model comprehension.

**C8 - Individuals.** [9] investigates preferences of individuals (i.e., cognitive styles) regarding alternative process representations, which have a positive effect on process model comprehension. In the context of business process variability, an empirical user study shows that neither complexity nor expertise in process modeling have a significant impact on process variant modeling [10]. Experience in modeling, as a crucial skill of individuals having a significant impact on the success of process modeling, is described in [11]. In turn, [22] provides evidence that the chosen process scenario representation form as well as individuals' characteristics result in similar levels of understanding, independent from whether subjects are confronted with familiar or unfamiliar process scenarios.

**C9 - Measurement Methods.** Eye tracking is increasingly used in research related to process modeling. [27] shows that reading process models changes pupil dilation as evidence for higher mental effort. Findings on how eye tracking might contribute to a deeper understanding of process models can be found in [28]. In [16], the existing research gap concerning the factors influencing process model comprehension tasks is investigated using eye tracking. [1] identifies performance improvement opportunities by determining the performances of individuals regarding different types of comprehension tasks. Finally, [8] proposes the use of visual cues in process models to improve their overall comprehensibility.

Regarding the comparison of process modeling languages, there exists several work. A review of process modeling languages can be found in [36]. Using a generic meta-model as benchmark, [25] evaluates seven modeling languages and their corresponding concepts. Further, [50] classifies existing process modeling languages. Finally, a literature review of the state-of-the-art on empirical research on process model comprehension is presented in [49].

# 5 Summary and Outlook

This paper gave insights into experiences we gathered in and the lessons learned from experiments on process model comprehension using eye tracking. To obtain these insights, process models in terms of four different modeling languages (i.e., BPMN, eGantt, EPC, and Petri Net) were considered in the experiments. To structure our discussion on the lessons learned, the gained insights were grouped into nine categories (cf. Fig. 4). Using this categorization, we are going to conduct a series of experiments to enhance the understanding on how the overall comprehension of process models can be fostered. Additionally, we will focus on process model creation (i.e., the process of process modeling). Thereby, particular emphasis will be put on *human factors*, especially on the cognitive processes involved. Altogether, using eye tracking for comparing different process modeling languages offers valuable insights into how process models are comprehended by individuals.

# References

1. Petrusel, R., Mendling, J., Reijers, H.A.: Task-specific visual cues for improving process model understanding. Inf. Softw. Technol. **79**, 63–78 (2016)
2. Martini, M., Pinggera, J., Neuratuer, M., Sachse, P., Furtner, M., Weber, B.: The impact of working memory and the process of process modelling on model quality: investigating experienced versus inexperienced modellers. In: Scientific Reports, vol. 6 (2016)
3. Moody, D.L.: Theoretical and practical issues in evaluating the quality of conceptual models: current state and future directions. Data Knowl. Eng. **55**, 243–276 (2005)
4. Mendling, J., Reijers, H.A., Cardoso, J.: What makes process models understandable? In: Alonso, G., Dadam, P., Rosemann, M. (eds.) BPM 2007. LNCS, vol. 4714, pp. 48–63. Springer, Heidelberg (2007). doi:10.1007/978-3-540-75183-0_4
5. Turetken, O., Rompen, T., Vanderfeesten, I., Dikici, A., Moll, J.: The effect of modularity representation and presentation medium on the understandability of business process models in BPMN. In: La Rosa, M., Loos, P., Pastor, O. (eds.) BPM 2016. LNCS, vol. 9850, pp. 289–307. Springer, Cham (2016). doi:10.1007/978-3-319-45348-4_17
6. Recker, J., Reijers, H.A., van de Wouw, S.G.: Process model comprehension: the effects of cognitive abilities, learning style and strategy. Commun. Assoc. Inf. Syst. **34**, 199–222 (2014)
7. Recker, J., Dreiling, A.: Does it matter which process modelling language we teach or use? An experimental study on understanding process modelling languages without formal education. In: Proceedings of ACIS 2007, pp. 356–366 (2007)
8. Petrusel, R., Mendling, J., Reijers, H.A.: How visual cognition influences process model comprehension. Decis. Support Syst. **96**, 1–16 (2017)
9. Figl, K., Recker, J.: Exploring cognitive style and task-specific preferences for process representations. Requirements Eng. **21**, 63–85 (2016)
10. Döhring, M., Reijers, H.A., Smirnov, S.: Configuration vs. adaptation for business process variant maintenance: an empirical study. Inf. Syst. **39**, 108–133 (2014)

11. Bandara, W., Gable, G.G., Rosemann, M.: Factors and measures of business process modelling: model building through a multiple case study. Eur. J. Inf. Syst. **14**, 347–360 (2005)

12. Ottensooser, A., Fekete, A., Reijers, H.A., Mendling, J., Menictas, C.: Making sense of business process descriptions: an experimental comparison of graphical and textual notations. J. Syst. Softw. **85**, 596–606 (2012)

13. Weber, B., Pinggera, J., Neurauter, M., Zugal, S., Martini, M., Furtner, M., Sachse, P., Schnitzer, D.: Fixation patterns during process model creation: initial steps toward neuro-adaptive process modeling environments. In: Proceedings of the 2016 49th Hawaii International Conference on System Sciences, pp. 600–609 (2016)

14. Mendling, J., Reijers, H.A., van der Aalst, W.M.P.: Seven process modeling guidelines (7PMG). Inf. Softw. Technol. **52**, 127–136 (2010)

15. Rodrigues, R.D.A., Barros, M.D.O., Revoredo, K., Azevedo, L.G., Leopold, H.: An experiment on process model understandability using textual work instructions and BPMN models. In: 29th Brazilian Symposium on Software Engineering, pp. 41–50 (2015)

16. Petrusel, R., Mendling, J.: Eye-tracking the factors of process model comprehension tasks. In: Salinesi, C., Norrie, M.C., Pastor, Ó. (eds.) CAiSE 2013. LNCS, vol. 7908, pp. 224–239. Springer, Heidelberg (2013). doi:10.1007/978-3-642-38709-8_15

17. Haisjackl, C., Barba, I., Zugal, S., Soffer, P., Hadar, I., Reichert, M., Pinggera, J., Weber, B.: Understanding declare models: strategies, pitfalls, empirical results. Softw. Syst. **15**, 325–352 (2016)

18. Recker, J.: Empirical investigation of the usefulness of gateway constructs in process models. Eur. J. Inf. Syst. **22**, 673–689 (2013)

19. Sánachez-González, L., Garcia, F., Ruiz, F., Mendling, J.: Quality indicators for business process models from a gateway complexity perspective. Inf. Softw. Technol. **54**, 1159–1175 (2012)

20. Kock, N., Verville, J., Danesh-Pajou, A., Deluca, D.: Communication flow orientation in business process modeling and its effect on redesign success: results from a field study. Decis. Support Syst. **45**, 562–575 (2009)

21. Figl, K., Mendling, J., Strembeck, M.: The influence of notational deficiencies on process model comprehension. J. Assoc. Inf. Syst. **14**, 312–338 (2013)

22. Recker, J., Dreiling, A.: The effects of content presentation format and user characteristics on novice developers' understanding of process models. Commun. Assoc. Inf. Syst. **28**, 65–84 (2011)

23. Figl, K., Strembeck, M.: Findings from an experiment on flow direction of business process models. In: International Workshop on EMISA 2015, pp. 59–73 (2015)

24. Figl, K., Laue, R.: Influence factors for local comprehensibility of process models. Int. J. Hum. Comput. Stud. **82**, 96–110 (2015)

25. List, B., Korherr, B.: An evaluation of conceptual business process modelling languages. In: Proceedings of the 2006 ACM Symposium on Applied Computing, pp. 1532–1539 (2006)

26. Pichler, P., Weber, B., Zugal, S., Pinggera, J., Mendling, J., Reijers, H.A.: Imperative versus declarative process modeling languages: an empirical investigation. In: Daniel, F., Barkaoui, K., Dustdar, S. (eds.) BPM 2011. LNBIP, vol. 99, pp. 383–394. Springer, Heidelberg (2012). doi:10.1007/978-3-642-28108-2_37

27. Dobesova, Z., Malcik, M.: Workflow diagrams and pupil dilatation in eye tracking testing. In: Proceedings of 13th International Conference on Emerging eLearning Techniques Applications, pp. 59–64 (2015)

28. Hogrebe, F., Gehrke, N., Nüttgens, M.: Eye tracking experiments in business process modeling: agenda setting and proof of concept. In: Proceedings of 4th International Workshop on Enterprise Modelling and Information Systems Architectures, pp. 183–188 (2011)

29. Mendling, J., Strembeck, M., Recker, J.: Factors of process model comprehension - findings from a series of experiments. Decis. Support Syst. **53**, 195–206 (2012)

30. Weitlaner, D., Guettinger, A., Kohlbacher, M.: Intuitive comprehensibility of process models. In: S-BPM ONE-running Processes, vol. 360, pp. 52–71 (2013)

31. Krogstie, J.: Model-Based Development and Evolution of Information Systems. Springer, London (2012)

32. Jošt, G., Huber, J., Heričko, M., Polančič, G.: An empirical investigation of intuitive understandability of process diagrams. Comput. Stand. Interface **48**, 90–111 (2016)

33. SMI: iView X Hi-Speed (2016). http://www.smivision.com/en/gaze-and-eye-tracking-systems/products/iview-x-hi-speed.html. Accessed 10 Feb 2017

34. Majaranta, P., Aoki, H., Donegan, M., Hansen, D.W., Hansen, J.P., Hyrskykari, A., Räihä, K.: Gaze Interaction and Applications of Eye Tracking: Advances in Assistive Technologies. IGI Global, Hershey (2011)

35. Reichert, M., Dadam, P.: Adept$_{flex}$ – supporting dynamic changes of workflows without losing control. J. Int. Inf. Syst. **10**, 93–129 (1998)

36. Wang, W., Ding, H., Dong, J., Ren, C.: A comparison of business process modeling methods. In: International Conference on Service Operations and Logistics, and Informatics, pp. 1136–1141 (2006)

37. Salvucci, D.D., Goldberg, J.H.: Identifying fixations and saccades in eye-tracking protocols. In: Proceedings of 2000 Symposium on Eye Tracking Research Application, pp. 71–78 (2000)

38. OMG: Business Process Management and Notation 2.0 (2016). www.bpmn.org. Accessed 11 Oct 2016

39. van der Aalst, W.M.P.: Formalization and verification of event-driven process chains. Inf. Softw. Technol. **41**, 639–650 (1999)

40. Person, J.L.: Petri Net Theory and the Modeling of Systems. Prentice Hall, Englewood (1981)

41. Sommer, M.: Zeitliche Darstellung und Modellierung von Prozessen mithilfe von Gantt-Diagrammen. Bachelors Thesis, Ulm University (2012)

42. Bernstein, V., Soffer, P.: Identifying and quantifying visual layout features of business process models. In: Gaaloul, K., Schmidt, R., Nurcan, S., Guerreiro, S., Ma, Q. (eds.) CAISE 2015. LNBIP, vol. 214, pp. 200–213. Springer, Cham (2015). doi:10.1007/978-3-319-19237-6_13

43. Schrepfer, M., Wolf, J., Mendling, J., Reijers, H.A.: The impact of secondary notation on process model understanding. In: Persson, A., Stirna, J. (eds.) PoEM 2009. LNBIP, vol. 39, pp. 161–175. Springer, Heidelberg (2009). doi:10.1007/978-3-642-05352-8_13

44. Zugal, S., Soffer, P., Haisjackl, C., Pinggera, J., Reichert, M., Weber, B.: Investigating expressiveness and understandability of hierarchy in declarative business process models. Softw. Syst. Model. **14**, 1081–1103 (2015)

45. Linden, D., Zamansky, A., Hadar, I.: How cognitively effective is a visual notation? On the inherent difficulty of operationalizing the physics of notations. In: Schmidt, R., Guédria, W., Bider, I., Guerreiro, S. (eds.) BPMDS/EMMSAD -2016. LNBIP, vol. 248, pp. 448–462. Springer, Cham (2016). doi:10.1007/978-3-319-39429-9_28

46. Reijers, H.A., Mendling, J., Dijkman, R.M.: Human and automatic modularizations of process models to enhance their comprehension. J. Inf. Syst. **36**, 881–897 (2011)
47. Koschmider, A., Reijers, H.A., Dijkman, R.: Empirical support for the usefulness of personalized process model views. In: Multikonf Wirtschaftsinformatik (2012)
48. Claes, J., Vanderfessten, I., Pinggera, J., Reihers, H.A., Weber, B., Poels, G.: A visual analysis of the process of process modeling. Inf. Syst. e-Business Manage. **13**, 147–190 (2015)
49. Figl, K.: Comprehension of procedural visual business process models. Bus. Inf. Syst. Eng. **59**, 41–57 (2017)
50. Mili, H., Tremblay, G., Jaoude, G.B., Lefebvre, É., Elabed, L., Boussaidi, G.E.: Business process modeling languages: sorting through the alphabet soup. ACM Comput. Surv. **43**, 1–56 (2010)

# An Experience Report on Teaching Business Process Modeling

# Teaching and Learning State-Oriented Business Process Modeling. Experience Report

Georgios Koutsopoulos and Ilia Bider[✉]

DSV - Stockholm University, Stockholm, Sweden
faerodin@hotmail.com, ilia@dsv.su.se

**Abstract.** Though experience on teaching and learning workflow-based business process modeling exists and is partly documented, this is not true for other types of business process modeling. Even if such experience exists, it is not documented in research publications devoted to process modeling or BPM education. This paper tries to fill the gap by reporting on experience of teaching and learning state-oriented business process modeling, which does not belong to the mainstream. The report gives both the teacher's and learner's perspective from a course where state-oriented process modeling was in the focus. The material is partly based on the reflections from the authors, one of whom is a learner, and the other - a teacher, and partly – on an investigation of opinions of other learners via interviews and a small-scale survey. The paper considers difficulties of teaching/learning state-oriented modeling, of which some does not exist for other types of process modeling, and gives suggestions on how they can be overcome.

**Keywords:** BPM · Education · Business process · Business process modeling · State-oriented

## 1 Introduction

Business Process Management (BPM) in the last 20–30 years became an established subject taught in at least some universities. Modeling of Business Process (BP) is an essential part of any BPM course, and there are plenty of books, e.g. [1], and other teaching materials, like videos for teaching/learning BP modeling. There is also some research literature related to the pedagogical aspects of teaching/learning BPM in general, and BP modeling in particular [2]. Nevertheless, the teaching/learning materials and the literature devoted to pedagogical aspects of BP modeling is limited to the mainstream operational view of considering a BP as a partially ordered set of activities/tasks, in other words workflow. For example, we could find quite a lot educational videos in English related to workflow view on YouTube, but very few that explain process modeling using IDEF0 notation [3] (though IDF0 is a bit more popular in Spanish and Russian). Moreover, in the last ten years the focus of BP modeling became even narrower – modeling BP using BPMN notation.

Summarizing the above, the research related to teaching/learning BP modeling does exist, but most, if not all, of it is focused on teaching/learning modeling based on an operation view on BP. Under the latter, we mean not only modeling workflows as

© Springer International Publishing AG 2017
I. Reinhartz-Berger et al. (Eds.): BPMDS/EMMSAD 2017, LNBIP 287, pp. 171–185, 2017.
DOI: 10.1007/978-3-319-59466-8_11

directed graphs, but also so-called declarative BP modeling in the narrow sense, which still considers a process as an ordered sequence of activities/tasks, but has other, more flexible ways of ordering them than via a directed graph. The problems related to teaching/learning other types of BP modeling and solution to them remains, if known, then unpublished. This paper aims to partly fill the gap by presenting an experience report on teaching/learning State-Oriented Business Process Modeling (StoBPM) [4, 5].

StoBPM has its origin in systems theory and follows the idea to represent a process instance as a point moving in a multidimensional state space. Thus, the most important step in StoBPM is constructing a process state space in which a trajectory of movement defines the lifeline of a possible process instance (case or run in other terminologies). The main criterion for the state space development serves a rule that any possible state of a process instance could be represented as a point in the space independently of in which way this state has been reached. The activities/tasks are defined as ways of movement in the state space. Even without tasks definition, the state space can be useful for following a BP instance development. This would be enough for modeling a flexible process in which the nature of activities is defined on the fly.

As StoBPM substantially differs from the mainstream modeling techniques, actual teaching/learning this modeling technique reveals different types of problems, which, naturally, require different kind of solutions. The experience presented in this paper is based on the first round of a course in which StoBPM is an essential part. The report is mainly based on the reflections of two participants, one of which was a learner and the other a teacher in this course round. These reflections could constitute a basis for a theory building according to [6]. In addition, opinions and reflections of several other learners have been gathered through interviews and small-scale survey. The report presents the problems discovered, and discusses possible solutions.

The rest of the paper is structured as follows. In Sect. 2, we give the background for the rest of the paper, which consists of (a) short description of the course the first round of which provided insights in the problems; (b) short description of the state-oriented view on business process; (c) short overview of the literature devoted to teaching/learning BP modeling. Section 3 contains reflections from the teacher. Section 4 presents reflections of the learner. Section 5 presents findings from interviews conducted with other learners. Section 6 summarizes lessons learned and lists suggestions for improvements.

## 2 Background

### 2.1 Course Description

A course discussed in this paper is called Business Process and Case Management (BPCM); it is given by Department of Computer and Systems Sciences (DSV) of Stockholm University. BPCM is a Master level course developed in 2016 for an international on-line MS program called "Open eGovernment"; it is also open for enrolment of MS students from other program at DSV, such as Information Systems Management and IT project management. The student audience is diverse, some have their background in social sciences, others in humanities, the third in engineering. Some students have prior knowledge on BP, acquired from previous courses, for others this is the first course related to BP. In addition, very few students have practiced modeling of any kind outside the classroom. The course amounts to 7, 5 ECTS points (5 weeks of fulltime study) and has duration of 10 weeks. Most students take another course in parallel to BPCM, many of them also have a part time job.

The objective of the course is to give the students broad view on BP, including that there are different approaches to BP modeling, and development, and that the choice of which to adopt depends on the context and task at hand. The course presents to the students two modeling methods in details, workflow modeling with BPMN and StoBPM, while giving a short overview of some other modeling techniques, alongside with how to choose the one that fits the context and task at hand [7]. The course also takes such issues as agile vs. traditional business process development, process architecture and adaptive case management.

For each topic taken in the course, the students get resources in form of research articles, chapters from books, slides and sometimes video recordings of presentations at research and industrial conferences. For more traditional topics, e.g. BPMN related issues, links to short videos from YouTube are provided. There are no lectures recordings prepared specifically for this course.

The goal of the course is to give the student knowledge that they can use in practice. This goal is reflected in the examination which consists of two parts both with focus on application of the theoretical knowledge to practice. The first part is a project that the students do individually during the course. The project concerns creating an executable process model that functions as a prototype for a Business Process Support (BPS) system. Currently, the students use *iPB* [8] as a tool for completing the project, but this may change in the future. *iPB* uses a kind of StoBPM technique for designing executable BP models. The project assignment follows the idea of apprenticeship simulation [9], and does not include a textual description of the process. The students are presented with a number of recorded interviews with stakeholders, and information on the web about the stakeholders and their line of business.

The second part of the examination is a home exam (6 h long), were the students get a textual description of a BP, and need to do 5 practical assignments, including modeling and choosing modeling technique suitable for some tasks. An exam assignment does not include pure theoretical questions.

Beside the project, which is a part of examination, the students do smaller assignments on each topic of the course, including modeling assignments. Each student chooses his/her own BP for completing assignments, e.g. a BP in which he/she participates/participated, or a BP for which the student has access to stakeholders to get information. The course also follows the idea of collaborative learning, the assignments are peer-reviewed, and the prototype created in the projects are tested by peers. Naturally, the teachers also provide feedback on submitted assignments and project progress. Most of feedback is not personal, but consists of summary of common misunderstandings and recommendations. Besides feedback on the assignments, there are forums to discuss various topics were both students and teachers participate. In addition, there are weekly virtual meetings between the teacher and students, but participation is voluntary. The summary of each meeting is usually posted later in the news for everybody.

So far, we run only one round of BPCM in autumn 2016 with around 30 active students that have finished the course. The course material, and assignments were prepared more or less in parallel with running the course, adding more material and examples to the resources based on the teachers' assessment of submitted assignments and general feedback from the students. This can be considered as agile course development. Agile course development, though causing some disturbances, was not a major issue, and the round went successfully according to the feedback from the students. In this paper, we will not discuss further the content of BPCM, and the way it is being developed, but will focus on our findings regarding teaching/learning StoBPM.

### 2.2 State-Oriented View on Business Processes

As a state-oriented view on business processes is not a mainstream view, in this section, we provide a brief overview of its underlying concepts and principles as suggested in [4]. The origin of the state-oriented view on business processes lies outside the business process domain. In essence, the state-oriented view on business processes is an application of the theories and mechanisms worked out for modeling and controlling physical processes to the domain of business processes.

The main concept of the state-oriented view is a *state* of the process instance that is defined as a position in some state space. A state space is considered multidimensional, where each dimension represents some key parameter (and its possible values) of the business process. Each point in the state space represents a possible result of the execution of a process instance. If a time axis is added to the state space, then a trajectory (curve) in the space-time will represent a possible execution of a process instance in time. A process type is defined as a subset of allowed trajectories in space-time.

As an example, consider an order process from Fig. 1. Its state space can be presented as a set of numeric dimensions from Fig. 2 defined in the following way:

- First, there are a number of pairs of product-related dimensions <ordered, delivered>, one pair for each product being sold. The first dimension represents the number of ordered items of a particular product. The second one represents the number of already delivered items of this product. The number of such pairs of dimensions is not fixed but is less than or equal to the size of the company's product assortment.
- In addition, there is a pair of numeric dimensions concerning payment: invoiced (the amount of money invoiced) and paid (the amount of money already received from the customer).
- Each process instance of the given type has a goal that can be defined as a set of conditions that have to be fulfilled before a process instance can be considered as finished (i.e., end of the process instance trajectory in the space state). A state that satisfies these conditions is called a *final state* of the process. The set of final states for the process in Fig. 1 can be defined as follows: (a) for each ordered item *Ordered = Delivered*; (b) *To pay = Total + Freight + Tax*; (c) *Invoiced = To pay*; (d) *Paid = Invoiced*. These conditions define a surface in the state space of this process type.

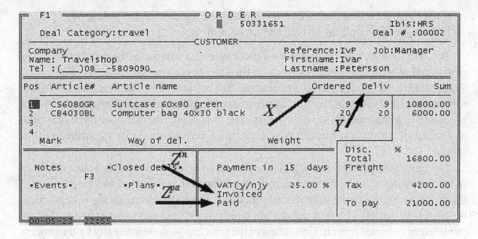

**Fig. 1.** Example of a process state as a mockup screen

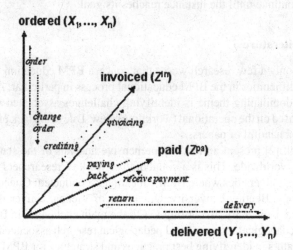

**Fig. 2.** State space dimensions as axes

The process instance is driven forward through *activities* executed either automatically or with human assistance. Activities can be planned first and executed later. A *planned activity* records such information as type of action (goods shipment, compiling a program, sending a letter), planned date and time, deadline, name of a person responsible for an action, etc.

All activities planned and executed in the frame of the process should be aimed at diminishing the *distance* between the current position in the state space and the *nearest* final state. The meaning of the term distance depends on the business process in question. Here, the term is used informally. For example, activities to plan for the process in Figs. 1 and 2 can be defined in the following manner:

– If for some item *Ordered* > *Delivered*, *shipment* should be performed, or
– If *To pay* > *Invoiced*, an *invoice* should be sent, etc.

All activities currently planned for a process instance make up the process plan. The plan together with the current position in the state space constitutes a so-called generalized state of the process, the plan being an "active" part of it. The plan plays the same role as the derivatives in the formalisms used for modeling and controlling physical processes in Mathematical systems theory. The plan shows the direction (type of action) and speed of movement (deadlines), just as first derivatives do in a continuous state space.

Using the concept of process plan, the control over a process instance can be defined in the following manner. First, an activity from the plan is executed and the position of the process instance in the state space is changed. Then, depending on the new position, the plan is corrected, i.e., new actions are added to the plan and some existing ones are modified or removed from it. Correction of the plan can be done manually by the process participants, automatically by a system that supports the process, or in a mixed fashion. The iterations continue until the instance reaches its goal.

## 2.3  Related Literature

We have found only a few research works that concern BPM education in general and challenges and difficulties in the BPM educational process in particular. As was already mentioned, the dominating theme is identifying challenges associated with teaching/learning BPM based on the operational (workflow) view. Due to the lack of space, below, we review only a handful of papers.

Bandara et al. [2] present a most comprehensive analysis of the state of the art in BPM education worldwide. This is a collaborative work of researchers that identified challenges in five universities where BPM education is conducted: Queensland University of Technology, Bentley University, University of Vienna, University of Praetoria and Georgia State University. According to [2], the main challenges in BPM education are (a) lack of pedagogical resources and pedagogical research associated with BPM so as to assist educators in identifying best practices and strategies for BPM education, (b) the diversity of the learners, (c) the dependency of the field on technology, which requires additional resources for having it in place and working, (d) the limited administrative willingness to assist in building BPM education interest, like lowering the requirements on the minimum number of students participating in a BPM course, (e) inclusion of the same BPM course in diverse educational programs, along with enrollment strength and high student expectations, and finally, (f) the unclear role of BPM professional.

Siau and Loo's research [10] is not related to BP modeling, but to the conceptual modeling with UML. However, it highlights challenges faced by students learning of modeling of any type, including StoBPM. Their main findings can be divided in three categories:

1. *Organizational/administrative difficulties*, like inconsistent course information, crowded classroom, lack of good textbook and unfriendliness of software tools.

2. *Prior knowledge.* For example, not only inexperienced students have problem understanding modeling, but also experienced students whose prior knowledge is interfering with the learning process.
3. *Difficulties associated with the modeling language.* In case of UML diagrams, it is unclear semantics, constructs with unclear definitions, inconsistencies and ambiguities of the respective concepts.

One last paper that is relevant for our study is [11], which is not directly associated with BPM or modeling. However, it provides certain educational concepts that are related to this research. In the paper, the notion of threshold concept is discussed and a conceptual framework is proposed. By the notion of threshold concept, the authors refer to a possibly transformative, integrative and irreversible conceptual gateway or portal that leads to a new way of thinking that was possibly troublesome and not accessible before the gateway. The notion is used in this paper to assist in identifying the nature of conceptual challenges faced by StoBPM learners.

## 3 The Teacher's Reflections

### 3.1 Reflections on the Nature of State-Oriented Modeling

StoBPM was developed as part of consulting practice of a Swedish consulting company *IbisSoft* based on the state-oriented view on business processes summarized in Sect. 2.2. StoBPM was used in business analysis projects, mostly for defining requirements on Business Process Support (BPS) systems. When using StoBPM, the main effort is directed to constructing a state space that can be used for tracing development of any process instance. A state space is always visualized as a mockup screen(s) of a possible BPS system, without any requirements that the actual system should follow up this design exactly. Beside the visualized state-space, the model includes conditions on proper finishing the instance, and description of activities used for movement in the state space. Such description includes:

- Conditions on when an activity can/should be used in terms of the state-space, e.g. which fields should be filled, and, possibly, with which values.
- What are the expected results of the execution of activity in real world.
- What changes are to be made in the position of the process instance in the state space after execution, which field will be changed, and, possibly, with which values.
- Who are to execute the activities in terms of organizational roles.

There is an essential difference between StoBPM and workflow modeling. The latter consists of the level of abstraction required when building a StoBPM model is higher than when building a workflow model. A workflow model consists of activities connected to each other. Both the list of activities and connections between them is possible to obtain from observations and/or interviewing the process participants. The typical question here could be "What do you do first/next/in case". It is not that easy to discover the elements (dimensions) of the state space. Sometimes the elements could be derived when studying structured documents/forms used in the process. For example, most of the elements of the state in Figs. 1 and 2, can be devised based on studying the structure of packing lists and invoices. However, if such structured documents do not exist, then other means need to be employed for constructing a state space, e.g. interviews or facilitated workshops with process participants.

To get information for building a State-oriented Model (StoM), more detailed questions need to be asked than just "What you do next?". In simple cases, it would be enough to ask "Why do you do it?" and/or "What is the intended result of this action". For example, ... *Next, we send a copy of this document to the boss. "Why we do this?" - The boss always needs to be informed when a document of this type is received.* This dialogue will result in getting a checkbox *Chef informed* in the visual representation of the process state space.

Summarizing the deliberation above, building a StoM requires higher level of abstraction than building a workflow model. Also, it requires more information on the nature of the process in question than when building a workflow diagram. In other words, it is quite possible to derive a workflow model from a StoM, but the reverse, in general, is not true. Under the level of abstraction, here, we understand the difference between what is observed, and the actual model.

### 3.2 Reflections on the Experience from the First Round of BPCM

As an outsider (from the mainstream), StoBPM, does not have much literature that discusses and explains this type of modeling. However, there are a number of published papers with examples of modeling projects, e.g. [5, 12], and unpublished consulting reports. These were used as resources for the students for the topic of StoBPM in the first round of BPCM. In particular, paper [5] with two examples of application of StoBPM in practice served as an introduction into StoBPM. In addition, an article which considered several different BP modeling techniques was given to the students [7], in which an example from [5] has been presented using several different modeling techniques.

As it is usual for published papers, the papers chosen as resources are concentrated on presenting the results (models) rather than on how they were achieved. Therefore, understanding the papers does not automatically translate in acquiring knowledge on how to build a model in another domain. To compensate the lack of instructions an example of building a StoM has been added which includes a process description and deliberation on the way to building a model. Two models where presented in this example: a deep model in form of Fig. 2, and more detail visual model as a form to be filled when following a process instance. In addition, Q&A sessions have been held, synchronously (through the conference systems), and asynchronously (forums and emails). Additional examples were added, some of them in the same domain as students' processes. General recommendations on how to improve a model were produced based on the review of typical problems in the students' models.

While in the end, most students understood the ideas behind StoBPM and managed to go through the exam, many of them had difficulties to grasp these ideas. These difficulties were of another type than when they learned workflow modeling, where they mostly struggled with formal rules of BPMN notation. For StoBPM, the misunderstandings were on the conceptual level. Some students tried to copy elements from the presented examples, instead of looking what is needed for their own processes, others disregarded construction of the state space and jumped to creating state-transition diagrams that were only complementary to the state space design. An example of building a deep model based on abstract dimensions showed to be confusing, and recommendations were made to disregard it and concentrate on visual state representation.

Summarizing the experience of the first round of the course, it looks like the concept of state space and movement in it belongs to the class of difficult knowledge (in teaching/learning) called threshold concepts [11]. The course managed the difficulties that arose in an agile manner adding materials on the fly and interacting with the students. This may work satisfactory as long as one of the teachers has substantial experience in StoBPM (being its inventor in this case). To facilitate self-learning and provide less experienced teachers with proper material, there is a need for detailed investigation of the best way of introducing the threshold of StoBPM concepts to the learners. This in turn requires uncovering the difficulties of understanding these concepts by the learners, which is, at some extent, done in the next two sections.

## 4 The Learner's Reflections

This section presents the reflections of the first author who participated in the first round of the BPCM course without previous exposure to BPM. Reflections are done based on the constructivist view on knowledge acquisition, see, for example, [13].

Participation in the BPCM course with no previous experience in BP modeling provides an opportunity for a student to become familiarized with BP modeling on a deep and comprehensive level. Students with previous BP modeling experience get an opportunity to deepen and broaden their knowledge of the field by getting exposed to alternative views on BP that are different from the workflow view.

Though the course includes many (maybe too many) topics the main factor that provides the abovementioned opportunities is exposure to StoBPM, in theory and practice. In addition to providing an alternative approach to BP modeling, which expands the learner's knowledge on BP modeling as such, StoBPM also assists in comprehending the concept of BP, its parameters and environment on a deeper level. The notion of process evolves as the course advances. As StoBPM requires a deeper understanding of BP from the learner, it facilitates the learner to expand the definition of BP in his/her mind. However, this does not come without an effort. StoBPM can be considered as an approach that rewards its learner and practitioner with a more sophisticated mental model of the BP concept, but considerable mental efforts are required for constructing this mental model.

One advantage of StoBPM is that it is possible to include into a multidimensional state space any number of factors associated with the internal and external process elements. Therefore, a StoM can adapt the level of abstractness in order to allow more or less deviations dependent on the nature of the given process and its environment. Though StoBPM is more appropriate for representing flexible BPs where a significant number of unpredictable deviations is considered a norm, it can also be used for representing highly structured processes. However, the advantages of using StoBPM in this case may disappear, as a workflow model for a highly standardized process that allows few procedural deviations is easier to appreciate and implement in practice.

StoBPM demands a deeper and, probably, more time-consuming inquiry in the nature of the BP being modeled. The tasks completed in the frame of the process need to be identified, and their connection should be understood, as it is also done in workflow modeling. However, while workflow requires to connect the tasks through (partially) ordering them, building a StoM requires uncovering and depicting the relationships between the tasks and the BP's internal and external environment elements. This is needed in order to succeed in constructing a corresponding multidimensional state space, and describing the tasks as movements in it.

Understanding the concepts and meaning of StoBPM is not easy. The first practical exercise while learning StoBPM requires the learner to design a form or a set of forms as a visual representation of a state space for a BP model. Each form includes a set of widgets, e.g. radio button groups, checkboxes and text fields that are well-known elements of software systems user interfaces. At this point, a StoM is easily confused with a software system prototype or a mockup. Perceiving the created form(s) as part of BP model requires the learner to unlearn, to a small degree, his/her experience with software interfaces, and see the form(s) in a different light. At this moment, the existing familiarity with software interfaces may help to acquire the concept of multidimensional state space for a student who has no prior knowledge of it. The notion of multidimensional state space, being the first challenge, is the learner's main milestone towards being able to practice StoBPM. It can be considered as a conceptual gateway or a threshold concept [11] in learning StoBPM.

Once the notion of multidimensional state space has been conquered, a different challenge emerges for a BPCM participant. The absence of a standard on modeling language notation and guidelines for StoBPM is a serious issue. An inexperienced learner feels lost when considering how to improve the first draft of a model. How many forms should be used, which elements need to be included and in which form to place them, how a BP element should be presented, especially if there are several appropriate choices, the size of the state space and the associations between the model's elements are only a few examples of the issues that may prove to be troublesome for a learner.

Taking into consideration the flexibility of the approach, a standard modeling language notation may be difficult to provide. However, the total absence of any guidelines presents a gap between theory and practice. The conceptual difficulties of understanding StoBPM discussed above suggest that a new modeling language notation consisting of totally unfamiliar elements would not benefit the learner and practitioner. The design elements used in its current form are familiar and easy to use. What may bridge the gap between theory and practice of StoBPM is providing the learners with a methodological framework of design principles, in the form of a structured set of rules and guidelines that would guarantee a safe transition from theory to practice and mitigate confusions.

Once the forms are created, the student needs to define the process goal and rules of movement in the state space aimed at achieving it. While this task seems significantly easier that the creation of forms, perceiving the goals and rules and conceiving them as part of the model is as confusing as using the forms to represent a BP in the beginning.

This difficulty is also associated with the concept of the multidimensional state space. Once properly conceived, the process goal and rules are nothing more than definition of the desired BP trajectories in the state space.

The next step in learning StoBPM was exposure to *iPB* for converting a StoM into an executable model. The notion of executable model, which is perceived more as a prototype than a BP model, amplified the confusion of the nature of StoMs. A significant number of clarifications was needed in order to fully understand the difference between the interlinked and thus confusing notions of BP model, executable model and prototype. The tool itself has great potential. Its core features are not only adequate, but also well-suited for creation of an executable StoM. What actually slightly undermined the learning process was the existence of a number of minor omissions and system bugs that caused unexpected results. They have all been discussed in the course forums and are expected to be fixed until the next course instance. The general outcome of using *iPB* was a highly positive experience.

What played an important role in the positive experience from the course was the combination of using *iPB* with a collaborative learning educational approach and the apprenticeship simulation [9]. This combination created a highly dynamic active educational environment where a model was being built based on the interviews with a client, and tested by peers playing the roles of different BP actors. This environment was inspiring and promotional for further engagement in BPM studies in general, and, in studies related to BP modeling theory and practice, in particular.

## 5    Difficulties and Challenges Experienced by Other Learners

In order to gain further insights on the learners' difficulties and challenges associated with StoBPM, four semi-structured interviews were conducted and complemented by a small-scale survey. The interviews were conducted asynchronously via email. All BPCM participants were invited to participate in the survey, ten of which responded by filling a questionnaire consisting of multiple choice and open ended questions. Participation was voluntary and anonymous. Manual thematic analysis was performed on the collected data in correspondence to the qualitative nature of the research. Besides the StoBPM survey, a general course evaluation survey was conducted at the end of the course. 12 students participated in this survey, however, the size of intersection between the students who participated in both surveys remains unknown. Due to the space limitations we only present a short overview of our findings related to the students' opinions and suggestions.

The BPCM students have diverse educational background: engineering, social, humanities, finance, management, economy, hybrid and multidisciplinary studies, along with Information Technology (IT) studies, which is the most common background among the participants. Participating students represent the entire range of MS programs where BPCM is mandatory or optional, and different age groups; also both full-time and part-time students were represented. The wide range of backgrounds assisted in identifying a wide range of challenges and difficulties.

Only half of the participants had previous experience with BP modeling, yet, the majority find the field very interesting. StoBPM is also considered an interesting approach, though none of the participants had any previous knowledge of it. Only one student had experience with the threshold concept of multidimensional state space before the course. The majority evaluates their understanding of StoBPM as average or above average. At the same time they consider that understanding the theory of StoBPM and acquiring practical modeling skills is harder than for workflow modeling. Half of the participants would like to enhance their knowledge on StoBPM.

Most students had difficulties in understanding the theory and practice of StoBPM, only one experiencing no difficulties at all. This case is of significance, since it concerns the only student who had previous exposure to the concept of multidimensional state space, a fact supporting the concept being a threshold concept.

There is no consensus in students' opinion on the *helpfulness of provided materials*, especially *examples*. Some consider them helpful, others - not helpful or somewhat helpful. This reflects the diversity of backgrounds, and lack of diversity in the examples. Some students pointed to this fact in their comments, e.g. "examples outside my frame of reference". The survey participants also provided a number of suggestions related to examples that are included in the discussion in the next session. Note that in the course evaluation survey the quality of material provided in the course in general was rated as above average.

There also is lack of consensus regarding *usefulness of iPB*. Some students consider it helpful for understanding the theory and practice of StoBPM, others not helpful or only somewhat helpful. This partly reflects the diversity of the students, and partly experimental nature of *iPB*, and the fact that it was developed as a tool for supporting system development in the first place, rather than for process modeling.

Regarding the helpfulness of *apprenticeship simulation*, the vast majority of the participants consider it well-chosen for the particular context and quite helpful for understanding StoBPM. Some students complained, however, with not enough individual feedback. This somewhat contradicts the course evaluation survey, in which the majority of participants rated the quantity and quality of teachers help as above average.

Finally, the notion of *collaborative learning*, while not included in the survey questionnaire, kept being mentioned by the participants as a solution to the initial confusion caused by theoretical concepts. Discussing not only with the teachers but also among the students themselves provided valuable clarifications and explanations.

It is worth mentioning that the interviews and surveys have not reveal exceptional difficulties and challenges faced by the students in understanding the notion of BP in general, identifying and documenting a BP, defining process goals and rules in the model, which is a bit in contrast with the learner's reflections presented in Sect. 4.

## 6   Lessons Learned and Suggested Actions

Based on own reflections and opinions from the learners, we can conclude that difficulties and challenges in teaching/learning StoBPM are of two sorts: general, i.e. the ones already reported in the literature, especially [2], and specific for StoBPM. The general challenges belong to the areas listed below. In the list, we refer to the letters under which the areas are mentioned in Sect. 2.3 when reviewing paper [2].

1. Resource material challenges, e.g. lack of adequate resources – (a)
2. The diversity of learners' educational and practical background – (b)
3. Technology and, specifically *iPB*, challenges – (c)
4. The unwillingness of administration to give additional resources for the course in terms of teaching hours – (d). This is connected to the wrong presumption that an online course, when designed, does not require much effort on the part of the teachers.
5. Inclusion of the course in diverse programs – (e)

There are two specific areas of challenges in teaching/learning StoBPM:

6. Presence of a number of concepts that belongs to the threshold concept type [11] for the majority of students. In particular, the notion of multidimensional state space and representing a process as a point moving in it is the main hurdle in understanding StoBPM.
7. A gap between theory and practice, which means that understanding the concepts does not automatically translate into being able to create a StoM. This gap is much smaller for workflow modeling due to its less abstract nature than StoBPM.

As general challenges 2, 4, 5 are outside our control, we need to work with general challenges 1 and 3 to meet specific challenges of teaching/learning StoBPM. In addition, we need to concentrate on enhancing the educational means that proved to be helpful and useful for, at least some, students, such as usage of examples, technology, collaborative learning, and apprenticeship simulation.

As far as specific challenge 1 is concerned, considering the diversity of learners and programs, it is difficult to meet it by increasing focus on the theory alone. The possible solution here is to expose the students to practice as early as possible, and improve the pedagogical means related to practice. As it seems that the workflow is easier to understand for the majority of students, more focus can be made on contrasting StoBPM and workflow modeling. Note, however, that the first paper that introduces state-oriented concepts [13] is built on this contrast. In Table 1, we list possible measures for improving the pedagogical means to be employed in teaching/learning StoBPM. The list includes suggestions that came from the learners, which are marked with letter (L).

Though all areas of improvement listed above are important, in our opinion, the priority should be given to the area of practice, especially to developing a methodology and guidelines. This will be done based on the reflections presented in Sects. 4 and 5.

In conclusion, we would like to mention that in our opinion, lessons learned from our experience could be of interest not only for StoPBM, but for any non-mainstream modeling to be taught. For example, they can be relevant for artifact-based BP modeling, data-centered BP modeling, etc.

**Table 1.** Suggestions for improvement.

| Area | Suggestions for improvement |
|---|---|
| General | Diminish the number of topics taken in the course to increase time for teaching/learning StoBMP (L) |
| | Provide video recordings for various learning moments as a complement for other resources, e.g. articles. In particular have recordings for:<br>• Explaining theoretical concepts (L)<br>• Explaining examples of models (L)<br>• Presenting a step by step creation of a model (L)<br>• Demo of the tool (*iPB*) |
| | Introduce teaching/learning based on *analysis of most common errors*/mistakes through the whole diapason of learning moments, theory (misconceptions), practice (wrongly built models (L)), tool usage, etc |
| Theory | • Provide better clarification of the concepts, especially, multidimensional state space, but also the difference between model, executable model and prototype<br>• Make more detailed comparison with workflow, in particular show how a workflow model can be obtain from a StoM |
| Examples | • More and diverse examples (in different domains) (L)<br>• Better connection to theory in the examples (L)<br>• Examples of incorrect StoMs (L)<br>• More examples of models in both StoBPM and workflow (L) emphasizing on similarities and differences of the two approaches |
| Practice | Provide step by step methodology of building a StoM. The question on whether such methodology would be helpful was posed in the survey, and the majority of students consider that such a methodology would be helpful or very helpful |
| | Provide guidelines for visual representation of the state space, e.g. which widgets to use dependent on what need to be represented |
| | Provide criteria on the correctness and adequateness of a StoM |
| | Introducing the tool (*iPB*) at the earliest opportunity (L) |
| Collaborative learning | Introduce detailed instructions on how to test and review a StoM created by somebody else (based on the criteria of correctness and adequateness) |
| Apprenticeship simulation | Introduce earlier in the course (L) |
| | Provide detail instructions on how to test executable models in *iPB* |
| Technology *iPB* | • Provide better documentation, especially more explicit connection to StoBPM (L)<br>• Fix bugs and issues as much as possible (L)<br>• Check whether other appropriate tools exist |

**Acknowledgements.** This work could not have been completed without the students from the first round of BPCM volunteering to participate in interviews and surveys. The authors appreciate very much the time they spent and comments they provided.

# References

1. Dumas, M., La Rosa, M., Mendling, J., Reijers, H.A.: Fundamentals of Business Process Management. Springer, Heidelberg (2013)
2. Bandara, W., Chand, D., Chircu, A., Hintringer, S., Karagiannis, D., Recker, J., van Rensburg, A., Usoff, C., Welke, R.: Business process management education in academia: status, challenges, and recommendations. CAIS **27**, 747–776 (2010)
3. NIST: Integration definition for function modeling (IDEF0), Draft Federal Information Processing Standards, Publication 183 (1993). www.idef.com/downloads/pdf/idef0.pdf. Accessed Feb 2015
4. Khomyakov, M., Bider, I.: Achieving workflow flexibility through taming the chaos. In: 6th International Conference on Object Oriented Information Systems, OOIS 2000, pp. 85–92 (2000)
5. Andersson, T., Andersson-Ceder, A., Bider, I.: State flow as a way of analyzing business processes - case studies. Logistics Inf. Manage. **15**(1), 34–45 (2002)
6. Mott, V.: Knowledge comes from practice: reflective theory building in practice. In: Rowden, R.W. (ed.) Workplace Learning: Debating Five Critical Questions of Theory and Practice, pp. 57–63. Jossey-Bass, San Francisco (1996)
7. Bider, I., Perjons, E.: Evaluating adequacy of business process modeling approaches. In: Handbook of Research on Complex Dynamic Process Management: Techniques for Adaptability in Turbulent Environments, pp. 79–102. IGI (2009)
8. IbisSoft: iPB Reference Manual. http://docs.ibissoft.se/node/3. Accessed 2009
9. Bider, I., Henkel, M., Kowalski, S., Perjons, E.: Simulating apprenticeship using multimedia in higher education: a case from the information systems field. Interact. Technol. Smart Educ. **12**(2), 137–154 (2015)
10. Siau, K., Loo, P.: Identifying difficulties in learning UML. Inf. Syst. Manage. **23**, 43–51 (2006)
11. Meyer, J., Land, R.: Threshold concepts and troublesome knowledge (2): epistemological considerations and a conceptual framework for teaching and learning. High. Educ. **49**(3), 373–388 (2005)
12. Perjons, E., Bider, I., Andersson, B.: Building and exploiting a business process model for lobbying: experience report. Commun. IIMA CIIMA **7**(3), 1–14 (2007)
13. Biggs, J., Tang, C.: Teaching for Quality Learning at University, 4th edn. Open University Press, New York (2011)

# Evaluation and Comparison of Modeling Languages and Methods

# On the Requirement from Practice for Meaningful Variability in Visual Notation

Dirk van der Linden[✉], Irit Hadar, and Anna Zamansky

Department of Information Systems, University of Haifa, Haifa, Israel
{djtlinden,hadari,annazam}@is.haifa.ac.il

**Abstract.** This research-in-progress paper proposes the need for a move towards more *meaningful variability* of visual notations. Evidence accumulated via an online survey on the requirements practitioners have for visual notations, indicate the need for variability of a modeling language's visual notation. Widely used modeling languages in practice such as UML and BPMN do not support redesign of the visual notation of core constructs without modifying or extending the underlying abstract syntax and semantics (e.g., UML stereotypes, BPMN extensions). The expressed need to vary commonly used visual notations depending on particular users or contexts, while not changing the underlying modeling language itself, poses a set of research challenges discussed here.

**Keywords:** Conceptual modeling · Requirements · Visual notations · Variability · Concrete syntax · Practitioner · Empirical study

## 1 Introduction

Visual notation, or concrete syntax, is the main way people interface with models. Whether models convey their meaning effectively and accurately depends on their visual design [14], as well as the cognitive makeup of the person looking at them [24]. Consequently, a model used among developers or technical experts would have different requirements towards its visual representation being effective than a model used to communicate with other stakeholders such as users, business experts and domain experts.

This paper will show that many practitioners who employ conceptual modeling techniques require the ability to vary the visual representation (i.e., the concrete syntax) of their models depending on the audience they target. This does not mean they are interested in modifying the language itself, whether by extending the meta-model or creating specialized extensions. In particular, when developers communicate with customers or business stakeholders they prefer using less technical or complicated displays for the same model, such as using rich pictures or clear iconography.

This implies the need for a certain *variability* in the way models are represented: changing the way the visual notation appears. However, at the same time practitioners use general-purpose languages which remain visually abstract, and

© Springer International Publishing AG 2017
I. Reinhartz-Berger et al. (Eds.): BPMDS/EMMSAD 2017, LNBIP 287, pp. 189–203, 2017.
DOI: 10.1007/978-3-319-59466-8_12

offer little to no support for on-the-fly variation of their visual notation. Short of creating specialized notations, e.g., by stereotyping in UML or extension creation in BPMN, there is no easy way to vary only the visual representation of the notation.

This paper is focused on understanding how we can give practitioners what they want. In particular, how the visual notation of a single modeling language can accommodate a diverse audience of model users, including non-experts with no experience with modeling. Based on an ongoing empirical study into the requirements practitioners have for visual notations, we describe the need for a move towards a *meaningful variability* of visual notation use. We discuss the challenges stemming from the requirement to change parameters of a visual notation on-the-fly to suit different audiences, in particular when these changes to accommodate non-experts are non-trivial and require rethinking existing models.

## 2   Defining Variability of Concrete Syntax

Variability in the context of modeling languages has received attention in literature, such as the need for systematic ways to create dialects of enterprise modeling languages [3]. However, such work remains primarily on the level of meta-models describing which entities exist, namely the abstract syntax. To define or describe a modeling language fully this is not sufficient, as both semantics (what things mean) and the concrete syntax, or visual notation (how things look), are important [8]. Meta-modeling approaches grounded in the OMG Meta-Object-Facility (MOF) [20] have been proposed to extend the degree to which visual notations are systematically captured and linked to their meta-models [6,17]. Related, approaches to detect inconsistencies between such definitions of visual notations and meta-models have been proposed [1]. Some of this work has explicitly noted the option of having multiple visual notations for a single meta-model [8], concluding that multiple visual notations can be used as long as the underlying meta-model is well defined and serves as a common (abstract) representation of the actual information represented in the model.

However, these studies predate insights from more recent theory on visual notation design [14], which shows diagram-level aspects of design known to be important for ensuring that non-experts can parse models effectively. In particular, it is now understood that *meaningful* variations in concrete syntax to bridge the expert/non-expert gap amount to more than mere differences in symbols or color schemes used. Some examples of such variation are [14]:

- Targeted iconographic design to suggest meaning: non-experts are aided by the use of rich pictures that suggest their underlying concepts' meaning clearly.
- Use of visual complexity management mechanisms: non-experts may find it hard to parse models that do not incorporate any mechanisms to abstract and hide information, having to mentally 'chunk' elements into sub-diagrams.
- Variation in the number of visual variables used to discriminate between visual elements: non-experts may benefit from graphical symbols being distinguished on more than just shape or color.

– Variation in size of the visual vocabulary: non-experts are challenged by notations with a high number of distinct graphical symbols.

These aspects of visual notation design are not addressed by the earlier work
mentioned, and pose additional challenges for the ease with which a visual notation may be selected and used on-the-fly, as will be further discussed in Sect. 5.3.

## 3    Empirical Study

The original objective of the empirical study was to elicit data on the requirements that practitioners hold for visual notations, and analyze how these compare to the Physics of Notations (PoN) [14], a widely used design theory for
cognitively effective visual notations. We then aimed to determine whether some
requirements are considered more important than others, depending on professional context.

While the assessment of the relative importance of the PoN requirements was
done in a quantitative fashion, We took a qualitative approach [18] to explore
practitioners' views on what is important in visual notations. Specifically, we
used exploratory coding [22] to analyze the views elicited from practitioners.

### 3.1    Research Questions

Our general research question is: *what requirements do practitioners have for
visual notations?* For a satisfactory answer to this question, we need not only to
understand what requirements practitioners might find important, but also to
what degree these requirements are found important, which ones are perceived
to be the least addressed, and so on. To this end, we concretely investigate:

1. What requirements do practitioners have for visual notations?
2. To what extent does the existing theory for visual notation design adequately
   cover practitioners' requirements?
3. Which requirements, if any, are considered more high priority than others?
   Can we correlate this to a domain or focus of modeling?
4. To what extent do existing modeling languages satisfy these requirements?
   How can this be improved?

### 3.2    Research Design

**Participants.** We used LinkedIn to approach practitioners employing conceptual modeling techniques. In particular, we solicited participation in the study
via relevant professional groups. We searched first for groups based on keywords
including "conceptual modeling", "requirements", "business analyst", "software
architect/engineer", "enterprise architect/engineer". After joining a group, we
posted a message asking group members for their input on requirements for
visual notations.

**Materials.** To assess requirements for visual notations we used the summary of the PoN principles [14] given in [15]. For each principle we displayed the summary with a 5-point Likert scale ranging from "very important" to "not important at all." Although these results are not discussed in this paper, we mention them as they are used to contextualize the qualitative questions on any additional requirements practitioners may have.

**Pilot.** Before setting out the survey on LinkedIn, we piloted an initial version among four professionals with expertise in conceptual modeling techniques. Their feedback was used to verify the estimated time needed to complete the survey (attempting to keep it short in order to stimulate participation), and remove any potential misunderstandings in the phrasing. Two participants in the pilot indicated that they would have different answers for how important each requirement was depending on whether they interacted with experts or non-experts. As a result of this feedback we adapted the survey to be of two parts, investigating the importance of requirements for visual notations used – first among experts, and second among non-experts such as business professionals. This version was piloted again with the same group, after which no more ambiguities were found.

**Procedure.** We invited people to participate in the survey voluntarily, with no incentive given. The questionnaire first elicited some general demographic data, as well as some information about their modeling experience asking:

– What country do you work in?
– How many people are employed in your organization? [Less than 100, Less than 1000, Less than 10.000, More than 10.000]
– How many years have you used modeling languages in a professional setting? [Less than 5 years, 5 to 10 years, More than 10 years]

This was followed by specific demographics, asking:

– What do you mostly model? [Processes, Goals/Motivations, Information/Data, Requirements, Architecture (Software), Architecture (Enterprise), Other: ...]
– What is the typical purpose of your models? [...]
– What modeling language(s) do you have significant experience with? [...]
– What domain do you currently work in? [Services, Manufacturing, Telecom, Financial, Health, Government, Academic, IT/Software, Other: ...]

Next, participants were presented the one-line summaries of each PoN principle and asked to rate them on a 5-Point Likert scale. This was done twice, first asking participants to consider their requirements for visual notations used among fellow modelers, followed by the question:

– Are there any requirements you feel are not covered by the ones you just saw, specific to the use of a visual notation among fellow modeling experts? And then, considering their requirements for non-modeler experts, followed by the question:

– Are there any requirements you feel are not covered by the ones you just
  saw, specific to the use of a visual notation among other stakeholders with
  no expertise in modeling?

## 3.3   Data Analysis

The data described in this paper is based on the first **85** responses received.
One response was discarded on suspicion of non-serious data, with all Likert
Scale data repeating the same value, and any open question containing only
meaningless repeating characters. The data we analyze in this paper results from
the open questions, yielding qualitative data. We used a qualitative approach for
coding this data, using iterative coding in which all three authors coded the data
independently. Coding of the data describing the purpose of modeling involved
two iterations of coding, after which we agreed on a limited set of codes that
arose similarly out of our analyses. For the data on missing requirements we
separately encoded whether one of the PoN principles addressed the presented
requirement and/or whether the requirement was instead related to a different
factor, such as tool support or semantic quality instead of the visual notation.
After discussion these coding sessions led to the results shown in Tables 1 and 2.

## 3.4   Threats to Validity

The primary threats to validity in this study are construct validity and participant fit. In the survey, requirements are presented as the one-sentence summary
given by the PoN itself. It is possible that they would be interpreted differently than intended, however, given the ambiguous nature of the PoN itself [11],
even if given full details of the principles as presented in [14] such differences in
understanding could arise. Nonetheless, these high-level descriptions represent
the summarized overall 'spirit' of the principle, and are widely used by different
applications of the PoN. We therefore work under the assumption they serve as
an adequate representation of the principles.

Whether participants actually know if, and to what degree, these requirements are important for them is another matter. We targeted participants with
experience in conceptual modeling, specifically capturing their years of professional experience, in order to have a grounded assumption that they had been
exposed to the use of modeling languages long enough to develop an internal
set of high-priority requirements. In an analog to Henry Ford's quote on the
development of the first cars, "if I asked anyone at the time what they wanted,
they would have said faster horses," we do acknowledge that the importance of
these requirements might not be understood or underwritten by all participants.

The fit of participants to the study was ensured as much as possible by
limiting the participant recruitment to relevant groups of LinkedIn, our own
professional network, and academic mailing lists, in order to target only those
with experience in conceptual modeling. The profile built by the questions given
above further helped to (de)select only those participants with relevant and
significant experience. Furthermore, we specifically targeted those with primary

industrial experience, and specifically, ensured in the datasets that there were no participants whose primary experience was solely of an academic nature.

A final threat to validity is the potential self-selection bias, as we only elicit responses from those practitioners willing to respond. However, in our experience setting out these surveys on LinkedIn, we encountered several groups where one or more participants enthusiastically replied to the survey and stimulated others to join, emphasizing the potential benefit of the insight the study could also bring for their community.

# 4    Study Results

## 4.1    Demographic Data

While the dataset at this point in time cannot yet be considered to be significant enough to generalize (given $n = 84$), we established some basic demographic data to ensure that the data represents a heterogeneous sample of participants (see Fig. 1).

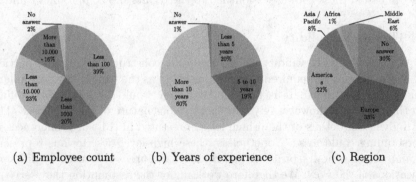

(a) Employee count        (b) Years of experience            (c) Region

**Fig. 1.** General demographics.

For modeling-specific demographics we list the domains in which participants operated. Practitioners typically only operated in a **single** domain (see Fig. 2).

As for what is actually modeled: most participants were involved in modeling multiple foci, the median being **three**. Fig. 3 shows how many participants modeled each focus.

## 4.2    Used Visual Notations

A large number of modeling languages (**36**) was reported to be used by the respondents: BPMN, UML, xtUML, SysML, SimuLink, Stateflow, SDL, MARTE, ERD, ORM, BPEL, FSA, ArchiMate, IDEF0, IDEF1x, CMMN, Viso, RDF/OWL, GRAPES BPM, i*, IE, DMN, MODAF, GSN, EPC, C4, and more.

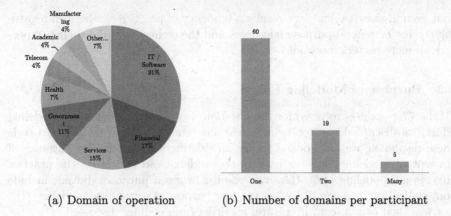

(a) Domain of operation            (b) Number of domains per participant

**Fig. 2.** Domains in which participants operate.

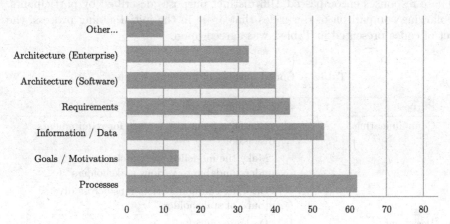

**Fig. 3.** Different foci modeled by participants. The x-axis is number of participants, running up to the $n$ of 84.

However, most of these notations were reported to be used by very few participants. By far the most used visual notations reported on were UML (**49** counts) and BPMN (**32** counts), followed at a big distance by ArchiMate (**12** counts) and SysML (**8** counts).

Of particular interest is that the two most frequently used visual notations are general-purpose languages, seemingly wielded and adapted to many domains and purposes. Interestingly, dataflow diagrams (DFDs) and entity-relationship diagrams (ERDs) were noted only **once** and **four** times, respectively. Compared to a study from 2006 which found DFDs and ERDs [4] among the most used notations in practice, this could point towards changing attitudes.

As noted, there are limitations to keep in mind when considering these data, most notably self-reporting bias and selection bias. However, given the wide spread of LinkedIn groups targeted and different domains reached, we believe that even in these preliminary results a tendency of practice can be seen regarding the use of general-purpose languages and the eschewing, from their perspective, of more esoteric notations.

## 4.3    Purpose of Modeling Efforts

Of the **77** responses received for the question regarding the purpose of modeling effort, we discarded one for being irrelevant (stating solely "UML"). To code these responses, we first looked to use an existing set of codes for purposes of conceptual modeling, such as used in two widely-cited papers on the practice conceptual modeling [4,5]. However, the list of given purposes did not include communication, commonly seen as the core purpose of conceptual modeling [21], nor was their origin (e.g., literature, resulting from coding) discussed.

Thus, we decided to have each author code all **76** responses independently. These responses encompassed **106** distinct purposes described by participants. Following comparison of the codes that arose in the initial coding process, the set of codes presented in Table 1 was agreed upon.

**Table 1.** Coded purpose of modeling efforts

| Purpose | # | Exemplary quote(s) |
| --- | --- | --- |
| Communicating | 25 | "Common point of reference for requirements discussions" |
| | | "Make the modelled system clear and understandable to various stakeholders" |
| | | "Bridging communication gaps across diverse groups of stakeholders" |
| Designing | 23 | "Designing new software" |
| | | "Systems design" |
| Understanding | 20 | "Simplification of complex concepts/solutions" |
| | | "High level understanding of the system and purpose" |
| Supporting development | 13 | "Guide me when actually writing the software" |
| | | "Supporting decisioning, and instructioning designers" |
| Visually representing | 13 | "Visualisation of architectural metadata" |
| | | "Visualizing design" |
| Engineering requirements | 12 | "Represent knowledge at different levels of abstraction to look for missing, incorrect, and unnecessary requirements" |

### 4.4   Additional or Missing Requirements

We processed the data elicited on missing requirements with a coding schema with the three researchers independently coding the data marking whether, and if so, which PoN principle addressed the proposed requirements. A total of **49** remarks were coded: **six** remarks were irrelevant to the posed question; **five** remarks were excluded due to their ambiguous nature; and, **eleven** remarks were not related to the principles, reflecting requirements related to a tool rather than the visual notation itself. Of the remaining **27** remarks, only two dealt with something not clearly or directly addressed by a PoN principle: how to display visually overlapping relationships. The remaining **25** remarks were found to be addressed by one or more PoN principles, as summarized in Table 2 below.

**Table 2.** Requirements covered by each principle.

| PoN principle | # | Exemplary quote(s) |
|---|---|---|
| Cognitive fit | 8 | "I cannot do the formal models without 'artist impressions' or rich pictures tailored to specific stakeholders or stakeholder groups, even fellow modeling insiders/experts" |
| | | "My responses are coloured by my desire to use these diagrams to collaborate with non - experts, those most familiar with the problem domain" |
| | | "Highlight how important is to have flexibility to communicate to several audiences perhaps incorporating a more complex visual design. The simplicity of the visual design of UML could be perfect for a software engineer but very cold for a Business User" |
| | | "Flexibility in presentation" |
| Complexity management | 6 | "Visual representation capabilities like zooming in or out" |
| | | "Visual simplication techniques" |
| | | "Provide different views of complexity level" |
| | | "Use of abstraction (e.g. a high-level overview)" |
| Semantic transparency | 5 | "I think [the] biggest detractor to existing [notations] are that they are conceptually abstract and have steep learning curves" |
| Semiotic clarity | 3 | "Precision and unambiguous" |
| Dual coding | 1 | "Visual notation needs to have a textual counterpart" |
| Perceptual discriminability | 1 | "The size and usability of the symbols" |
| All (PoN overall) | 2 | "The modeling notation should be empirically founded on cognitive theories of visualisation" |

The responses in Table 2 show a link to the aspects in which non-experts are perceived by our participants as more cognitively challenged during model usage, such as the notion of personalizing the notation for different audiences, and ensuring that the used visual representation be as simple as possible. In an earlier study the first author performed on model-aided decision making in Enterprise Architecture [10], numerous responses were found that corroborate this tendency to require simplicity when dealing with modeling non-experts. For example, one architect noted that PowerPoint, Excel and Visio were more suitable for non-technical audiences, and another architect noted that in dialogues with management stakeholders, they did not use any modeling languages or techniques.

## 5    Toward Meeting Practitioners' Requirement for Visual Variability

### 5.1    The Need

The presented results sketch a clear view on the research question *what requirements practitioners have towards visual notations,* as well as showing that *existing theory for visual notation design adequately covers practitioners' requirements.* What seems particularly salient in Table 2 is practitioners' requirements to support the purpose of models in communicating with non-experts, and bridging the cognitive gap between modeling experts and non-experts. This means, specifically, that a meaningful visual variability is indeed required: varying the (properties of the) visual notation depending on the audience. However, this need seems to not yet be accommodated by the main modeling languages that are used in practice: UML and BPMN.

**Fig. 4.** Example of a stereotyped entity from the UML standard [19].

### 5.2    Why This Need Is Not Accommodated

To concretely answer the research question *To what extent does the existing theory for visual notation design adequately cover practitioners' requirements?,* let us look at the two most used modeling languages among our participants. UML allows a designer to adapt the notation to a specific context by using stereotyping, which enables both the use of *specific terminology,* and *[visual] notation* [19, Sect. 12.3.3.4]. The extent to which a new notation can be introduced is limited though, to primarily new symbols and coloring. Stereotyped entities can have symbols appended to them as markers, or be displayed as that symbol entirely, as shown in Fig. 4.

This allows at least for the use of rich pictures: the use of detailed icono-graphic representation for domain concepts. However, there is a significant lim-itation in that these visual modifications only seem to be allowed over stereo-typed elements. This means that new elements in the abstract syntax have to be created, and semantics defined, instead of allowing for simple visual vari-ability in the representation. The existence of numerous tool-specific extensions to allow for modification and coloring of core elements (e.g., in Visual Studio) seems to be a clear hint at people implementing this need themselves. Similar to UML, BPMN extensions' primary means of visual modification in practice seems to be coloring and the addition of markers to existing graphical elements [12]. There are concrete instructions in the standard for BPMN [20] when it comes to extending its notation. Particularly salient are:

- "A new shape representing a kind of Artifact MAY be added to a Diagram, but the new Artifact shape SHALL NOT conflict with the shape specified for any other BPMN element or marker."
- "An extension SHALL NOT change the specified shape of a defined graph-ical element or marker (e.g., changing a square into a triangle, or changing rounded corners into squared corners, etc.)."

The same restriction as in the UML standard is found again: that existing ele-ments may not be meaningfully changed. Shape, color, and line style of existing core constructs are all protected. This impacts the ability to create a meaningful variability in the visual notation, as properties of the core constructs would be modified to deal with practitioners' needs. An argument may be brought that allowing to make changes to core constructs' representation would impact the *mutual intelligibility* of created models. However, as practitioners clearly indicate such variability would be used to communicate from an expert audience (e.g., developer, technical analysts) to a non-expert audience (e.g., business stakehold-ers, management, end-users), there is no need for these two groups to read the same underlying model in the visual representation optimal for the other group. Therefore, the challenge of mutual intelligibility does not come into play.

The ability to create meaningful visual variability in UML and BPMN thus lags behind the ability to create meaningful semantic variability.

## 5.3   The Challenges

Finally, we reflect on *what can be done*. Some aspects required to implement variability in the concrete syntax to accommodate the expert/non-expert divide are seemingly trivial, although they would require incorporation into the rele-vant modeling language's standard to be truly effective. However, other aspects require more careful thought.

The aspects needed for *meaningful variability* to target non-experts as described in Sect. 2 lead to a number of challenges for the implementation and use of visual variability. In particular, the last three require thought on how to redraw models: when adding or removing complexity management mechanisms, when changing the number of visual variables used to discriminate between sym-bols, and when changing the total number of graphical symbols used.

**Challenge 1: Complexity Mechanisms.** It is known that non-experts are more challenged by visual complexity on models due to a lack of "chunking strategies." [2]. This means that non-experts find it more challenging to mentally group together closely related entities and effectively perceive them as sub-diagrams. When changing the visual notation for a non-expert audience, one would thus have to incorporate such mechanisms. However, how do we decide which parts of the model to group together and hide without expert (modeler) oversight? The meta-model has to enforce encoding of meta-data that represents whether, and to which, sub-diagram an element may be collapsed. Determining the boundaries for this is challenging, as over-zealous encoding of sub-diagram potential may lead to diagrams with little actual information, with all meaningful semantic elements hidden away in sub-diagrams. Furthermore, the "chunks" of a model should ideally also be represented in a rich visual way. This poses an additional challenge for the iconographic design of these chunks, as the chunked sub-diagram not only requires complicated iconography (e.g., representing in a realistic way the chunked concept of "financial handling", which is composed of say "payment request," "payment receiving," "payment registration," "payment reminder") but also has to be relatable to the *rich pictures* used for all the underlying elements when the sub-diagram is unfolded into all of its constituent parts.

**Challenge 2: Variation in Visual Variables.** To assist non-experts in clearly discriminating between different elements in a model, we can use visual variables. However, the more visual variables that are used, the more cognitively complicated it will be to assess which elements are distinct. If only shape is used to distinguish between different elements, most people would see so quickly. However, with the complexity of realistic models, more variables are needed to distinguish between all possible different elements, going up as high as using e.g., the unique combination shape, color, texture and size to determine an element's uniqueness. How can we redraw a model for non-experts, requiring using fewer combinations of visual variables as a unique separation? This requires the incorporation of evidence-driven data, showing exactly which visual variables are most distinguishable, and then in particular which instantiations thereof, as recently proposed for e.g., color schemes [23]. However, for other visual variables such data is needed too, showing e.g., optimal schemes of most distinct textures, shapes, orientations.

**Challenge 3: Variation in Visual Vocabulary Size.** Visual notations use many different graphical symbols. While experts may be trained to deal with this complexity, for non-experts not trained or familiar with the use of such models, limiting the size of the visual vocabulary is important. Practically, this means not exceeding the established threshold of $7 \pm 2$ distinct symbols [13]. However, the two most used notations exceed this by far, with UML going up as high as 60 distinct symbols for some diagrams [16], and BPMN as high as 171 [7]. When presenting a model to a non-expert, this requires one to thus either use a very limited subset of the notation, as in the case of BPMN's "core" constructs, or dynamically concatenating semantic elements to be represented by a similar visual element. When we have a model using, say, 35 distinct elements, and we want to apply a visual notation for non-experts that reduces that down to seven, how do we decide which semantic elements to represent by the same visual element? This, again, requires either extensive additional meta-data, grounded in e.g., ontological or psycholinguistic work establishing the similarity or "closeness" of these concepts [9] – or expert (modeler) oversight establishing clear rationale for the used grouping.

## 6 Concluding Outlook

In this research-in-progress paper we have described initial results from an ongoing study into the requirements practitioners have for visual notations, clearly showing the need from practice for meaningful variability in visual notations. In particular, variability in aspects that make diagrams easier to read for non-experts. Allowing for such variability poses some challenges to on-the-fly re-representing models, often demanding either expert (modeler) oversight and clear rationale, or grounding in additional meta-data of the modeled elements.

The contribution of this work so far is in its empirical findings providing insight into requirements from modeling practice, and how those may clash with prevailing research efforts. For example, the findings diverge from previous studies in the past decade [4], pointing towards changing attitudes in what modeling languages are most commonly used. Furthermore, it re-emphasizes the lack of widespread acceptance of specialized, niche notations for specific foci, showing that practitioners commonly use UML and/or BPMN instead of domain-specific notations. Perhaps as a consequence, participants stressed the yet unsatisfied requirement for visual notations to allow for variability in its visual notation. In particular, for design that allows for models to be effectively used with non-experts (i.e., end-users, business stakeholders).

Our further work in this area will center around implementing this kind of *meaningful variability* in the visual notation of general-purpose modeling languages. To do so, we will focus on (i) systematic formulation of visual notation dialects that account for design aspects important for non-expert understanding, (ii) mechanisms to allow OMG specifications to use multiple visual notations linked to one core meta-model (or abstract syntax), and finally (iii) an evidence-driven approach for systematically capturing (structures for) meta-data in the meta-model of a modeling language that can inform the on-the-fly rendering into varying visual notations.

## References

1. Baar, T.: Correctly defined concrete syntax for visual modeling languages. In: Nierstrasz, O., Whittle, J., Harel, D., Reggio, G. (eds.) MODELS 2006. LNCS, vol. 4199, pp. 111–125. Springer, Heidelberg (2006). doi:10.1007/11880240_9

2. Blankenship, J., Dansereau, D.F.: The effect of animated node-link displays on information recall. J. Exp. Educ. **68**(4), 293–308 (2000)
3. Braun, R., Esswein, W.: Designing dialects of enterprise modeling languages with the profiling technique. In: 2015 IEEE 19th International Conference Enterprise Distributed Object Computing (EDOC), pp. 60–67. IEEE (2015)
4. Davies, I., Green, P., Rosemann, M., Indulska, M., Gallo, S.: How do practitioners use conceptual modeling in practice? Data Knowl. Eng. **58**(3), 358–380 (2006)
5. Fettke, P.: How conceptual modeling is used. Commun. Assoc. Inf. Syst. **25**(1), 43 (2009)
6. Fondement, F., Baar, T.: Making metamodels aware of concrete syntax. In: Hartman, A., Kreische, D. (eds.) ECMDA-FA 2005. LNCS, vol. 3748, pp. 190–204. Springer, Heidelberg (2005). doi:10.1007/11581741_15
7. Genon, N., Heymans, P., Amyot, D.: Analysing the cognitive effectiveness of the BPMN 2.0 visual notation. In: Malloy, B., Staab, S., van den Brand, M. (eds.) SLE 2010. LNCS, vol. 6563, pp. 377–396. Springer, Heidelberg (2011)
8. Kleppe, A.: A language description is more than a metamodel. In: Fourth International Workshop on Software Language Engineering (ATEM 2007) (2007)
9. van der Linden, D., Proper, H.A.: Category structure of language types common to conceptual modeling languages. In: Bider, I., Gaaloul, K., Krogstie, J., Nurcan, S., Proper, H.A., Schmidt, R., Soffer, P. (eds.) BPMDS/EMMSAD -2014. LNBIP, vol. 175, pp. 317–331. Springer, Heidelberg (2014). doi:10.1007/978-3-662-43745-2_22
10. van der Linden, D., Van Zee, M.: Insights from a study on decision making in enterprise architecture. In: PoEM (Short Papers), vol. 1497, pp. 21–30 (2015)
11. van der Linden, D., Zamansky, A., Hadar, I.: How cognitively effective is a visual notation? On the inherent difficulty of operationalizing the physics of notations. In: Schmidt, R., Guédria, W., Bider, I., Guerreiro, S. (eds.) BPMDS/EMMSAD -2016. LNBIP, vol. 248, pp. 448–462. Springer, Cham (2016). doi:10.1007/978-3-319-39429-9_28
12. van der Linden, D., Zamansky, A., Hadar, I.: On the need for more requirements towards visual notation design of BPMN extensions. In: Caise Radar 2016, University of Ljubljana (2016)
13. Miller, G.A.: The magical number seven, plus or minus two: some limits on our capacity for processing information. Psychol. Rev. **63**(2), 81 (1956)
14. Moody, D.L.: The "physics" of notations: toward a scientific basis for constructing visual notations in software engineering. IEEE Trans. Softw. Eng. **35**(6), 756–779 (2009). <GotoISI>://WOS:000272172800003
15. Moody, D.L., Heymans, P., Matuleviius, R.: Visual syntax does matter: improving the cognitive effectiveness of the i* visual notation. Requirements Eng. **15**(2), 141–175 (2010)
16. Moody, D., van Hillegersberg, J.: Evaluating the visual syntax of UML: an analysis of the cognitive effectiveness of the UML family of diagrams. In: Gašević, D., Lämmel, R., Wyk, E. (eds.) SLE 2008. LNCS, vol. 5452, pp. 16–34. Springer, Heidelberg (2009). doi:10.1007/978-3-642-00434-6_3
17. Muller, P.-A., Fleurey, F., Fondement, F., Hassenforder, M., Schneckenburger, R., Gérard, S., Jézéquel, J.-M.: Model-driven analysis and synthesis of concrete syntax. In: Nierstrasz, O., Whittle, J., Harel, D., Reggio, G. (eds.) MODELS 2006. LNCS, vol. 4199, pp. 98–110. Springer, Heidelberg (2006). doi:10.1007/11880240_8
18. Myers, M.D.: Qualitative research in information systems. Manage. Inf. Syst. Q. **21**(2), 241–242 (1997)
19. (OMG) O.M.G.: Unified modeling language (UML), version 2.5 (2015). www.omg.org/spec/UML/2.5/

20. (OMG) O.M.G.: Meta object facility (MOF) version 2.5.1 (2016). http://www. omg.org/spec/MOF/2.5.1/
21. Robinson, S., Arbez, G., Birta, L.G., Tolk, A., Wagner, G.: Conceptual modeling: definition, purpose and benefits. In: Proceedings of the 2015 Winter Simulation Conference, pp. 2812–2826. IEEE Press (2015)
22. Saldana, J.: The Coding Manual for Qualitative Researchers. Sage, London (2015)
23. Stark, J., Braun, R., Esswein, W.: Systemizing colour for conceptual modeling (2017)
24. Wilmont, I., Hengeveld, S., Barendsen, E., Hoppenbrouwers, S.: Cognitive mechanisms of conceptual modelling. In: Ng, W., Storey, V.C., Trujillo, J.C. (eds.) ER 2013. LNCS, vol. 8217, pp. 74–87. Springer, Heidelberg (2013). doi:10.1007/978-3-642-41924-9_7

# Balanced Scorecard for Method Improvement: Approach and Experiences

Kurt Sandkuhl[1,2(✉)] and Ulf Seigerroth[2(✉)]

[1] University of Rostock, Albert-Einstein-Str. 22, 18059 Rostock, Germany
kurt.sandkuhl@uni-rostock.de
[2] School of Engineering, Jönköping University, Box 1026, 55111 Jönköping Sweden
{kurt.sandkuhl,ulf.seigerroth}@ju.se

**Abstract.** Modelling methods provide structured guidance for performing complex modelling tasks including procedures to be performed, concepts to focus on, visual representations, tools and cooperation principles. Development of methods is an expensive process which usually involves many stakeholders and results in various method iterations. This paper aims at contributing to the field of method improvement by proposing a balanced scorecard based approach and reporting on experiences from developing and using it in the context of a method for information demand analysis. The main contributions of the paper are (1) a description of the process for developing a scorecard for method improvement, (2) the scorecard as such (as a tool) for improving a specific method, and (3) experiences from applying the scorecard in industrial settings.

**Keywords:** Method improvement · Balanced scorecard · Method engineering · Information demand analysis method

## 1 Introduction

Modeling methods provide structured guidance for performing complex modeling tasks including procedures to be performed, concepts to focus on, visual representations for capturing modeling results, tools and cooperation principles (see Sect. 2.1). Method engineering (ME) is an expensive and knowledge intensive process, which usually involves many stakeholders and results in various engineering iterations. This paper aims at contributing to the field of method engineering and especially method improvement by proposing a balanced scorecard (BSC) based approach and reporting on experiences from using the method and the BSC in the context of a method for information demand analysis.

The primary perspective for method improvement taken is that of an organization using the method for business purposes and aiming at improving the contribution of the method to business objectives. In this context, approaches from the field of "business value of information technology" (BVIT) are relevant and were investigated. Most of the BVIT approaches currently existing originated in a demand from enterprises to evaluate the contribution of IT to the business success. Section 2.2 includes an overview to BVIT approaches.

I. Reinhartz-Berger et al. (Eds.): BPMDS/EMMSAD 2017, LNBIP 287, pp. 204–219, 2017.
DOI: 10.1007/978-3-319-59466-8_13

One of the general approaches for measuring BVIT is to capture indicators for different perspectives of the business value in a scorecard with different, balanced perspectives. Our proposal is to apply this approach for method improvement as it allows for combining different aspects relevant for business value, such as quality of the results achieved by using the method, quality of the method documentation and quality of the work procedures included in the method. The application of the scorecard is illustrated using the method for information demand analysis (the IDA-method [12]). For the organizations using the IDA-method in own projects, the scorecard was supposed to be a management instrument for the operational use of the method.

Main contributions of the paper are (1) a description of the process for developing a scorecard for method improvement, (2) the scorecard as such (as a tool) for improving the IDA-method, and (3) experiences from applying the scorecard in industrial settings. The remainder of this paper is structured as follows: Sect. 2 summarizes the foundation for our work from method engineering and business value of IT research. Section 3 introduces the research approach taken. Section 4 describes the development process of the BSC and the resulting "method scorecard". Section 5 is dedicated to experiences related to the use of the scorecard. Section 6 summarizes the results and gives an outlook on future work.

## 2  Theoretical Foundation

### 2.1  The Notion of Methods

Methods are often used as instrumental support for development of enterprises, e.g. for enterprise modeling (EM), information systems design etc. According to our view the use of methods is to be regarded as artifact-mediated actions where different prescribed method actions will guide our development work. A method as an artifact is something that is created by humans and the artifact can't exist without human involvement either by design or by interpretation (c.f. [9, 11]). An artifact can therefore be instantiated as something with physical- and/or social properties which also needs to be taken into consideration during method improvement. Method-mediated actions are diverse in nature and can also be tacit in character. Guidance for actions can also be found in the solution space in terms of artifacts like best practices, which also can be instantiated through different patterns. Methods are in many cases also implemented in computerized tools to facilitate the modeling process.

Our focus is on methods, method engineering, and method improvement. We acknowledge the ISO/IEC 24744:2014 standard and this definition of methods. During modeling activities, there is usually a need to document various aspects, and many methods include rules for representation, usually referred to as modeling techniques or notation rules. Methods also provide procedural guidelines (work procedures), which often are tightly coupled to notation. The work procedures involve meta-concepts such as process, activity, information, and object, as parts of the prescribed actions. The work procedures are also parts of the semantics of the notation. Concepts are to be regarded as the cement and bridge between work procedures and notation.

When there is a close link between work procedures, notation, and concepts, it is referred to as a method component. The concept of method component is similar to the concept of method chunk [2, 3] and the notion of method fragment [4]. A method component therefore gives instructions of how to perform a certain work step, e.g. a method component is executed through the work procedures – notation rules – and the concepts in focus. A so called "method" is often a compound of several method components into what is often referred to as a methodology [5] or a framework [1]. A framework gives a phase structure of method components, which guides us in us in terms of what to do, in what order, and what results to produce but instructions about how to do things is found in different method components.

## 2.2  Business Value of IT and Balanced Scorecard

During the last decades, numerous research activities from business administration, economics and computer science have addressed how to measure the business value of IT. Four typical examples of this are:

- Process-oriented approaches, like IT Business Value Metrics [20]. In process-oriented approaches the BVIT is demonstrated through process improvements. These approaches investigate how value is added to the business.
- Perceived value approaches, like IS Success Model [22]. These approaches bases BVIT evaluations on user perceptions rather than on financial indicators or measurements within technical systems.
- Project-focused approaches, like Information Economics [21]. This kind of approach basically tries to support decision making, whether an IT-project should be started by calculating a score for project alternatives.
- Scorecard-based approaches, like the balanced scorecard [13]. These approached try to include different perspective when evaluating the business value, including, e.g., financial, process-oriented and learning perspectives.

As stated in Sect. 1, the focus of our work is on improving the contribution of a method to the business objectives of an organization. All four types of BVIT approaches could potentially be tailored for this purpose. There are though differences between these approaches with respect to their suitability:

- the required method improvement approach has to include business value and coherence with business drivers like reduced lifecycle time or increased flexibility. These business drivers are measurable criteria reflected in control systems of many companies. Perceived value approaches do not cover these aspects sufficiently.
- method improvement requires monitoring of relevant indicators during a longer period of method use, i.e. capturing of performance indicators only once would not be sufficient. This requirement is hard to meet with project-centric approaches.
- process-oriented approaches are by nature quite specific for the individual company, as they require an understanding business processes, potential business impact and potential IT impact before starting the actual analysis of BVIT. This makes the

approaches quite expensive for method improvement in terms of efforts to be invested, as methods are expected to be used in many different organizations.

Among the scorecard-based approaches, the BSC proposed by Kaplan and Norton [13] is the most established. The BSC is a *management system*, i.e. it includes measurement approaches to continuously improve performance and results.

## 2.3  Method Engineering

Method engineering (ME) is an expensive and knowledge intensive process, usually involving many stakeholders and results in various engineering iterations. ME is defined by [6] as the engineering discipline to design, construct and adapt methods, techniques and tools for systems development, which is also is in line with the IEEE definition of software engineering (SE) and the ISO/IEC 24744:2014 standard. In the approaches for ME and there is a need for approaches in which SE can improve the success rate [6]. A ME approach that has received a lot of interest is situational method engineering (SME) (ibid). In this paper we have applied a phase-based ME process similar to the ISO/IEC 24744:2014 standard. In this we have especially acknowledged the iterative interplay between method generation and method validation (enactment) according to Fig. 1. In the ISO/IEC standard the main activities are Generation and Enactment. Generation is the act of defining and describing the method based on a defined foundation, often a meta model. Enactment is the act of validating the method through application. This standard also depicts roles like the Method engineer who is the person(s) who design, builds, extends, and maintains the method and the Developer who is the person(s) who during enactment applies the method. These two activities and roles are interlinked so that they in an interactive way can participate during both generation and enactment.

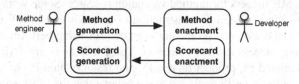

**Fig. 1.**  Method engineering process, based on ISO/IEC 24744:2014

In our ME process for the IDA-method, we developed and used a BSC as a tool for method improvement. This was done through generating and measuring different performance indicators in a BSC as part of the validation (enactment) of the method. In this the BSC has also gone through generation and validation as part of the total ME process (see Fig. 1), i.e., the generation and enactment of the BSC has been both interwoven in the ME-process and a parallel activity. This iterative interplay between generation and enactment for both the method and the BSC has called for a structured way to deal with this from the dimensions of both theoretical and empirical input and feedback. We followed the approach of Goldkuhl [18] proposing three levels to address during method generation and enactment (internal, theoretical, and empirical), see Table 1. This approach is similar to approaches, which also advocate theoretical and empirical dimensions of ME (c.f. [10, 19]). During our ME process we have performed different generation- and enactment activities illustrated in Table 1.

**Table 1.** Generation and enactment of the IDA-method and the scorecard

|  | Generation | Enactment (Validation) |
|---|---|---|
| Internally | Reflective discussions between method engineers and developers where the emerging internal structure and content of the method and the scorecard was questioned and developed | Evaluation of method and scorecard consistency in use in terms of structure and interrelationships of its various parts |
| Theoretically | Use of a method notion to provide a conceptual structure for the method Relating concept definitions to existing methods and established knowledge (e.g. BSC, BVIT, IDA etc.) | Comparison of the generated method against existing method notions and method theories Analysis of method and BSC in comparison to existing method- and BVIT practices |
| Empirically | Interview-based investigation for deriving method focus, conceptual foundation, and requirements. Practical application of the evolving method and BSC together with industrial partners. Development of support documentation (method- and BSC handbook) together with industrial partners | Several test cases for evaluating the usefulness of the method and BSC in industrial cases Industrial method use and evaluation by external parties by means of a method evaluation framework, NIMSAD Industrial use and evaluation of method- and BSC handbook |

According to our knowledge research about method validation through the use of BSC to measure ME success for method validation is scarce. Some work can be found in relation to the actual design or construction of methods e.g. in [6]. Harmsen [16] presents a more elaborated and promising approach for using performance indicators (PI) for measuring success in IS engineering. These indicators are divided into three groups: process-related PI, product related PI, and result related PI. Even though that this research has a focus on IS engineering we believe that the same principles can be useful for method validation during ME.

## 3    Research Approach

The research approach for development of the BSC and the engineering of the IDA-method combines design science (DS) [8] and action research (AR) [14]. In this combination, we have taken a stance in Technical Action Research (TAR) according to Wieringa and Morali [7]. In TAR the engineering process and the artifact design is the starting point and where the artifact is supposed to be validated in practice in a scaled-up sequence from test in controlled environment to full-fledged applications to solve a real practical problem in an enterprise (ibid). Our artifacts in this case are two folded, (1) the IDA-method, which is developed as a "treatment" to improve or solve information

challenges in enterprises in dimensions of information supply, provision, demand, logistics etc. and (2) the BSC, which is developed as a "treatment" for method improvement.
There are also earlier promising initiatives to combine DS and AR and one example of
this is Action Design Research (ADR) by Sein et al. [15]. Even though that the artifact
is in focus in ADR the approach still has a problem driven approach [15]. In our case
the TAR approach has been more convenient since the method is developed from the
notion that we have to handle information challenges in enterprises and the BSC from
the notion that there is a need for method improvement.

The work presented in this paper originates from a TAR research project with two
academic and five industrial partners aiming at development of a method for IDA. The
purpose with the IDA-method was to support identification, modeling and analyzing
information demand as a base for development of technical and organizational solutions
that provides a demand driven information provision. The ME process for the IDA-
method and the BSC is described in Fig. 2 below.

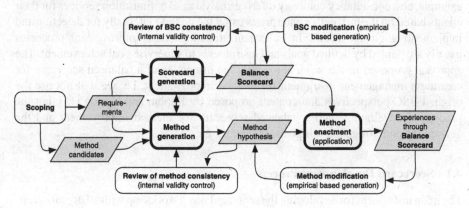

**Fig. 2.** Generation and validation via balance scorecard of the IDA method

In this study we focus on the enactment phase and the use of BSC as a tool for method
improvement. Five different IDA-cases were included:

- A metal finishing company (coordination of quality, technology and production)
- A municipality (handling of errands)
- The association for Swedish SAP users (coordination of information flow)
- A timber company (identification of information demand for test strategy)
- A gardening retailer (information demand for different organizational roles)

## 4   Development of BSC for Method Improvement

The BSC development is illustrated using the IDA-method which has its focus on
capturing, modelling and analysing the information demand of organizational roles in
order to improve the supply of information. This method has similarities to enterprise
modelling methods, but it only focuses on the information demand perspective (cf. [15]).
Part of the method is the use of information demand patterns, i.e. if the analysis process

discovers that a certain organizational role is similar to what has been found in earlier analysis projects in other organizations, the known pattern for this role might be used and adapted. The motivation behind the narrow focus on information demand and the pattern use was to contribute to reduction of time and efforts in projects aiming at improving information flow.

Among the users of the IDA-method are consultancy companies who perform many projects aiming at improved information flows in small and medium-sized enterprises. They consider the method as a kind of resource in their "production" process. These companies are interested to have control on the use of the method from an economic perspective, to find improvement potentials and to get at least an idea of the value for their business.

This means that the primary perspective for method improvement taken in our work is that of an organisation using the method for business purposes and aiming at improving the contribution to business objectives. Such an organisation could, for example, be a consultancy company offering analysis and optimisation services for their clients based on the method, or enterprises using the method internally for detecting and implementing change needs. In an organizational context, improvement processes usually are guided by defined goals and instruments to supervise goal achievement. The approach proposed in our work is to apply the principles of a balanced scorecard for creating a management instrument for method improvement, i.e. we will not use the original BSC perspectives and content proposed by Kaplan and Norton [15], but the process of developing such a balanced scorecard for method improvement and the general structure of goals, sub-goals, indicators, etc.

### 4.1 Scorecard Development Process

The main instrument for developing the scorecard was a workshop with all organizations planning to use the IDA-method. The workshop produced an initial scorecard version, which formed the basis for refinements and further development during the project. During the scorecard workshops, the following steps were taken:

The first step was to evaluate, whether the *perspectives* proposed by the original BSC approach (i.e. financial, internal business process, learning and growth, customer) are valid and appropriate for method improvement or should be changed. A starting point for identifying relevant perspectives were the strategic aims of the participating organizations. The result of this step was an initial agreement on perspectives to consider in the "method scorecard". For each perspective, *strategic goals* had to be defined and preferably quantified, as quantifying them helps to reduce the vagueness in strategic goals. Identifying strategic goals was again based on the organizations' strategy. The defined strategic goals were in a next step broken down in *sub-goals*. The objective was to define not more than 5–7 sub-goals per goal.

The last step related to strategic aspects was the identification of *cause-effect-relationships*. There might be strategic goals which cannot be achieved at the same time because they have conflicting elements. It is important to understand these conflicts or cause-effect relations between goals. After having covered the strategic aspects, focus was shifted on measurement issues:

For each sub-goal defined in the different perspectives, a way had to be found how to measure the current situation. For this purpose, *indicators* had to be defined contributing to capture the status with respect to the sub-goal. When defining indicators, one had to have in mind that there must be a practical way to capture these indicators. In this context, existing controlling systems or indicators (e.g. from quality management) were inspected and checked for possibilities to reuse information. For each indicator identified, the *measurement* or recording procedure was defined. A measurement procedure typically includes the way of measuring an indicator, the point in time and interval for measuring, the responsible role or person performing the measurement, how to document the measured results.

## 4.2 Method Validation Scorecard

The development process described in Sect. 4.1 resulted in four different perspectives in the scorecard with the following strategic goals:

1. Method Documentation Quality: the quality of the IDA-method handbook and aids
   Goal: To have a method which is easy to train and communicate
2. Pattern Quality: the quality of the information demand (ID) patterns
   Goal: To achieve patterns of high quality applicable with the method
3. Resource Efficiency: the efficiency of the process for understanding information flow problems in enterprises and developing an appropriate solution proposal.
   Goal: More efficient resource use for the analysis including a proposal for solution
4. Solution Efficiency: the efficiency of the solution implemented in an enterprise based on using the IDA method and ID patterns
   Goal: To propose a relevant and actable solution for the case at hand

**Indicator examples.** Our view that a method is a guide for actions, which often are artifact-mediated actions (see Sect. 2.1), affected the selection and definition of indicators. For brevity reasons, we will discuss sub-goals, criteria and indicators only on the basis of one of the perspectives, the method documentation quality. The overall goal "To have a method which is easy to train and communicate" was divided into several sub-goals:

- Easy to teach the method and train future modelers (transferability)
- Provide a good documentation
- Method shall support the effective development of new patterns
- Method shall take into account that patterns need continuous improvement

The criteria and indicators derived from the sub-goals are captured in a tabular way including the following information:

- What to measure, i.e. the criteria to capture. Criteria are grouped into aspects.
- Motivation of this criteria and comments (not included in Table 2)
- Indicators reflecting the criteria. This is the actual value to measure.
- Indicator description: explanation related to the indicator name

- Practical implementation of capturing the indicators, i.e. how to measure, who will be responsible for measuring, when to measure and how to document the findings

**Table 2.** Excerpt from criteria and indicators for "method documentation quality" perspective

| Aspect | Criterion | Indicator Name | Indicator Description | How to capture indicators? |
|---|---|---|---|---|
| Documentation Quality | Learning Time | Average learning time for new analyst until "productivity" | How much time does it on average take until a person can be considered "productive"? | Captured during training sessions by method specialist |
| | | Average learning time for new trainers until "productivity" | How much time does it on average take until a new trainer for the method can be considered "productive"? | |
| | | Average learning time for participants in analysis projects until being able to participate in analysis projects | How much time does it on average take until a participant in analysis projects understands what she/he is contributing to? | |
| | Perceived quality of Method Documentation | Perceived quality of completeness, correctness, understandability, etc. on a suitable scale (e.g. 5 point Likert scale) | | |
| | Documentation maturity | Maturity level according to review status of different stakeholder groups, like consultant, method specialist or modelling facilitator | What maturity level between "draft" and "fully validated" is assigned in method reviews by domain experts? | |
| | | Number of improvements proposed by researchers | How many change requests were submitted for the method by researchers? | |
| | | Number of shortcomings detected in use | How many change requests were submitted by practitioners? | |

Table 2 shows an excerpt of the criteria and indicator table for "method documentation quality". This excerpt is focused on "documentation quality". Further aspects in this perspective are method documentation maturity, method support for pattern use and method support for pattern extension.

The other three perspectives included the following aspects:

- Pattern Quality: applicability, technical quality, extensibility
- Resource Efficiency: analysis process, analysis result (solution), delivery
- Solution Efficiency: strategic benefits, automation benefits, transformation benefits).

# 5    Method Scorecard in Use

The method scorecard was applied in two different contexts: for improving the IDA method and the enterprise modeling method 4EM [17]. When applying the scorecard in the context of IDA-method, two groups of method users have to be distinguished:

- Members of the method development team. This group obviously consisted of experts in IDA and focused on finding method improvement potential,
- Method users from outside the development team who got a training in IDA and used the method on their own shortly after the training. This group is expected to have a more independent perspective on the utility of the IDA method.

Data collected for these different groups are discussed in Sects. 5.1 and 5.2. In order to investigate whether the method scorecard would also be suitable for other methods than IDA, the scorecard was applied in a few 4EM cases (see Sect. 5.3).

## 5.1    Scorecard Use by IDA-Method Developers

In total 4 different members of the method development team used the scorecard during 5 different IDA cases in a time frame of 10 months. The cases addressed information flow problems in a municipality and in enterprises from retail, automotive supplier, wood-related industry, and IT industry. In each case, several modeling activities were performed, scorecard data collected and observations noted down. The observations were discussed with the other members of the method development team. As a result of the observations when using the scorecard, several adjustments were made, all of them in the first 6 months of the scorecard use:

- initially, data capturing in the cases happened based on a printed version of the document describing the scorecard. Since entering this hand-written data into a spreadsheet was tedious, a software tool was developed for data capturing. This tool offered the possibility to capture experiences and remarks in free text form.
- the solution efficiency perspective of the scorecard proved very difficult to implement and in practice not applicable. The main obstacle was that data about resource consumption, time needed for certain activities or quality of activities "before" implementing improvements detected during use of the IDA method either did not exist or were not made available due to confidentiality reasons. As a consequence, the indicators of the solution efficiency perspective were no longer captured. Instead, two new indicators were introduced: "perceived solution quality from customer perspective" and "perceived solution quality from method expert perspective". Both were captured on a 5-point scale.

- many indicators needed refinements or adjustments. An example is "average learning time for new analyst until productivity" where clarification was required whether self-study time also should be included in learning time, and whether "productivity" means being able to contribute to IDA-method use or being able to use the method self-reliantly.

The indicator data collected with the scorecard were not only evaluated during info-FLOW, but also during use of the IDA-method in later years (see also Sect. 5.2). In every IDA use case, there were potentially four types of activities which correspond to the phases of the IDA-method: scoping, ID-context analysis, demand modeling, consolidation. Every activity type potentially requires multiple steps (i.e., activities). For each activity, scorecard indicators were captured. Example: if demand modeling required several modeling sessions with different focus areas and participants, for each of the workshops indicators were captured as separate activity.

For the presentation in this paper, we selected four indicators originating from the method documentation quality and resource efficiency perspectives of the scorecard. These four indicators were the ones preferred by the industrial partners in the infoFLOW project who intended to use the method for commercial purposes: perceived productivity, perceived method value, perceived result quality (method user) and perceived result quality (client). All indicators used the same scale: 5 - very good, 4 - good, 3 - acceptable, 2 - improvements needed, 1 - poor, 0 - don't know. When preparing the data for presentation, we used two approaches:

- For all activity types in a case, we calculated the activity average for the case. Using these activity averages for a case, we calculated the overall average for a case. The case averages are shown in Fig. 3. The purpose of the chart was to visualize the general tendency of the method perception, here expressed in the four indicators, in order to check whether improvements made in the method handbook or the training material had any visible effect.
- The activity type averages per case are shown in Fig. 4. Here the intention was to see differences between activity types: where should improvements have priority?

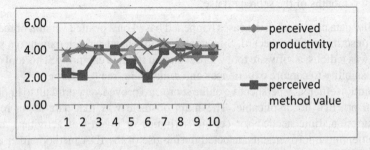

**Fig. 3.** Case averages of selected indicators.

Figures 3 and 4 are based on the same cases. Cases 1 to 5 were performed by method developers; cases 6 to 10 were performed by other method users. After case 2 and case 6, a new handbook version was released. Figures 3 and 4 are meant to illustrate the

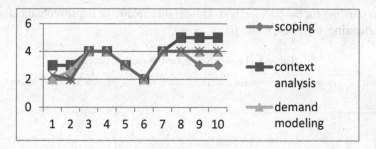

**Fig. 4.** Activity type averages.

indicator use in infoFLOW-2. They are not meant to prove any statistically significant developments or correlations.

The indicator development shows improvements for "perceived method value" after case 2 and case 6 when new handbook versions were released. "Perceived productivity" seems to be correlated to "perceived method value" seem to be correlated, which is not surprising. When the method was used its developers (case 1 to 5) the perceived result quality of the client was higher than of method users. When the method was used later by other method users, this is the opposite. This indicates that method developers are more critical to the results or have higher expectations.

One of the main intentions with the activity type averages was to detect which phase should have priority when working on improvements. In cases 1 and 2, the scoping, demand modeling and consolidation needed improvement. With the new handbook published after case 2, many of the problems were addressed. In demand modeling, to take one example, a notation for the demand model was included which earlier was missing. Case 5 and 6 represent the phase of transferring the method knowledge from method developer to method user. Case 5 was done in cooperation between developer and user; case 6 completely by a method user. The experiences from these first "external" uses resulted in the improvement of the handbook, i.e. from case 7 the new version was applied, which also is reflected in improved activity type averages. Currently, scoping seems to be in most need of improvement.

## 5.2 Scorecard Use by Project-External IDA-Method Users

In total 6 different persons were trained in the IDA-method and also used the scorecard in their information demand analysis cases, which came from logistics, manufacturing, higher education and IT industry. The scorecard indicators regarding learning time and perceived quality of the documentation were captured after the training. The other indicators were captured in every activity in each case (same as in Sect. 5.1). 5 different cases were the basis for this paper. Section 5.1 already presented the case averages and activity type averages (see case 6 to 10 in Figs. 3 and 4). Regarding learning time, Table 3 shows the time invested in training the different method user, separated into lecture-like training, self-study, working on examples or coaching in real cases. The table makes clear that training was intensified for later cases which probably improved the understanding for the IDA method. This might explain the improved indicator value when comparing, e.g., case 6 and 10.

**Table 3.** Learning time for the method users

| Method user (case #) Training part | Student 1 (7) | Student 2 and 3 (6) | Student 4 (8) | Student 5 (9) | Student 6 (10) |
|---|---|---|---|---|---|
| Lecture/ Presentation | 2 | 2 | 4 | 6 | 6 |
| Self-study of Handbook | 4 | 2 | 4 | 8 | 8 |
| Exercise/Example | 0 | 0 | 2 | 4 | 4 |
| Coaching on case | 2 | 0 | 4 | 4 | 4 |
| Total | 8 | 4 | 14 | 22 | 22 |

### 5.3   Scorecard Use by 4EM-Method Users

Three persons used the scorecard in enterprise modeling cases with the 4EM method. The main intention was to investigate what parts of the scorecard can be used without any changes for 4EM and where adaptations need to be made. Not in scope was the comparison of IDA and 4EM based on the scorecard values.

Before the method scorecard could be used for 4EM, all perspectives, aspects and indicators were checked for suitability for 4EM:

- Method documentation quality perspective: the aspects documentation quality and method maturity could remained unchanged. Method support for pattern use and method support for pattern extension are not suitable and were removed, since 4EM does not include the use of patterns.
- Pattern quality perspective was not used – 4EM does not use patterns
- Resource efficiency perspective: all three aspects analysis process, analysis result (solution) and delivery were kept. As "analysis process" uses criteria and indicators which capture effort and duration for the different IDA method phases, these criteria had to be adapted to the activities of 4EM modeling,
- Solution efficiency perspective was not used because of the experiences made in IDA-method improvement (see Sect. 5.1)

All three 4EM modelers managed to collect data about method documentation quality and resource efficiency which confirms the feasibility of using the method scorecard for 4EM. However, in future work it should be investigated whether additional scorecard perspectives tailored to 4EM should be included. An example could be a perspective directed to participative modeling, an essential feature of 4EM.

## 6   Summary and Future Work

Based on the industrial project infoFLOW-2, which aimed at improving information flow in organizations, the paper presented the development process of a scorecard intended to support method improvement. The paper also presented the perspectives, aspects and (excerpts of) criteria of the method scorecard and illustrated its use for the IDA-method, and its transfer to the 4EM method. Among the conclusions to be drawn from this work are two rather "obvious" ones:

- Feasibility of scorecard development and use as support for method improvement was demonstrated. Scorecard development helped to identify what criteria and indicators were important from the organizational method users perspective.
- The transfer of the scorecard from IDA to 4EM indicates that many aspects and criteria are transferable between methods, although criteria reflecting the method phases needed adaptation. More cases are needed to confirm and refine this.

The more "hidden" conclusions are related to the utility of a scorecard: What are the actual benefits of using the scorecard? Could we have reached the same effects without the scorecard (i.e., without collecting and evaluating data)? Our impression is that the answer to these questions depends on the number of method users and cases of method use. For a method used by many persons in many cases, i.e. a sufficiently big "sample", the data collected will help to identify elements of a method that might be candidates for improvement efforts. However, the scorecard indicators should not be considered as the "only source of truth", i.e. the scorecard should be taken as complementary means besides experience reports from method users. Section 5.1 shows an example: the indicators point at the scoping phase as a candidate for improving the method. This should be a motivation to investigate the scoping phase, but it does not mean that this part of the method really is the cause for the indicator values – there might be other causes, like e.g., the qualification of the modelers for "scoping" or the measurement procedure for the indicators might be inadequate.

Furthermore, some criteria and indicators of the scorecard need further investigation regarding their usefulness. Example is the average time required for the different phases of the IDA method. This time is partly dependent on modeler and complexity of the case. But if there are many projects and different modelers, the development tendency of the average values of this indicator can be relevant.

Our preliminary recommendations regarding the method scorecard can be summarized as follows:

- use the scorecard only for methods with many users and cases
- for indicators addressing the time or effort required for certain activities: find way to normalize the complexity of these different activities
- consider to reduce number of indicators, e.g., to 5 per perspective
- Use tool support for capturing and evaluating indicators
- Use scorecard as complementary means for method evaluation and improvement only. Very valuable information for improvement of methods usually comes from the method users
- Indicators can help in method evolution management

Future work will on the one hand consist of continued data collection regarding the IDA method, which will probably lead to further development of the scorecard, and further investigation of transferability of the scorecard to other methods. Furthermore, more work is needed on understanding from what number of method users and cases a scorecard use is recommendable. It also has to be investigated if a scorecard designed for method improvement in organisational purposes also can be applied as instrument in method engineering. This is to a large extent a question of generalisability of scorecard perspectives and indicators, i.e. is the scorecard for a specific organisational context also (in total or parts) valid for the general use of the method?

# References

1. Seigerroth, U.: Enterprise Modeling and Enterprise Architecture: the constituents of transformation and alignment of Business and IT. Int. J. IT/Bus. Alignment Gov. (IJITBAG) **2**, 16–34 (2011). ISSN 1947-9611
2. Ralyté, J., Backlund, P., Kühn, H., Jeusfeld, Manfred A.: Method chunks for interoperability. In: Embley, D.W., Olivé, A., Ram, S. (eds.) ER 2006. LNCS, vol. 4215, pp. 339–353. Springer, Heidelberg (2006). doi:10.1007/11901181_26
3. Mirbel, I., Ralyté, J.: Situational method engineering: combining assembly-based and roadmap-driven approaches. Requirements Eng. **11**(1), 58–78 (2006). http://dx.doi.org/10.1007/s00766-005-0019-0
4. Brinkkemper, S.: Method engineering: engineering of information systems development methods and tools. Inf. Softw. Technol. **38**(4), 275–280 (1996). http://dx.doi.org/10.1016/0950-5849(95)01059-9
5. Avison, D.E., Fitzgerald, G.: Information Systems Development: Methodologies, Techniques, and Tools. McGraw-Hill Education, Maidenhead (1995)
6. Henderson-Sellers, B., Ralyté, J., Ågerfalk, P., Rossi, M.: Situational Method Engineering. Springer, Heidelberg (2014)
7. Wieringa, R., Moralı, A.: Technical action research as a validation method in information systems design science. In: Peffers, K., Rothenberger, M., Kuechler, B. (eds.) DESRIST 2012. LNCS, vol. 7286, pp. 220–238. Springer, Heidelberg (2012). doi:10.1007/978-3-642-29863-9_17
8. Hevner, A.R., March, S.T., Park, J., Ram, S.: Design science in information systems research. MIS Q. **28**(1), 75–105 (2004)
9. March, S.T., Smith, G.: Design and natural science research on information technologies. Decis. Support Syst. **15**(4), 251–266 (1995)
10. Lincoln, Y.S., Guba, E.G.: Naturalistic inquiry, vol. 75. Sage (1985)
11. Lind, M., Seigerroth, U., Forsgren, O., Hjalmarsson, A.: Co-design as social constructive pragmatism. In: AIS Special Interest Group on Pragmatist IS Research (SIGPrag 2008) at International Conference on Information Systems (ICIS2008), France (2008)
12. Lundqvist, M., Sandkuhl, K., Seigerroth, U.: Modelling information demand in an enterprise context: method, notation and lessons learned. Int. J. Syst. Model. Design **2**(3), 74–96 (2011). IGI Publishing
13. Kaplan, R.S., Norton, D.P.: The Balanced Scorecard: Translating Strategy into Action. Harvard Business Press, Boston (1996)
14. Susman, G.I., Evered, R.D.: An assessment of the scientific merits of action research. Adm. Sci. Q. **23**(4), 582–603 (1978)
15. Sein, M.K., Henfridsson, O., Purao, S., Rossi, M., Lindgren, R.: Action design research. MIS Q. **35**(1), 37–56 (2011)
16. Harmsen, A.F.: Situational Method Engineering, Doctoral dissertation University of Twente. Moret Ernst & Young, Utrecht, The Netherlands (1997). ISBN 90-75498-10-1
17. Sandkuhl, K., Stirna, J., Persson, A., Wißotzki, M.: Enterprise Modeling: Tackling Business Challenges with the 4EM Method. Springer, Heidelberg (2014). ISBN 978-3662437247

18. Goldkuhl, G.: The grounding of usable knowledge: an inquiry in the epistemology of action knowledge. In: CMTO Research Papers, No. 1999:03, Linköping University (1999)
19. Siau, K., Rossi, M.: Evaluating techniques for system analysis and design modelling methods – a review and comparative analysis. In: Information System Journal. Blackwell Publishing Ltd. (2008)
20. Mooney, J., Gurbaxani, V., Kraemer, K.: A process oriented framework for assessing the business value of information technology. In: Proceedings of the 16th International Conference on Information Systems, Amsterdam, pp. 17–27 (1995)
21. Parker, M., Benson, R.: Information Economics. Prentice-Hall, Englewood Cliffs (1998)
22. DeLone, W., McLean, E.: Information system success: the quest for the dependent variable. Inf. Syst. Res. 3(1), 60–95 (1992)

# Modeling Exchange Agreements
# with DEMO/PSI and Core Component
# of Communication

Duarte Gouveia[(✉)] and David Aveiro

Madeira Interactive Technologies Institute, University of Madeira,
Caminho da Penteada, 9020-105 Funchal, Portugal
duarte.gouveia@m-iti.org, daveiro@uma.pt

**Abstract.** Intervac Home Exchange is an international club, created in 1953, where members exchange their house during a limited period without money transfers between them. Both parties negotiate and establish an exchange agreement with specific terms of the exchange. This club requested our collaboration to improve their existing online exchange agreement, as it doesn't fully satisfy their members. We show that it is hard to model this kind of exchange agreement with existing state of the art in enterprise engineering modeling methods (DEMO/PSI). We propose the usage of Core Component of Communication (CCC), which is an evolution of the existing DEMO/PSI theory done by the authors. We show how CCC can be applied to this real-life organization and better solve the challenges posed by this kind of agreements. Analytical evaluation is performed to compare both approaches.

**Keywords:** DEMO · PSI theory · Exchange agreement · Core component of communication

## 1 Introduction

Persons talk to each other to establish agreements regarding shared goals. Searl posted in 1969 [1] that the minimum unit of communication is a speech act. Speech acts can be expressed independently of the chosen media form. Speech acts are used in business transactions between parties to keep a inter-social state of the world among them. One case of business transaction is exchanging homes during holidays.

In 1953, the Intervac club [2] pioneered the concept of exchanging homes for your holidays [3]. The perceived benefit was lowering the cost of having international vacations, therefore its name: Intervac. To reach an exchange agreement, several traditional mail letters and phone calls were needed. With the advent of Internet, there was a Cambrian explosion of similar services enlarging the scope, range and amount of sharing services [4]. Although the media channels have changed, the ontological model of the business has not changed. Intervac pioneered the now prevailing concept of "sharing economy" [5]. We adhere to the definition of sharing economy given by Botsman [6]: "An economic model based on sharing underutilized assets from spaces to skills to stuff for monetary or non-monetary benefits." In the case of Intervac, the underutilized asset is the member's home.

© Springer International Publishing AG 2017
I. Reinhartz-Berger et al. (Eds.): BPMDS/EMMSAD 2017, LNBIP 287, pp. 220–236, 2017.
DOI: 10.1007/978-3-319-59466-8_14

When two club members want to do a home exchange, they first search through the web catalog. When they find a potential exchange partner, they interact with him through online messages. Only then they move to the detailed discussion of the specific terms of the exchange agreement, namely number of days, dates, number of persons and other details.

Exchange agreements can be achieved through speech acts between the club members without any participation of the club. The club role is just to provide mediation in case of future conflict. Different persons, with different cultures, can have different interpretations and expectations on others' behaviors regarding their houses. To reduce potential conflicts, it is on the club's best interest to have clear exchange agreement terms between members. Therefore, the club recommends that its members communicate through the website and fill the exchange agreement before the exchange. In case of conflict, the Intervac national representatives can rule on disputes.

At an ontological level [7], the exchange agreement happens between the members. Both parties must specify their desired terms and agree to the other party'.

This work, first addresses the research design options at Sect. 2. Then we describe the existing as-is solution in Sect. 3. Section 4 lists the existing problems for current solution. Section 5 succinctly describes DEMO/PSI [7] and Core Component of Communication (CCC) [8] in Literature Review. In Sect. 6 we model the exchange agreement with DEMO/PSI and discuss the difficulties that this case poses to DEMO/PSI assumptions and requisites. In Sect. 7 we propose a solution based on the CCC. In Sect. 8 we compare both solutions and we conclude in Sect. 9.

## 2  Research Design

In this work we perform an empirical study [9]. To make research design options explicit, we use the pattern presented in [10] and depicted in Fig. 1. The process starts with a research question, that will be presented in Sect. 4 – Problem Statement, and ends with research findings, which will be shown in Sect. 8 – Comparing Solutions. The chosen path is indicated by the checkboxes marked with gray.

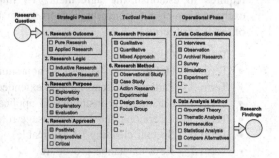

**Fig. 1.** Research path using decision-making structure adapted from [9]

## 3  Describing As-Is Solution

The description of the As-Is solution follows the public available information available on the Intervac blog [11–15].

After identifying potential interest between two club members, they can move on to the detailed discussion of the specific terms of the exchange agreement. Intervac describes its process as a four-step process: (1) Edit your terms; (2) Send terms to counterpart; (3) Accept terms from counterpart; (4) Sign the agreement. This description is a simplification of the actual process implemented on the website. The As-Is solution is depicted in Fig. 2 as perceived by the researcher. This figure is not part of Intervac's description of the process.

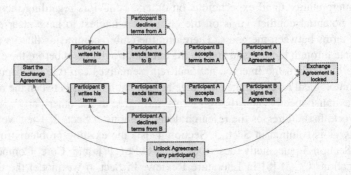

**Fig. 2.** As-Is exchange agreement on Intervac website

There are four kinds of steps, as described in Intervac blog [11]:

(1) **Edit your terms** [12]

The exchange agreement specific terms are the conditions that each member requires to establish the agreement. To improve the reader knowledge on exchange agreements concerns, a short summary is presented below with the set of ten typical terms.

- Term 1 – Contacts and house address
- Term 2 – Holiday dates (might be non-simultaneous exchanges)
- Term 3 – Participants (can include extended family or friends)
- Term 4 – Car usage & insurance (if applicable)
- Term 5 – Telephone and Internet usage rules
- Term 6 – Special cleaning (if applicable)
- Term 7 – Keys exchange procedure
- Term 8 – Pets & plants care (if applicable)
- Term 9 – Guests & family visits
- Term 10 – Other terms [15]

(2) **Send your terms** [13]

Terms must be explicitly sent to the counterpart and only then they become visible by the counterpart. After sending the terms, the terms author cannot re-edit its terms until the counterpart either Accepts or Declines them. Declining at least one of the terms gives editing rights back to the counterpart on all its terms.

(3) **Review your partner's terms** [13]

As both parties mirror steps 1 and 2, a member must review the terms sent by the counterpart. Each specific term requires an explicit acceptance that can only be Accept or Decline (with possible justification). A party cannot edit the counterpart terms. The author can revise its terms and resend them until eventual agreement.

(4) **Sign the agreement** [14]

When both parties have agreed upon all specific terms, it is necessary for both to review and sign the full exchange agreement. That conditions are depicted in Fig. 2 with dashed lines. Until signing the agreement any party can cancel at any time. [13] After both parties' sign, it is still possible to "Unlock Agreement". This can be done unilaterally and moves members get back to step 1, re-starting the process.

# 4  Problem Statement

We list the following problems in the current As-Is solution:

1. When a member refuses a specific term that forces to refuse all other terms. This is inefficient.
2. After sending the edited terms, the author can't change them until an acceptance or refusal by the counterpart. This is inefficient and confusing for members.
3. There is no clear and visual notion of the state of the process for exchangers. This is confusing for members.
4. Current solution allows to reopening signed exchange agreements unilaterally. This is unsecure and unreliable.
5. In non-simultaneous exchanges, some specific terms might not be defined when the agreement is signed, namely the specific dates when one (or both) segment will occur. This is not flexible enough.

Based on the stated problem set, the research question is: How to model the exchange agreement business process to solve these problems?

# 5  Literature Review

## 5.1  Demo/PSI

The foundational theory of Organizational Engineering field is the Design and Engineering Methodology for Organizations (DEMO) [7]. A core idea of DEMO is that to model business interactions we should use a communication-centric approach, instead of the dominant approach to the design of information systems that is the data-centric approach.

The communication-centric approach has its roots in the Action Workflow Loop [16] presented in Fig. 3, being "general and universal", models the core pattern of all successful interactions.

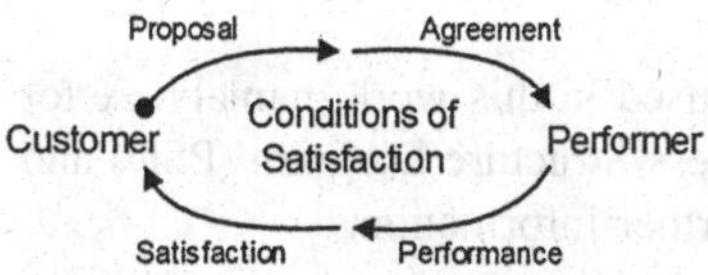

**Fig. 3.** Action workflow loop [16]

According to Denning and Medina-Mora [17], "Incomplete workflows invariantly cause breakdowns, and if they persist, they give rise to complaints and bad feelings that interfere with the ultimate purpose of work – to satisfy the customer."

DEMO extends this core loop through Performance in Social Interactions Theory (PSI) [7, 18]. It describes the world through a model based on transactions, each producing a single result, initiated by a set of actor roles and executed by one particular actor role. This result is the simplified pattern presented in Figs. 4 and 5 which uses a sequence of coordination acts surrounding a production (execute) act.

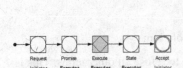

**Fig. 4.** Simplified pattern for a PSI transaction [7]

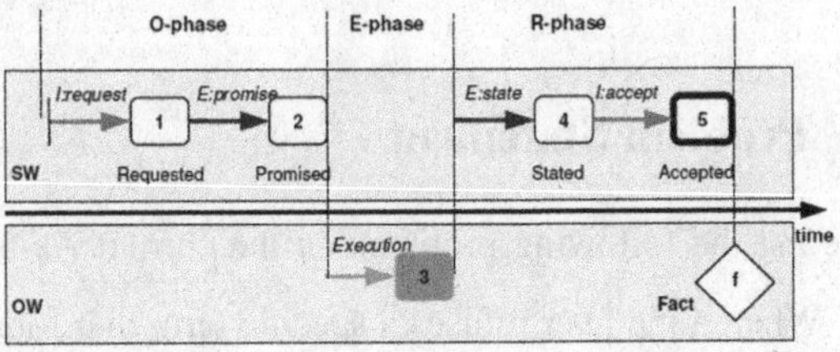

**Fig. 5.** Order, execution and result phases [19]

The transaction starts with a **request** by the initiator which includes the desired outcome in full detail. If the *executor* can fulfill that **request**, he will **promise** a delivery and then produce/**execute** the expected result and **state** its completion to the *initiator*. Assuming that the delivered result is as requested, the *initiator* will finish the transaction by **accept**ing the result. Therefore, this pattern assigns different acts to the *initiator* and the *executor* actor roles.

These core acts can be split into three phases, as can be seen in Fig. 5: order, execution and result [19]. This simplified description becomes more complex, as can be seen in Fig. 6, as additional revoke acts are needed and so are added to each phase [18]:

- The *initiator* can change his mind and **revoke** the request at any time.
- The *executor* can **decline** the initial request if he can't deliver as requested.
- The *executor* can **revoke** his previous **promise** act.
- The *executor* can **revoke** his previous **state** act.
- The *initiator* may **reject** the **state**d result.
- The *initiator* may **revoke** a previous **accept**.

As for revoking acts, either performed by the *initiator* or by the *executor*, contradict previously established expectations, the counterpart may allow the revoke or refuse it.

DEMO introduces several diagrams that will be used in this work, namely: Actor Transaction Diagram (ATD), Fact Model (FM), Process Structure Diagram (PSD) and Action Rules. Please refer to the literature [7] for further information.

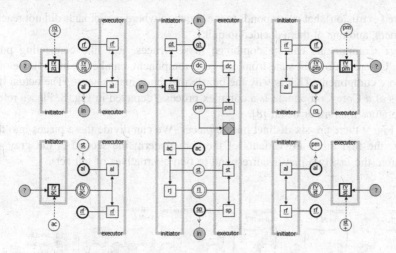

**Fig. 6.** DEMO/PSI version 3.4 complete transaction pattern

## 5.2 Core Component of Communication

The Core Component of Communication [8] is a previous work from the authors. It is an evolution to DEMO/PSI theory that tries to address some of its problems, namely: using a message based protocol instead of shared memory; allowing more than two participants; allowing flexible roles; allowing change of opinion before previous state opinions take effects.

DEMO/PSI transactions have two parties: the order and the result phase. CCC argues that each of these phases is a core component of the communication with its specific state machine. By splitting these phases, we can achieve more flexibility in modeling information systems using a communication-centric approach.

**Fig. 7.** Black-box model of CCC [8] (Color figure online)

CCC theory uses puzzle pieces as a metaphor to hide the complexity of the state machine for each phase. Each puzzle piece, as depicted in Fig. 7, is a black model.

The black-box model simplifies the internal state machine to a few visible states: initial state (yellow intrusion); answer states (simplified as red and green extrusions, corresponding to two possible answers No - blue and Yes - green); quit

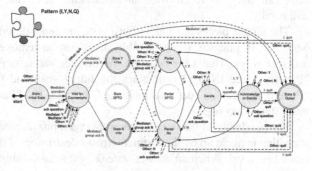

**Fig. 8.** White-box model of CCC [8]

state (red extrusion) that corresponds to the situation where participants did not reach an agreement, and one of them decided to quit.

Core Components can be combined in sequences, just like connecting puzzle pieces. One result or quit state from one core component, can be the initial state of the next core component. That is why the puzzle metaphor makes sense. The actual inner process of a Core Component is a complex process, depicted in Fig. 8. Please refer to the literature for further detail [8].

In Fig. 9 there are six distinct puzzle pieces. We can divide these pieces into three groups: the first three are variants of the core pattern; the second is the gray state extension; the last two pieces correspond to two alternatives of tell acts.

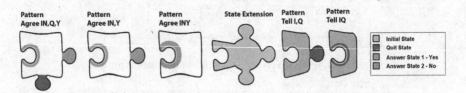

**Fig. 9.** CCC variant patterns used to model the Exchange Agreement (Color figure online)

The puzzle piece metaphor uses several assumptions. Each puzzle piece is a black box that hides much of its complexity, only showing some of its states in the intrusions and extrusions of the puzzle piece. On each puzzle piece, there is only one single intrusion that corresponds to the initial state, identified with the letter I and represented with the yellow color. The extrusions on the puzzle pieces correspond to possible result states, which can either be the Answer States or a Quit state.

The Answer states, can have several possible results. The most typical is having: Yes and No, respectively represented in green and the letter Y or with the blue color and the letter N. Any answer state can only be reached with an agreement between the participants – either an agreement on Yes answer or an agreement on the No answer.

The Quit state, represented in red, can be reached when any of the parties unilaterally quits. The Quit answer is not equivalent to the No answer because the No answer state can only be reach with an agreement, while the Quit state can be forced unilaterally.

The puzzle pieces have an internal state machine, described for the general case in Sect. 5.2. In practice, those possible states can be removed or be joined together in different ways. That's how we get the distinct variants. For example, in Fig. 9, the "Pattern Agree IN,Q,Y", combines the Initial state and the No Answer State. The "Pattern Agree IN,Y" does not have the Quit state. The "Pattern Agree INY" combines three states into one.

Independently of the internal states that each puzzle piece has, there is also a macro state, that is made up by the distinct intrusion/extrusion of the puzzle pieces seen at the black box level. When an answer state or quit state combine with the initial state, that means that there might be a new fact generated by a decision, but at the macro level there is no state change.

We might wish to connect several puzzle pieces to the same extrusion of a puzzle piece. To enable that we introduce the state extension puzzle piece, colored in gray in Fig. 9. This puzzle piece does not have internal events or internal states.

The events that happen inside each puzzle piece internal machine do not have any impact on the macro state of transactions. Only when Quit or Answer states are reached, and those states correspond to a new extrusion there is a change in state at the macro level.

If the macro state is equal to the initial state of some puzzle pieces, it is possible to have events happening at those puzzle pieces' internal state machines.

Finally, the last two puzzle pieces presented in Fig. 9 represent variants of tell acts. The difference between them is just if the Quit answer leads to a new macro state ("Pattern Tell I,Q") or keeps the macro state the same ("Pattern Tell IQ"). The tell acts have just two possible internal events: Tell and Acknowledge. The Tell act is performed unilaterally.

# 6   Modeling the Exchange Agreement with DEMO/PSI

Modeling this Exchange Agreement requires handling five topics that will be addressed separately to reduce complexity. Those five topics are (1) The main transaction; (2) Agreement on terms; (3) Fulfillment; (4) Unlock agreement; (5) Handling complaints. Section 6.1 addresses the first three topics. Sections 6.2 and 6.3 address respectively the remaining two topics 4 and 5.

## 6.1   The Main Transaction, Agreement on Terms and Fulfillment

**First attempt** - We notice that the fundamental business transaction is the Exchange Agreement between two parties. We can model it with a single transaction (T101), as depicted in Fig. 10.

In this first attempt, there is a negotiation between both parties regarding specific terms that takes place before the first coordination act, which is a **request**, as determined by theory. As all detailed negotiation is before the beginning of the transaction, the **request-promise** pair is some mere proforma, as the actual agreement was established elsewhere. One of the exchangers takes the initiative and will be the initiator; the other will be the executor. When both exchangers made their houses available to the counterparts, both parties can **state** and **accept**, leading the exchange agreement to a good ending.

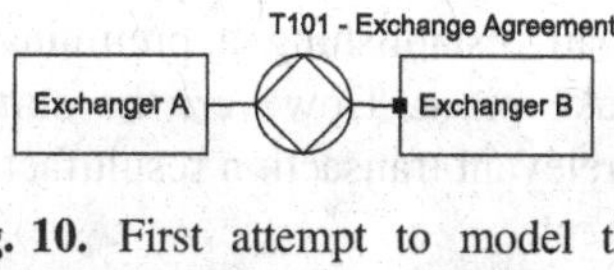

One clear problem with this first attempt is that all the complexities of discussing the terms and approving each term by both parties are left out of the model. This option may make the diagram compact, but also makes it useless.

T101 - Exchange Agreement

Exchanger A ◇ Exchanger B

**Fig. 10.** First attempt to model the Exchange Agreement – Actors Transactions Diagram

Additionally, only having Exchangèr B **executing** and **stat**ing deviates from the established theory, as both exchangers are executor – both share their house.

**Second attempt** - We will now attempt to model the exchange agreement with two transactions, as can be seen in Fig. 11. Deciding on modeling the main agreement with either one or two transactions is a difficult decision.

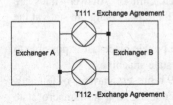

T111 - Exchange Agreement

Exchanger A          Exchanger B

T112 - Exchange Agreement

**Fig. 11.** Second attempt to model the Exchange Agreement – Actors Transactions Diagram

Having two transactions with the same name and result fact type (T111 and T112) also deviates from theory. The purpose is to uniquely identify the Actor Roles Exchanger A and Exchanger B and therefore make clear that both transactions are established between the two.

With this modeling option, each exchanger can establish its terms and send them to the counterpart (**request**).

The counterpart can then **promise**. This improves the solution from first attempt, depicted in Fig. 10, as the **request** - **promise** are no longer pro-forma acts. This however poses a new problem: the business description, presented in Sect. 3, each owner tells the terms for his house (**request**) and not the counterpart.

This second attempt poses additional problems, as **promise** from T111 cannot be performed before **promise** from T112 and vice-versa. The solution provided by DEMO for this problem is to leave it to the action rules, since there is still no formal grammar to represent then, anything can be put under that rug.

Just like in the first attempt, the second attempt adds nothing regarding the modeling of each specific exchange agreement term.

**Third Attempt -** The third attempt gets back to a single transaction, just like the one depicted in Fig. 10, and assumes that there are two instances of transaction T101, with participants taking opposing roles (initiator-executor) in each transaction.

To solve the promise dependency, it would have to rely on queries on the fact model, to design some implementation solution.

This third attempt, although better following what is prescribed in the theory, inherits the problems of both attempt one and two without solving any of its problems.

**Forth Attempt** - To solve the mutual promise dependency, we need another transaction that takes place before the already existing ones. In this fourth attempt, depicted in Fig. 12, we called transaction T121 as "Elicit mutual interest in Exchange Agreement". This option maps what happens as described in Sect. 3, as the Exchange Agreement only starts after that preliminary agreement.

Transaction T121 acts as the **request-promise** pair, establishing a preliminary agreement before the precise terms discussion can take place. However, the **state-accept** pair in transaction T121 is meaningless, as the relevant transaction result fact is that there is an intention to reach an exchange agreement.

The right side of Fig. 12, with transactions T122 and T123 is equivalent to the second attempt, except for the transaction name change, that now focus on the

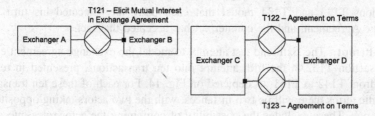

**Fig. 12.** Forth attempt to model the Exchange Agreement – Actors Transactions Diagram

agreement on terms. We have used the solution proposed in the first attempt, as the problem that this forth attempt solved – the promise dependency – is solved by transaction T121 and not by the right side of the picture.

The actor roles in T122 and T123, Exchanger C and D, will be fulfilled by the same actor, as Exchanger A and B. Those actors take different names to comply with the DEMO rule that each actor role can only be the executor of one transaction.

This forth attempt solves the promise dependency problem, but does not solve the handling of the agreement on terms.

**Fifth Attempt** - In this fifth attempt to model the exchange agreement, depicted in Fig. 13, we handle the problem of reaching agreement on each specific exchange agreement term and the fulfilment.

Transaction T131 on Fig. 13 exists to solve the promise dependency, just like in forth attempt.

Transaction T132 uses the single transaction approach, described in the third attempt, to model each individual agreement os specific terms. Following the description on Sect. 3, each exchanger has to fill 10 specific terms, which means that 20 specific instances of T132 would be created for each exchange agreement. We named the actor roles as Exchanger C, D, E and F, but those roles would be fulfilled by the same actors that fulfill the actor roles of Exchanger A and B. We could have chosen to model T132 as distinct transactions, one for each specific term.

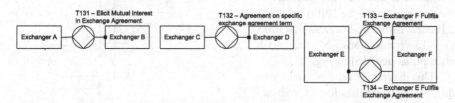

**Fig. 13.** Fifth attempt to model the Exchange Agreement – Actors Transactions Diagram

Finally, transaction T133 and T134, depicted in Fig. 13, is the fulfillment of the exchange agreement by both parties. The request-promise acts for transactions T133 and T134 can only take place when the twenty instances of particular exchange agreement terms reach the accepted state, but they are implicit as no additional information is added in those coordination acts. The state-accept coordination acts for transactions T133 and T134 model that each party has executed his turn of the Exchange Agreement, and the counterpart has accepted that fact.

**Sixth Attempt** - The sixth and last attempt to model the exchange agreement extends the transaction T132 in the fifth attempt into ten transactions, presented in resumed format, from T142 to T151, as depicted on Fig. 14. For each of these ten transactions on specific terms there will be two instances, with the two actors taking opposite roles on each one. These excludes the possibility of combining the actor roles into a composite actor role and therefore almost all of these transactions are islands that cannot be connected to each other.

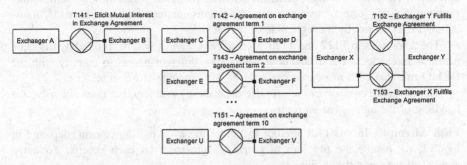

**Fig. 14.** Sixth attempt to model the Exchange Agreement – Actors Transactions Diagram

This sixth attempt continues with the difficult discussion on either to keep transactions simpler with increase the number of instances or specialize transactions into a more thinner grain. There is a benefit to specialization that exists in this sixth attempt and that was not possible in the previous five – the ability to create a Process Structure Diagram that links the 13 transactions of the sixth attempt, as depicted in Fig. 15.

This diagram is only possible now due to the specialization of transactions. This option is the major benefit of the sixth attempt, although it has unexpected implications that will be described in Sect. 6.2.

As a general analysis of the sixth attempt for a DEMO solution for

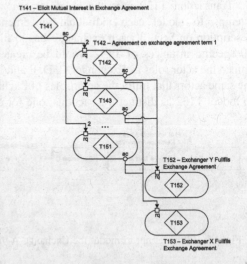

**Fig. 15.** Sixth attempt to model the Exchange Agreement – Process Structure Diagram

modeling the exchange agreement, we believe that the Figs. 14 and 15 do not bring insights or model particularly well the state of an exchange agreement, nor the possible actions that each actor can take at each situation. The existence of implicit acts in T141, 152 and 153 raise the question of adaptability of the DEMO method to model this problem.

The two participants need to agree at several levels to model the exchange agreement.

## 6.2 Unlock Agreement

Unlocking an agreement, as specified in Sect. 3, corresponds in DEMO to revoking acts in any of the transactions used. In this section, we will follow up based on the proposed solutions for the sixth attempt in Sect. 6.1.

After accepting a revoke request or revoking promise of T141, all dependent transactions should also be revoked, and the acceptance should be implicit. The state and accept of T141 is meaningless, as explained in Sect. 6.1 – fourth attempt, therefore its revocation is also pointless.

Transactions T152 and T153 handle the fulfillment of the exchange agreement. The request-promise pair of those transactions can be implicit because they do not add any new information, as explained in Sect. 6.1 – the fifth attempt. This option makes revoking these acts meaningless. Revoking those transactions state or accept only changes its internal state, not affecting any other transaction.

A more complex situation occurs when any revoke act happens for transactions T142 to T151. Any accepted revoke to a transaction forces a revoke to both T152 and T153, as there are dependencies from accepting all specific exchange agreement terms to start T152 and T153. The impact of this dependency is too high with undesirable consequences. For example, since exchange agreements from both parties can happen at different times, it might be the case that one of the segments as already happen, but then there is an exchange request for an "inoffensive" term on the other segment. Even if the term change is accepted, a cancelation on T152 and T153 had to happen, and eventually reintroduced again. This would be a problem for the transaction that models the segment that was already executed and accepted.

The ability of linking transactions that the sixth attempt allowed – Sect. 6.1 – seemed to be a positive improvement, but introduced unexpected difficulties to handle to revoking of terms. The current DEMO modeling does not provide a comprehensive solution to model revocation without a significant work left for implementation.

## 6.3 Handling Complaints

Any of the exchangers can file a complaint with Intervac. The complaint is collectively handled by the Complaint Committee, as depicted on Fig. 16, which is composed of all national representatives that were involved in the exchange agreement.

Figure 17 shows the Fact Model for handling the complaints. Although both exchangers are stakeholders for this transaction, DEMO only allows the person that filed the complaint to be part of the transaction. It is also not clear in DEMO literature how the executor role is collectively performed by more than one person.

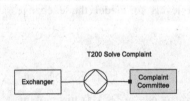

T200 Solve Complaint

**Fig. 16.** Transaction to solve complaint - Actor Transaction Diagram

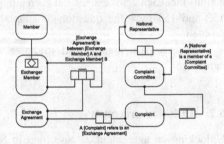

**Fig. 17.** Fact Model to model transaction to solve complaint (T200)

## 7 Modeling the Exchange Agreement with CCC

Figure 18 shows the modeling of the Exchange Agreement with CCC. At the top left we have C01 which is the only puzzle piece with an vacant intrusion. That corresponds to the initial state of the macro transaction. All extrusions that are not connected to any other puzzle pieces are terminal stated for the macro state machine.

The Component C01 uses the "Pattern Agree IN,Q,Y" for eliciting interest in the change agreement. From initial state the discussion might lead to a quit state in the case of no interest in the exchange, and therefore terminating the Exchange Agreement. It might also lead to a No answer state, where no interest is elicited for now, but that might be changed in the future. The answer state Yes leads to new macro state – "discussion macro state".

The component C04 Sign Agreement, that uses the "Pattern Agree IN,Y", allows reaching a new macro state through the Yes answer – the "agreement macro state". Using the same pattern it is possible to get back to the discussion macro state through the C05 Re-open Negotiation.

### 7.1 Discussion Macro State

While in the "discussion macro state" it is possible to establish the concrete agreement on the ten terms for each party with the components C11–C20 and C21–C30. All these components uses the "Pattern IYN" that makes agreements on specific exchange terms without modifying the macro-state. From that macro state it is possible to unilaterally cancel an established agreement on a specific term using the components C31–C50. These components use the "Pattern Tell IQ". Since there is global signed agreement, agreeing on specific terms is always dependent on the current context of negotiation. Changes in negotiation context allow unilateral changes of positions without violating the claim to sincerity and justice [7].

Also from the "discussion macro state" this design allows termination through components C02 and C03. Both components have similar function ending the exchange agreement transaction. While C02 performs a unilateral quit using "Pattern Tell I,Q", C03 performs a quit through agreement with the "Pattern Agree IN,Y", which is a more polite alternative of terminating the exchange agreement discussion.

## 7.2 Agreement Macro State

After the "agreement macro state" has been reached, through the component C04 – Sign Agreement, it is possible to fulfill both parties of the agreement, present a complain to the national organizers or close the agreement. It is also possible to reopen negotiation through component C05 as presented before.

Fulfilling each part of the exchange agreement is achieved with components C06 and C07. They use the "Pattern Agree INY" allowing to register that part of the

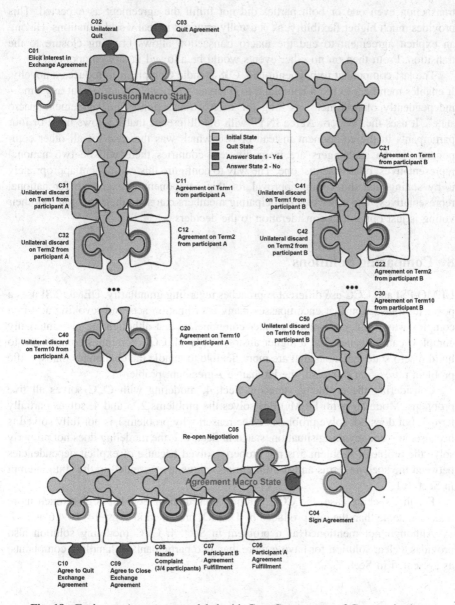

**Fig. 18.** Exchange Agreement modeled with Core Components of Communication

agreement was fulfilled. Agreeing that one of expected fulfillment happened does not change the macro state. Closing the exchange agreement only happens through an explicit agreement – either C09 or C10.

Both C09 and C10 use the "Pattern Agree IN,Y" that allows reaching a terminal state. The difference is that C09 is an agreement to close, that is indicating that parties agree that the macro transaction terminated successfully, while C10 is an agreement to end the transaction, although the macro transaction did not end successfully.

Notice that this design options allow to establish agreements to close the macro transaction even one or both parties did not fulfill the agreement as expected. This provides much higher flexibility, as is usually required in real world situations. Having an explicit agreement to end the macro transaction allows bringing closure to the transition. From then on no other events would be allowed in any component.

The last component to be mentioned, C08 Handle Complaint introduces a novelty. It enables members to file a complaint to Intervac's national organizers, at any time – independently of fulfilment, as long the macro transaction is in "agreement macro state". It uses the "Pattern Agree INY" with the difference that it allows three or four participants in the component instead of two which was the case for all other components. If the exchangers are from different countries there will be two national representatives, otherwise just one. The way to configure this component appropriately is by stating that the voting approval for this component is exclusive for national representatives. The other two participating members can state their opinion, but their voting is just opinion to consideration to the deciders.

## 8   Comparing Solutions

DEMO/PSI and CCC use different approaches regarding granularity. DEMO/PSI uses a powerful transaction that encompasses many coordination acts and revoking acts in a complex way. CCC uses much smaller components, that although are also internally complex, can be handled at a higher abstraction level. CCC combines components to build macro state machines that are more flexible to handle the challenges that specific problem poses – in this case, the Exchange Agreement problem.

Considering the problems stated in Sect. 4, modeling with CCC solves all five problems. Modeling with DEMO/PSI solves the problems 2, 3 and 4, solves partially term 1, but does not solve problem 5. The reason why problem 1 is not fully solved is because, in some revoking situation, stated in Sect. 6.2, the modeling does not properly solve the problem. Problem 5 is not properly solved because of explicit dependencies between the specific terms and fulfilling transactions, as presented in the sixth attempt in Sect. 6.1.

For this specific case, the CCC solution presented in Fig. 18, is also much more understandable than the one produced by DEMO, presented in Figs. 14, 15, 16 and 17.

Although not mentioned as a problem in Sect. 4, CCC modeling solution also provides a clear solution for having more than two participants in handling complaints, as presented in Sect. 7.2.

# 9   Conclusions and Future Work

This work shows evidence that modeling with CCC is a better modeling solution than DEMO/PSI for this Exchange Agreement problem. It presents several benefits in terms of flexibility, clearness and efficacy, while keeping the same high level proficiency in terms of security and reliability.

The authors believe that these benefits are likely to be found in other businesses problem, especially if they involve several interdependent transactions that are prone to change requests, and therefore requiring revoke acts with many and complex dependencies. We will follow that research path.

**Acknowledgments.** This work was partially funded by FCT/MCTES LARSyS (UID/EEA/50009/2013 (2015–2017))

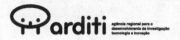

This work was developed with financial support from ARDITI (Agência Regional para o Desenvolvimento da Investigação, Tecnologia e Inovação), in the context of project M14-20 09–5369-FSE-000001- Bolsa de Doutoramento.

# References

1. Searle, J.R.: Speech Acts: An Essay in the Philosophy of Language, vol. 626. Cambridge University Press, Cambridge (1969)
2. http://intervac-homeexchange.com. Accessed 4 Dec 2016
3. http://en.intervac-homeexchange.com/facts-about-intervac. Accessed 4 Dec 2016
4. Cohen, B., Kietzmann, J.: Ride on! Mobility business models for the sharing economy. Organ. Environ. **27**(3), 279–296 (2014)
5. Botsman, R., Rogers, R.: What's Mine is Yours: How Collaborative Consumption is Changing the Way We Live. Collins, London (2011)
6. Botsman, R.: The sharing economy lacks a shared definition. Fast Company (2013). http://www.fastcoexist.com/3022028/the-sharing-economy-lacks-a-shared-definition/1. Accessed 4 Dec 2016
7. Dietz, J.L.G.: Enterprise Ontology – Theory and Methodology. Springer, Heidelberg (2006)
8. Gouveia, D., Aveiro, D.: Core Component of Communication. CIAO DC (2016). https://www.researchgate.net/publication/308622176_Core_Component_of_Communication
9. Basili, V.R., Shull, F., Lanubile, F.: Building knowledge through families of experiments. Softw. Eng. IEEE Trans. **25**(4), 456–473 (1999)
10. Wohlin, C., Aurum, A.: Towards a decision-making structure for selecting a research design in empirical software engineering. Empirical Softw. Eng. **20**(6), 1427–1455 (2015)
11. http://blog.intervac-homeexchange.com/guide/arranging-an-exchange/exchange-agreements/1-starting-an-agreement.html. Accessed 4 Dec 2016
12. http://blog.intervac-homeexchange.com/guide/arranging-an-exchange/exchange-agreements/2-filling-out-the-form.html. Accessed 4 Dec 2016
13. http://blog.intervac-homeexchange.com/guide/arranging-an-exchange/exchange-agreements/3-sending-and-reviewing-terms.html. Accessed 4 Dec 2016

14. http://blog.intervac-homeexchange.com/guide/arranging-an-exchange/exchange-agreements/4-signing-your-exchange-agreement.html. Accessed 4 Dec 2016
15. http://blog.intervac-homeexchange.com/guide/arranging-an-exchange/exchange-agreements/collected-questions.html Accessed 4 Dec 2016
16. Medina-Mora, R., Winograd, T., Flores, R., Flores, F.: The action workflow approach to workflow management technology. In: Proceedings of the 1992 ACM Conference on Computer-Supported Cooperative Work, pp. 281–288. ACM, December 1992
17. Denning, P.J., Medina-Mora, R.: Completing the loops. Interfaces **25**(3), 42–57 (1995)
18. Dietz, J.L.G.: DEMO-3 Way of Working (2009)
19. Van Reijswoud, V.E., Mulder, H.B., Dietz, J.L.: Communicative action-based business process and information systems modelling with DEMO. Inf. Syst. J. **9**(2), 117–138 (1999)

# Modeling Approaches to Support Decision Making

# Towards a Decision-Support System for Selecting the Appropriate Business Process Modeling Formalism: A Context-Aware Roadmap

Afef Awadid[1]([⊠]), Selmin Nurcan[1], and Sonia Ayachi Ghannouchi[2]

[1] CRI, University of Paris 1 Pantheon-Sorbonne, Paris, France
afef.awadid@malix.univ-parisl.fr,
nurcan@univ-parisl.fr
[2] RIADI Laboratory, University of Manouba, Manouba, Tunisia
s.ayachi@coselearn.org

**Abstract.** Business Process Modeling (BPM) is the cornerstone of the Business Process Management field, which has become a crucial topic in the competitiveness of enterprise information systems. The importance of BPM to Business Process Management can be justified by the serious problems, which may arise in the latter, if the former is not conducted correctly. This can take place, inter alia, when an inappropriate choice of a BPM formalism for a given BPM context has been made. Such an improper choice is due not only to the availability of a huge number of BPM formalisms but also to the lack of guidelines assisting in the selection process. Our aim in this paper, is to propose a context-aware roadmap with associated methodological guidelines underpinning the selection of the appropriate BPM formalism. To this end, a systematic literature review (SLR) of studies on BPM formalisms quality has been undertaken. The contribution of this paper is threefold viz. the SLR itself, a context-aware roadmap, along with a context model inspired by the Zachman framework, and is a first step towards a decision support system for selecting the appropriate BPM formalism.

**Keywords:** BPM formalism · Context-aware selection · Methodological guidelines · SLR · Context model · Roadmap

## 1 Introduction

Through a better understanding obtained by an explicit representation of business processes (BPs), the management community aims to improve organization performance via BP reengineering whereas the IS engineering community aims to design/redesign the IT solution that best fit the reengineered BPs [1]. The reasons behind the popularity of BPM go beyond its usefulness in enabling BPs definition and documentation [2]. It is further an important and key phase of the Business Process Management lifecycle. The latter has as aim to support the analysis, modeling, enactment and improvement of BPs and has become a crucial topic in the competitiveness of

© Springer International Publishing AG 2017
I. Reinhartz-Berger et al. (Eds.): BPMDS/EMMSAD 2017, LNBIP 287, pp. 239–256, 2017.
DOI: 10.1007/978-3-319-59466-8_15

enterprise information systems (IS), with several patents issued [1]. The importance of BPM to the BPM field can be justified by the serious problems, which may arise in other BPM phases, if the modeling phase is not conducted correctly [12]. This can take place, inter alia, when an inappropriate choice of BPM formalism has been made. In fact, a plethora of formalisms for modeling BPs exist. Since each of them allows to highlight different features of a given process [3, 4], and may restrict the ways in which a BP can be described, the choice of the BPM formalism can affect the success of the Business Process Management lifecycle [5].

Although the easiness to produce a domain specific language, avoiding then the selection issue, it seems more efficient to capitalize on the advantages of existing formalisms rather than systematically developing new ones [79] for each specific situation. Nonetheless, selecting the appropriate formalism from existing ones has become a convoluted task for modelers/engineers in the field of BPM [7]. This is due not only to the availability of a huge number of formalisms, but also to the lack of guidelines assisting in the selection process. Thereby, developing a decision support system that helps modelers in selecting the appropriate BPM formalism in a given modeling context will arguably be beneficial to all of them. As a first step towards doing this, this paper attempts to answer the overall question: How to define methodological guidelines to be implemented in such a decision support system? It proposes a context-aware roadmap (high-level methodological guidelines) deduced from a SLR of studies on BPM formalisms quality.

In the following, Sect. 2 outlines the theoretical background and the related work. Section 3 is dedicated to present the SLR we have conducted. Section 4 is devoted to highlight the proposed context-aware roadmap. We conclude our paper, discuss the limitations of our work and comment on future research directions in Sect. 5.

## 2  Background and Related Work

The key concepts that will be used throughout the paper are the following:

*Context:* In BPM, context is usually defined as the minimum set of variables containing all relevant information that impact either the design and execution of a business process" [9, 76] or the decision-making [10]. The corresponding phenomenon is scientifically referred to as context-awareness.

*Context Related Knowledge:* (CRK) is any information being part of the modeling context, and having impact on the decision of selecting or not a given BPM formalism. The fact that a practitioner (e.g. a banker) is not able alone to determine the relevant CRK to be considered when selecting a BPM formalism can lead him to make an improper choice affecting the BPM in his enterprise and hence the competitiveness of the banker's information system. Note that with regard to CRK, the approach we are presenting in this paper is based on the assumption that organizations aim for providing the ideal documentation instead of some documentation in a fast way.

*Quality:* "the total of characteristics of a product or service that are relevant for satisfying specific requirements and obvious necessities" (the definition given by the International Standards Organization). In our case, these properties and characteristics are the quality criteria, and the "product" or "service" is the BPM formalism.

A *primary study* refers to an empirical study investigating a specific research question.

Examining the research efforts pertaining to the selection of the appropriate BPM formalism, one is able to perceive that it is an attractive topic of investigation, in which researchers have been increasingly interested. Several frameworks have been proposed for this purpose. They can be broadly classified into two categories based on their prevalence. The first category includes the widespread frameworks, viz. the workflow patterns [14] where the selection is based on the expressiveness of the BPM formalisms, the Bunge-Wand-Weber (BWW) representation model [15] where the selection is based on their representational capability, and the Semiotic Quality (SEQUAL) Framework [78] which is more generic, so that the selection can be made based on several quality criteria. In the second category, we found the newly proposed frameworks. For instance, [2] proposes a comparative framework based on five quality criteria, viz. flexibility, ease of use, understandability, simulation and expressiveness, as basis for evaluating BPM formalisms and generating selection procedures. Similarly, [11] suggests a comparative framework in which each of the considered BPM formalisms is characterized regarding a number of quality criteria, which is nearly tripled, compared to [2]. [6] introduces a measurement framework towards determining the suitability of a BPM formalism for a particular application. It is based on more than ten quality criteria, including the five introduced in [2]. As well in [12], a multi criteria framework for selecting a BPM formalism is put forward with a large basis of quality criteria (about sixty).

The perceived differences in the number of quality criteria between the research works, can offer a conclusive proof that the criteria to be considered, for selecting the appropriate BPM formalism, must be context-dependent. Highlighting all pertinent CRK seems vital for guiding the selector in making her decision about the BPM formalism. Nevertheless, the aforementioned frameworks consider that it is up to the selector to decide which quality criteria to consider, and hence which BPM formalism to choose, mainly based on her modeling purpose(s) including amongst others (i) facilitating the coproduction of a group of BP actors and BP modelers to share their understanding of the BP, (ii) supporting BP improvement and reengineering though BP analysis and simulation or (iii) enabling communication between stakeholders. As arguably, CRK cannot be narrowed down to the modeling purpose (i.e. to a single kind of CRK); research works are still insufficient regarding the critical ability of providing guidance to the selector. Thus, the proposed frameworks can not form a basis towards a decision support system since they consider only partially the modeling context, although many are the efforts revealing the impact of context for better decision-making and recognizing that "combining context-awareness and decision-making in one system makes of it more desirable to users" [10].

# 3  Systematic Literature Review

Constructing a sound basis for developing a decision support system for selecting the appropriate BPM formalism is hampered, at a first stage, by three issues. The first one concerns the elicitation of the exhaustive *CRK*. The second consists in gathering a significant set of *relevant quality criteria* upon which the selection process can be based; the decision of selecting a given formalism depends on its perceived quality in a given modeling context. The third issue consists in specifying the methodological process itself. A prominent way to overcome the two first issues is to conduct a SLR on BPM formalisms quality. This choice is justified in [16] by its capability to collect/synthetize evidence related to a specific research area, and to provide a consolidated theoretical framework based on empirical evidence. As far as we are aware of, none SLR has been yet performed on the same topic. Given the impact of the appropriateness of BPM formalisms on BPM, and hence on the competitiveness of enterprise information systems, conducting such SLR seems us an important gap to fill.

We performed a SLR on BPM formalisms quality, with those research questions: RQ1: Which quality criterion/criteria is/are being highlighted by researchers? (*This is about extracting quality criteria on which the selection process can be based*). RQ2: What can be considered as a CRK in each primary study? (*To facilitate CRK elicitation, we use the definition of the CRK outlined in* Sect. 2, *and we examine the title, abstract and keywords of the primary studies (i.e. knowledge judged important by the authors). In case no relevant CRK was found, the corresponding field was marked with* "-"). RQ3: Which BPM formalism(s) is/are being evaluated/compared? RQ4: How quality of BPM formalism(s) is being assessed?

Although the problem of selecting the appropriate conceptual modeling formalism is of a broader scope, we put emphasis on it in the area of BPM field marked by its specificity regarding, inter alia, the quality assessment of formalisms. We investigated all English-language articles on BPM formalisms quality published between 2000 and 2016. This choice is relied on our assumption that by excluding the period before 2000, we will exclude only a petty fragment of potentially·relevant studies. We included papers comparing BPM formalisms or methods. Publications analyzing or evaluating BPM or execution formalism(s) were also included. We excluded any publication with a different focus than BPM formalism or BPM method as subject to quality assessment or analysis e.g. papers dealing with the quality of BPs, BP models, the standards or PAISs (Process-Aware ISs). We also omitted papers, where the quality criteria, the BPM formalism(s) or the means used for assessment were not explicitly defined. Aside from books and doctoral dissertations, papers tackling BPM formalism(s) improvement (mainly transformations between formalisms, quality framework(s) revision and formalisms extension) were also excluded.

To perform the automated search process for primary studies, we used Google Scholar, IEEE Xplore, ACM Digital Library, Science Direct, and Scopus Database, which were recommended in [17] as relevant within the research community. These databases were selected by assuming that they index papers published in well-reputed conferences and journals within the areas of business process and IS engineering. We used the same search strings for all search engines stated above. However, the search fields were different. Indeed, while in Google Scholar, all fields were concerned with the search; only title, abstract and keywords were chosen as search fields for the rest. The search strings used in Google Scholar are: *(evaluation OR comparison OR assessment "business process modelling languages"–translation –transformation –extension –extending)* published between 2000 and 2016. In the search process we also used the term *modeling* as synonym to *modelling*, and the terms *language, formalisms, formalism, techniques, technique, methods* and *method* as synonyms to *languages*. Similarly, the terms quality evaluation, quality comparison and quality assessment have been considered as synonyms to respectively evaluation, comparison and assessment.

The initial search run in March 2016 returned 1081 papers in total. First, we quickly examined titles and abstracts. Irrelevant or duplicate papers were eliminated. This left us with 61 papers, which were ultimately included in the review (Table 1). The significant reduction of the number of papers can be explained by the discarding of studies dealing with model quality rather than language quality. Due to the high number of papers in the field of BPM, it is arguably possible to miss some publications. Nonetheless, given the fact that those included address the core of the topic of the present SLR (viz. BPM formalisms quality), we are confident that the selected primary studies can be deemed to be at least sufficiently representative.

## 3.1 Data Extraction

For each one of the 61 remaining papers, quality criterion/criteria (**RQ1**), CRK (**RQ2**), BPM formalism(s) (**RQ3**), and means/way(s) for assessment (**RQ4**) were extracted (see Table 1[1]). We summarize here, the descriptions of quality criteria outlined in Table 1, column 2. **Effectiveness**: *(BPM formalism's)* capability of achieving user's modeling purposes [6]. **Efficiency**: capability of designing BP models by using the minimum possible number of concepts [18]. **User satisfaction**: a user subjective criterion referring toto which extent users (modelers and BP actors) accept a BPM formalism

---

[1] Acronyms used in Table 1: Specific Modeling Purpose (SMP) (focus on a single specific modeling purpose), Generic Modeling Purpose (GMP) (emphasis on a collection of modeling purposes), Business Process Modeling Notation (BPMN), Unified Modeling Language- Activity Diagram (UML-AD), UML-State Diagram (UML-SD), Event-driven Process Chain (EPC), Workflow-net (WF-net), Yet Another Workflow Language (YAWL), Extended Enterprise Modeling Language (EEML), Data Flow Diagram (DFD), Integration Definition for Function Modeling (IDEF), extended Event-Process Chain (eEPC), Role Activity Diagram (RAD), Business Use Case (BUC), Business Object Interaction Diagram (BOID), Coordination, Cooperation and Communication (C3) method, Architecture of Integrated Information Systems (ARIS), Business Modeling Language (BML), XML Process Definition Language (XPDL), Business Process Execution Language (BPEL), Business Process Modeling Language (BPML), Web Service Choreography Interface (WSCI), Web Services Choreography Description Language (WS-CDL), Actor Role (AR) diagram, Enterprise Knowledge Development –Change Management Method (EKD-CMM), BPEL for Web Services (BPEL4WS), Entity Relationship (ER) diagram, Business Process Specification Shema (BPSS), Semantics of Business Vocabulary and Rules (SBVR), Production Rule Representation (PRR), Simulation Reference Markup Language (SRML), and Semantic Web Rule Language (SWRL).

**Table 1.** The extracted data from primary studies.

| Ref. | Quality criteria (RQ1) | CRK (RQ2) | BPM formalism (RQ3) | Assessment means (RQ4) |
|---|---|---|---|---|
| [2] | Flexibility, ease of use, understandability, simulation, expressiveness | GMP | Flow charts, Petri nets, DFD, RAD, BPMN, BUC, BOID | A case study |
| [6] | Completeness, complexity, understandability, ease of use, concision, effectiveness, efficiency, expressiveness, flexibility, formality, tool support | GMP | BPMN, EPC, UML-AD | A measurement framework |
| [11] | Expressiveness, understandability, ease of use, flexibility, popularity, formality, effectiveness, tool support, learnability, concision, innovation inducer, evolutionary, collaborative work support | GMP | BPMN, EPC, UML-AD, RAD, IDEF | A quantitative scale |
| [18] | Effectiveness, efficiency, user satisfaction | Business users | BPMN, UML-AD | A survey |
| [19] | Representational capability | – | BPMN | The BWW representation model + series of interviews |
| [20] | Learnability | Users without formal education | BPMN, EPC | An experimental study |
| [21] | Inter-process dependency support | Integrated processes | WF-net, YAWL, UML 2.0-AD, BPMN, EPC | A set of inter-process dependencies |
| [22] | Effectiveness | An insurance company | UML 2.0-AD, BPMN, EEML | The SEQUAL framework |
| [23] | Understandability | People not familiar with process modeling | BPMN, UML2.0-AD | A controlled experiment |
| [24] | Ease of use | SMP: to trim SW maintenance and operational costs | BPMN, UML | A set of complexity metrics |
| [25] | Expressiveness | – | DFD, BPMN, UML-AD, IDEF0 | A case study |
| [26] | Expressiveness, ease of use, simulation | – | IDEF0, eEPC | A multidimensional framework |
| [27] | Performance evaluation support | A manufacturing process | IDEF0 | A case study |
| [28] | Expressiveness | Large and mid-sized enterprises | BPMN, UML-AD, EPC | BWW representation model+ workflow patterns |

(*continued*)

**Table 1.** (*continued*)

| Ref. | Quality criteria (RQ1) | CRK (RQ2) | BPM formalism (RQ3) | Assessment means (RQ4) |
|------|------------------------|-----------|---------------------|------------------------|
| [29] | Flexibility, tool support, performance evaluation support | Environmental protection | EPC, BPMN, UML-AD | Three case studies |
| [30] | Expressiveness, ease of use, popularity | Small and mid-sized enterprises | BPMN, eEPC, C3 | An interdisciplinary framework |
| [31] | Formality, understandability, business goals description support, completeness, performance evaluation support, simulation | BP Reengineering (BPR) phases | IDEF, UML, ARIS | A qualitative scale |
| [32] | Confidentiality, formality, effectiveness, expressiveness | Cross-organizational BPs (CBP) | UML, Petri nets, BPMN, EPC | A qualitative scale |
| [33] | Expressiveness | – | EPC, UML-SD, BML | A metamodel |
| [34] | Ease of use, understandability | – | BPMN | The SEQUAL framework |
| [35] | Expressiveness | – | BPMN, EPC, IDEF3, Petri nets, RAD, UML-AD | A metamodel |
| [36] | Level of exceptions support | SMP: Workflow processes execution | XPDL, BPEL, BPMN | Patterns for exception handling |
| [37] | Representational capability | – | Petri net, EPC, ebXML, BPML, WSCI, WS-BPEL, BPMN | The BWW representation model |
| [38] | Graphical modeling quality | Complex processes | BPMN, EPC, UML-AD | Moody's quality criterion |
| [39] | Completeness, effectiveness | SMP: to support BP understanding | IDEF0, IDEF1, IDEF3, Petri nets, RAD, EPC | A qualitative scale |
| [40] | Understandability, completeness, expressiveness, tool support, portability | SMP: to represent a unified process | UML-AD, EPC, BPMN | A qualitative scale |
| [41] | Expressiveness | – | BPMN, RAD, EPC, UML-AD, IDEF3 | A unified business process metamodel |
| [42] | Completeness, ease of use, understandability | SMP: to support BP improvement | UML | A questionnaire |
| [43] | Ease of use, understandability, flexibility, formality, performance evaluation support | Small and mid-sized companies + Novice and experienced users | Flowchart, RAD, DFD | Surveys |
| [44] | Choreography modeling capability | Cross-organizational BPs | BPMN | The SEQUAL framework |
| [45] | Choreography modeling capability | Collaborative BPs | BPEL, WS-CDL | Patterns for services interactions |

(*continued*)

**Table 1.** (*continued*)

| Ref. | Quality criteria (RQ1) | CRK (RQ2) | BPM formalism (RQ3) | Assessment means (RQ4) |
|---|---|---|---|---|
| [46] | Cognitive effectiveness | Experts and novices | BPMN | Evidence-based principles |
| [47] | Inter-model consistency support | Multi-perspective modeling | AR, RA and Objects diagrams | Consistency rules |
| [48] | Flexibility | SMP: to design flexible BPs | EKD-CMM, ARIS, UML | A benchmarking framework |
| [49] | Effectiveness, efficiency, learnability, user satisfaction, ease of use, memorability | Students as modelers | EPC, UML | The framework for Usability Evaluation of Modeling Languages (FUEML) |
| [50] | Expressiveness | – | UML, DFD, Petri nets, EPC, IDEF3, BPMN | A framework based on the BWW representation model |
| [51] | Flexibility | Knowledge-intensive processes | YAWL | Three case studies |
| [52] | Complexity, confidentiality, understandability, evolutionary, flexibility | Healthcare domain | BPEL, WS-CDL | An evaluation framework |
| [53] | Expressiveness | Collaborative BPs | BPEL4WS | A case study |
| [54] | Representational capability | – | IDEF, EPC, UML, BPMN, WS-BPEL, ebXML | BWW representation model + Curtis's Framework |
| [13] | Expressiveness | GMP | Flowcharts, DFD, ER, IDEF0, Petri nets, RAD | An evaluation framework |
| [55] | Representational capability | – | UML | BWW representation model |
| [56] | Expressiveness | – | UML | A metamodel for BWW ontological constructs |
| [57] | Representational capability | – | Petri nets, BPEL4WS, DFD, EPC, IDEF3, BPMN, BPML | BWW representation model |
| [58] | Expressiveness, representational capability | – | BPMN | BWW model+ workflow patterns |
| [59] | Choreography modeling capability | SMP: to enable application integration | BPEL4WS | Workflows and communication patterns |
| [60] | Performance evaluation support | SMP: to analyze BP models | BPMN | A Petri net approach |
| [61] | Representational capability | Inter-organizational workflows | UML | BWW representation model |

(*continued*)

**Table 1.** (*continued*)

| Ref. | Quality criteria (RQ1) | CRK (RQ2) | BPM formalism (RQ3) | Assessment means (RQ4) |
|---|---|---|---|---|
| [62] | Representational capability | – | EPC | BWW representation model |
| [63] | Choreography modeling capability, representational capability | SMP: to obtain a clear and complete representation of the electronic commerce domain | ebXML BPSS | BWW representation model |
| [64] | Choreography modeling capability, representational capability | SMP: to obtain a clear and complete representation of process interoperation | ebXML BPSS, BPML, BPEL4WS, WSCI | BWW representation model |
| [65] | Understandability | SMP: to improve understandability | ER diagrams | An ontological model |
| [66] | Expressiveness | Workflow processes | Petri nets | A formal framework |
| [67] | User satisfaction | People familiar with process modeling | BPMN | A survey |
| [68] | Representational capability | – | Petri nets | BWW representation model |
| [69] | Expressiveness | – | UML2.0- AD | Workflow patterns |
| [70] | Expressiveness | – | BPMN | Workflow patterns |
| [71] | Representational capability | – | BPMN, SBVR, PRR, SRML, SWRL | BWW representation model |
| [72] | Expressiveness | Workflow processes | XPDL | Workflow patterns |
| [73] | Effectiveness | SMP: to implement BPR and ERP | IDEF3, eEPC, RAD, DFD | An evaluation framework |
| [74] | Expressiveness, representational capability | – | BPMN, UML-AD | Workflow patterns + BWW representation model |

and have the intention to use it again [67]. **Expressiveness**: capability of designing BP models for any number and type of applications [6]. **Learnability**: easiness to be learnt (i.e. less effort is required to the modelers and BP actors to master and to be productive in its use) [20]. **Inter-process dependency support**: capability to support dependencies among a set of BPs [21]. **Understandability**: the extent to which a BPM formalism can be understood by modelers [2]. **Ease of use**: the degree to which a BPM formalism can be easily used (i.e. it is not complicated to model BPs using this formalism) [24]. **Simulation**: capability of dynamically simulating a BP [2]. **Performance evaluation support**: capability of empowering users to define performance measures or indicators for supporting the performance evaluation of BPs [27]. **Flexibility**: easiness to make evolve BP models (built by instantiating the BPM formalism) in response to internal and external changes [51]. **Popularity**: to which extent the BPM formalism can be considered as mainstream [30]. **Formality**: rigor in the semantics of the BPM formalism reducing ambiguities in the interpretation of BP models [31]. **Tool**

**support**: availability of suitable tools supporting the use of a BPM formalism for building BP models [29]. **Concision**: capability of depicting various facets of a BP using a smaller set of concepts [6]. **Innovation inducer**: ability to induce modelers to discover new solutions and modeling practices [11]. **Evolutionary**: possibility of a BPM formalism to be extensible (i.e. updated and extended in the future) [11]. **Collaborative work support**: capability to support the modeling of collaborative activities in a BP (e.g. meetings) [11]. **Business goals description support**: ability to depict business goals [31].**Completeness**: capability to cover all relevant BPM perspectives that are required by an organization and/or by the nature of BPs [39]. **Confidentiality**: ability to support security requirements in BPs [32]. **Complexity**: capability to model complex BPs [6]. **Level of exceptions support**: capability to anticipate/handle exceptions in BPs [36].**Graphical modeling quality**: relevance of the formalism for producing "good" BP models [38]. **Portability**: tool-independence of the BPM formalism [40]. **Choreography modeling capability**: capability to represent the interactions between multiple organizations or organizational units involved in a common BP [44]. **Cognitive effectiveness**: the speed, ease and accuracy for a human mind to process the visual notation of a BP model [46]. **Inter-model consistency support**: capability to inhibit contradiction in a set of BP models depicting the same BP [47]. **Memorability**: capability to be memorized after a period of non-use provided a user has already learned it [49]. **Representational capability**: ability to provide clear and complete descriptions of a real-world domain [19].

## 3.2   Analysis of the Results

Based on Table 1, we identified 30 quality criteria stemmed from the SLR **(1)** and dispersed over the 61 primary studies. These criteria can be an exhaustive and broader basis for evaluating BPM formalisms, and hence for selecting the appropriate one **(2)**, since such evaluation is needed either for their improvement or for selecting one among them. Analyzing their distribution among the selected studies, we observe (Fig. 1) that *expressiveness* is the most used criterion for evaluating the quality of BPM formalisms (22 of 61; 36%), followed by the criterion of *representational capability* (13 of 61; 21%). About 50% of primary studies (31 of 61) were interested at least in one of these two criteria, often without defining the CRK (i.e. both seem to be considered 'context independent'). This empowers both of them to be viewed as prioritized in any context. Criteria like *portability, cognitive effectiveness,* and *memorability* are the least used ones (all with the same percentage 1.64%). Thus, contrarily to the expressiveness and representational capability, these criteria can be considered as overlooked or deemed less important. Since comparison is the cornerstone for selecting the appropriate BPM formalism, the comparison criteria with higher priority (i.e. the most important ones) according to the modeling context should be determined **(3)**.

By focusing on columns 2–3 of Table 1, we see that their values vary conjointly. Hence, the CRK seems to affect the decision about the appropriate BPM formalism to be selected, by facilitating the identification of higher priority quality criteria **(4)**. Furthermore, we notice that a single CRK (60 of 61: 98%) or multiple ones (1 of 61; 2%) can aid in determining the prioritized criterion/criteria **(5)**. Similarly, a single

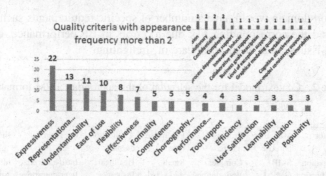

**Fig. 1.** Frequency of quality criteria in primary studies

criterion (41 of 61; 67%) or several ones (20 of 61; 33%) can be regarded as prioritized for comparing BPM formalisms **(6)**.

A closer look at column 3 of Table 1 allows us revealing seven facets based on which CRK can be classified. The first is related to *who can be selector* including her occupation (e.g. business users, students as modelers), and her qualifications (users without formal education, people familiar with BPM, novices and experienced users). The second facet focuses on *modeling purposes* (including SMP and GMP). The third is pertaining to the *process nature* (complex processes e.g. integrated processes), well-defined BPs where all activities to be executed and their schedule are known in advance (e.g. workflow processes, manufacturing processes), ill-defined BPs where it is not possible to predict neither the activities to be executed nor their schedule (e.g. knowledge-intensive processes). The fourth defines the *type of enterprise* (small, mid-sized, large). The fifth defines the application domain (e.g. healthcare or insurance). The sixth addresses the *location* (inter-organizational workflows, CBP). The seventh facet puts emphasis on Business Process Reengineering *(BPR) phases* (see Table 2).

The aforementioned facets seem complementary and allow providing a complete and thorough picture of the BPM context. This reminded us Zachman's framework [75], which offers a complete picture of the Enterprise Architecture (EA) and allows analyzing and structuring the related information. From here, comes our idea of using Zachman's interrogative pronouns (what, when where, how and why) for structuring the deduced facets as shown in Table 2. Row 1 of this table includes the context aspects (the interrogatives pronouns), row 2 includes the context facets (CRK defined at a high level of abstraction), and row 3 includes the context attributes (CRK defined at a detailed level). The role of each context attribute (i.e. a CRK) is to filter the number of quality criteria so that only that or those qualified as the most important (by means of weights to be assigned to them) is/are maintained. At this stage of work, the context attributes are those extracted from primary studies. In the near future, we intend to realize an empirical study with practitioners in order to judge the impact of each potential context attribute, and hence to assign weights to the quality criteria. This will also allow us to identify the specific requirements in terms of the most appropriate BPM formalism for each application domain (healthcare, education, etc). For instance, the application domain would have a number of specific requirements such as security of persons and the corresponding risk due to errors in BP performance, or the crisis management issues, such as in healthcare or firefighting.

**Table 2.** Context model for the selection of the appropriate BPM formalism

| Context aspects | Who | Why | What | | | | Where | When |
|---|---|---|---|---|---|---|---|---|
| Context facets | Selector | Modeling purpose | Process nature | Enterprise type | Application domain | | Location | BPR phases |
| Context attributes | Occupation Qualification | SMP GMP | Complex Well-defined Ill defined | Small mid-sized Large mid-sized | Healthcare Insurance | | Intra-enterprise Inter-enterprise | Identification Analysis Redesign Evaluation Implementation Improvement |

The examination of column 4 of Table 1 reveals that 62.3% of studies (38 of 61) focus on evaluating a set of BP formalisms, rather than evaluating a single formalism or notation (37.7%; 23 of 61). This means that majority of researchers opt for comparing a set of BPM formalisms as a fundamental activity, not only for selecting the most appropriate one, but also for improving those presenting some deficiencies (**7**). In fact, based on the comparison result, a BPM formalism can be selected (**8**). The taxonomy of BPM formalisms presented in [54] classifies BPM formalisms into four categories; Traditional process modeling formalisms (e.g. Petri nets, IDEF family, RAD, EPC), Object-oriented modeling formalisms (e.g. UML family), Dynamic process modeling formalisms (e.g. BPMN, BPML, WS-BPEL) and Process integration formalisms (e.g. ebXML, WS-CDL). We can notice that all these categories have been covered by the primary studies. Therefore, the diversity in the types of BPM formalisms has a significant importance in the process of selecting the appropriate one, since it can guarantee the coverage of different BPM requirements, and hence a context-aware selection process (**9**).

Analyzing column 5 of Table 1, we notice that there are two possible ways for assessing BPM formalisms: by using a single means (90%; 55 of 61) or by combining multiple ones (10%; 6 of 61) (**10**). Given the variety of means, their classification is highly demanded. In order to classify them, we have relied on a thorough taxonomy presented in [77], which classified evaluation methods into three categories, viz. feature comparison (including mainly the check List), theoretical and conceptual investigation (e.g. ontological evaluation, conceptual framework, meta modeling), and empirical evaluation (e.g. surveys, experiments, case studies). In the works listed in Table 1, 80% of researchers based their evaluation of BPM formalisms on theoretical and conceptual investigation, against 20% who opted for an empirical evaluation. There are mainly three straightforward reasons explaining this result; theoretical and conceptual investigation is less subjective, well defined and does not require empirical data [77].

An important point to put over is that the findings numbered (1), (2) ... (10) in this section will be used in the next one to construct the roadmap.

# 4   A Context-Aware Roadmap

The motivation behind constructing a context-aware roadmap (with its context-aware methodological guidelines) is to get a sound theoretical basis for developing a decision support system assisting the BP modelers to make decision about the formalism to be adopted. Such system is needed for mainly two reasons: (i) the number of BPM formalisms increases more and more rapidly, and (ii) the selection of the appropriate BPM formalism is a context-aware process. We advocate that the Map formalism [8] seems an ideal candidate to set up such roadmap thanks to its capability to support a context-aware decision-making since it is grounded on a decision-driven navigational structure. A Map is a goal-driven formalism, which aims to capture the intentions (goals) of an enterprise, system, or method and to determine the strategies contributing to the fulfillment of these intentions. As shown in Fig. 2, a map is a labeled directed graph with intentions as nodes and strategies as edges between intentions. A map consists of a number of sections each of which is a triplet <*source intention Ii, target intention Ij, strategy Sij*>. Since the next intention and the strategy to achieve it are selected dynamically, each map incorporates three types of guidelines: (1) Intention Selection Guidelines (ISG) whose role is to guide the selection of the intention to achieve in the next step, (2) Strategy Selection Guidelines (SSG) whose role is to assist the selection of a strategy among those connecting two given intentions, and (3) Intention Achievement Guidelines (IAG) whose role is to support the execution of any map section.

Based on the SLR presented in the above section, we identified the intentions and strategies constituting a sketch of our higher-level map (see Fig. 2). The intentions represent the main milestones towards making the decision about the BPM formalism to adopt in a given context and are deduced from our findings (Sect. 3.2) numbered (1), (2), (3), (4), (6) and (7). The strategies are deduced from the findings (5), (8), (9) and (10). The strategy "by using existing recommendations" is derived from our modest experience in the field of BPM. Thus, at this stage of our ongoing work, we have defined high-abstraction-level Intention Achievement Guidelines (which refer to the map sections in Fig. 2). Moreover, we have operationalized the section <"Start", "Get a significant set of quality criteria", "By undertaking a SLR approach">. Besides, sets of quality criteria, CRK, BPM formalisms, and assessment means have been identified. The two formers are needed for operationalizing, as example the section <"Get a significant set of quality criteria", "Determine prioritized criteria with respect to modeling context", "By considering a single CRK">. However, the two latters are needed for instance for operationalizing the section <"Determine prioritized criteria with respect to modeling context", "Compare BPM formalisms against prioritized criteria", "By considering different types of BPM formalisms and by using different assessment means">.

The roadmap presented in Fig. 2 is just a starting point; some sections are too complex and should be refined in lower abstraction level maps such is the case for the section <"Determine prioritized criteria with respect to modeling context", "Select the appropriate BPM formalism", "By using existing recommendations">. To implement

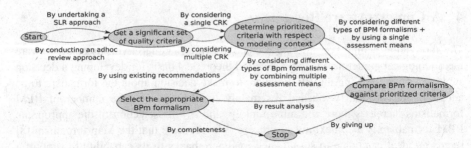

**Fig. 2.** A context-aware roadmap underpinning the selection of the appropriate BPM formalism

the methodological guidelines in a decision support system, all guidelines associated with this roadmap should be operationalized (i.e. specified in the operational level).

## 5 Conclusion and Limitations

This paper reports on an ongoing work to develop a decision support system for the selection of the appropriate BPM formalism in a given context. It provides a SLR of studies on BPM formalisms quality. The latter allowed us to define high-level methodological guidelines as a theoretical basis for developing the targeted system, and to get the key data (viz. sets of quality criteria, CRK, BPM formalisms and assessment means), which are a prerequisite for operationalizing and implementing the proposed roadmap. As it is inherent in any literature review that something can be missing because of the used databases, search strings, time period, etc, our present SLR suffers from some limitations: (i) due to space limitation, the quality evaluation of primary studies has not been considered; (ii) the approach used for analyzing the extracted data (mainly the quality criteria) has not been linked to literature that can guide such analysis. This led us to an unmanageable number of criteria, which should be sorted out and reduced in number, especially since some criteria are overlapped (e.g. understandability and ease of use). To overcome these limitations, we will extend the current SLR in which, (i) the search process and sources selection will be described in a detailed way, (ii) the idea of a context-aware selection of modeling formalisms will be more deeply developed, (iii) the quality evaluation of primary studies will be included and (iv) a structuration of the analysis of the extracted data by referring to the grounded theory method proposed in [80] will be carried out. As a next step towards developing the targeted system, we plan to perform an empirical study in the form of interviews with practitioners (BP actors as modelers) in order to (i) further validate the proposed theoretical basis or to adjust it according to practical needs and (ii) to assign weights to quality criteria in accordance with each CRK. This will enable us to operationalize sections (i.e. to specify the associated methodological guidelines) including the term "CRK" such as <*"Get a significant set of quality criteria", "Determine prioritized criteria with respect to modeling context", "By considering multiple CRK"*>, and hence to specify all methodological guidelines associated to the Map in order to implement the targeted decision support system.

# References

1. Campos, C.S., Daher, S.F.D., Almeida, A.T.: New patents on business process management information systems and decision support. Recent Pat. Comput. Sci. **4**(2), 91–97 (2011)
2. Aldin, L., de Cesare, S.: A comparative analysis of business process modelling techniques. In: Proceedings of the UK Academy for Information Systems (2009)
3. Li, Y., Cao, B., Xu, L., Yin, J., Deng, S., Yin, Y., Wu, Z.: An efficient recommendation method for improving business process modeling. IEEE Trans. Ind. Inform. **10**(1), 502–513 (2014)
4. Tan, W., Xu, W., Yang, F., Xu, L., Jiang, C.: A framework for service enterprise workflow simulation with multi-agents cooperation. Enterp. Inf. Syst. **7**(4), 523–542 (2013)
5. Luo, W., Alex Tung, Y.: A framework for selecting business process modeling methods. Ind. Manag. Data Syst. **99**(7), 312–319 (1999)
6. Geyer, R.W., Fourier, C.J.: Determining the suitability of a business process modelling technique for a particular application. S. Afr. J. Ind. Eng. **26**(1), 252–266 (2015)
7. Glassey, O.: A case study on process modelling—three questions and three techniques. Decis. Support Syst. **44**(4), 842–853 (2008)
8. Rolland, C., Prakash, N., Benjamen, A.: A multi-model view of process modelling. Requir. Eng. **4**(4), 169–187 (1999)
9. Rosemann, M., Recker, J.C.: Context-aware process design: exploring the extrinsic drivers for process flexibility. In: Proceedings of Workshops and Doctoral Consortium (CAISE 2006), pp. 149–158. Namur University Press (2006)
10. Yousfi, A., Dey, A.K., Saidi, R., Hong, J.H.: Introducing decision-aware BPs. Comput. Ind. **70**, 13–22 (2015)
11. Pereira, J.L., Silva, D.: Business process modeling languages: a comparative framework. In: Rocha, Á., Correia, A., Adeli, H., Reis, L., Mendonça Teixeira, M. (eds.) New Advances in Information Systems and Technologies. AISCLNCS, vol. 444, pp. 619–628. Springer, Heidelberg (2016). doi:10.1007/978-3-319-31232-3_58
12. Scanavachi Moreira Campos, A.C., de Almeida, A.T.: Multicriteria framework for selecting a process modelling language. Enterp. Inf. Syst. **10**(1), 17–32 (2016)
13. Giaglis, G.M.: A taxonomy of business process modeling and information systems modeling techniques. Int. J. Flex. Manuf. Syst. **13**(2), 209–228 (2001)
14. van Der Aalst, W.M., Ter Hofstede, A.H., Kiepuszewski, B., Barros, A.P.: Workflow patterns. Distributed Parallel Databases **14**(1), 5–51 (2003)
15. Wand, Y., Weber, R.: An ontological model of an information system. IEEE Trans. Soft. Eng. **16**(11), 1282–1292 (1990)
16. Kitchenham, B.: Procedures for Performing Systematic Reviews, vol. 33, pp. 1–26. Keele University, Keele (2004)
17. Keele, S.: Guidelines for performing systematic literature reviews in software engineering. In: Technical report, Ver. 2.3 EBSE Technical report. EBSE (2007)
18. Birkmeier, D., Kloeckner, S., Overhage, S.: An empirical comparison of the usability of BPMN and UML activity diagrams for business users. In: ECIS, vol. 2 (2010)
19. Recker, J. C., Indulska, M., Rosemann, M., Green, P.: How good is BPMN really? Insights from theory and practice (2006)
20. Recker, J.C., Dreiling, A.: Does it matter which process modelling language we teach or use? An experimental study on understanding process modelling languages without formal education. In: 18th Australasian Conference on Information Systems (2007)

21. Grossmann, G., Schrefl, M., Stumptner, M.: Modelling and enforcement of inter-process dependencies with business process modelling languages. J. Res. Pract. Inf. Technol. **42**(4), 289 (2010)
22. Nysetvold, A.G., Krogstie, J.: Assessing business process modeling languages using a generic quality framework. Adv. Top. Database Res. **5**, 79–93 (2006)
23. Peixoto, D., Batista, V., Atayde, A., Borges, E., Resende, R., Pádua, C.I.P.S.: A comparison of BPMN and UML 2.0 activity diagrams. In: VII Simposio Brasileiro de Qualidade de Software, vol. 56 (2008)
24. Recker, J.C., zur Muehlen, M., Siau, K., Erickson, J., Indulska, M.: Measuring method complexity: UML versus BPMN. Association for Information Systems (2009)
25. Tangkawarow, I.R.H.T., Waworuntu, J.: A comparative of business process modelling techniques. In: IOP Conference Series: Materials Science and Engineering, vol. 128(1), p. 012010 (2016)
26. Tsironis, L., Anastasiou, K., Moustakis, V.: A framework for BPML assessment and improvement: a case study using IDEF0 and eEPC. BPM J. **15**(3), 430–461 (2009)
27. Tsironis, L., Gentsos, A., Moustakis, V.: Empowerment the IDEF0 modeling language. Int. J. Bus. Manag. **3**(5), 109 (2009)
28. Patig, S., Casanova-Brito, V.: Requirements of process modeling languages-results from an empirical investigation. In: Wirtschaftsinformatik, vol. 39 (2011)
29. Opitz, N., Erek, K., Langkau, T., Kolbe, L., Zarnekow, R.: Kick-starting green business process management–suitable modeling languages and key processes for green performance measurement (2012)
30. Nielen, A., Jeske, T., Schlick, C., Arning, K., Ziefle, M.: Interdisciplinary assessment of process modeling languages applicable for small to medium-sized enterprises. In: 8th International Conference on Computing, Communications and Control Technologies: CCCT, pp. 47–52 (2010)
31. Bertoni, M., Bordegoni, M., Cugini, U., Regazzoni, D., Rizzi, C.: PLM paradigm: how to lead BPR within the product development field. Comput. Ind. **60**(7), 476–484 (2009)
32. Ziemann, J., Matheis, T., Freiheit, J.: Modelling of cross-organizational business processes-current methods and standards. EMISA, 87–100 (2007)
33. Söderström, E., Andersson, B., Johannesson, P., Perjons, E., Wangler, B.: Towards a framework for comparing process modelling languages. In: Pidduck, A.B., Ozsu, M.T., Mylopoulos, J., Woo, C.C. (eds.) CAiSE 2002. LNCS, vol. 2348, pp. 600–611. Springer, Heidelberg (2002). doi:10.1007/3-540-47961-9_41
34. Wahl, T., Sindre, G.: An analytical evaluation of BPMN using a semiotic quality framework. Adv. Top. Database Res. **5**, 94–105 (2006)
35. List, B., Korherr, B.: An evaluation of conceptual business process modelling languages. In: Proceedings of the 2006 ACM symposium on Applied Computing, pp. 1532–1539. ACM (2006)
36. Russell, N., Aalst, W., Hofstede, A.: Workflow exception patterns. In: Dubois, E., Pohl, K. (eds.) CAiSE 2006. LNCS, vol. 4001, pp. 288–302. Springer, Heidelberg (2006). doi:10.1007/11767138_20
37. Recker, J., Rosemann, M., Indulska, M., Green, P.: Business process modeling-a comparative analysis. J. Assoc. Inf. Syst. **10**(4), 1 (2009)
38. Johansson, L.O., Wärja, M., Carlsson, S.: An evaluation of business process model techniques, using Moody's quality criterion for a good diagram. In: BIR12. CEUR Workshop Proceedings, CEUR-WS.Org, vol. 963 (2012)
39. Mili, H., Tremblay, G., Jaoude, G.B.: Business process modeling languages: sorting through the alphabet soup. ACM Comput. Surv. (CSUR) **43**(1), 4 (2010)

40. Kelemen, Z.D., Kusters, R., Trienekens, J., Balla, K.: Selecting a process modeling language for process based unification of multiple standards and models. Technical report TR201304, Budapest (2013)
41. Heidari, F., Loucopoulos, P., Brazier, F., Barjis, J.: A unified view of business process modelling languages. 1 (2012)
42. Kock, N., Verville, J., Danesh-Pajou, A., DeLuca, D.: Communication flow orientation in business process modeling and its effect on redesign success: results from a field study. Decis. Support Syst. 46(2), 562–575 (2009)
43. Aksu, F., Vanhoof, K., De Munck, L.: Evaluation and comparison of business process modeling methodologies for small and midsized enterprises. In: Intelligent Systems and Knowledge Engineering (ISKE), pp. 664–667. IEEE (2010)
44. Cortes-Cornax, M., Dupuy-Chessa, S., Rieu, D., Dumas, M.: Evaluating choreographies in BPMN 2.0 using an extended quality framework. In: Dijkman, R., Hofstetter, J., Koehler, J. (eds.) BPMN 2011. LNBIP, vol. 95, pp. 103–117. Springer, Heidelberg (2011). doi:10.1007/978-3-642-25160-3_8
45. Barros, A., Dumas, M., ter Hofstede, A.H.M.: Service interaction patterns: towards a reference framework for service-based business process interconnection. Faculty of IT, Queensland University of Technology (2005)
46. Genon, N., Heymans, P., Amyot, D.: Analysing the cognitive effectiveness of the BPMN 2.0 visual notation. In: Malloy, B., Staab, S., Brand, M. (eds.) SLE 2010. LNCS, vol. 6563, pp. 377–396. Springer, Heidelberg (2011). doi:10.1007/978-3-642-19440-5_25
47. Awadid, A., Nurcan, S.: Towards enhancing business process modeling formalisms of EKD with consistency consideration. In: RCIS Conference. IEEE, Grenoble (2016)
48. Daoudi, F., Nurcan, S.: A benchmarking framework for methods to design flexible business processes. Softw. Process Improv. Pract. 12(1), 51–63 (2007)
49. Schalles, C., Creagh, J., Rebstock, M., Ave, R.: Exploring usability-driven differences of graphical modeling languages: an empirical research report (2012)
50. Rima, A., Vasilecas, O., Šmaižys, A.: Comparative analysis of business rules and business process modeling languages. Comput. Sci. Tech. 1(1), 52–60 (2013)
51. Di Ciccio, C., Marrella, A., Russo, A.: Knowledge-intensive processes: an overview of contemporary approaches. In: 1st International Workshop on Knowledge-intensive Business Processes, KiBP 2012, Rome (2012)
52. Afrasiabi Rad, A., Benyoucef, M., Kuziemsky, C.E.: An evaluation framework for business process modeling languages in healthcare. J. Theor. Appl. Electron. Commer. Res. 4(2), 1–19 (2009)
53. Jang, J., Fekete, A., Greenfield, P., Kuo, D.: Expressiveness of workflow description languages. In: ICWS, pp. 104–110 (2003)
54. Mohammadi, M., Mukhtar, M.B.: Theoretical and conceptual approach for evaluation business process modelling languages. J. Converg. Inf. Technol. 8(4), 372–384 (2013)
55. Opdahl, A.L., Henderson-Sellers, B.: Ontological evaluation of the UML using the Bunge–Wand–Weber model. Softw. Syst. Model. 1(1), 43–67 (2002)
56. Rosemann, M., Green, P.: Developing a meta model for the Bunge–Wand–Weber ontological constructs. Inf. Syst. 27(2), 75–91 (2002)
57. Rosemann, M., Recker, J., Indulska, M., Green, P.: A study of the evolution of the representational capabilities of process modeling grammars. In: Dubois, E., Pohl, K. (eds.) CAiSE 2006. LNCS, vol. 4001, pp. 447–461. Springer, Heidelberg (2006). doi:10.1007/11767138_30
58. Recker, J., Rosemann, M., Krogstie, J.: Ontology-versus pattern-based evaluation of process modeling languages: a comparison. Commun. Assoc. Inf. Syst. 20(1), 48 (2007)

59. Wohed, P., van der Aalst, W.M., Dumas, M., ter Hofstede, A.H.: Pattern based analysis of BPEL4WS. QUT Technical report, Queensland University of Technology, Brisbane (2002)
60. Ou-Yang, C., Lin, Y.D.: BPMN-based business process model feasibility analysis: a petri net approach. Int. J. Prod. Res. 46(14), 3763–3781 (2008)
61. Dussart, A., Aubert, B.A., Patry, M.: An evaluation of inter-organizational workflow modelling formalisms. J. Database Manag. (JDM) 15(2), 74–104 (2004)
62. Green, P., Rosemann, M.: Integrated process modeling: an ontological evaluation. Inf. Syst. 25(2), 73–87 (2000)
63. Green, P.F., Rosemann, M., Indulska, M.: Ontological evaluation of enterprise systems interoperability using ebXML. IEEE Trans. Knowl. Data Eng. 17(5), 713–725 (2005)
64. Green, P., Rosemann, M., Indulska, M., Manning, C.: Candidate interoperability standards: an ontological overlap analysis. Data Knowl. Eng. 62(2), 274–291 (2007)
65. Gemino, A., Wand, Y.: Complexity and clarity in conceptual modeling: comparison of mandatory and optional properties. Data Knowl. Eng. 55(3), 301–326 (2005)
66. Kiepuszewski, B., ter Hofstede, A.H., van der Aalst, W.M.: Fundamentals of control flow in workflows. Acta Inform. 39(3), 143–209 (2003)
67. Recker, J.C.: Why do we keep using a process modelling technique? (2007)
68. Recker, J.C., Indulska, M.: An ontology-based evaluation of process modeling with petri nets. IBIS – Internat. J. Interoperability Bus. Inf. Syst. 2(1), 45–64 (2007)
69. Russell, N., van der Aalst, W.M., Ter Hofstede, A.H., Wohed, P.: On the suitability of UML 2.0 activity diagrams for business process modelling. In: Proceedings of the 3rd Asia-Pacific Conference on Conceptual Modelling, vol. 53, pp. 95–104. Australian Computer Society, Inc. (2006)
70. Wohed, P., Aalst, W.M.P., Dumas, M., Hofstede, A.H.M., Russell, N.: On the suitability of BPMN for business process modelling. In: Dustdar, S., Fiadeiro, J.L., Sheth, A.P. (eds.) BPM 2006. LNCS, vol. 4102, pp. 161–176. Springer, Heidelberg (2006). doi:10.1007/11841760_12
71. Zur Muehlen, M., Indulska, M.: Modeling languages for business processes and business rules: a representational analysis. Inf. Syst. 35(4), 379–390 (2010)
72. van der Aalst, W.M.: Patterns and xpdl: a critical evaluation of the xml process definition language. BPM Center report BPM-03-09, BPMcenter.org, pp. 1–30 (2003)
73. Ning, K., Li, Q., Chen, Y.L.: Study of evaluation technology of business process modeling methods. Jisuanji Jicheng Zhizao Xitong/Comput. Integr. Manuf. Syst. (China) 8(10), 792–796 (2002)
74. Eloranta, L., Kallio, E., Terho, I.: A notation evaluation of BPMN and UML activity diagrams. Special course in information systems (2006)
75. Zachman, J.A.: A framework for information systems architecture. IBM Syst. J. 26(3), 276–292 (1987)
76. Saidani, O., Nurcan, S.: Towards context aware business process modelling. In: 8th Workshop on Business Process Modeling, Development, and Support (BPMDS 2007), CAiSE, vol. 7, p. 1 (2007)
77. Siau, K., Rossi, M.: Evaluation techniques for systems analysis and design modelling methods–a review and comparative analysis. Inf. Syst. J. 21(3), 249–268 (2011)
78. Krogstie, J.: Evaluating UML using a generic quality framework. In: Favre, L. (ed.) UML and the Unified Process. Idea Group Publishing, Hershey (2003)
79. Letsholo, K.J., Chioasca, E.V., Zhao, L.: An integrative approach to support multi-perspective business process modeling. Int. J. Serv. Comput. 2(1), 11–24 (2014)
80. Wolfswinkel, J.F., Furtmueller, E., Wilderom, C.P.: Using grounded theory as a method for rigorously reviewing literature. Eur. J. Inf. Syst. 22(1), 45–55 (2013)

# Designing a Decision-Making Process for Partially Observable Environments Using Markov Theory

Sérgio Guerreiro[1,2]($\boxtimes$)

[1] Instituto Superior Técnico, University of Lisbon,
Av. Rovisco Pais 1, 1049-001 Lisbon, Portugal
sergio.guerreiro@tecnico.ulisboa.pt
[2] INESC-ID, Rua Alves Redol 9, 1000-029 Lisbon, Portugal

**Abstract.** This paper is motivated by the problem of deciding how to proceed in a business process when a workaround occurs. In addition to this problem, most of the times, the exact state of the business processes is not fully available to the industrial organization. Therefore, it means that something wrong happens during automatic (or manual) operation; however, the managers do not know exactly the state of the operating systems. Usually, the combination of these problems drives to management decision without enough information and thus error prone. This paper integrates Markov theory with business processes design to predict the impact of each decision in the operational environment. The solution is tested in an agro-food industrial company that transforms fresh fruit to preparations that are sold to others companies. The paper shows that anticipating the production processes changes has the benefit of minimizing lot infections or stock disrupts. The main identified limitations are the compute intensive process involved and the effort required to estimate the business processes details. In future research, this work might be *(i)* extended to friendly software interfaces in order to facilitate the interaction with end-users, *(ii)* optimized to the algorithm of informed decision-making computation, and *(iii)* automatic estimation of business processes details using machine learning techniques.

**Keywords:** Actuation · Business processes · Instances · Markov theories · Models · Observation

## 1 Introduction

There are multiple endogenous and exogenous factors pressuring an organization, and consequently promoting the need to take decisions while business processes operate [21], *e.g.*, changing requirements, legal changes or attempted fraud in electronic invoicing and payments between enterprises. In response to these multiple changes, it is necessary to have native capabilities that continuously find innovative solutions to adapt the business processes to be more efficient and

© Springer International Publishing AG 2017
I. Reinhartz-Berger et al. (Eds.): BPMDS/EMMSAD 2017, LNBIP 287, pp. 257–271, 2017.
DOI: 10.1007/978-3-319-59466-8_16

effective. In this context, the existence of mechanisms to enable an informed decision-making [36] are key competences for the success of the organization's management.

This paper addresses the problem of decision-making in partially observable [27] environments[1] orchestrated by business processes. Business processes execution environments, *e.g.* operation of ERPs, CRMs or business intelligence, are by nature, complex systems with partially observable properties [24]. The stakeholders involved with this problem are the business processes decision makers: the business managers and the enterprise architects. Many evidences of this problem are corroborated in related research [20,23,32]. Our solution, aids the decision makers, providing causal maps that express the impacts of change on the organizational operation. Therefore, it minimizes the risk of making wrong decisions (*e.g.*, incorrect change of business processes [38]) and could power up a positive impact on the national economy services industry. Therefore, the challenge raised by this paper, is not only located in the scope of technology, but also, in the scope of business informatics: the intersection between the business management knowledge with the informatics required to support the enterprise's operation. So forth, the innovation of this paper is located in the integration, conceptual and technological, between two disjoints domain of knowledge: *(i)* the business processes in enterprise information systems, and *(ii)* the computational approaches to estimate the future behavior in partially observable environments. The ultimate goal is to make available to the organizational managers, a set of maps with impact estimation of their actions in the operational reality of the organization throughout time.

Regarding the methodological approach, this paper applies the principles of the design science research (DSR), as in [2,37,40], as a way to identify the constraints and the boundaries for the problem at hand. Figure 1 exhibits the essential DSR phases. Firstly, the design objective of supporting the Human decision in partially observable environments is motivated. Afterwards, the second DSR phase, involves the design of a solution using Markov theory integrated with business transaction models. Thirdly, an argumentative evaluation about the results delivered by an agro-food case study, using the principles proposed by [26], are presented. Designing and then evaluating the design is a research initiative that aims at discovering the future research opportunities. Furthermore, when decoupling the conceptual layer of the solution from the specific technological implementation details, it allows a future technological independent development.

This paper is organized as follow. Firstly, Sect. 2 compares our approach with others. After that, the solution design is presented in Sect. 3. Afterwards, Sect. 4 discusses the previous introduced design using a case study to support the results. Then, Sect. 5 evaluates the results obtained in the previous section. Finally, Sect. 6 concludes and identifies future work to follow up this research.

---

[1] Referred in the literature as the opposite of *"a system is completely observable if every state variable of the system affects some of the outputs"* [13], *i.e.*, *"a system is partially observable if some state variable of the system affects some of the outputs"*.

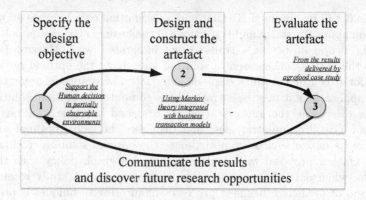

**Fig. 1.** Essential design science research (DSR) phases.

## 2  Related Work

This section summarizes work related to design and operation of decision making concerning partially known transactional environments and discusses how our contributions differ from that work.

Nowadays, the enforcement of decision making solutions where the states are not precisely defined, are primarily management-driven with few detail regarding business processes dynamics. Some evidences of this phenomenon could be found, *e.g.*, in the initial exploration of [36] using a probabilistic approach from descriptive and prescriptive decision theories to classify the utility of the different actions. Developing this idea, later, [24] argues that probabilistic approaches should be integrated with model definition to analyze the decision problems with more information. More recently, the process mining scientific domain [1, 29, 34] is an appropriate application example where new results and insights from business process executions are demanded. However, even in this domain, the solutions are mainly related with analyzing the past executions, grounded in the data mining techniques, and not with forecasting next executions using intelligent systems. By the contrary, our research is forecast-oriented. Moreover, process mining is usually exclusive based on petri nets, while our proposal depends on a tuple $S = <Actor, State, StateTransition, ControlRule>$ definition that could be derived from any business process notation, language or ontology. Finally, the amount of data required to use our solution is much lower than the large data sets used by process mining, this evidence is corroborated by the small amount of data obtained in the presential meetings and in the BPMN modelling.

Still in this line of reasoning, the work of Elovici and Braha [11] use an *ex-post* approach to provide an economic perspective towards the value of extracted knowledge to the organization, rather than our paper that uses an *ex-ante* approach. Comparing the benefit offered by our paper is the ability to forecast the impact of the current organization' decisions in the future, and therefore anticipate the reward that will be obtained. To that end, our solution only requires an *a priori* estimation about the states and transitions of the business process models.

In the scope of business transactions integrated with Markov Decision Process, the authors [35] present a solution for solving the optimal recommendations for executing product data models [28]. These authors refer that for real-life applications it may be intractable to compute the optimal solution. To overcome this issue, the authors attempts a second heuristic solution with a number of local decision strategies, that dismisses the global optimal solution, but where its outcome closely approximate the optimal solution calculated by a MDP. On our proposal we calculate the control graph policy with the current data, when data changes the graph is recomputed. A study towards the comparison of predictive business processes monitoring techniques is presented in [22]. The authors present results about machine learning, constraint satisfaction and QoS aggregation, but do not refer to the promising field of Markov theory. Moreover, Guerreiro [17] presents a solution to elicit the most valuable business transaction redesign in relation with a set of a priori defined alternatives. This work reduces the states explosion problem using the concept of business transaction space. However, the problem of non-observable states is not addressed and a single enterprise ontology for business transactions is used. Finally, Bonhomme [5] addresses the scope of unobservable transitions; however it is applied to the strict sense of petri nets, rather than to the abstract perspective of any business processes as proposed by our paper.

## 3   Formalization: The Design

This section presents a formalization towards the design of decision making solution in partial known transactional environments. Firstly, a set of intensional[2] definitions are presented to state the agreed meaning of each term. Afterwards, two propositions, grounded on the previous definitions, are presented. These propositions are the primary bearers of truth and falsity of this paper, and were the object of discussion during the course of this research. Section 4 grounds on these propositions to argue about the obtained results. The definitions and propositions are described textually and in addition, for some particular aspects, mathematical notation is used and properly referenced. Following related research [18] that proposes a separation between abstraction (model) and its representation (instantiation), Fig. 2 distinguishes design from operation. Moreover, an overall representation of the definitions and propositions is also depicted.

**Definition 1.** *Actor.* Could be human or machine, is an active part of the enterprise and is organized in a network where the individual and collective views of the enterprise coexist [10]. Actors have action freedom and act accordingly with their purposes and orchestrations [39], organized in a social system. Some portions of the enterprise tasks can be automated by software systems while human

---

[2] Intensional is usually defined as: giving the essence of a term.

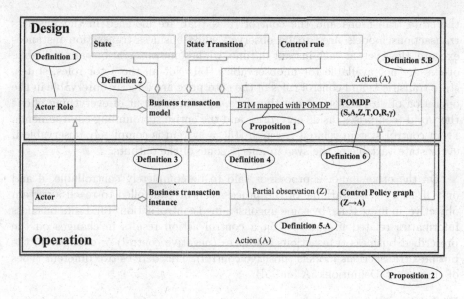

**Fig. 2.** Decision-making UML domain specification: separating the design and operation. Definitions and propositions are annotated.

actors perform others. An actor executes different activities over time. For performing an activity, an actor should fulfill tacitly or explicitly, an actor role. Therefore, an actor is an instance of an actor role. An actor is autonomous in deciding what to do next.

**Definition 2.** *Business transaction model.* Is the result of applying design constraints for a particular organizational reality, valid over a given period of time, and is used to share a common understanding between the stakeholders that have a diverse interpretation of it [16]. As defined by related research [9], a business transaction aggregates: *(i)* the actor roles, in order to specify who is responsible for each part of the transaction, who initiates it and who executes it, *(ii)* the states, specifying the set of allowable states of a system, *(iii)* the state transitions, specifying the set of allowable sequences of transitions of a system and *(iv)* the control rules, specifying what, and how, should be performed each state transition.

**Definition 3.** *Business transaction instance.* Is a realization of one or more business transaction models, by one or more actors, and is only revealed while the actors perform their actions. Therefore, the actors are responsible to instantiate the business transaction models. Many instances of a business transaction model could be executed at the same time in an organization. In line with this definition, related research has shown the need to decouple the model from its instances [8].

**Definition 4.** *Business transaction instance observation.* Observation is a core concern for controlling any system. To enable control, the actor roles, the states, the state transitions and the control rules that are modeled in the business transactions models need to be observed while business transaction instances execute. However, at each instant in time, while some observations are available, others are not available (or unobservable) [13]. Not all the actor roles, states, state transitions and control rules of the enterprise are directly observable in the operation of an enterprise; and therefore, not aware about of everything about the world (comprises inside enterprise and the entire surrounding environment). From control system related research [13], a system is completely observable if every state variable of the system affects some of the outputs.

On the other hand, a process is said to be completely controllable, if and only if, every state variable of the process can be controlled to reach a certain objective, in finite time, by some unconstrained control action [13]. From business informatics related literature [16], a control action results in changes on the prescribed business transactions instances (negative control) or changes on the business transactions models (positive control). This derives two different types of change, *cf.* Definitions 5A and 5B:

**Definition 5A.** *Business transaction instance change.* Constitutes the negative control counterpart, the currently running business transactions instanced are changed to mitigate the impact of unintended operations, *e.g.*, because something is currently wrong in operation.

**Definition 5B.** *Business transaction model change.* Constitutes the positive control counterpart, innovation is recognized as positive and the deviations from prescribed transactions models are incorporated as new prescriptions, constituting continuous organizational learning, *e.g.*, due to bad design or due to business processes transformation.

**Definition 6.** A *POMDP* stands for acronym of partial observable Markov decision process. In probabilities theory, a Markov process is a stochastic process that satisfies the Markov property [30]: if the transition probabilities from any given state depend only on the actual state and not on previous history. In other words, the predictions for future are solely based on its present state; future and past are independent. Markov theories are applied to systems that are controlled or uncontrolled (autonomous) *versus* observable or partial observable, as summarized in Table 1.

**Table 1.** Markov for controllable/uncontrollable *vs* observable/partial observable systems.

|                            | Observable system             | Partial observable system                              |
| -------------------------- | ----------------------------- | ------------------------------------------------------ |
| Non-controllable system    | Markov chain                  | Hidden Markov model (HMM)                              |
| Controllable system        | Markov decision process (MDP) | Partially observable Markov decision process (POMDP)   |

In detail, a Markov chain is used to refer to a process which has a countable and discrete set of state spaces, yet not controllable. When the states of process are only partial observable, then an hidden Markov model (HMM) should be used. A Markov decision process (MDP) is able to solve the problem of calculating an optimal policy in an accessible and stochastic environment with a known transition model [27]. A MDP is defined by the tuple $(S, A, T, R, \gamma)$. In partial accessible environments, or whenever the observation does not provide enough information to determine the states or the associated transition probabilities, then the hidden Markov model (HMM) or partially observable Markov decision process (POMDP) solutions should be considered. The difference is that HMM is applied to uncontrolled systems and POMDP to controlled systems. A POMDP solution provides a rich framework for planning under uncertainty [15]. A POMDP finds a mapping between observations (not states) to actions. In practice, two different states could appear to be observed equally. A POMDP is defined by the tuple $(S, A, Z, T, O, R, \gamma)$, where:

$S$ is a set of states, representing all the possible underlying states the process can be in, even if state is not directly observable;

$A$ is a set of actions, representing all the available control choices at each point in time;

$Z$ is a set of observations, consisting of all possible observations that the process can emit;

$T : A \times S_{start} \times S_{end} \rightarrow \prod(S)$ is a state transition function, where $\prod(.)$ is a probability distribution over some finite set, encoding the uncertainty in the system state evolution, *i.e.*, the probability to transit from $S_{start}$ to $S_{end}$ with a given action $A$;

$O : A \times S_{end} \times Z \rightarrow \prod(Z)$ is an observation function, relating the observations to the underlying state, *i.e.*, the probability of observing $Z$ for a particular action $A$ and an ending state $S_{end}$;

$R : A \times S_{start} \times S_{end} \times Z \rightarrow \mathbf{R}$ is an immediate reward function, giving the immediate utility for performing an action of the underlying states;

$\gamma$: discounted factor of future rewards, meaning the decay that a given achieved state suffers through out time.

The realization of a POMDP definition is given by a control policy graph in the form: $Z \rightarrow A$, *cf.* represented in Fig. 2.

**Proposition 1.** *Business transaction model* $\mapsto$ *POMDP.* To map the business transaction model definition with the POMDP specification, this paper formalizes a tuple $S$ definition containing all the concepts aggregated by the business transaction model, *cf.* Definition 2:

$S = <ActorRole, State, StateTransition, ControlRule>$

However, considering a partial observable system, each observation cannot be directly related with a specific $S$. By other words, what we observe from a state is not the same as the state itself. For instance, the state of order deliver could be partially observed by a signed document by the customer. Therefore, the order deliver state is an abstraction, that by its turn, is instantiated in the operation of the organization, when a document is signed. Leaving to the manager the difficult task of relating a signed document with the achievement of a given state. In this sense, our solution, follows the POMDP premise that an observation does not correspond to a $1:1$ state definition. In POMDP, each observation is used to compute the state where the system is believed to be (belief state).

The pseudo-code of the informed decision-making solution is given in Algorithm 1. The method starts by modeling the business transactions using a methodology with (at least) the capabilities of modeling the transition, the state and actor role spaces, *e.g.*, DEMO [9], SBPM [12], BPMN [14], *etc.* Afterwards, the business transactions models are instantiated in a set of memory less tuples as introduced previous in this section (*cf.* Definition 3). The advantage of decoupling steps 1 and 2 is because, in practice, is easier to instantiate the tuples $S$ after producing the business transactions model $M$. Then, step 3, $P$ is populated with the POMDP tuple estimation. Usually, it corresponds to a file creation in the POMDP format [6]. After that, from step 4 until 11, the POMDP is computed: (1) execute the action that the current node tells us; (2) receive the resulting observation from the world; (3) transition to next node based on the observation; (4) repeat to step (1). In the end, a policy graph mapping $Z \rightarrow A$ is delivered (*cf.* shadowed ellipse area in Fig. 3). Finally, the policy graph is rendered using any graphical tool.

---

**Algorithm 1.** Method to compute the informed decision-making process.

---

**Require:** Business transaction prescriptions
**Ensure:** Control policy graph $(Z \rightarrow A)$
1: **Set** $M \leftarrow$ Model the prescribed business transactions.
2: Instantiate $M$ in a set of tuples:
        $S =< Actor, State, StateTransition, ControlRule >$.
3: $P \leftarrow$ POMDP tuple $(S, A, Z, T, O, R, \gamma)$ estimation.
4: **for all** node of $P$ **do**
5:      **for each** $Z$ **do**
6:          Calculate $Prob(Z)$
7:          Calculate Belief State
8:          Calculate **R**
9:          Calculate $A$
10:     **end for**
11: **end for**
12: Render the computed policy graph $(Z \rightarrow A)$ using a graphical tool.

---

**Proposition 2.** *Business transaction model* run-time compliance control. To design and implement decision making the following POMDP solution is presented. For a POMDP, at each period, the environment is in some state $s \in S$. The manager takes an action $a \in A$, which causes the environment to transition to state $S'$ with probability $T(S'|S, a)$. And because the manager does not know the exact state the system is then the manager must estimate a probability distribution, known as *belief state*, over the possible states $S$. This estimation is used as a seed to be refined by the POMDP executions.

Figure 3 presents a diagram with one system transiting from state $S$ to $S'$, supported in partial observations, and using a belief state to achieve the reward on $S'$. Without knowing the actual state $S$ at time $t$ (cf. Fig. 3), the partial observation triggers the possibility of having one or more belief states. The challenge of solving a POMDP is to maximize the reward of a given action $A$ achieving the state $S'$ at time $t+1$, from the belief states. In the end, a control policy will yield the greatest amount of utility over some number of decision steps.

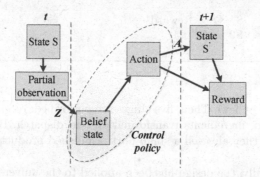

**Fig. 3.** State transition from state $S$ to state $S'$: the POMDP solution.

## 4   Case Study: Discussion

This section instantiates and discusses the design introduced in Sect. 3 following the presented Algorithm 1 supported by an industrial case study. The methodology followed to obtain the business transaction model is also presented.

The universe of discourse of this case study is summarized as follow. The client is an agro-food industrial company focusing the transformation of fresh fruits to preparations that are sold to other companies is herein considered. Its clients are industries of milk-based products, ice creams, cakes and beverages products. To guarantee the product quality, fruit producers are subject to a ratification process before starting supplying fruit. The fruit passes through three stages: *(i)* raw material, *(ii)* ingredients after raw material preparation, and *(iii)* finished product after ingredients transformation. Until reaching the end consumer, a complex value chain is executed including the actor roles of: client, fruit producer, raw material receptionist, ingredient preparator (*e.g.*, weighing and cleaning), ingredient transformer (*e.g.*, mixing components, adding water, sugar or other products accordingly with the recipe), finished product transporter and storage company (when the agro-food company is not able to locally store all the production). The production starts when a client order is received

**Listing 1.1.** POMDP file format example

```
1   discount : 0.05
2   values : reward
3   states : S1 , S2, S3, ...
4   actions : A1, A2, A3, ...
5   observations : O1, O2, O3, ...
6   # One textual row for each matrix cell
7   # A      S     S'   Probability
8   T: A1 : S1 : S2    0.98
9   ...
10  # A      S     O   Probability
11  O: A1 : S1 : O1 0.9700
12  ...
13  # A      S     S' O     Reward
14  R: A1 : S1 : S2 : O1   1
15  ...
```

(produce to order policy). Then, five stages are performed: receive supply, ingredients preparation, ingredients transformation and dispatch. Besides selling to other companies, they also sell a small part of finished products directly to the end consumer.

Methodologically, the design has been applied to the universe of discourse of this industrial case study, starting with face-to-face meetings to elicit the requirements of the business processes. After that, the requirements are transformed in business transactions models using BPMN specification language [25]. Many models were created and presented in a workshop session where the advantages and pitfalls of each model were discussed. A final model is reached as the result of group discussion. Afterwards, the parameters $(S, A, Z, T, O, R, \gamma)$ from Algorithm 1 were estimated by an iterative process between the research team and the agro-food company. At this stage, the company' knowledge about their past experiences is of key importance to estimate the $T$ and $O$ matrices. To obtain this knowledge, non-structured questions were posed to the company. For instance, *during the last year, how many trucks had problems while transporting the finish product to storage?*

In implementation terms, the POMDP configuration for this case study is loaded in a text file using a standard POMDP format [6] (an example is depicted in Listing 1.1). To facilitate the generation of the POMDP file (summing up to 7500 configuration lines in our case study) a JAVA application was specially developed for this purpose. For computation, the APPL toolkit [6], which is a recent C++ implementation running in Linux environment was used. But, currently, a set of others POMDP solvers are available to compute POMDP [7, 31,33].

For demonstration purposes, this paper describes a simulation scenario that is performed for a specific use case scenario regarding the subset of *"receive supply from the fruit producer"* tasks (usually considered in the industry as supplier). Within this subset, two scenarios are considered: *(1)* ratification process triggered (more complex involving more tasks related with lot inspection) and *(2)* no ratification process involved (simpler: only receiving the fruit and transform it).

The result is delivered by a control policy graph mapping the observations ($Z$) into actions ($A$), maximizing the reward, and yielding the greatest amount of utility over the different decisions through out a time-wide horizon, as depicted by Fig. 3. Whenever a decision is needed, this control policy graph is, by the manager, as a decision map which forecasts the impact of each $A$ in the organizational operation.

From the management perspective, two findings were obtained during the course of this research. On the one hand, the policy graph visualization must fit a legibility criteria, *i.e.*, the POMDP probabilities configuration for scenario 2 is simpler resulting in a smaller control policy graph. For scenario 1, 4095 nodes and 4084 branches are obtained, whereas scenario 2, contains only 6 nodes and 8 branches. Scenario 2 provides a clearer visualization for the manager to have a better insight on actions, and their impact on the decision process. To solve this issue, if the policy graph is consulted manually then complexity reduction is suggested. Otherwise, if the policy graph is exported to any automatic decision-support system (DSS), *e.g.* PRO/M or DISCO, then all the branches are recommended.

On the other hand, the graph computation is intensive with growing complexity. Considering the setup from our case study, a growth in terms of nodes and branches along with the linear growth of the graph depth is exhibited. Therefore, taking this aspect in consideration, a POMDP implementation should *(i)* minimize the control policy depth and *(ii)* repeat the calculation process whenever new observations are acquired.

From the business processes modeling perspective, we remark that only 28,57% BPMN tasks transitions were considered for demonstration of this POMDP simulation. A full coverage of the BPMN model is possible, but, too extensive to be included in the scope of this paper. Moreover, scenario 1 uncovers the complexity that is usually inherited when a single BPMN model is designed. The operation of a BPMN model could have an explosive combination of states leading to an unmanageable situation.

In regard Proposition 1 (*Business transaction model $\mapsto$ POMDP*), this research identifies that the solution may be used to evaluate other set of business processes from any organization context, given the fact that POMDP evaluation method only depends on the estimation process that is defined for each business process reality and on the integration with $Z, T, O$ and $R$ matrices. Nevertheless, estimation effort is required; however, this is not a counterpart because management already uses it for decades. Moreover, this approach, has many similarities with management estimation approaches, *e.g.*, COCOMO2 [4], where the manager needs to analyze the *(i)* requirements and the *(ii)* major indicators related with software requirements, in order to receive an accurate effort estimation. The more detail analyzed, the better estimation results are obtained.

In regard, Proposition 2 (*Business transaction model* run-time compliance control), this research explores the benefits of using a stochastic approach supporting business processes management decisions, *e.g.*, business processes design or re-engineering. This paper defeat the idea that this goal can be achieved if decision makers are empowered with all pertinent information to forecast the impacts of their decisions in the near future of the organization. In this sense, decision makers could simulate different configurations (and evaluate them) before its implementation, and subsequently understand the impact of their actions in the operation of the enterprise. Moreover, with this paper, and based on related research that defines enterprise governance as: *"the organizational competence for continuously exercising, guiding the authority over enterprise strategy and architecture development, and the subsequent design, implementation and operation of the enterprise"* [19], we are designing and operating run-time compliance control, by prescribing a real implementation for observing, measuring, deciding and acting in the operation of the enterprise and thus improving enterprise governance.

## 5   Evaluation

Following the rigor imposed by DSR methodology, the conceptual map is analysed using the four principles of *(i)* abstraction, *(ii)* originality, *(iii)* justification and *(iv)* benefit as proposed by [26]. In light of this, the previous conceptualization and instantiation is argued and the following results are delivered:

1. *Abstraction* (**the solution must be applicable to a class of problems**) - the presented conceptualization and instantiation could be applied to other business processes, considering the following facts: *(i)* our experiment used an implementation independent language: BPMN (which is founded in petri nets theory) showing that any BPMN model is easily integrated with the discrete Markov theory; *(ii)* we found in the related literature other successfully attempts to use Markov theory with business processes, however, our proposal's innovation is the ability to predict future behavior from incomplete execution environments; and *(iii)* the conceptualization (six definitions and two propositions) is grounded in the General Systems Theory [3], which is widely used to systems analysis.

2. *Originality* (**the solution must substantially contribute to the advancement of the body of knowledge**) - by our knowledge there is no other solution that is able to predict the impact of management decisions in the operation of business transactions using a probabilistic approach with incomplete execution environments. Moreover, the solution conceptualization facilitates the communication of this solution between practitioners and academics.

3. *Justification* (**the solution must be justified in a comprehensible manner and must allow validation**) - the conceptualization, as depicted in Fig. 2, decouples the concepts of modeling (the Design part) from operating

concerns (the Operation part), thus facilitating the understanding of concepts and relations between the design and operation. UML specification language helps in communicating the domain of concern in decision-making. A highlight is given for the relation between operation and design: actor role is a generalization of an actor; business transaction model is a generalization of business transaction instance; and POMDP is a generalization of a control policy graph $Z \rightarrow A$. By its turn, $Z \rightarrow A$ is associated with two concepts: business transaction instance and business transaction model. The first association is triggered when the action $A$ recalling for a change in *run-time*, while the second association recalls to an action $A$ changing the *design-time*. Moreover, the delivered policy graph $Z \rightarrow A$ could be used to validate whether the solution fits the problem or deviates from goal. Nevertheless, to present large policy graph (as the one obtained in our case study) is still required more effort to transform the results in a purposeful way.

4. *Benefit* (**the solution must deliver benefit, immediately or in the future for the respective stakeholder groups**) - a major innovation of this proposal is the ability to predict future behavior in incomplete observable execution environments. In the future, further improvements for the policy graph visualization will benefit the stakeholder's with the correct information at the correct time.

# 6 Conclusion

Business managers, enterprise architects, and other decision makers, at their different competence layers, need to take decisions that are based upon the available observations at each instant in time. Because of partially available information, these observations do not fully describe the actual state of the organization and sends to decision makers the problem of guessing what is the state that organization actually is. Markov theory is conceived to solve exactly this problem. However, to enforce Markov theory in the decision making process, many constructional details of the organization dynamics' is demanded. This paper overcome this problem using BPMN business transaction models. Afterwards, BPMN is combined with Markov theory. The main benefit delivered is to predict the future behavior of business transaction instances in partially observable execution environments.

This paper delivers the following: *(i)* an UML decision-making design delivering the definitions, propositions and their relationships; and thus, conceptualizing our domain of interest, and *(ii)* an algorithm to calculate the informed decision-making process; and thus, allowing the reproducibility of results.

Regarding future work, the estimation of $T$ and $O$ matrices is actually a complex task that will require the development of automatic tools. Besides this, the more integration between POMDP and business transactions models is needed. Moreover, the visualization and computation of the control policies also offer new research challenges to future improvements.

**Acknowledgments.** This work was supported by national funds through Fundação para a Ciência e a Tecnologia (FCT) with reference UID/CEC/50021/2013.

# References

1. van der Aalst, W.M.P.: Process Mining: Discovery, Conformance and Enhancement of Business Processes. Database Management & Information Retrieval. Springer, Heidelberg (2011)
2. von Alan, R.H., March, S.T., Park, J., Ram, S.: Design science in information systems research. MIS Q. **28**(1), 75–105 (2004)
3. Bertalanffy, L.V.: General Systems Theory. George Braziller, New York (1969)
4. Boehm, B.W., Madachy, R., Steece, B., et al.: Software Cost Estimation with Cocomo II with Cdrom. Prentice Hall PTR, Upper Saddle River (2000)
5. Bonhomme, P.: Marking estimation of p-time petri nets with unobservable transitions. IEEE Trans. Syst. Man Cybern. Syst. **45**(3), 508–518 (2015)
6. Cai, P.: Approximate POMDP planning (appl) toolkit (2010). https://github.com/petercaiyoyo/appl
7. Cassandra, A.R.: POMDP solver (v53 2005). http://www.pomdp.org/code/index.shtml
8. De Bruyn, P., Huysmans, P., Oorts, G., Mannaert, H., Verelst, J.: Using entropy's justificatory knowledge for a business process design theory. In: 2014 47th Hawaii International Conference on System Sciences (HICSS), pp. 3717–3726. IEEE (2014)
9. Dietz, J.L.G.: Enterprise Ontology: Theory and Methodology. Springer, Heidelberg (2006)
10. Dietz, J.L., Hoogervorst, J.A., Albani, A., Aveiro, D., Babkin, E., Barjis, J., Caetano, A., Huysmans, P., Iijima, J., van Kervel, S., et al.: The discipline of enterprise engineering. Int. J. Organ. Des. Eng. **3**(1), 86–114 (2013)
11. Elovici, Y., Braha, D.: A decision-theoretic approach to data mining. IEEE Trans. Syst. Man Cybern. Part A Syst. Hum. **33**(1), 42–51 (2003)
12. Fleischmann, A., Stary, C.: Whom to talk to? A stakeholder perspective on business process development. Univ. Access Inf. Soc. **11**(2), 125–150 (2012). http://dx.doi.org/10.1007/s10209-011-0236-x
13. Franklin, G., Powell, J., Emami-Naeini, A.: Feedback Control of Dynamic Systems, 2nd edn. Addison-Wesley Publishing Company, Reading (1991)
14. Group, O.M: BPMN specification 1.2. pdf available in internet, January 2009
15. Guerreiro, S.: Decision-making in partially observable environments. In: 2014 IEEE 16th Conference on Business Informatics (CBI), vol. 1, pp. 159–166, July 2014
16. Guerreiro, S., Tribolet, J.: Conceptualizing enterprise dynamic systems control for run-time business transactions. In: European Conference on Information Systems (ECIS) 2013, paper 5 (2013)
17. Guerreiro, S.: Business rules elicitation combining Markov decision process with demo business transaction space. In: 2013 IEEE 15th Conference on Business Informatics (CBI), pp. 13–20 (2013)
18. Guizzardi, G.: On ontology, ontologies, conceptualizations, modeling languages, and (meta) models. Front. Artif. Intell. Appl. **155**, 18 (2007)
19. Hoogervorst, J.A.: Enterprise Governance and Enterprise Engineering. The Enterprise Engineering Series. Springer, Heidelberg (2009)
20. Johnson, P., Ullberg, J., Buschle, M., Franke, U., Shahzad, K.: An architecture modeling framework for probabilistic prediction. Inf. Syst. e-Bus. Manag. **12**(4), 595–622 (2014)

21. Laudon, K.C., Laudon, J.P., et al.: Essentials of Management Information Systems. Pearson, Upper Saddle River (2011)

22. Metzger, A., Leitner, P., Ivanovi, D., Schmieders, E., Franklin, R., Carro, M., Dustdar, S., Pohl, K.: Comparing and combining predictive business process monitoring techniques. IEEE Trans. Syst. Man Cybern. Syst. **45**(2), 276–290 (2015)

23. Mikaelian, T., Nightingale, D.J., Rhodes, D.H., Hastings, D.E.: Real options in enterprise architecture: a holistic mapping of mechanisms and types for uncertainty management. IEEE Trans. Eng. Manag. **58**(3), 457–470 (2011)

24. Montiel, L., Bickel, J.: A simulation-based approach to decision making with partial information. Decis. Anal. **9**(4), 329–347 (2012)

25. OMG: Business process model and notation (2011). http://www.omg.org/spec/BPMN/2.0/

26. Österle, H., Becker, J., Frank, U., Hess, T., Karagiannis, D., Krcmar, H., Loos, P., Mertens, P., Oberweis, A., Sinz, E.J.: Memorandum on design-oriented information systems research. Eur. J. Inf. Syst. **20**(1), 7–10 (2011)

27. Puterman, M.L.: Markov Decision Processes: Discrete Stochastic Dynamic Programming. Wiley, New York (1994)

28. Reijers, H.A., Limam, S., van der Aalst, W.M.P.: Product-based workflow design. J. Manag. Inf. Syst. **20**(1), 229–262 (2003)

29. Rozinat, A., van der Aalst, W.M.P.: Conformance checking of processes based on monitoring real behavior. Inf. Syst. **33**(1), 64–95 (2008). doi:10.1016/j.is.2007.07.001

30. Russell, S., Norvig, P.: Artificial Intelligence: A Modern approach. Artificial Intelligence, 3rd edn. Prentice Hall, Englewood Cliffs (2010)

31. Smith, T.: ZMDP software for POMDP and MDP planning (2007). https://github.com/trey0/zmdp

32. Sommestad, T., Ekstedt, M., Johnson, P.: A probabilistic relational model for security risk analysis. Comput. Secur. **29**(6), 659–679 (2010)

33. Spaan, M.: Perseus randomized point-based approximate value iteration algorithm (2004). http://users.isr.ist.utl.pt/mtjspaan/software/index_en.html

34. van der Aalst, W.M.P., et al.: Process mining manifesto. In: Daniel, F., Barkaoui, K., Dustdar, S. (eds.) BPM 2011. LNBIP, vol. 99, pp. 169–194. Springer, Heidelberg (2012). doi:10.1007/978-3-642-28108-2_19

35. Vanderfeesten, I., Reijers, H.A., Van der Aalst, W.M.P.: Product-based workflow support. Inf. Syst. **36**(2), 517–535 (2011)

36. Weber, M.: Decision making with incomplete information. Eur. J. Oper. Res. **28**(1), 44–57 (1987)

37. Wieringa, R.J.: Design Science Methodology for Information Systems and Software Engineering. Springer, London (2014)

38. Wilf, J., Port, D.: Decisions and disasters: modeling decisions that contribute to mishaps. In: 2016 49th Hawaii International Conference on System Sciences (HICSS), pp. 5635–5641. IEEE (2016)

39. Winograd, T.: A language/action perspective on the design of cooperative work. In: Proceedings of the 1986 ACM Conference on Computer-Supported Cooperative Work, pp. 203–220. ACM (1986)

40. Winter, R.: Design science research in Europe. Eur. J. Inf. Syst. **17**(5), 470–475 (2008)

# Know-How Mapping – A Goal-Oriented Approach and Evaluation

Arnon Sturm[1,2(✉)], Eric Yu[1], and Sadra Abrishamkar[1]

[1] University of Toronto, Toronto, Canada
eric.yu@utoronto.ca, sadrayan@gmail.com
[2] Ben-Gurion University of the Negev, Beer Sheva, Israel
sturm@bgu.ac.il

**Abstract.** Information system developers have to cope with a continually changing technological landscape. Knowing what each kind of technique or technology can do and how well they perform under various conditions constitute an important kind of know-how that systems professionals seek. In this paper, we claim that such know-how information can be structured as a map, so as to facilitate understanding and decision making about what technology to adopt or develop. Recent work has proposed to use a goal-oriented approach to address the challenge of constructing such a map. In this paper, we examine the hypothesis that a goal-oriented approach can be used for mapping and analyzing technological domains. First, we apply the approach to several domains, to verify the applicability and expressiveness of the approach. Second, we perform a feature-based analysis and examine the extent to which the approach addresses the desired characteristics of a know-how map. Third, we conduct a controlled experiment in which the comprehension of goal-oriented know-how maps in comparison to a textual summary from a literature review was examined. The evaluation results indicate that the goal-oriented know-how maps have sufficient expressiveness, are easy to read and understand, and address a number of desired characteristics.

## 1 Introduction

Information technologies have greatly accelerated the rate of knowledge production and dissemination. In some domains, knowledge is said to be doubling every few years, making it hard for practitioners and even researchers to keep pace. In technology areas, we are especially concerned with know-how, the kind of knowledge that guides action towards practical objectives, prescribing solutions to technical problems [5, 13].

Within technical fields such as information systems engineering, new techniques are constantly being invented and evaluated, as reported in research conferences and journals. While there have been enormous strides at the infrastructure level to the extent that we have almost instant access to published literature online, there has been little advance in how a body of know-how is organized for easier access and understanding. To learn quickly about a technology area and its latest developments, we are most likely to use text-string based searches in online repositories, not different from searching for any general piece of information. Thus, we are not able to use the

© Springer International Publishing AG 2017
I. Reinhartz-Berger et al. (Eds.): BPMDS/EMMSAD 2017, LNBIP 287, pp. 272–286, 2017.
DOI: 10.1007/978-3-319-59466-8_17

means-ends structure of technical know-how to seek potential solutions to problems, or to gain an overall understanding of the state-of-the-art of the domain.

In information systems engineering, goal-oriented techniques have been introduced to guide systems development to meet stakeholder needs and requirements [11, 19]. Goal-oriented requirements engineering (GORE) techniques rely fundamentally on means-ends knowledge which offer alternate ways for achieving goals while contributing positively or negatively to "non-functional" properties. While means-ends knowledge are used in requirements engineering to achieve goals for a particular system or project, the same conceptual structure can potentially be adapted to organize and manage a body of means-ends knowledge for a technology domain.

In earlier work, a goal modeling approach has been proposed for mapping the know-how of a technology domain [7]. In this paper, we outline the know-how mapping technique based on *i\**, illustrating the technique as applied to the knowledge domain of web mining. We analyze the technique with respect to several desirable characteristics, and evaluate how well the know-how map facilitates domain comprehension compared to a textual literature review in a controlled experiment.

The paper is organized as follows. Section 2 introduces the Goal-Oriented Knowledge Mapping (GOKM) approach and elaborates on its application to the Web mining domain. Section 3 reviews alternative approaches for knowledge mapping and compares it to the GOKM approach. Section 4 presents the feature analysis of the GOKM approach, whereas Sect. 5 elaborates on the controlled experiment we performed in order to test the comprehension of a GOKM map. Finally, Sect. 6 concludes and sets plans for future research.

## 2    The Goal-Oriented Know-How Mapping Approach

The GOKM approach adopts a subset of *i\** [20] for mapping out a knowledge domain. The subset of *i\** notations was selected to capture the means-ends relationships among the available solutions and problems in the knowledge domain. A major reason for selecting a subset of the *i\** capabilities is to keep the mapping approach as simple as possible. It should be emphasized that the aim of GOKM is to **_map_** and highlight the means-ends structure of the knowledge domain. It is not meant for describing the details of mechanisms, behaviors, and processes of alternative solutions. The novelty introduces by the GOKM approach is the use of *i\** for representing the structure of the knowledge of a domain (e.g., as presented in technical papers) rather than for modeling and analyzing a system. We use a subset of *i\** constructs as follows: A *goal* is used to represent a problem to be addressed. For example in Fig. 1, which presents a partial view of the web mining map, *Information to be extracted from web data* is a goal. Another goal in that map is *Web template to be detected*. Note that while the former represents the overall purpose of the map/domain, the latter arises as part of a solution required to achieve a higher goal. Solutions are represented as *tasks* that are proposed for achieving a goal. There may be multiple solutions to a goal, which means there is more than one way of achieving the goals. *Soft-goals* are used as evaluation criteria of solutions, serving to support tradeoff analysis of solutions. In the context of GOKM, soft-goals are qualitative values that are attached to the solution, which describe benefits or shortcomings of the solution. The support that each solution contributes to each of the desired criteria is indicated using the *i\* contribution links*. These links can be of type: hurt, some-, break, unknown, help, some+, make.

The domain we chose to demonstrate GOKM in this paper is web mining as it is well suited to illustrating our objective of mapping out a technology domain. The know-how map can be constructed in a top-down or bottom-up fashion. When using the top-down approach, one may take advantage of secondary sources that already provides some kind of structuring or classification (e.g., a review article or a textbook on the topic area). In the bottom-up approach, the mapping begins with a single primary source. As additional sources are being mapped, the know-how map expands and evolves. In this paper, we adopted the top-down approach. We used [10] as a secondary source of knowledge to map out the web mining domain. The references to the primary source for each node appear in the map in square brackets (these primary sources are not part of this paper).

The partial map described in Fig. 1 consists of the following. The main goal of *Information to be extracted from web data* consists of two sub-goals: *Information to be searched and retrieved* and *Web information to be prepared for web mining*. The latter can be addressed by three alterative goals: *Text and web pages to be pre-processed*, *Web information to be removed from data*, and *Information blocks to be extracted from web page*. The first goal can be achieved by *Stemming*, *Duplicate detection*, and *Stop word removal*. Each of the solutions contributes differently to various soft-goals which are essential criteria for evaluating these solutions. These include *precision*, *recall*, *smaller index*, *SEO*, and *Phrase search*.

Having constructed such a map, one can query or reason about it with various questions like what are the properties that need to be discussed in relation to mining web information? what are the required actions? what solutions and techniques exist? what are the tradeoff in using these solution and techniques? and where improvement be introduced?

Querying technical domains is generally done through formal text queries. However, understanding the meaning of research concepts remains the major source of error in retrieving good quality results from such queries. The know-how map presents a short form description of the goals and solutions available in the domain. Having a visual view over a domain, the identification of the goals and solutions are becoming easier. In particular, the concepts provided by the GOKM approach facilitate the querying and reasoning by outlining the means-end relationships of the goals and available solutions in a specific knowledge domain.

An important aspect of reasoning is the ability to identify the means-end relationship. This task is generally dependent on the researcher/experts of the domain to outline those relationships. For example, based on the partial map of the domain in Fig. 1, we can reason about the task of *Stemming*, which is considered to a part of the solution to the goal *Text and web-page to be pre-processed*. Further, the effects of the solution can be evaluated based on the qualitative relation of the solution and its related soft-goals.

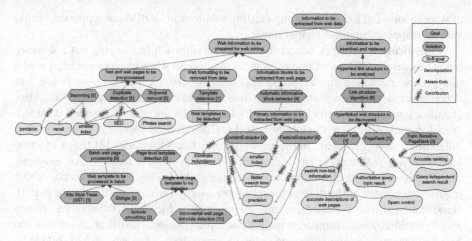

**Fig. 1.** A partial view of the web mining map

We applied GOKM to various domains including agent-oriented software engineering, architecture description languages (ADL), data mining, customer retention, and variability in business process. We found that in its current form the GOKM has sufficient expressiveness for the mapping purposes we set out above.

## 3    Other Approaches to Knowledge Mapping

Knowledge mapping has emerged from various areas [1]. In the following, we present techniques that can be utilized for the purpose of knowledge mapping and analyzing these in light of desired properties: ease of use, expressiveness, evolution, reasoning capabilities, and process support.

**Tabular representation (TAB)** is a prevalent approach to summarize and map out a domain or a sub set of it. Tables present selected features in some table dimensions and approaches in another. Once constructed, tables are typically easy to overview. However, tabular representations have limitations. Tables, while offering some reasoning, for example, to choose a best possible alternative, do not include the rationale for selecting the features according to which approaches are compared nor is the rationale for evaluations or ranking easily given. Also, it is not possible to show relevant relationships among approaches, making tabular representations less expressive. Tables are typically resilient to change. Yet, some evolution needs are supported such as the addition of rows or columns to add approaches, and/or features to include in a comparison. Deeper "taxonomical" changes to the feature set used to compare and contrast, typically require reworking the whole table. Finally, from a process point of view, a table helps to systematically guide a reviewer, such as, what features to look out for when analyzing a new approach, however, no guidance is offered in identifying features relevant for the comparison.

The GOKM approach is more flexible and allows for changes during its evolution. As it has a precise meaning of its concepts, mappers are provided with some guidelines of what to look for. Relations among existing solutions in GOKM are supported via the various mapping language relationships.

**Classification (CLS)** is similar to the tabular approach in mapping out a domain, but is less detailed. Classification is, in particular, useful when clustering related works into groups exhibiting similar properties. Usually, classification is easy to use, but expressiveness to differentiate between related works and studies is limited. Also, classification is sensitive to changes, i.e., when the classification is changed there is a need for re-classification all classified works. Classification approaches come in four different variants: hierarchy, trees, paradigm, and faceted analysis [8]. Each of these has, however, problems when dealing with complex subject matters. For example, classification cannot deal with works that require multiple classification criteria, or that involve knowledge at the different level of granularity (level of abstraction or detail); classification also have limited explanatory power [8], which limits the ability to reason about classified works. Similar to the tabular representation, classification offers some help in systematizing reviews, once classifications have been established, however, little support is given in establishing classifications themselves during the review of a domain.

Classification in GOKM can be achieved by focusing on a sub-graph of the know-how map. As it maps out each contribution separately, an analysis and reasoning about each contribution and the relationships among these can be easily achieved.

**Hierarchical Value Maps (HVM)** were developed to represent properties of product and service in commercial settings and placed them in higher contexts of human needs. More specifically, HVMs connect through means-ends links product or service attributes, to perceived benefits or costs, and to higher level values that represent customer believes and that guide the customer's choices [6]. HVM could be used to map out problems and solutions during an exploration of an engineering domain. When keeping to the structure proposed by HVMs the result would offer a description of problems and solutions at a high-level of abstraction. Once HVM has been constructed, they are typically easy to understand. However, the initial construction may be harder, given the fixed level of means-end chains offered. HVMs also lack constructs in highlighting the difference between alternative solutions to problems. Resilience to change, evolution of HVM and reasoning with such maps seem to be supported.

In relation to HVM, GOKM facilitates the mapping of criteria that can be used to analyze the tradeoff among solutions.

**Cause maps (CM)** can be seen as a variant of HVMs, without however restricting levels of chained concepts. CMs are directed graphs which most often take some form of cause and effect graph [4]. Cause maps are often used to analyze decision-making process, which are differently affected by preconditions values. In terms of our evaluation criteria, CMs are essentially similar to HVM. Cause maps are constructed using nodes and links thereby offering flexibilities in mapping domains. However, using cause maps also has limitations in mapping engineering domains. Cause maps do not distinguish between problems and desirable properties associated with problems and thus are lacking in an essential goal of a know-how map which is a tradeoff analysis among alternatives.

With respect to CM, GOKM facilitates the identification of solutions and problems and their associated properties that can be used for analyzing the domain. GOKM also provides a mapping over a domain that can be used for various purposes, whereas CM aim at providing rules for decision making.

**Conceptual graphs (CG)** [15] is composed of concepts and conceptual links which were formalized to support the inference in a database. Later on, the notion of semantic networks was introduced [16] and a large number of conceptual graph variants have been proposed including less formal variants, such as concept maps [12], mind mapping [3], claim oriented graphs [14], and graphical design rationale models [2]. CGs offer a graphical representation to capture concepts and relationships among concepts to capture domain knowledge. Concepts are connected with labeled arrows, which are sometimes visually presented in a downward-branching hierarchical structure. CGs maps help to explore knowledge "chunks" in a domain of interest. To analyze CGs in terms of the aforementioned properties it is useful to distinguish between formal and less formal CG approaches. Formal approaches offer concept types and formal relationships that facilitate different kinds of reasoning, while informal approaches, such as concept maps, only offer one type of node and link, which can however be informally labeled arbitrarily. Informal CGs are consequently easier to use, but also offer only limited reasoning support. Both groups support evolution to a large extent. Given the flexibility of CGs in how they can be used, they only offer limited guidance during the mapping process.

With respect to the conceptual graph, GOKM bridges the gap between the informal and the formal CG approaches by providing meanings to elements and allows analysis and reasoning, yet, keeping the simplicity of informal approaches.

**Formal knowledge representations approaches** are approaches that offer sophisticated logical machinery to represent and analyze knowledge [9]. Such approaches could in principle be utilized to represent and capture knowledge included in technical domains. However, formal knowledge representation approaches are typically heavy weight, making them hard to use and understand. Offering formal knowledge representation approaches to researchers and practitioners would require tailored and simplified user interfaces to support capturing technical knowledge. Furthermore, such approaches are often neutral in relation to the type of knowledge they capture, and hence the appropriate meta model or ontologies would need to be predefined before particular user interfaces could be furnished and technical knowledge captured.

With respect to formal approaches, the GOKM approach provides a generic (i.e., domain independent) reasoning mechanism and further ease the use of the know-how mapping due to its low number of modeling constructs.

## 4   A Feature Analysis of GOKM

In this section we analyze GOKM in light of the properties stated above, namely: Ease of Use that refers to the ease of creating and understanding maps; Expressiveness that refers to the level of which the approach is sufficient to be used for mapping knowledge, including clustering and differentiation; Evolution that refers to the support of map advancement; Reasoning that refers to the whether the approach semantics allow for reasoning; and Process Support that refers to the guidance of knowledge elicitation and modeling during mapping efforts.

*Ease of use:* As the GOKM modeling language consists of only a subset of *i\** - resulting in a small number of modeling constructs with clear semantics, we believe that it would be easy to use and understand.

*Expressiveness:* Based on our experience with GOKM in various domains we found that it supports the capturing of problems and solutions through goals and tasks, their qualification through soft-goals, the relationships among problems and solutions, through achieved-by and consists-of links, and trade-offs among solutions through contribution links. Furthermore, the rationale of the various elements could be explicated via contribution links. Nevertheless, it might be useful to add constructs that allow for logical relationships among concepts.

*Evolution:* As the GOKM is based on a connected graph, elements of any type can be deleted, changed, and added at any stage of the mapping process, while having only local effects, without the need for major mapping rework. This means that in case contribution changes, only relevant links would be changed. In case an element is updated, nothing is required to be changed. In case an element is deleted, its related links are omitted too, yet all other elements remain unchanged. Thus, we believe that the GOKM has a good support for maps' evolution.

*Reasoning:* We found that given the semantics of GOKM, different kinds of reasoning can be performed. For example, to select the best alternative based on the contribution links, to find gaps, where problems exist while no solution has been proposed, or where contribution link negatively affect certain qualities, without solutions that have positive contributions to that quality.

*Process Support:* Akey driver during the constructing GOKM is intentionality: what is the intent behind a solution or a solution element. This helps in continuously question the motivation for each of the mapped elements (to ask why), and thus guide the map creator/developer in critical thinking, which in turn is an essential aspect of mapping a domain.

## 5   A Controlled Experiment with GOKM

Having described the GOKM approach we were interested in confirming its benefits. To examine that, we conducted a controlled experiment. In the following, we describe the objectives of the experiment, its design process and execution, as well as the results, their analysis and a discussion.

**Objectives.** The main objective of the controlled experiment was to evaluate the effectiveness of understanding a knowledge domain by comparing it to a widely used technique – a written review. A written review is the baseline for all other means for knowledge mapping. The written review is designed to mimic a short literature review of the domain. We compared the two approaches in terms of the level of understanding of the domain, and the relative time it takes users to find answers to given questions. A by-product of the experiment is to check the extent to which one understands a know-how map generated by others. We also analyzed how the familiarity of the participants with goal-oriented concepts affected the comprehension of the domain.

**Hypotheses.** The objective of the experiment was to examine the effectiveness of understanding a knowledge domain. We had the following two hypotheses regarding the GOKM approach:

- GOKM facilitates a ***better*** understanding of a domain than a written review. The reason for the hypothesis is that GOKM can help navigating domains more effectively, as it follows a set of clear relationships among know-how concepts, and thus provide a better understanding of the domain.
- GOKM facilitates a *faster* understanding of a domain than a written review. The reason for the hypothesis is that GOKM illustrates key points of the domain by focusing on the relationships between the problems and solutions in a domain allowing for easier navigation.

We further examine the above hypotheses with respect to four dimensions: identifying problems, identifying solutions, evaluating alternative solutions, and finding knowledge gaps.

Another facet we aimed to explore is whether the familiarity with goal-oriented concepts and modelling approach affects the results. Our hypothesis is that the participant's performance over time and comprehension of the domain is positively affected, if they have a background in goal-oriented concepts and modelling.

**Experiment design.** In order to test the comprehension of a domain, we first design a written review and a GOKM map. The written review is designed to represents a short survey of the knowledge domain of two pages long. To have comparable artifacts, the written review and the GOKM map shared the same lexical space. Furthermore, the written review is structured to contain equivalent amount of information with the clear relations of the problem statements and proposed solutions. We also kept the written review to contain the minimal required information although usually such a review is written more as a prose rather than as a structured text. Next, we devise a questionnaire (partially appears in the Appendix) to examine the comprehension of the domain from various aspects: finding problems, finding alternatives, evaluating alternative solutions, evaluating the solution's effects, and finding knowledge gap. The questionnaire was framed in such way to simulate the information need of the user when looking for an answer in the knowledge domain. The experiment setting follows a similar experiment design as discussed in [18].

Specifically, we designed the experiment to have three groups: *G1*- Participants with no goal-oriented background working with the know-how map; *G2*- Participants with goal-oriented background working with the know-how map and G3 - Participants working with the written review.

The experiment form includes (1) a section collecting background information of the participants; (2) a section dealing with the domain comprehension task comprised of open-ended questions about the web mining domain; and (3) a section that had reflection questions, which ask participants about their experience with retrieving information while doing the experiment.

While designing the main comprehension task we followed the principles of: (1) Information equivalence – we checked that the information provided in both the know-how map and the written review is equivalent and both groups are provided with the information needed to answer the questions; (2) Gold standard solution – before the experiment took place we prepared a solution with grading scheme to avoid bias when checking the participant forms; and (3) Ethics – before executing the experiment we got the approval of the university ethic committee.

**Experiment execution.** The participants in the experiment were voluntary recruited and were motivated by a monetary compensation for completing the experiment. The participants were academics which are familiar with scholarly search and are used to look for solutions to existing problems. We were able to recruit 12 participants and assign them to the three groups.

**Training.** The participants of both G1 and G2 groups were given a ten minutes' interactive demo on a simple GOKM graph to familiarize them with basic concepts of GOKM. This demo was required for both groups since even though G2 participants had goal-oriented knowledge, the GOKM components and approach were new to them. The demo focused on demonstrating the problem-solution aspect of GOKM and explained the means-ends and decomposition relationships among the components.

**Task.** The primary task of participants in this experiment was to explore and navigate the domain material in order to answer questions about the domain. Participants have to refer to the domain material (either the GOKM map or the written review) to answer the questions. While answering the questions, participants also had to record the start and end time for each of the questions.

**Table 1.** Overall results per question per group

| Q# | G1 | | G2 | | G3 | |
|---|---|---|---|---|---|---|
| | Correctness average (%) | Average time (sec) | Correctness average (%) | Average time (sec) | Correctness average (%) | Average time (sec) |
| 1 | **100** | 105 | 75 | **73** | 93 | 96 |
| 2 | 100 | 79 | 100 | **54** | 100 | 127 |
| 3 | 50 | 97 | **100** | 48 | **100** | 82 |
| 4 | 75 | 79 | **100** | 48 | **100** | 116 |
| 5 | 100 | **52** | 50 | 56 | 50 | 123 |
| 6 | 100 | **51** | 100 | 56 | 100 | 63 |
| 7 | **100** | 72 | **100** | 88 | 30 | 107 |
| 8 | 0 | 184 | 25 | 215 | **60** | 316 |
| 9 | **95** | 161 | 74 | 131 | 43 | **130** |
| 10 | 55 | 176 | **65** | 166 | 35 | **97** |
| 11 | 25 | 289 | **75** | **104** | 25 | 124 |
| Tot | 72.72 | 1345 | **78.55** | **1039** | 66.9 | 1381 |

**Results.** Table 1 presents the averages for each question for each group in terms of the correctness and the time it took to answer the questions. The table clearly shows that the groups used the GOKM approach outperform the group used the written review both in the comprehension level (73% and 79% versus 67%) and in time it took to achieve those results (1345 and 1039 versus 1381 s). The results indicate that the GOKM approach provides a good basis for mapping out a domain so one can facilitate understanding of that domain. Also, it facilitates this understanding much quicker than a written review.

It is also demonstrated that the participants that were familiar with the goal-oriented approach achieved better results - a fact that indicates that using the approach requires further training and guidance.

To further analyze the results, we grouped the answers following the aspects we would like to examine as follows: Identifying Problems (Q3–Q4), Identifying Solutions (Q1–Q2), Evaluating Alternative Solutions (Q5–Q10), and Finding Knowledge Gaps (Q11). Table 2 shows the results per examined aspect, which we analyzed in the following.

**Table 2.** Overall feature results

| Aspect | G1 | | G2 | | G3 | |
|---|---|---|---|---|---|---|
| | Correctness average (%) | Total average time (sec) | Correctness average (%) | Total average time (sec) | Correctness average (%) | Total average time (sec) |
| Identifying problems | 62.5 | 176 | **100** | **96** | **100** | 198 |
| Identifying solution | **100** | 184 | 87.5 | **127** | 96.5 | 223 |
| Evaluating alternative solutions | **75** | **696** | 69 | 712 | 53 | 836 |
| Finding knowledge gaps | 25 | 289 | **75** | **104** | 25 | 124 |

- Regarding the ability to identify problems, G1 achieved lower results then G2 and G3 group. This result indicates that there is a need to better train the goal-oriented approach to novice users. With respect to the time, it shows that using the GOKM approach requires less efforts, in particular when you have enough knowledge on goal-oriented modeling. When drilling down to check lower performance by G1 we found out that for two subjects the differences between problems and soft-goal were not clear.
- Regarding the ability to identify solutions it seems that there was limited difference in identifying alternative solutions. Yet, having the information presented as a know-how map results in less time required to answer the questions. We attribute that fact to the visualization which positively contributes to understanding, as well as, to the explicit construct of the means end link that indicates alternatives.

- Regarding the ability to evaluate alternative solutions, it seems that using the GOKM approach the participants gained more understanding and with less time. Moreover, the participates of G1 who did not have previous knowledge on goal-oriented modeling succeeded the most.

In the following we analyze the related results by question and its goals.

- The goal of question 5 was to examine the understanding of the means-end relationship. G1, the group that used GOKM and were not familiar with goal-orientation, outperformed the other two groups. It seems that as the participants in that group were new comers to the approach they strictly followed the guidelines provided them during the short training. For G3, who used the written literature review, the means-end relationships were implicitly stated within the text, which might explain the lower performance. For G2, it seems that the results are due to lack of attention, as the time to perform the task was rather low, a fact that might indicate that they were sure about their answers.
- The goal of questions 6 and 7 was to examine the understanding of the solution effects. As question 6 was focused, all participants provided the right answer, however, in question 7 which was more open ended, the goal-oriented groups outperformed the literature review group. The straight forward hypothesis regrading that results is that the GOKM provides explicit guidance for such questions.
- The goal of question 8 was to examine the understanding of tradeoffs among solutions. It appears that the literature review group outperformed the others. When examining the answers of the GOKM groups, we found out that their mapping of the question to the GOKM concepts were wrong. For some reason they refer to the goal-solution relationship rather to the soft-goals. Thus, it seems that further training and explanation is still required.
- The goal of questions 9 and 10 was to examine the understanding of evaluation of alternative solution. The GOKM groups outperformed the other group, probably as the questions were more focused and thus easily mapped to GOKM concepts.

- Regarding the ability to find knowledge gaps, experiencing with goal-oriented modeling results in better identification of such gaps. This further indicate that additional training is required.

**Reflection questions.** To better understand the participants' experience regarding the use of two approaches (GOKM and written review) we asked them to answer a set of questions (as part of their task) and rank their experience in a Likert scale (1(low)-5 (high)). The questions and the average ranking appears in Table 3.

In general, the participants provide a positive feedback regarding the usefulness of the GOKM approach for comprehending a domain and their subjective evaluations are in line with the objective results.

When asking the participates to provide areas for improvement, five of the eight participants suggested that there is a need for classification mechanism to manage complexity and for scaling up the approach.

**Table 3.** Participants answer to reflection questions

| Questions | G1 | G2 | G3 |
|---|---|---|---|
| The taken approach helps a newcomer to a domain to learn a domain in a short amount of time | 3 | 4 | 2.75 |
| The taken approach facilitates a newcomer to learn a domain comprehensively | 3.25 | 2.75 | 3.25 |
| The approach enables researchers to identify knowledge gaps in a short amount of time | 3.25 | 4.5 | 2.75 |
| The approach enables researchers to easily identify knowledge gaps | 3.5 | 4.25 | 3 |

**Threats to validity.** The experiment reported in this paper is exploratory in nature and thus the results should be cautiously reviewed. In particular, the following threats to validity exist:

- The participant's background in the web mining domain can potentially be a threat to the validity of the overall results. This can skew the results in favor of those with the previous knowledge of the domain. However, we believe that this threat is minimized in this experiment because of the following. First, the focus of the experiment is on the understanding of knowledge components and links in GOKM, and not the knowledge domain itself. Second, web mining is a large domain with many specializations; therefore, background knowledge of the participants is not enough to skew the results. Third, the questions were specific to the material provided to the participants; thus, we assume that participants would prefer to base their answers on the provided material.
- The number of participants is low. Although the number of participants was more than experiments of a similar kind (e.g., [18]), it is still not enough to make a definite conclusion or generalized these.
- The questionnaire emphasis the notion of know-how structure, thus the questions might be biased towards the GOKM approach. Nevertheless, we double checked that all information can be easily extracted from the written review as well (this sometimes resulted in too condensed review).
- As the questions were open-ended, their evaluation and ranking might be subjective. To reduce that threat, we used a gold standard solution to rank the answers, and also have two of the authors grade the questionnaire independently based on the gold standard solutions. We found out that out of the 132 graded answers, differences occurred only in 4 and after a short discussion we reached an agreement regarding those grading.
- It might be that the different levels of abstraction used in the experiment (i.e., visual vs. textual) are the actual cause for the differences found. Nevertheless, we believe that the mean-end structure used in GOKM did cause the difference as the review was rather small and the answers were easy to find.

# 6    Conclusion and Future Work

In this paper, we evaluate the use of goal modeling for the purpose of know-how mapping. In particular, we have demonstrated its use via a specific domain, the web mining domain. We analyze the proposed approach via a set of criteria, and we examine the comprehension of the outcomes of using the approach. The various evaluation has shown the great potential of using the approach, including its sufficient expressiveness and the ease of understanding of goal-oriented maps. Nevertheless, the evaluation indicated places for improvement. These include the clarification of the differences between goals and tasks in the context of know-how mapping, the goal-task hierarchy, and the role of soft-goals. In fact, following those results, we devise a slightly different mapping approach, which we called Means-end knowledge map (ME-Map) [17], which aims at resolving the limitations we found. We also showed there that the feature analysis performed in this paper is supported to a large extent by external validators.

As we demonstrated that the GOKM approach better support the understanding of a domain or a problem at hand, it further facilitates the decision making process as it highlights the tradeoffs among alternatives.

In the future we further plan to develop the approach, review its core concepts and further refines these, provide additional guidelines of how to develop goal-oriented maps, supplement the approach with formal semantics to allow reasoning, and to provide tools to increase its pragmatics. We also plan to explore ways of integrating other $i*$ concepts (such as actor) so they can contribute to the process and artifacts of know-how mapping. As for the evaluation of the GOKM, we are considering comparing it to other mapping approaches.

# Appendix

**The comprehension questions.**

1. What are the alternative methods for discovering hyperlinked web structure?
2. What are the alternative methods for text and web page pre-processing for data mining?
3. What is the problem that HITS and SALSA methods aim to solve?
4. What is the problem that the Feature Extractor method aims to solve?
5. Solutions to the web template detection problem include batch web page processing and page level template detection. Are both of these techniques required to address this problem?
6. How do Site Style Trees (SST) affect noise data in the web page?
7. Describe the effects of "stopword" removal.
8. Provide a summary of the solution trade-offs when crawling the web for specific topics.
9. Which of the alternative techniques for batch web template processing has the advantage? Please explain.

10. What are the distinguishing effects of focused crawlers and context-focused crawlers?
11. In the provided material, can you identify any gaps in the knowledge in this domain? Explain how you are able to identify these gaps (if any).

**The reflection questions (in scale of strongly disagree to strongly agree).**

1. The approach helps a <u>newcomer</u> to a domain learn about the domain in a short amount of time.
2. The approach helps a <u>newcomer</u> to obtain an overview of the domain <u>comprehensively</u>.
3. The approach enables <u>researchers</u> to identify knowledge gaps in a short amount of <u>time</u>.
4. The approach enables <u>researchers</u> to easily identify knowledge gaps.

# References

1. Balaid, A., Abd Rozan, M.Z., Hikmi, S.N., Memon, J.: Knowledge maps: a systematic literature review and directions for future research. Int. J. Inform. Manage. **36**(3), 451–475 (2016)
2. Bracewell, R., Wallace, K., Moss, M., Knott, D.: Capturing design rationale. Comput. Aided Des. **41**(3), 173–186 (2009)
3. Budd, J.W.: Mind maps as classroom exercises. J. Econ. Educ. **35**(1), 35–46 (2004). Taylor & Francis Ltd
4. Eden, C., Ackermann, F., Cropper, S.: The analysis of cause maps. J. Manage. Stud. **29**(3), 309–324 (1992)
5. Garud, R.: On the distinction between know-how, know-why, and know-what. Adv. Strateg. Manage. **14**, 81–101 (1997)
6. Gengler, C.E., Reynolds, T.J.: Consumer understanding and advertising strategy: analysis and strategic translation of laddering data. J. Adv. Res. **35**, 19–33 (1995)
7. Gross, D., Sturm, A., Yu, E.: Towards know-how mapping using goal modeling. In: iStar, pp. 115–120 (2013)
8. Kwasnik, B.: The role of classification in knowledge representation and discovery. Libr. Trends **48**, 22–47 (1999)
9. Lenat, D.: CycL. http://www.cyc.com/cyc/cycl/syntax. Accessed April 2013
10. Liu, B.: Web Data Mining: Exploring Hyperlinks, Contents and Usage Data. Springer, Heidelberg (1995)
11. Mylopoulos, J., Chung, L., Yu, E.: From object-oriented to goal-oriented requirements analysis. Commun. ACM **42**(1), 31–37 (1999)
12. Novak, J.D., Cañas, A.J.: The Theory Underlying Concept Maps and How To Construct and Use Them, Institute for Human and Machine Cognition (2006)
13. Sarewitz, D., Nelson, R.R.: Progress in know-how: its origins and limits. Innovations **3**(1), 101–117 (2008). MIT Press
14. Shum, S.B., Motta, E., Domingue, J.: ScholOnto: an ontology-based digital library server for research documents and discourse. Int. J. Digital Libr. **3**(3), 237–248 (2000)
15. Sowa, J.F.: Conceptual graphs for a data base interface. IBM J. Res. Dev. **20**(4), 336–357 (1976)

16. Sowa, J.F.: Semantic Networks, Encyclopedia of Artificial Intelligence. Wiley, New York (1992)
17. Sturm, A., Gross, D., Wang, J., Nalchigar, S., Yu, E.: Mapping and usage of know-how contributions. In: Nurcan, S., Pimenidis, E. (eds.) CAiSE Forum 2014. LNBIP, vol. 204, pp. 102–115. Springer, Cham (2015). doi:10.1007/978-3-319-19270-3_7
18. Uren, V., Shum, S.B., Bachler, M., Li, G.: Sensemaking tools for understanding research literatures: design, implementation and user evaluation. Int. J. Hum. Comput. Stud. **64**(5), 420–445 (2006)
19. Van Lamsweerde, A.: Requirements Engineering: from System Goals to UML Models to Software Specifications. Wiley Publishing, Chichester (2009)
20. Yu, E., Giorgini, P., Maiden, N., Mylopoulos, J.: Social Modeling for Requirements Engineering. MIT Press, Cambridge (2011)

# Behavioral Specification and Business Process Modeling

# Controlled Experiment in Business Model-Driven Conceptual Database Design

Drazen Brdjanin[(⊠)], Goran Banjac, Danijela Banjac, and Slavko Maric

Faculty of Electrical Engineering, University of Banja Luka,
Patre 5, 78000 Banja Luka, Bosnia and Herzegovina
{drazen.brdjanin,goran.banjac,danijela.banjac,
slavko.maric}@etf.unibl.org

**Abstract.** The paper presents the initial results of a controlled experiment that we conducted with professional database designers in order to evaluate an approach to automated design of the initial conceptual database model based on collaborative business process models. The source business process model is represented by BPMN, while the target conceptual model is represented by UML class diagram. The preliminary results confirm already obtained results in case-study based evaluation, as well as the results of an earlier controlled experiment conducted with undergraduate students. The evaluation implies that the proposed approach and implemented automatic generator enable the generation of the target conceptual model with a high percentage of completeness and precision.

**Keywords:** BPMN · Collaborative business process model · Conceptual database model · Evaluation · Experiment · Model-driven · UML

## 1 Introduction

Data modelling is a very important part of information system design. The process of data modelling is often time consuming and not straightforward, meaning it often requires many iterations before designing the final model. Therefore, automatic generation of data models is very appealing and has been the subject of research for many years. Although the idea of model-driven design of data models is almost 30 years old, the survey [1] shows that only a small number of papers present the implemented automatic model-driven generator of the data model and the corresponding evaluation results.

In this paper, we present the initial results of the controlled experiment that we started with professional database designers in order to evaluate an approach to automated synthesis of the conceptual database model (CDM) based on the collaborative business process model (BPM). The source BPM is represented by BPMN [2], while the target CDM is represented by the UML class diagram [3]. The initial case-study based evaluation of the proposed approach [4] implies that the approach and implemented generator enable generation of the target model with very high precision. In order to do a more extensive evaluation, we conducted a

© Springer International Publishing AG 2017
I. Reinhartz-Berger et al. (Eds.): BPMDS/EMMSAD 2017, LNBIP 287, pp. 289–304, 2017.
DOI: 10.1007/978-3-319-59466-8_18

controlled experiment with our undergraduate students two years ago. Based on those experiences, in the last year we started a new controlled experiment with professional database designers. This paper presents the initial results obtained in this experiment and compares those results with the results obtained in the case-study based evaluation [4] and the previous controlled experiment [5].

The paper is structured as follows. After the introduction, the second section presents the related work. The third section presents a short overview of the evaluated approach to automatic synthesis of the initial CDM based on the collaborative BPM. The fourth section describes the experiments. The results are analysed in the fifth section. The final section concludes the paper.

## 2   Related Work

The survey [1] shows that the current approaches to the model-driven synthesis of data models (MDSDM) can be classified as: *function-oriented*, *process-oriented*, *communication-oriented*, and *goal-oriented*. In most papers, a process-oriented model (POM) is used as the source model. The survey [1] shows that the semantic capacity of POMs has still not been sufficiently identified to enable automatic synthesis of the complete target data model.

The BPMN is used in [4,6–19] as the starting point for MDSDM. There are two QVT [20]-based proposals [9,12], but with modest achievements in the automated generation of analysis level class diagrams, and there are also several proposals [7,8,11,15,17] for semi-automated generation. A MDSDM based on BPMN is also considered in [13,14,17], but without implementation. A large majority of all proposals are based on an incomplete source model, i.e. single diagram (a real model contains a finite set of diagrams). Only [19] considers a set of interrelated BPMs, but with no explicit rules or implementation. This overview does not contain approaches based on other POMs, although there is a paper [21] considering a finite set of interrelated BPMs represented by UML activity diagrams. An overview of BPMN-based MDSDM approaches is given in Fig. 1.

The formal rules for automated CDM synthesis based on BPMN are presented in [4], and partially in [16,19]. Other papers consider only the

**Fig. 1.** Overview of BPMN-based MDSDM approaches

guidelines that do not enable automated CDM synthesis. In this paper, we evaluate the approach for automated CDM synthesis presented in [4] and further improved after the controlled experiment conducted with students.

There are no papers presenting experiments for evaluation of automatically generated CDMs based on POMs. There are two papers [4,21] presenting case-study based evaluation of POM-based approaches. There is also a paper [22] presenting a controlled experiment which compares two techniques for deriving conceptual models from requirements models, but none of them is a POM.

## 3 Overview of the Evaluated Approach

The semantic capacity of the collaborative BPM represented by BPMN and the corresponding rules for automatic CDM synthesis are presented in [4]. In this section we only give a brief overview of the proposed mapping rules (Fig. 2).

**Classes.** There are three bases for the generation of classes: *participants, objects,* and *activation of existing objects* (objects that are not created in the given business process). Each participant from the source BPM is to be mapped into the corresponding class of the same name in the target CDM (rule $T_1$). Lanes are to be mapped into the corresponding classes in the target CDM as well. Since some lanes belonging to different pools may have the same name, generated classes should be named differently (e.g. concatenation of the parent pool name and the lane name). During the execution of the business process, participants perform tasks and exchange messages. Each task may have a number of input and output objects that can be in different states. Each different type of objects from the source BPM is to be mapped into the corresponding class of the same name in the target CDM $(T_2)$. Due to similar semantics of objects and messages, the same rule is to be applied to message flows as well. An activation represents the fact that some existing object constitutes the input in some task that changes its state. Activated objects have similar semantics as generated objects and they need to be represented with a corresponding class (activation class) that is named by concatenation of the object name and the state name $(T_3)$.

**Associations.** There are three types of associations in the CDM: *participant-participant, participant-object,* and *object-object. Participant-participant* associations originate from the fact that a pool may contain several lanes representing different business roles. This implies that class representing a pool should have associations with classes representing corresponding lanes $(T_4)$. Process patterns that have the semantic potential for the generation of *participant-object* associations are: creation and subsequent usage of generated objects $(T_5)$, exchange of messages $(T_6)$, and activation and subsequent usage of activated objects $(T_7)$. Every mentioned fact is to be represented by corresponding association(s) with multiplicities 1:* or 0..1:*. There are two bases for the generation of *object-object* associations: (i) activation $(T_8)$, which is represented

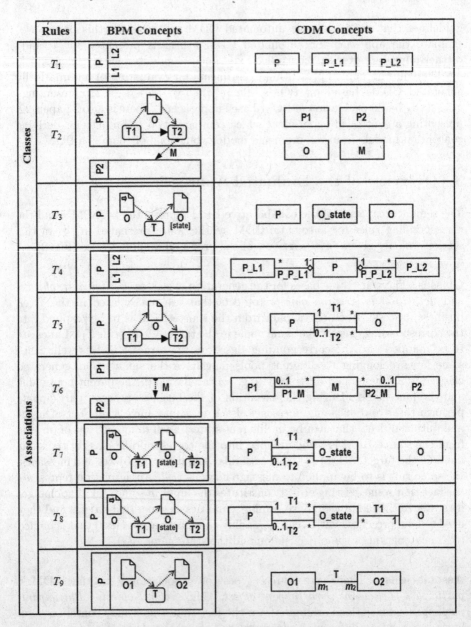

**Fig. 2.** Mapping of BPM concepts into CDM concepts

with an association between the class that represents the existing object and
the class that represents its activation, and (ii) tasks having input and output
objects of different types ($T_9$), where the association end multiplicities depend
on the nature of the objects (if they are generated, non-activated existing or
activated existing objects).

# 4    Experiment Design

This section describes the design of the experiments, including the experimental context, variables, as well as the subjects, settings and assignments.

## 4.1    Experimental Context

**Experiment with Undergraduate Students.** We conducted our first controlled experiment with students of the fourth-year undergraduate study programme *Computing and Informatics* at our University. The experiment included 24 students who took an elective course in the final year. Before doing the experiments, we had to teach the students to be able to achieve approximately the same level of knowledge. The training lasted four weeks and included both theoretical and practical classes (a short overview of database modelling by using UML class diagrams and BPMN training). The students had four assignments during the semester and each assignment was done individually.

**Experiment with Professional Database Designers.** After the experiment with students, we started a similar controlled experiment with professional database designers. A total of 135 candidates have been invited to participate voluntarily in the experiment. All invited candidates are graduate engineers with years of practical experience in database design and development of database-intensive software systems. All candidates are acquaintances of the authors and most of them are graduates of our University. The vast majority live and work locally, but there are also candidates who live and work abroad. Table 1 shows the total number of invited candidates and their answers to the invitation for participation in the experiment. This controlled experiment started last year and is still in progress. So far, the participants have finished two assignments each. Every assignment was done individually.

**Table 1.** Candidates and their responses to the invitation for participation

| Category | Number |
|---|---|
| Total number of candidates invited to participate in the experiment | 135 |
| Total number of candidates who expressed consent to participate | 67 |
| Total number of candidates who expressed conditional consent to participate | 28 |
| Total number of candidates who did not agree to participate | 14 |
| Total number of candidates who did not respond to the invitation for participation | 26 |

## 4.2  Variables

According to [23], we identified appropriate response variables and parameters.

**Response Variables.** The quantitative outcome of an experiment is referred to as a response variable. The response variable of an experiment must reflect the data that is collected from experiments so it can be used in the analysis. Appropriate measures and metrics need to be used in order to acquire the values of the response variables. There are no metrics or measures for the quantitative evaluation of automatically generated CDMs based on POMs, but there are some metrics and measures for the evaluation of automatic CDM generators based on natural language processing (NLP). Some of NLP metrics and measures can be used to perform the quantitative evaluation of the implemented generator. We have adopted some of them that were introduced in [24,25] and later adjusted in [26].

The most commonly used metrics for quantitative evaluation of automatically generated CDMs are: $N_{generated}$ (the total number of automatically generated concepts), $N_{correct}$ (the number of correctly generated concepts that can be kept in the target model), $N_{incorrect}$ (the number of incorrectly generated concepts that cannot be kept in the target model), $N_{excessive}$ (the number of excessively generated concepts that should not be kept in the target model), and $N_{missing}$ (the number of missing concepts that should be in the target model, but are not generated). In this experiment we use *recall* and *precision* as response variables used for the evaluation of automatically generated CDMs.

*Recall* represents the percentage of the target CDM that is automatically generated (the estimated percentage of automatically generated concepts in the total number of concepts in the target model). It may be defined as

$$Recall = \frac{N_{correct}}{N_{correct} + N_{missing}} \cdot 100\%. \tag{1}$$

*Precision* represents the percentage of correctly generated concepts in an automatically generated model (the percentage of correctly generated classes and the percentage of correctly generated associations). It may be defined as

$$Precision = \frac{N_{correct}}{N_{correct} + N_{incorrect}} \cdot 100\%. \tag{2}$$

**Parameters.** Qualitative or quantitative characteristics that are invariable in an experiment are called parameters. Such characteristics are to be fixed so they do not influence the results of the experiment. We established the following:

- *Modelling language* used for modelling BPMs: BPMN.
- *Modelling language* used for modelling CDMs: UML class diagram in the controlled experiment with students, while professionals were able to use different notations due to their preferences and experience.
- *Modelling tool: Topcased* with *BPMN Modeler* plugin in the controlled experiment with students, while professionals were able to use different tools.

## 4.3   Subjects, Settings and Assignments

**Experiment with Students.** Four experiments have been completed within the controlled experiment with students.

The goal of **Experiment #1 (SE-1)** was to compare an automatically generated CDM with a manually designed CDM for the same business system. In this experiment, students had to manually create a CDM based on a collaborative BPM representing *Order processing*. Eight students participated but only six models were considered for evaluation (two models were incomplete). The time for modelling was limited to 90 min. The students were in the same laboratory during the experiment and a teacher was also present in order to preserve the validity of the experiment and, if necessary, help the students to understand the source model. The students' individual work resulted in different CDMs for the same BPM, making the comparison of automatically generated and manually designed CDMs very challenging. We tried to find an equal or equivalent concept in manually designed CDMs for each concept in the automatically generated model. If an equal or equivalent concept was found in a manually designed CDM, it was considered suitable and retained in the target CDM without any change. If an equal or equivalent concept was not found in a manually designed CDM, the given concept was considered a surplus. Missing concepts are the relevant concepts that exist in the manually designed CDMs but are missing from the automatically generated CDM. All CDMs were evaluated by at least two teachers.

The setup of **Experiment #2 (SE-2)** was similar to SE-1. The students had to create CDMs based on a collaborative BPM representing *E-mail voting*. The source model is taken from the BPMN specification [27]. It is very complex and provides examples for many of BPMN features. A total of 14 students participated and six manually created CDMs were considered for evaluation. Other models were evaluated as incorrect. The main difference between SE-1 and SE-2, in addition to the source model complexity, is that SE-2 was done as homework (students had more time to do it). The automatically generated and manually designed CDMs were compared in the same way as in SE-1.

**Experiment #3 (SE-3)** was different compared to the first two. In this experiment, the students analysed the CDM which was automatically generated based on the *E-mail voting* BPM. The goal of the experiment was to compare the results of the initial evaluation [4,28] and the results of the students' evaluation. The students evaluated the CDM from the database designer's point of view. For each concept (class or association) in the generated CDM, they had to determine whether the concept should be retained unchanged, or if it should be retained with corrections (if it was generated incorrectly) or if it should not be contained in the model (if it was redundant). The students evaluated the same generated model within a 60-minute time frame. They were in the same laboratory during the experiment and teachers were also present in order to preserve the validity of the experiment and help the students to understand the model. During the experiment, the students also had the source BPM (*E-mail voting*) at their disposal. We did not accept all evaluations, because some of them were incorrect. Thirteen students participated in the experiment, but only six models were considered for evaluation, since the source BPM was too complicated for some students.

The goal of **Experiment #4 (SE-4)** was to test the generator [4,28] on a set of different BPMs. Each student had to create his/her own BPM representing a real business process and use that model as the source model to create a target CDM manually. They had to choose and model different processes. Fifteen students participated in SE-4 and seven models were considered for evaluation. The experiment was also done as homework. We used the generator to create target CDMs based on the students' BPMs, which we compared with the manually designed CDMs in the same way as in SE-1 and SE-2.

**Controlled Experiment with Professional Database Designers.** We have completed two experiments with database professionals.

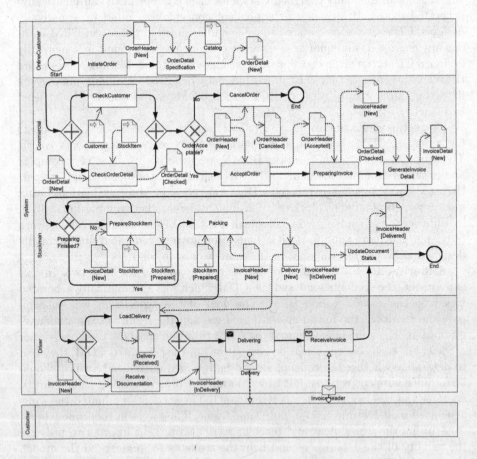

**Fig. 3.** BPMN model used in experiments as a starting basis for CDM design

**Experiment #1 (PE-1)** was conducted in two phases. In the first phase, participants manually designed CDMs based on the BPMN model (Fig. 3), which is very similar to the BPM used in SE-1. Unlike in the students' experiment, professionals were invited to finish the task as a homework. Before starting manual CDM design, they were asked to estimate the required time. They were also asked to measure the time spent for manual design of the target CDM. We sent the assignment and the evaluation form to all candidates who expressed consent and conditional consent for participation (95 candidates). All invited candidates were asked to complete the assignment and submit the manually designed CDM and completed evaluation form within 15 working days (this deadline was caused by their voluntary participation and work overload). All received manually designed CDMs and evaluation forms were reviewed by at least two teachers. If any cardinal mistakes and/or shortcomings were found, the participants were asked to revise the model and/or evaluation form. Most of the participants submitted the appropriate model and evaluation form in the first iteration, while the others completed the assignment in the second iteration. At the end of this phase, a total of 36 completed manually designed CDMs and evaluation forms were received. The remaining 59 candidates either did not complete the required modifications or did not submit the required CDM and evaluation form at all.

In the second phase, all participants who completed the first phase were invited to evaluate their manually designed CDMs against the CDM (Fig. 4), which was automatically generated based on the same BPM. They were asked

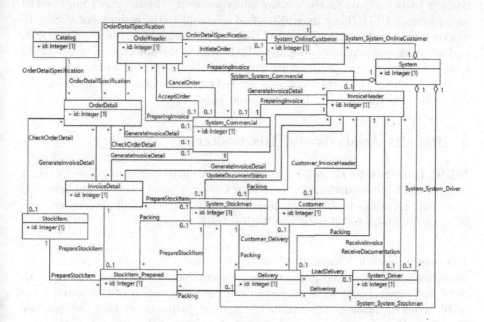

**Fig. 4.** Automatically generated CDM based on BPMN given in Fig. 3

**Table 2.** Candidates and participants in the experiment with professionals

| Category | PE-1 | PE-2 (CG) |
|---|---|---|
| Total number of candidates invited to participate | 95 | 36 (59) |
| Total number of participants who completed the assignment | 31 | 23 (8) |

to complete the evaluation within 15 working days. A total of 31 participants completed the assignment.

All participants who completed the first phase of PE-1 were invited to participate in **Experiment #2 (PE-2)**. They were asked to manually design new CDMs meeting the information requirements of the same business process (*Order Processing*), but in SE-2 they were asked to take the automatically generated CDM (Fig. 4) as a starting point. They were able to retain correctly generated concepts, drop excessively generated concepts, correct incorrectly generated concepts, and add missing concepts. They were asked to complete the assignment within 15 working days. Like in PE-1, they were asked to estimate the required time, as well as to measure the spent time. They were also asked to evaluate their new manually designed CDMs against the automatically generated CDM. A total of 23 participants completed the assignment.

The same experiment (manual CDM design based on the automatically generated CDM) was also conducted with a control group (CG). The invitation for participation in the CG was sent to all candidates (59) who initially expressed consent to participate in the controlled experiment, but did not complete the assignment in PE-1. They were also asked to complete the assignment within 15 working days, including the required time estimation, spent time measurement, and evaluation of manually designed CDMs against the automatically generated CDM. A total of eight participants completed the assignment in the CG.

Table 2 shows the total number of invited candidates and participants in the controlled experiment with database professionals.

## 5    Results Analysis and Discussion

**Initial Case-Study Based Evaluation.** The initial case-study based evaluation [4,28] of the automatically generated CDMs implied that the implemented automatic generator is able to automatically generate very high percentage (over 90%) of the target CDM with very high precision (over 85%).

**Experiment with Students.** Due to the space limitations, we present only summary results obtained in the experiment conducted with students (Table 3).

These experiments with students confirmed the results of the initial case-study based evaluation. The results of the experiments imply that the specified transformation rules cover the automated generation of the majority of concepts of the target CDM. The average values of recall and precision for classes are

**Table 3.** Summary results for the controlled experiment with students

| Experiments | Classes | | Associations | |
| --- | --- | --- | --- | --- |
| | Recall [%] | Precision [%] | Recall [%] | Precision [%] |
| SE-1 | 96.43 | 100.00 | 88.35 | 92.78 |
| SE-2 | 95.56 | 100.00 | 83.54 | 77.76 |
| SE-3 | 94.45 | 100.00 | 87.47 | 89.98 |
| SE-4 | 98.09 | 100.00 | 91.86 | 85.79 |
| Mean | **96.13** | **100.00** | **87.81** | **86.58** |

very high (>95%) and slightly lower for associations (>85%). Almost each single value of recall and precision is greater than the average respective value in all experiments, except in SE-2. The main reason for lower precision for associations in SE-2 is the source model complexity. Taking into account the high complexity of the source model (four complex loops, two sub-processes, etc.), recall and precision are still very high (>77%).

The results of comparing the automatically generated and manually designed CDMs in all four experiments show that the objectified evaluation does not significantly differ from the initial case-study based evaluation. The participants concluded (in all experiments) that all automatically generated classes could be retained in the generated CDMs. They also evaluated a low percentage of automatically generated associations as incorrect because of partially incorrect cardinalities (i.e. incorrect multiplicity of one association end). The main reason for this are some control patterns that are presently not covered by the rules.

During the review, we found out more about the influence of alternate process flows on the end multiplicities of generated associations. We used these findings to improve the rules and generator before the controlled experiment with database professionals (the rules presented in Sect. 3 are a modified version in comparison to the original rules [4]).

**Experiment with Professional Database Designers.** The evaluation results of the controlled experiment with database professionals are given in Table 4 (evaluation of generated classes) and Table 5 (evaluation of generated associations). The presented data constitutes average values of the data collected from the completed evaluation forms in PE-1 and PE-2.

The PE-1 experiment confirmed the Conway's Law [29] that independent work of $n$ database designers results by $n$ different CDMs for the same system. This is the main reason why the values of recall and precision in PE-1 are lower than in PE-2. Although the recall and precision in PE-1 are lower in comparison with PE-2 and similar students' experiment SE-1, these measures are still high (around or above 70%), while the precision of automatically generated associations is 85%! The participants evaluated all excessive classes as incorrect

**Table 4.** Evaluation of automatically generated classes in PE-1 and PE-2

| Average metrics and measures | PE-1 | PE-2 (CG) |
|---|---|---|
| Number of classes in manually designed CDMs | 12.80 | 12.00 (12.13) |
| Number of matching classes in manually designed CDMs and automatically generated CDM | 8.80 | 10.52 (10.75) |
| Number of missing classes in automatically generated CDM | 3.73 | 1.52 (1.38) |
| Number of excessive classes in automatically generated CDM | 4.33 | 3.43 (3.25) |
| Recall [%] | 76 | 89 (88) |
| Precision [%] | 68 | 76 (77) |

in both experiments. This is the reason for the lower precision of automatically generated classes.

During the review of the manually designed CDMs and completed evaluation forms, we concluded that some participants modelled roles by applying a different design pattern. This is the reason for considering some automatically generated classes as excessive. A relatively high percentage of automatically generated associations was evaluated as excessive in both experiments ($\sim$50% in PE-1 and $\sim$40% in PE-2). Although almost half of the generated associations were evaluated as excessive, a large majority of excessive associations are correctly generated redundant associations.

The results obtained in PE-2 confirm the results obtained in case-study based evaluation [4,28] and controlled experiment with students. The average recall is above 80% (for classes $\sim$90%). The average precision for automatically generated classes is above 75% (since all excessive classes were evaluated as incorrect), while the average precision for associations is also about 90%. It is also very important to emphasise very high results matching with the control group.

Apart from the fact that the generator is able to automatically generate a very high percentage of the target CDM with very high precision, this experiment with professionals confirms that the automatically generated CDM can also be efficiently used as a starting point for manual design of the target CDM. Table 6 presents some participants' self-evaluation data, which implies that manual CDM design from scratch is more time consuming than CDM design based on automatically generated CDM, despite more extensive experience and higher level of expertise of database designers. It is obvious that CDM design based on automatically generated CDM almost bisects the design efforts. It is also very important to emphasise very high results matching with the control group, since the estimated and spent times are very similar and independent of previous experience in CDM design for the same system – designers in the CG did not have previous experience in CDM design based on the given BPM in comparison with participants who previously completed manual CDM design from scratch.

Finally, apart from the qualitative and quantitative evaluation, the majority of participants expressed subjective feedback about the automatically generated

**Table 5.** Evaluation of automatically generated associations in PE-1 and PE-2

| Average metrics and measures | PE-1 | PE-2 (CG) |
|---|---|---|
| Number of associations in manually designed CDMs | 17.30 | 22.05 (26.38) |
| Number of matching associations in manually designed CDMs and automatically generated CDM | 11.33 | 18.05 (21.38) |
| Number of incorrect associations in automatically generated CDM | 2.61 | 2.71 (1.75) |
| Number of missing associations in automatically generated CDM | 5.43 | 2.95 (4.75) |
| Number of excessive associations in automatically generated CDM | 18.83 | 16.10 (14.13) |
| Recall [%] | 71 | 83 (83) |
| Precision [%] | 85 | 89 (91) |

**Table 6.** Participants self-evaluation in PE-1 and PE-2

| Average metrics | PE-1 | PE-2 (CG) |
|---|---|---|
| Experience in database design [years] | 7.19 | 5.96 (5.50) |
| Level of expertise in database design [0–5] | 3.42 | 3.39 (2.83) |
| Level of expertise in BPMN modelling [0–5] | 2.33 | 2.43 (1.67) |
| Estimated time required for manual CDM design [hours] | 5.75 | 2.07 (2.00) |
| Time spent for manual CDM design [hours] | 4.54 | 1.89 (2.50) |

CDM. Many participants were fascinated with the completeness and precision of the automatically generated CDM and did not believe that the given CDM was automatically generated.

## 6    Conclusions and Future Work

In this paper we presented the results of two controlled experiments we conducted in order to evaluate a business model-driven approach to automated conceptual database model. The source business process model is represented by BPMN, while the target conceptual model is represented by UML class diagram.

The initial case-study based evaluation of the automatically generated CDMs implies that the implemented generator is able to generate very high percentage of the target CDM with very high precision. In order to do a more extensive evaluation, we conducted a controlled experiment with undergraduate students. Currently, we are doing an even more extensive evaluation of the approach with professional database designers. This paper presents the conducted experiments, as well as the results of the experiments with students and the initial results obtained in experiments with professional database designers.

The results obtained in the experiment with students confirm the results of the initial case-study based evaluation. In the experiment with students, recall and precision for classes are very high (>95%) and slightly lower for associations (>85%). During the experiments with students, we further identified how alternate process flows influence the association end multiplicities in the target CDM. We used these findings to improve the rules and the generator before conducting the experiment with professional database designers.

The initial results of the experiments with professional database designers also confirm the results of the initial case-study based evaluation, as well as the results obtained in the controlled experiment conducted with students. The average recall in the controlled experiment with database professionals is above 80% (for classes almost 90%). The average precision for automatically generated classes is above 75%, while the average precision for associations is also about 90%. Apart from the fact that the generator is able to automatically generate very high percentage of the target CDM with very high precision, this experiment also confirms that the automatically generated CDM can also be efficiently used as a starting point for manual design of the target CDM, since it significantly shortens the time required for CDM design.

The results of the experiments imply that the specified transformation rules cover the automated generation of the majority of concepts of the target CDM. Experiments also show that generated CDM can be efficiently used as starting point for manual design of the target CDM. Therefore, the presented results indicate that the proposed approach can be used in practice for automatic generation of the initial CDM.

Apart from continuing the started controlled experiment with professional database designers, the future work will focus on the further identification of the semantic capacity of BPMs for automated CDM design and additional improvement of the implemented generator as well.

**Acknowledgments.** We would like to express our sincere gratitude to all participants of the controlled experiment for their voluntary participation and valuable contribution.

# References

1. Brdjanin, D., Maric, S.: Model-driven techniques for data model synthesis. Electronics **17**(2), 130–136 (2013)
2. OMG: Business Process Model and Notation (BPMN), v2.0. OMG (2011)
3. OMG: Unified Modeling Language (OMG UML), v2.5. OMG (2015)
4. Brdjanin, D., Banjac, G., Maric, S.: Automated synthesis of initial conceptual database model based on collaborative business process model. In: Bogdanova, M.A., Gjorgjevikj, D. (eds.) ICT Innovations 2014: World of Data. AISC, vol. 311, pp. 145–156. Springer International Publishing, Cham (2015)
5. Banjac, D., Brdjanin, D., Banjac, G., Maric, S.: Evaluation of automatically generated conceptual database model based on collaborative business process model: controlled experiment. In: Stojanov, G., Kulakov, A. (eds.) ICT Innovations 2016. AISC. Springer (2016, in press)
6. Rungworawut, W., Senivongse, T.: From business world to software world: Deriving class diagrams from business process models. In: Proceedings of the 5th WSEAS International Conference on Applied Informatics and Communications, WSEAS, pp. 233–238 (2005)

7. Rungworawut, W., Senivongse, T.: Using ontology search in the design of class diagram from business process model. PWASET **12**, 165–170 (2006)
8. Brambilla, M., Cabot, J., Comai, S.: Automatic generation of workflow-extended domain models. In: Engels, G., Opdyke, B., Schmidt, D.C., Weil, F. (eds.) MODELS 2007. LNCS, vol. 4735, pp. 375–389. Springer, Heidelberg (2007). doi:10.1007/978-3-540-75209-7_26
9. Rodríguez, A., Fernández-Medina, E., Piattini, M.: Towards obtaining analysis-level class and use case diagrams from Business Process Models. In: Song, I.-Y., Piattini, M., Chen, Y.-P.P., Hartmann, S., Grandi, F., Trujillo, J., Opdahl, A.L., Ferri, F., Grifoni, P., Caschera, M.C., Rolland, C., Woo, C., Salinesi, C., Zimányi, E., Claramunt, C., Frasincar, F., Houben, G.-J., Thiran, P. (eds.) ER 2008. LNCS, vol. 5232, pp. 103–112. Springer, Heidelberg (2008). doi:10.1007/978-3-540-87991-6_15
10. Vara, J.L., Fortuna, M.H., Sánchez, J., Werner, C.M.L., Borges, M.R.S.: A Requirements Engineering Approach for Data Modelling of Process-Aware Information Systems. In: Abramowicz, W. (ed.) BIS 2009. LNBIP, vol. 21, pp. 133–144. Springer, Heidelberg (2009). doi:10.1007/978-3-642-01190-0_12
11. Brambilla, M., Cabot, J., Comai, S.: Extending conceptual schemas with business process information. Adv. Softw. Eng. **2010**, Article ID 525121 (2010)
12. Rodriguez, A., Guzman, I.G.-R., Fernandez-Medina, E., Piattini, M.: Semi-formal transformation of secure business processes into analysis class and use case models: an MDA approach. Inf. Softw. Technol. **52**(9), 945–971 (2010)
13. Zhang, J., Feng, P., Wu, Z., Yu, D., Chen, K.: Activity based CIM modeling and transformation for business process systems. Int. J. Softw. Eng. Knowl. Eng. **20**(3), 289–309 (2010)
14. Nikiforova, O., Pavlova, N.: Application of BPMN instead of GRAPES for two-hemisphere model driven approach. In: Grundspenkis, J., Kirikova, M., Manolopoulos, Y., Novickis, L. (eds.) ADBIS 2009. LNCS, vol. 5968, pp. 185–192. Springer, Heidelberg (2010). doi:10.1007/978-3-642-12082-4_24
15. de la Vara, J.L.: Business process-based requirements specification and object-oriented conceptual modelling of information systems. PhD Thesis, Valencia Polytechnic University (2011)
16. Cruz, E.F., Machado, R.J., Santos, M.Y.: From business process modeling to data model: a systematic approach. In: Proceeding of QUATIC 2012, pp. 205–210. IEEE (2012)
17. Drozdová, M., Mokryš, M., Kardoš, M., Kurillová, Z., Papán, J.: Change of paradigm for development of software support for e-learning. In: Proceeding of ICETA 2012, pp. 81–84. IEEE (2012)
18. Rhazali, Y., Hadi, Y., Mouloudi, A.: Transformation method CIM to PIM: from Business Processes Models defined in BPMN to use case and Class Models defined in UML. Int. J. Comput. Inf. Syst. Control Eng. **8**(8), 1334–1338 (2014)
19. Cruz, E.F., Machado, R.J., Santos, M.Y.: Deriving a data model from a set of interrelated Business Process Models. Proc. ICEIS **2015**, 49–59 (2015)
20. OMG: MOF 2.0 Query/View/Transformation Specification, v1.0. OMG (2008)
21. Brdjanin, D., Maric, S.: Towards the automated business model-driven conceptual database design. In: Morzy, T., Harder, T., Wrembel, R. (eds.) Advances in Databases and Information Systems. AISC, vol. 186, pp. 31–43. Springer, Heidelberg (2013). doi:10.1007/978-3-642-32741-4
22. Espana, S., Ruiz, M., Gonzalez, A.: Systematic derivation of conceptual models from requirements models: a controlled experiment. In: Proceeding of RCIS 2012, pp. 1–12. IEEE (2012)

23. Juristo, N., Moreno, A.: Basics of sOftware Engineering Experimentation. Springer, New York (2001)
24. Harmain, H., Gaizauskas, R.: CM-builder: a natural language-based CASE Tool for object-oriented analysis. Autom. Softw. Eng. **10**(2), 157–181 (2003)
25. Omar, N., Hanna, P., McKevitt, P.: Heuristics-based entity-relationship modelling through natural language processing. Proc. AICS **2004**, 302–313 (2004)
26. Brdjanin, D., Maric, S.: An approach to automated conceptual database design based on the UML activity diagram. Comput. Sci. Inf. Syst. **9**(1), 249–283 (2012)
27. OMG: BPMN 2.0 by Example, v. 1.0. OMG (2010)
28. Banjac, G.: Automated synthesis of conceptual database model based on collaborative business process model. Master thesis, University of Banja Luka (2014)
29. Conway, M.: How do committees invent? Datamation (1968)

# Incorporating Data Inaccuracy Considerations in Process Models

Yotam Evron[✉], Pnina Soffer[✉], and Anna Zamansky[✉]

University of Haifa, Mount Carmel, 3498838 Haifa, Israel
{yevron,spnina,annazam}@is.haifa.ac.il

**Abstract.** Business processes are designed with the assumption that the data used by the process is an accurate reflection of reality. However, this assumption does not always hold, and situations of data inaccuracy might occur which bear substantial consequences to the process and to business goals. Until now, data inaccuracy has mainly been addressed in the area of business process management as a possible exception at runtime, to be resolved through exception handling mechanisms. Design-time analysis of potential data inaccuracy has been mostly overlooked so far. In this paper we propose a conceptual framework for incorporating data inaccuracy considerations in process models to support an analysis of data inaccuracy at design time and empirically evaluate its usability by process designers.

**Keywords:** Data inaccuracy · Business process management · Business process modeling

## 1 Introduction

Business processes are designed with the assumption that the data used by the process and its supporting information system is an accurate reflection of reality. Based on this assumption, process aware information systems (PAIS) can operate as a closed system and actions can be triggered based on the data values in the system, without a need to actually "sense" the values in the real world. Nevertheless, it is a well-known fact that the data stored in the database of an information system is not always completely reliable [4], and data values might not match the real-world values they should reflect, thus creating a situation commonly known as "data inaccuracy" [21]. Those inaccurate data values may affect the ability to reach the business process goals.

Until recently, data inaccuracy has mainly been addressed in the area of business process management as a possible exception at runtime [15]. Our main premise in this paper is that considering potential data inaccuracy situations during process design can alleviate their consequences at runtime. We are hence taking a step towards supporting process designers in this task. Our aim in this paper is to propose a formal representation that would facilitate human reasoning about potential data inaccuracy situations and their potential consequences. While several works have addressed the issue of data quality at process design, as [14], they provide only limited support for reasoning about potential data inaccuracy at design time due to a lack of formal semantics of the notations

© Springer International Publishing AG 2017
I. Reinhartz-Berger et al. (Eds.): BPMDS/EMMSAD 2017, LNBIP 287, pp. 305–318, 2017.
DOI: 10.1007/978-3-319-59466-8_19

used. A first step in this direction was taken in [21], where a notion of data and real world synchronization points in processes was introduced. The idea is to consider the information system dependent process and its environment as (sometimes) independent sub-domains, which operate concurrently. These sub-domains merge at synchronization points, where the process "senses" not only the data items, but also the real values which the data items represent. Identifying such points at *design time* can better inform an analysis of the consequences and risks of data inaccuracy, and is therefore instrumental in further developing tools for supporting automatic as well as manual analysis of potential data inaccuracy.

In this paper we further extend the notion of synchronization point and propose a conceptual framework for its incorporation into process models. As our intention is to provide a basis for human reasoning at design time, we consider the usability of the proposed model a critical issue. To evaluate this usability, we conducted an empirical study, in which participants were asked to identify synchronization points in a given process model. The preliminary results indicate that participants were mostly able to correctly identify synchronization points in a given process model.

The rest of the paper is organized as follows: Sect. 2 provides the conceptual analysis of data inaccuracy through an example. Section 3 incorporates considerations of data inaccuracy into process models. In Sect. 4 the empirical evaluation is described, including, in particular, research settings, data analysis, and the results of the evaluation. In Sect. 5 discussion and limitations are provided. Section 6 discusses related work. Finally, in Sect. 7, conclusions and future work are discussed.

## 2     Conceptual Analysis of Data Inaccuracy

Following the data inaccuracy notions introduced by [21], we build on the state-based view of a process suggested by the Generic Process Model (GPM) [19, 20]. According to GPM a process takes place in a domain which is typically captured by a set of state variables, whose values at a given moment reflect the domain state at that moment. State variables obtain values (in the physical world) and data items are updated in the information system (IS) to reflect these changes. We assume that all relevant domain variables are represented by corresponding data items in the information system, thus corresponding couples $<x_i, d_i>$ relate to a state variable $x_i$ and the data item $d_i$ that reflects it. A subdomain is a part of the domain described by a subset of the domain state variables. Note that there are many ways to partition a given domain into sub-domains and different partitions can reflect different views of the process domain. A process is viewed as a sequence of state transitions, which are governed by a transformation law. However, not all state variables are relevant in order to make a transition. Thus, the domain may be decomposed into independent subdomains in some parts of the process.

*Observation 1.* A process may involve multiple sequences of transitions in several independent subdomains.

As explained in [20], subdomains which operate in parallel or independently, may reach a state where there is a dependency between them so the activation of next transition relies on combined information from all subdomains. Considering the threads of transitions in these subdomains, such states are termed synchronization points.

*Observation 2.* Sequences of transitions which take place concurrently in independent subdomains merge at synchronization points.

We focus on a specific decomposition of the process domain into two sub-domains: one which for some states may rely only on state variables (of the physical world), oblivious of the information system and its data values, and another, whose transitions at some states rely only on the values of data items, under the assumption that these reflect corresponding domain variables[1]. However, as already noted above, this assumption is not always realistic:

*Observation 3.* A discrepancy between the value of a state variable $x_i$ and its corresponding data item $d_i$ might occur. Such discrepancy is termed *data inaccuracy*.

As long as, e.g., a subdomain relying only on a data item $d_i$ operates independently of a subdomain which contains the corresponding state variable $x_i$, the existence of data inaccuracy for $d_i$ may not be recognized (unless noticed by chance). When these two subdomains merge at a synchronization point, data inaccuracy will necessarily be recognized. However, this may be too late for avoiding consequences, and the process might get "stuck", or some compensating action would be needed. Therefore, the exact location of a synchronization point matters for mitigating risks of data inaccuracy.

Note, there are processes where the two subdomains (one relying only on data items and the other manipulating domain variables) do not merge throughout the process. In such cases no synchronization points exist and data inaccuracy might remain unnoticed. If these data items are later on used by other processes, consequences might materialize then.

As a running example illustrating our observations, consider a process of a company organizing and executing business parties for customers. From the company's perspective, the goal of the process is reaching a state where the business party is completed successfully and paid for. Let us assume a customer met the company's representatives, who recorded the agreed upon details of the party (such as date, type of food, price etc.) as data in the company's IS. From now on, the company can execute the process on its own without a need for any further information from the customer in order to proceed. This reflects Observation 1: the company executes a part of the process in an independent subdomain, depending solely on the IS data items, without "sensing" their values outside the IS (e.g., by comparing the date registered in the IS to the actual date as known to the customers). At some point, however, when the party eventually takes place, the company's independent subdomain and the customer's subdomain merge, coming to a synchronization point (Observation 2). Now consider a scenario, in which the planned date has been falsely recorded in the IS and does not reflect the actual agreed upon date. This is

---

[1] We make a basic assumption here that the IS data structure is well-designed, which means that all relevant domain variables are represented by corresponding data items.

a manifestation of data inaccuracy (Observation 3). As noted, it is not recognized as long as each subdomain operates independently, but it will necessarily be detected at the synchronization point: the company will have everything ready for the planned date recorded in the IS, while the guests will arrive at the meeting point on the agreed upon date as they know it. Since these do not match, the party cannot take place.

Another possible scenario is a situation where the type of food has been falsely recorded, so the IS does not reflect the actual requirement of the customers. In this case we may need to deal with two possible situations: (1) Customer's food requirement is vegetarian but was recorded as non-vegetarian in the IS, and food preparations are made accordingly. (2) Customer's food requirement is non-vegetarian but was recorded as vegetarian; food preparations are made accordingly.

Suppose that situation (1) is not acceptable for the vegetarian customers and they would rather cancel the party than have non-vegetarian food. Thus, if discovered too late when corrections can no longer be made, the party arrangements should be cancelled. In contrast, situation (2) might be acceptable, but may still have consequences. Specifically, it may result in a reduced price as a compensation for not meeting the requirement. Note that while the consequences of data inaccuracy may differ for different values assumed by the data item, in both scenarios, these consequences depend on the time of detection. If detected early enough, plans can still be changed and the party can be executed satisfactorily. However, if data inaccuracy is not detected until the time of the party, full consequences will materialize (see "Party execution" in Fig. 1).

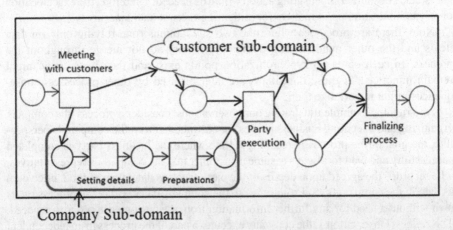

**Fig. 1.** Illustration of two independent sub-domains in the running example

Figure 1 provides an illustration of how the process as viewed by the company (as a Petri net in the company's subdomain) has in fact a concurrent part, taking place independently at the customer sub-domain. This part is marked by a cloud in the figure, as its details are not visible to the company. Yet, the transition of *Party execution* requires tokens from two input places – one from each of the sub-domains. Thus this transition synchronizes these two sub-domains, and requires inputs from both. If discrepancies exist between them (namely, data inaccuracy), the transition might not be possible to activate as planned.

This example highlights the important role synchronization points play in the detection and handling of data inaccuracy situations. For instance, the mismatch of the planned dates has significant consequences, some of which could have been avoided if detected at earlier stages. Therefore, incorporating synchronization points into process models can form the basis for a formal design time analysis of how data inaccuracy may manifest itself in the process. While a full method for such analysis is out of scope of this paper, here we focus on proposing a conceptual framework for this incorporation. We consider an explicit representation of synchronization points in a process model an essential basis for such analysis.

## 3   Incorporating Considerations of Data Inaccuracy into Process Models

To incorporate considerations of data inaccuracy into process models, we extend a specific representation formalism. Workflow-net based formalisms, which have well-defined formal semantics, as well as numerous tools for computational analysis, can form an adequate basis for our purposes.

**Definition 1 (WF-net).** [1] A Petri net $N = \langle P, T, F \rangle$ consists of two disjoint non-empty, finite sets $P$ of places and $T$ of transitions and of a flow relation $F \subseteq (P \times T) \cup (T \times P)$. $N$ is a Workflow net (WF-net) if and only if:

- There is a single source place i, i.e., $\{p \in P | \bullet p = \emptyset\} = \{i\}$
- There is a single sink place o, i.e., $\{p \in P | p \bullet = \emptyset\} = \{o\}$
- Every node is on a path from i to o, i.e., for any $n \in P \cup T : (i, n) \in F^*$ and $(n, o) \in F^*$ where $F^*$ is the reflexive-transitive closure of relation F.

WF-nets have been extended with data in [18] using a finite set $D = \{d_1, \ldots d_m\}$ of data elements. A WFD-net is basically a WF-net extended with conceptual read/write/delete data operations. WFD-net also allows transition guards, which are logical conditions defined on data items, upon which the execution of the guarded transition may be dependent. More formally:

**Definition 2 (WFD-net).** [18] A workflow net with data $N = \langle P, T, F, rd, wt, del, grd \rangle$ consists of

- A WF-net $\langle P, T, F \rangle$,
- A reading data labelling function $rd : T \to 2^D$,
- A writing data labelling function $wt : T \to 2^D$,
- A deleting data labelling function $del : T \to 2^D$, and
- A guard function $grd : T \to \vartheta_\Pi$ assigning guards to transitions.

In what follows we adapt the formalism of Workflow-nets with data (WFD-nets) and integrate into it the basic concepts related to data inaccuracy introduced in Sect. 2. The idea is to complement the WF-net view with notions based on the Generic Process Model (GPM) [19, 20], which allows us to reason about process models in terms of their real world meaning (which is not captured in a WF-net model). Soffer et al. [20] provided an explicit mapping of WF-nets to GPM-based concepts. For instance, a set of states of a sub-domain is mapped to a place; a transition is mapped to a change of state of a sub-domain, etc.

As opposed to control-flow synchronization that is normally depicted in WF-nets as two or more input places of a transition [2], and can be viewed as an "internal" synchronization, our notion is that of "external" synchronization. The difference is that the former is a point in the process where multiple parallel threads (within the process domain) converge into one single thread. In contrast, the latter is a point where the process domain and its environment converge. Consequently, a data item and the corresponding state variable are equalized. Therefore, we extend the WFD-nets to incorporate the new notion of external synchronization. We assume a finite set $D = \{d_1, \ldots d_m\}$ of data items.

**Definition 3 (S-WFD net).** A Synchronizing workflow net with data $N = \langle P, T, F, \Delta_D, \vartheta_D, rd, wt, del, grd, sp \rangle$ consists of

- A WF-net $\langle P, T, F \rangle$,
- A set $\Delta_D$ of synchronization points of the form $\Delta(d)$ where $d \in D$,
- A set $\vartheta_D$ of guards over D,
- A reading data labelling function $rd:T \to 2^D$,
- A writing data labelling function $wt:T \to 2^D$,
- A deleting data labelling function $del:T \to 2^D$,
- A guard function $grd:T \to \vartheta_D$ assigning guards to transitions, and
- A synchronizing function $sp:T \to 2^{\Delta_D}$ assigning synchronization points to transitions.

The main addition in the above definition is the explicit representation of synchronization points, which are labels of the form $\Delta(d)$ (where d is a data item) assigned to transitions of the WFD-net. The semantics of these labels is that they signify a merging point between the process explicitly captured by the WFD-net, and its external environment, which naturally is out of the scope of the model.

Note, as $\Delta$ is a label, it does not change the execution semantics of the WFD-net as presented in [18]. The control flow of a S-WFD net is the same as in a WFD-net, since the $\Delta$ label does not manipulate the data or the control flow during run time. Its role is to explicitly mark synchronization points for the modeler in order to support reasoning about possible consequences of data inaccuracy.

Let us demonstrate the new notions using our running example. The *Party execution* is a synchronization point with respect to the data items *ed* (event date) and *fr* (food requirement), because at this point the event date and food requirement data items "meet" the state variables they should reflect, and if the values do not match, namely, if data inaccuracy exists, it will be revealed. Therefore, we mark the transition *Party execution* with $\Delta$(ed) and $\Delta$(fr). The *Meeting with customer* and *Payment* are also synchronization points with respect to the data items *md* (meeting date) and *p*(price), respectively. They are therefore marked with $\Delta$(md) and $\Delta$(p) respectively. The *Meeting with customer* is a synchronization point with respect to data item *md* since at this point the recorded *md* and its corresponding state variable (which stands for the actual agreed upon meeting date) should match for the meeting to take place. The *Payment* is a synchronization point for the price since if the *p* was falsely recorded the actual payment will not match the expected. The Preparations transition, in contrast, is a stage at which the real values of the state variables reflected by these data items are not "sensed", and so it is not marked as a synchronization point for any variable (Fig. 2).

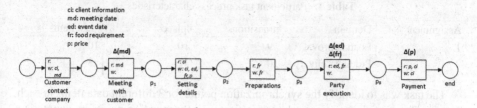

**Fig. 2.** The running example model using S-WFD net

In summary, we have proposed a formal representation of synchronization points and incorporated them into WFD-net based formalism. Using this formalism, process designers can make synchronization points visible, so reasoning about potential data inaccuracy becomes possible. Yet, a main concern remains whether designers of process models can correctly identify and place the synchronization point labels. This is what we explore in the next section.

## 4  Empirical Evaluation

In the previous section we have introduced a conceptual framework in which data inaccuracy considerations can be captured. As discussed, the goal of this conceptual framework is to support process designers during process design and to constitute a basis upon which additional analysis methods with respect to data inaccuracy can be developed. The concept of synchronization points, which is a key concept in our framework, is abstract, and developed using a GPM view. A main concern, therefore, is the usability of the framework: can process designers identify synchronization points when they exist in the process, and correctly place them in the process model? We consider the establishment of satisfactory usability of the proposed model an essential prerequisite for further analysis methods to be developed based on it.

Following this, our research question is whether process designers can correctly identify synchronization points in a given process model. To answer this question, we conducted an empirical study which is described next.

## 4.1 Data Collection

The participants in this study were 20 information systems students (17 undergraduate and 3 graduate students), enrolled to an elective course of business process management at the university of Haifa. The prerequisite of this course is a course in information systems analysis, which covers the basics of modelling with Workflow-nets.

The participants were introduced to S-WFD nets and handed out a task sheet, which included two S-WFD models, as defined in Definition 3, as well as textual descriptions of the processes and the data used in them. Structural characteristics of the processes are given in Table 1.

**Table 1.** Participant task process characteristics

| Assignment | Domain | #transitions | #places | #data items |
|---|---|---|---|---|
| 1 | Loan approval | 9 | 10 | 10 |
| 2 | Product delivery | 10 | 12 | 8 |

The task was to identify the synchronization points for 3 different data items in each process. The participants were asked to indicate synchronization points by annotating the model and to textually explain their choice. They were also instructed that in case a synchronization point is not found, this should be explained and justified textually.

Prior to handing out the task sheets, we gave a brief introduction of the conceptual framework to the participants, showing how WFD-net extend the standard WF-net formalism and introducing the concepts of data inaccuracy and the notion of synchronization point (without referring to GPM). We demonstrated these terms using an example (which was modelled using S-WFD net).

## 4.2 Data Analysis

Using the conceptual framework of GPM, we have manually labelled the two process models with synchronization points for the three data items in each example as a baseline for the evaluation. For a transition $t$ in $T$ and a data item $d$, let $BaseLine(t, d) = 1$ if $\Delta(d)$ in $sp(t)$, and $BaseLine(t, d) = 0$ otherwise. For a participant $p$, we denote by $Choice_p$ the classification function of $p$, that is $Choice_p(t, d) = 1$ if the participant labelled $t$ with $\Delta(d)$, and $Choice_p(t, d) = 0$ otherwise.

For each participant $p$, we define:

$$TP_p = \left\{(t, d) \mid BaseLine(t, d) = Choice_p(t, d) = 1\right\} \text{ (true positives)}$$

$$TN_p = \left\{(t, d) \mid BaseLine(t, d) = Choice_p(t, d) = 0\right\} \text{ (true negatives)}$$

$$FP_p = \left\{(t, d) \mid BaseLine(t, d) = 0, Choice_p(t, d) = 1\right\} \text{ (false positives)}$$

$$FN_p = \left\{(t, d) \mid BaseLine(t, d) = 1, Choice_p(t, d) = 0\right\} \text{ (false negatives)}$$

Using the above notions, we computed for each participant the standard metrics of Precision, Recall, F-measure and Accuracy [9]:

$$Precision_p = \frac{TP_p}{TP_p + FP_p}, Recall_p = \frac{TP_p}{TP_p + FN_p}, Accuracy_p = \frac{TP_p + TN_p}{TP_p + TN_p + FP_p + FN_p}$$

$$F-measure_p = 2 * \frac{Precision_p * Recall_p}{Precision_p + Recall_p}$$

The average values obtained for the metrics (for all participants, all tasks) were:

Precision = 67%, Recall = 76%, F-measure = 71% Accuracy = 95%.

For a more fine-grained analysis, aiming to identify the synchronization points that were less obvious for the participants, we computed the precision, recall, f-measure and accuracy for each task (related to a data item) separately (disregarding two tasks, 1.3 and 2.1, where no synchronization points existed in the process).

As can be seen from Table 2, the lowest precision-recall values are attributed to task 2.2. In this task the participants were asked to identify a synchronization point for the data item of shipment amount in the product delivery process. According to the textual description of the process handed to the participants, the transition of *package goods* requires using a package of a size that matches the right shipment amount as recorded in the information system. The participants were expected to understand that at this point any discrepancy between the package size, selected according to the data item value, and the physical goods to be shipped, will be revealed. Thus they were expected to indicate this transition as a synchronization point. The inherent difficulty in this task was that it required the participants to visualize the connection between the data item value (the amount) in the IS and its corresponding value in reality (the physical amount), via the package size. Evidently, this was not straightforward, especially considering that they were relying on a textual description of a process which was not familiar to them otherwise.

**Table 2.** Precision-Recall metrics for each task ·

| Tasks | 1.1 | 1.2 | 2.2 | 2.3 |
|---|---|---|---|---|
| Precision | 0.9 | 0.78 | 0.38 | 0.95 |
| Recall | 0.9 | 0.8 | 0.4 | 0.95 |
| F-measure | 0.9 | 0.79 | 0.39 | 0.95 |
| Accuracy | 0.99 | 0.95 | 0.9 | 0.99 |

Considering the remaining tasks (1.1, 1.2, and 2.3) led to the following average results:

Precision = 71%, Recall = 88%, F-measure = 78% Accuracy = 96%.

Thus for tasks where less domain knowledge was required and the connection between the recorded data item and the state variable was evident from the activity labels, the notion of synchronization point was more clear and correctly identified by the participants in most cases.

## 5  Discussion

The results of our analysis show that the abstract notion of synchronization points is identifiable by process designers, suggesting that the proposed framework has the potential to be useful as a basis for analysis of data inaccuracy at design time. However, the success of the participants in identifying synchronization points was not uniform, suggesting that some synchronization points are harder to identify than others. In particular, domain knowledge may play a role in the assessment of whether a transition involves a synchronization point or not. Furthermore, the activity labels are not sufficient for this assessment, and an in-depth consideration of how a transition (an activity) is actually performed and what data is used are needed. This also raises an interesting question whether choosing different labels for transitions can have an effect on designers' identification of synchronization points. Further qualitative analysis of the open-ended questions and the textual justifications given by the participants can help shed light on this question.

The limitations of our experimental settings can be discussed while assessing its construct, internal, and external validity. Regarding construct validity – we wanted to measure the extent to which modelers correctly use the notion of synchronization point and identify such points in a process model. To this end we treated our participants as human classifiers, classifying each transition in the model as a synchronization point or not. We then used metrics which are commonly used for classifiers (precision/recall). Moreover, the textual answers explaining the decisions served for triangulation with the actual selection, ensuring that arbitrary selections were not accounted for. As to internal validity – based on the detailed analysis reported above, it is possible that the phrasing of some of the labels affected the identification of synchronization points. Still, even with less careful label phrasing the results show that synchronization points are identifiable. Last, external validity could be compromised due the use of students as participants and the limited number of process models used. We believe, however, that the identification of synchronization points would be easier for experienced process designers than for students, especially considering that process designers should normally be familiar with the domain at hand. Hence, we expect even higher success rates for professionals. Nevertheless, we plan to study this further, using additional process models.

## 6  Related Work

Data quality has been extensively addressed outside the context of business processes [3, 4, 22]. For instance, Wang et al. [23] defined the notion Data Quality as "fitness for use", i.e., the ability of the data to meet users' requirements. Moreover, they explained that in order to improve data quality, we have to understand what the data means to those who consume it. They conducted the first large-scale study which empirically identified fifteen dimensions of data quality in information systems, claiming that there is no consensus on what constitutes a good set of data and on an appropriate definition of each dimension. Nevertheless, there are several fundamental dimensions which are common in most studies: accuracy, completeness, timeliness, consistency and reliability. Orr [13] indicated that data quality is of high priority in every enterprise, and that the general quality can be improved by changing data usage. Some studies discussed the quality of data simply as the ability to meet requirements [8, 23], while others stressed the importance of referring to the data elements during the design-time of the database in order to ensure data quality at the execution time of the process.

In the context of business processes, limited work concerning data quality has been done. For example, Sadiq et al. [16] claimed that in the area of business process design and business process analysis, the specification of data requirements and specification of the data flows between process activities is required, since they have a significant impact on the process activities. They argued that in order to understand the impact of the data on a process and its results, an evaluation against the process goal is needed. Moreover, they proposed a method for supporting process designers in the selection of actions that should be adopted in consideration of data quality requirements when designing business processes. Rodriguez et al. [6, 14] introduced a data quality-aware model. They presented a BPMN 2.0 extension, allowing business analysts to specify data quality requirements in business process models. This extension allows business analysts to be aware of data quality issues and also provides a systematic way for data quality management. However, their approach is not formally anchored and does not support a detailed and systematic analysis of potential data quality issues in a business process. Gharib et al. [10] introduced a goal-oriented approach to model and analyze information quality (IQ) requirements in business processes from a socio-technical perspective. Their work is based on an extended version of secure Tropos [12] that is able to model and analyze IQ requirements in their social and organizational context, and then map these requirements into workflow net with actors. Some studies, such as [11, 14] attempted to address data quality concepts at process design. The main goal of these studies is to help predict how changes in the business processes and transactions would influence the data quality and support process designers in the selection of actions that should be adopted in the (re)design of business processes, with respect to data quality requirements. Their methods do not involve automated actions and require high human involvement. Cappiello et al. [5, 7] also proposed a data quality improvement strategy that aims to identify potential source of errors at runtime or design time. In order to manage such enhancement, they used the notion of Data Quality block [17] which addresses the issues related to the design of the blocks and to their positioning inside a process.

Analyzing data inaccuracy at business process design time has been suggested by Soffer [21] who also provided formal definitions of the problem and an explanation of its underlying mechanism. Moreover, Soffer discussed the potential consequences of data inaccuracy in business processes and demonstrates possible scenarios of data inaccuracy in business processes. Additionally, Soffer introduced a notion of data and real world synchronization points in processes. Basically, the information system dependent process and its environment as independent sub-domains, operate concurrently. These sub-domains merge at synchronization points where the process needs to scrutinize not only the data items, but also the real values which the data items represent in order to proceed. An idea which is close to the notion of synchronization point has been presented in [24] in the context of requirement engineering. They discussed the importance of identifying which actions are controlled by the system (resemblance to the IS sub-domain), which actions are controlled by the environment (environment sub-domain) and which actions of the environment are shared with the system (synchronization point). This identification helps explain the nature of requirements, specifications, domain knowledge and the relationships among them. Furthermore, it assists in establishing minimum standards for what information should be represented in a requirements language.

The work presented here broadens Soffer's ideas by extending WFD-nets with the notion of synchronization points, thus providing a formal model which explicitly represents these points. This model provides a basis for a formal design time analysis of potential data inaccuracy in the process.

# 7 Conclusions

Data has an enormous impact on business processes. Until now, data inaccuracy has mainly been addressed in the area of business process management as a possible exception at runtime [15]. However, anticipating data inaccuracy situations as part of process design can help alleviating some of the possible consequences and mitigate the associated risks.

In this paper, we have proposed a conceptual framework for incorporating data inaccuracy considerations in process models. This was done by introducing the concept of synchronization points as part of an extension of the WFD-net formalism to support an explicit representation of such points while designing a process. This framework constitutes a basis upon which formal analysis methods of potential data inaccuracy will be developed. The applicability of the model was examined through an empirical evaluation. In this empirical study we discovered that process designers can identify correctly the right spots of synchronization points in a given process. Moreover, this new notion adds an additional layer to process design in the sense of the real world values and data inaccuracy consequences that might take place in a process. This can assist process designer in designing more robust process with respect to data inaccuracy.

Future research will build on this model for designing manual and automated analysis methods that should enable designing more resilient business processes, where the consequences of potential data inaccuracy would be reduced. In particular, we will alleviate the labeling of synchronization points in a model for indicating when data is used in "safe" modes, when its value is verified, and when it is used unsafely, so data inaccuracy might bear full consequences.

**Acknowledgement.** The first and the second authors are supported by the Israel Science Foundation under grant agreement no. 856/13. The third author is supported by the Israel Science Foundation under grant agreement no. 817/15.

# References

1. Aalst, W.M.: The application of Petri nets to workflow management. J. Circ. Syst. Comput. **8**(01), 21–66 (1998)
2. Aalst, W.M., Ter Hofstede, A.H., Kiepuszewski, B., Barros, A.P.: Workflow patterns. Distrib. Parallel Databases **14**(1), 5–51 (2003)
3. Aebi, D., Perrochon, L.: Towards improving data quality. In: CiSMOD, pp. 273–281 (1993)
4. Agmon, N., Ahituv, N.: Assessing data reliability in an information system. J. Manage. Inf. Syst. **4**, 34–44 (1987)
5. Cappiello, C., Pernici, B.: Quality-aware design of repairable processes. In: ICIQ (2008)
6. Cappiello, C., Caro, A., Rodriguez, A., Caballero, I.: An approach to design business processes addressing data quality issues. In: ECIS, p. 216 (1987)
7. Cappiello, C., Pernici, B., Villani, L.: Strategies for data quality monitoring in business processes. In: Benatallah, B., Bestavros, A., Catania, B., Haller, A., Manolopoulos, Y., Vakali, A., Zhang, Y. (eds.) WISE 2014. LNCS, vol. 9051, pp. 226–238. Springer, Cham (2015). doi: 10.1007/978-3-319-20370-6_18
8. Falge, C., Otto, B., Österle, H.: Data quality requirements of collaborative business processes. In: 2012 45th Hawaii International Conference on System Science (HICSS). IEEE (2012)
9. Fawcett, T.: An introduction to ROC analysis. Pattern Recogn. Lett. **27**(8), 861–874 (2006)
10. Gharib, M., Giorgini, P.: Modeling and reasoning about information quality requirements in business processes. In: Gaaloul, K., Schmidt, R., Nurcan, S., Guerreiro, S., Ma, Q. (eds.) CAISE 2015. LNBIP, vol. 214, pp. 231–245. Springer, Cham (2015). doi:10.1007/978-3-319-19237-6_15
11. Heravizadeh, M., Mendling, J., Rosemann, M.: Dimensions of business processes quality (QoBP). In: Ardagna, D., Mecella, M., Yang, J. (eds.) BPM 2008. LNBIP, vol. 17, pp. 80–91. Springer, Heidelberg (2009). doi:10.1007/978-3-642-00328-8_8
12. Mouratidis, H., Giorgini, P.: Secure tropos: a security-oriented extension of the tropos methodology. Int. J. Softw. Eng. Knowl. Eng. **17**(02), 285–309 (2007)
13. Orr, K.: Data quality and systems theory. Commun. ACM **41**(2), 66–71 (1998)
14. Rodríguez, A., Caro, A., Cappiello, C., Caballero, I.: A BPMN extension for including data quality requirements in business process modeling. In: Mendling, J., Weidlich, M. (eds.) BPMN 2012. LNBIP, vol. 125, pp. 116–125. Springer, Heidelberg (2012). doi: 10.1007/978-3-642-33155-8_10
15. Russell, N., Aalst, W., Hofstede, A.: Workflow exception patterns. In: Dubois, E., Pohl, K. (eds.) CAiSE 2006. LNCS, vol. 4001, pp. 288–302. Springer, Heidelberg (2006). doi: 10.1007/11767138_20
16. Sadiq, S., Orlowska, M., Sadiq, W., Foulger, C.: Data flow and validation in workflow modeling. In: Proceedings of the 15th Australasian Database Conference, ADC 2004, vol. 27, pp. 207–214 (2004)
17. Shankaranarayanan, G., Wang, R.Y., Ziad, M.: IP-MAP: representing the manufacture of an information product. IQ 2000
18. Sidorova, N., Stahl, C., Trčka, N.: Workflow soundness revisited: checking correctness in the presence of data while staying conceptual. In: Pernici, B. (ed.) CAiSE 2010. LNCS, vol. 6051, pp. 530–544. Springer, Heidelberg (2010). doi:10.1007/978-3-642-13094-6_40
19. Soffer, P., Wand, Y.: On the notion of soft goals in business process modeling. Bus. Process Manage. J. **11**(6), 663–679 (2005)
20. Soffer, P., Kaner, M., Wand, Y.: Assigning ontological meaning to workflow nets. J. Database Manage. **21**(3), 1–35 (2010)

21. Soffer, P.: Mirror, mirror on the wall, can i count on you at all? Exploring data inaccuracy in business processes. In: Bider, I., Halpin, T., Krogstie, J., Nurcan, S., Proper, E., Schmidt, R., Ukor, R. (eds.) BPMDS/EMMSAD -2010. LNBIP, vol. 50, pp. 14–25. Springer, Heidelberg (2010). doi:10.1007/978-3-642-13051-9_2
22. Wand, Y., Wang, R.Y.: Anchoring data quality dimensions in ontological foundations. Commun. ACM **39**(11), 86–95 (1996)
23. Wang, R.Y., Strong, D.M.: Beyond accuracy: what data quality means to data consumers. J. Manage. Inf. Syst. **12**(4), 5–33 (1996)
24. Zave, P., Jackson, M.: Four dark corners of requirements engineering. ACM Trans. Softw. Eng. Methodol. (TOSEM) **6**(1), 1–30 (1997)

# Structured Behavioral Programming Idioms

Adiel Ashrov[1], Michal Gordon[2], Assaf Marron[3], Arnon Sturm[1(✉)], and Gera Weiss[1]

[1] Ben Gurion University of the Negev, Beer Sheva, Israel
{ashrov,geraw}@cs.bgu.ac.il, sturm@bgu.ac.il
[2] Holon Institute of Technology, Holon, Israel
michaligordon@gmail.com
[3] The Weizmann Institute of Science, Rehovot, Israel
assaf.marron@weizmann.ac.il

**Abstract.** Behavioral Programming (BP) is a modelling and programming technique proposed for specifying and for implementing complex reactive systems. While effective, we report on a weakness that stems from the verbosity and from the complexity of the programming constructs in BP. Our analysis, described in this paper, shows that developers who work with BP use specific patterns that allow them to control the complexity of their specification. Thus, the main contribution of this paper is a set of specification constructs that represent those patterns. We report on the design of the new idioms, termed *structured constructs for behavioral programming* and on an empirical evaluation in a controlled experiment that proved their effectiveness. In particular, the experiment examined the comprehensibility differences between behavioral specifications with non-structured BP programming idioms and with the structured ones. The results indicate that the new structures improve the comprehension of the behavioral specification.

**Keywords:** Behavioral modeling · Behavioral specification · Behavioral programming · Experimentation · Abstraction · Comprehension

## 1 Introduction

Behavioral specifications play a crucial role in systems' specifications, in particular, reactive ones. Such specifications are rich and complex and both the research and industry communities are in continuous search for balancing the expressiveness and ease of use of languages and methods that support behavioral specification. A major tool for addressing this challenge is the use of abstraction.

While abstractions, as provided, e.g., by structured idioms, may help developers, they may also be counterproductive in some cases. In [1], for example, the authors show, via empirical evaluation, that the abstraction provided by software visualizations can provide measurable benefits in program comprehension tasks. In [2], however, the authors found that the abstraction provided by object-oriented design documents may be less effective than traditional design documents. The challenge is, of course, to identify those abstractions and structures that simplify the specification without sacrificing the naturalness of the semantics. See, for example, [3] where implementations of a specific set of solutions to problems in several languages are compared.

I. Reinhartz-Berger et al. (Eds.): BPMDS/EMMSAD 2017, LNBIP 287, pp. 319–333, 2017.
DOI: 10.1007/978-3-319-59466-8_20

In a sense, introducing modelling idioms that encapsulate existing idioms but subject them to certain design patterns, facilitates, and encourages the use of, such patterns [4]. This has been demonstrated by many studies on design and programming patterns including proposals for programming structures, for teaching methodologies, for supporting tools, etc. [5–8]. Usually, reports on the effects of patterns are available in anecdotal form from various practitioners [5], yet there are also cases that contain quantitative assessments and include empirical studies [9, 10].

The focus of this paper is on extracting patterns and structures in a particular behavioral specification approach called behavioral programming (BP) [11]. BP is an approach to software development, designed to allow developers to align their implementation with how people often describe a system's behavior. BP is an extension and generalization of scenario-based programming originally introduced with the visual language of live sequence charts (LSC) [12, 13], which has been implemented in several textual/procedural/imperative programming languages including Java [14], C++, Erlang, C, Javascript, and Blockly [15].

The structured idioms that we propose in this paper are in the context of behavior threads in an imperative language as proposed in [14]. In this context, developers specify short concurrent procedures, using standard imperative programming idioms that jointly specify how the system should respond to external events. In this paper, we propose a set of structured idioms for BP and evaluate them in an experiment. For the experiment, we use the Blockly library [15] that allows behavioral specification with a graphical interface through which subjects (software engineering students) construct imperative programs by dragging and dropping blocks (which combine text and graphic cues) on a canvas. Beyond shortening the learning phase and allowing us the flexibility to introduce the structures in a systematic manner, the use of an environment that the subjects were unfamiliar with contributes to the generality of our conclusion (that structures help developers) as the experiment by passes prejudiced preferences or habits.

The contribution of the paper is twofold: (1) A new set of idioms for BP specification is proposed. (2) An empirical evaluation that validates the improvement in comprehension of the new idioms in comparison to the existing idioms is reported upon.

The rest of the paper is organized as follows: In Sect. 2, we introduce the general principles of BP and their application to Blockly as well as the new structured idioms we devised. In Sect. 3 we described the empirical evaluation of the structured idioms in comparison to the previous, direct idioms. Finally, in Sect. 4 we conclude and outline a plan for future research.

## 2    Behavioral Programs and Specification Idioms

A behavioral program consists of a set of independent components called behavior threads (b-threads for short) that control the flow of events and synchronize via an enhanced publish/subscribe protocol, as follows. Each b-thread is a procedure running in parallel to the other b-threads. When a b-thread reaches a synchronization point, it waits until all other b-threads also reach synchronization points in their own flow. When entering a synchronization points, each b-thread refers to three sets of events:

1. **Requested** events - the thread proposes that these events be considered for triggering, and asks to be notified when any of them occurs;
2. **Waited-for** events - the thread does not request these events, but asks to be notified when any of them is triggered; and
3. **Blocked** events - the thread forbids triggering of these events.

When all b-threads are at a synchronization point, an event that is requested by at least one b-thread and not blocked by any other b-thread is chosen. The selected event is then triggered by resuming all the b-threads that either requested or waited for it. Each of these resumed b-threads then proceeds with its execution, all the way to the next synchronization point, where it again presents new sets of requested, waited-for, and blocked events. The other b-threads remain at their last synchronization points, oblivious to the triggered event, until an event that they have requested or are waiting for is selected. When all b-threads are again at a synchronization point, the event selection process repeats. The translation between inputs, and the events that represent them, and between program-driven events and program outputs are handled by separate sensor and actuator code which of secondary importance in the present discussion.

In this work, to enable experimenting with subjects who have minimal background in BP, we used the Blockly library [15] to implement a BP workbench and developed a tutorial that introduces this environment. Blockly is a library for building Scratch-like [16] visual programming environments. In the Blockly environment, we initially introduced the most basic BP idiom, bSync, shown below, very similarly to the way it is used by b-threads in the textual language implementations of BP (Java, C++, etc.) to declare the sets of requested, waited-for and blocked events:

With this construct, developers can set the b-threads as ordinary software procedures, as follows. Each b-thread procedure consists of internal computations and bSync blocks. In the internal computation, the b-thread has access to the all events in the model and, when ready, it can declare requested, waited-for, and blocked events by plugging them into the empty slots in the bSync construct. For example, assume that we want to program a robot (drawn as a pegman) to reach a target (drawn as an inverted-drop-shaped icon) moving along a desired path in a maze:

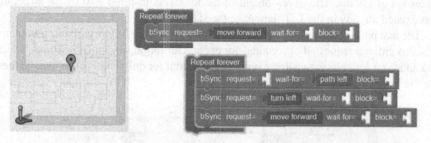

Each of the two disconnected groups of blocks represents a function that acts as a b-thread. The first (top) function always requests a '**move forward**' actuation event.

The second (bottom) b-thread, waits for a '**path left**' sensor event and, when it is triggered, requests a '**turn left**' followed by a '**move forward**' actuation events. The joint execution of these two b-threads is as follows:

1. Both b-threads run in parallel until both reach their first **bSync**. The first b-thread requests the event '**move forward**' and the second b-thread waits for the event '**path left**'.
2. The event '**move forward**' is triggered
3. The first b-thread is resumed and returns to the same **bSync**. The second b-thread is not resumed because the triggered event is neither requested nor is waited-for.
4. The above two steps are repeated while a hidden actuator causes the pegman to step forward every time the '**move forward**' event is triggered. After several such rounds, a hidden sensor causes the triggering of the event '**path left**' when the pegman arrives at a location where there is a path to its left.
5. The triggering of the '**path left**' event causes the second b-thread to advance to its second state where it requests the event '**turn left**'. At this point, two events, namely '**turn left**' and '**move forward**', are requested and none of them is blocked. When there are several possible events, the present mechanism triggers the first event in a predetermined order: sensing events come first, then turn events, and then the '**move forward**' event. In our case, the '**turn left**' event is selected. (In other implementations, event selection priorities are replaced, e.g., by additional b-threads that block the selection of events that would be undesired at that state).
6. In the next step, both b-threads request the '**move forward**' event so it is selected. Note that subject to the event selection process described above, the two concurrent requests are satisfied by one triggering of the event, a mechanism termed *unification* of events (see [13] for a detailed discussion on the power of event unification).
7. The run continues similarly until the pegman is at its goal, at which point a corresponding sensor and actuator display an appropriate message and stop the run.

This demonstrates the coding style before the idioms proposed in this paper were introduced, only with the, so-called, bSync idiom. The motivation for designing a new set of idioms for BP came from an examination of how the bSync idiom set is used in practice. We noticed that developers, ourselves included, utilized several patterns while developing applications (see [14, 15]). We then proceeded to extract these patterns into a new set of idioms. The development of the idioms is inspired also by the structures that existed already in the LSC language (see [12, 13, 17]).

The first pattern we noticed was that developers often use bSync with one parameter, which is either a requested or a waited-for event. Our initial simplification, then, was to add an idiom for only requesting events and an idiom for only waiting-for events; these are the Request and Wait-for idioms:

These two idioms are similar to *executed* and *monitored* events in LSC [17].

While the use of only `Wait-for` and `Request` idioms may suffice for specifying simple b-threads, we did find examples where these alone are not enough:

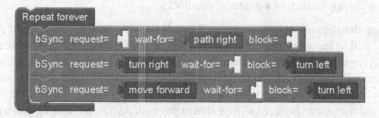

Specifically, we identified cases, as seen in the above example, where developers used more than one parameter of a **bSync**. We then tried to categorize the needs for such usage, and came with two specific patterns as follows. The desired behavior, implemented above, is to complete a right turn while forbidding left turns. A right turn maneuver is composed of two requested events, '**turn right**' and '**move forward**'. The desired behavior is implemented by blocking the event '**turn left**' in every synchronization point that takes place while the right turn process is happening. More generally, the pattern is a sequence of **bSync** declarations with an unwanted event being blocked in each declaration.

Once such a pattern was identified, we designed a language structure to facilitate its use. Specifically, we propose the `Blocking` structure. The `Blocking` structure can be specified with an event and be associated with a scope of a sequence of blocks stacked together. The idiom specifies that the unwanted event is implicitly declared as blocked in each synchronization point under its scope. In the following, we see an equivalent to the b-thread shown above where the **bSync** was transformed to wait-for and request and event blocking declarations are specified using the new structure:

The structure demonstrated in the above specification forces discipline in the sense that it does not allow for developers to specify arbitrary blocking declarations, except for the form of a construct that specifies a scope for each blocking specification.

The second construct proposed in this paper originated from the following issue: We saw in various behavioral specifications that developers deal with situation where an event triggers some fragment of behavior but, before the fragment of the behavior is completed, some other event indicates that the fragment needs to be aborted. For example, imagine two b-threads in a system:

1. A b-thread for handling a right turn by blocking '**turn left**' while turning right.
2. A b-thread that requests the '**turn left**' event. (In this example, this b-thread is purposely "naïve", in that it does not block any event, and, in particular, does not cause the appearance of a potential deadlock).

When the pegman is faced with a T-junction, both '**path left**' and '**path right**' will be triggered and both b-threads will be notified about the appropriate event and will progress to the next synchronization point. The b-thread responsible for making a left turn will be blocked by the first b-thread and, as a result, the pegman will turn right. When the first b-thread finishes the turn, it will no longer block the '**turn left**' and the second b-thread will be able to proceed. As a result, the pegman will turn left and try to move forward. However, it is unknown if there is a path to the left at the updated location of the pegman. Clearly, this delayed left turn was not intended.

There is a need for stopping and breaking from a block of specification if there is a change in the assumed state for the operation. An example that uses standard Blockly control-flow constructs for the pattern that we want to enforce is the following:

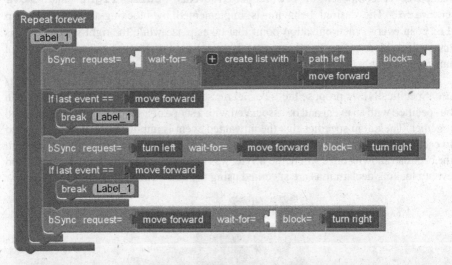

Here, the "if last_event==" construct is used together with the "break" command to test the last event and skip the rest of the sequence of requests if needed.

In general, the pattern we identified is a fragment of the specification in which the developers wish to abort preemptively when a certain event arrives. To allow this, we propose the idiom of 'break-upon'. The specification below has the same logic presented above. We wait-for a 'path left' event and then perform two requests in order to turn left. These instructions are under the scope of the break-upon idiom specified with '**move forward**'. This induces a wait-for '**move forward**' declaration in each of the nested synchronization points. If this event is triggered, the flow breaks from the break-upon scope and go back to the beginning of the loop.

Note that the semantics of the two idioms allow nesting:

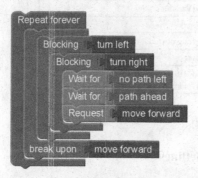

Formally, the semantics (and the implementation) of the new idioms is as follows: `Request` and `Wait for` are defined as a bSync call with two of the event sets being empty; the `blocking` idiom adds the blocked events to the blocked-event set in each synchronization point within its scope; and, the `break-upon` idiom adds to the waited-for event set in each of the synchronization points in its scope the referenced event, and adds after each such synchronization point the statement "if `lastEvent==<the break-upon event>` then `break`". A synchronization point can be nested in several scopes, as shown in the above example, in which case multiple such actions may apply to it.

To summarize, in this paper we are proposing new idioms for behavioral programming specification. These idioms where identified by an examination of behavioral specification and of the needs of developers that work with the language. We have proved that the new set of idioms, called structured idioms below, is equivalent in expressive power to the base language, called **bSync** (see the Appendix).

## 3 Evaluating BP Structured Idioms

To evaluate the benefits of using the BP structured idioms introduced before, we conducted a controlled experiment to compare the usage of the **bSync** and the **Structured** idioms with respect to the comprehension of a BP specification. In particular, we were interested in comparing two issues related to comprehension. The first is the execution semantics, i.e., the order of handled events and the second is the intention behind the developed specification. Our initial conjecture was that with respect to execution semantics comprehension, the results would be in favor of the **bSync** idioms since the statements are explicated in one block, in particular, in simple cases. With respect to the comprehension of the specification intention, our hypothesis was that the results would be in favor of the **Structured** idioms as the specification is more organized. We followed the experiment model that appears in Fig. 1.

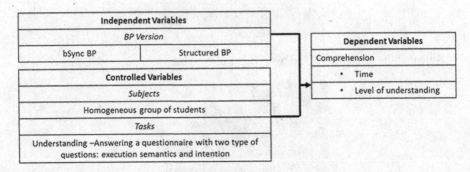

**Fig. 1.** The experiment model

## 3.1   The Experiment Settings

**The Independent Variable.** As the objective of the experiment was to evaluate the comprehension of the two BP versions over a set of dependent variables, the independent variable is the BP version used, i.e., **bSync** versus **Structured**.

**The Dependent Variables.** Following the experiment goal, the dependent variables are the level of understanding a behavioral specification and the time it takes to reach that understanding. The level of understanding was determined by a set of multiple-choice questions and the time was self-measured by the subjects.

**Subjects.** In the experiment, 49 software engineering students in their third year of studies participated; 22 were assigned to the **Structured** based specifications and 27 were assigned to the **bSync** based specification. They were randomly assigned to the specific set of idioms. Examining both the students' GPA and their grade in the "Topics in Software Engineering" course (from which the students were volunteered), we found no statistically significance differences (T-test: $p > 0.51, p > 0.69$). All subjects were at an advanced stage in their studies and already took courses related to programming and modeling. The participation in the experiment was on a voluntary basis. Yet, in order to motivate and encourage the subjects to participate (and in an effective way), they were told in advance that they would get a bonus in the aforementioned course based on their performance in the experiment. In addition, all participants signed a consent form on which they were explicitly informed that they could withdraw from the experiment at any time.[1]

---

[1]   The experiment design and execution was also approved by an ethical committee.

**Training.** In the beginning of the semester, the students were provided with a lecture about behavioral specification. In addition, the first part of the experiment was devoted to introduce the subjects with their assigned behavioral specification idioms set. It was an online tutorial to Behavioral Programming using a Maze[2] application, which we mentioned in the previous section. The main purpose of the tutorial was to teach BP principles using the assigned set of idioms. We believe that the fact that Blockly and BP are not common development environments that students interacted with during their studies, freed them from existing knowledge and beliefs, and allowed them to experience the tutorial from a fresh point of view. The tutorial consisted of nine challenges (levels) in solving mazes where every challenge introduced new concepts/idioms. In every challenge, the goal was to develop a behavioral specification, which will lead a pegman to a destination.

**Task.** Upon completing the introductory tutorial, the subjects were requested to answer a questionnaire consisting of questions about their perceptions over BP, in general, and to its specific concepts and mechanisms, followed by 16 BP specification questions[3]. The latter were classified as appears in Table 1.

**Table 1.** BP specification question classification

|  | Execution | Intention |
|---|---|---|
| Request + Wait (RW) | Q1, Q9, Q4, Q12 |  |
| Request + Wait + Blocking (RWBL) | Q3, Q11 | Q5, Q13 |
| Request + Wait + Breaking (RWBR) | Q2, Q10 | Q6, Q14 |
| Request + Wait + Blocking + Breaking (RWBLBR) |  | Q7, Q8, Q15, Q16 |

**Execution.** The experiment took place in several sessions within a lab, in which the subjects started with a tutorial demonstrating and teaching the BP concepts and then answered the questionnaire. Each session (including the tutorial) lasted one and half-hour long.

## 3.2 Experimental Results

We first review the students' perception over the knowledge and understanding of BP. Table 2 summarizes the results, where the average of the scores given by the students is in the scale of [0-4], are shown for each question and for each version of BP. It seems that from the lecture on BP the students who were assigned the **bSync** version perceived their understanding of BP a bit better than those who were assigned with the **Structured** version (yet, this was not statistically significant). This might be because the **bSync** version is related to the code version shown in class. Nevertheless, based on the tutorial, it seems that the students that were trained with the **Structured** version perceived their BP understanding higher than those who were trained with the **bSync** version. Applying

---

[2] https://bp-new-blockly-exp-2.appspot.com/static/apps/mazeBP/index.html? version=1(version=2). Designed to work with the Firefox web browser.

[3] The questionnaires can be found in https://tinyurl.com/h3bzphs, https://tinyurl.com/zah4ap3.

the Mann-Whitney test, we found that the differences were statistically significant. In general, in both groups, the students perceived their understanding of the BP concepts in the order for high to low comprehension level: blocking, breaking out, multiple events, and the execution mechanism.

**Table 2.** Students Perecptions over BP

| Question | Structured | bSync | Sig. (M-W) |
|---|---|---|---|
| To what extent did you understand the concept of BP from that lecture? | 1.64 | 1.78 | 0.497 |
| Do you perceive the BP tutorial helpful? | 2.55 | 2.04 | **0.004** |
| Do you understand the execution mechanism of BP (i.e., how events are chosen)? | 2.59 | 2.00 | **0.000** |
| Do you understand the concept of having the same event requested by multiple threads/scenarios? | 2.77 | 2.30 | **0.012** |
| Do you understand the concept of event blocking? | 3.14 | 2.41 | **0.001** |
| Do you understand the concept of "breaking out" from a scope in the program? | 2.86 | 2.41 | **0.002** |

Next, we review the results of the questions that objectively examined the students' understanding of BP. As shown in Table 3, in general, the level of understanding of BP (measured by the number of correct answers) both with respect to the execution semantics and with respect to the intention was in favor of the students who were trained and questioned with the **Structured** version. Those differences were also statistically significant. Nevertheless, no statistical significant differences were found with respect to the time it took to answer the various questions.

**Table 3.** Comprehension average scores (and standard deviation) on BP specification questions

| | Level of understanding | | | Time (min) | | |
|---|---|---|---|---|---|---|
| | bSync | Structured | Sig. (T-test) | bSync | Structured | Sig. (T-test) |
| Total | 7.41 (2.17) | 10.91 (2.83) | **<0.001** | 24.30 (8.02) | 23.23 (6.39) | 0.61 |
| Execution semantics | 3.19 (1.39) | 4.95 (2.06) | **<0.001** | 9.48 (3.77) | 9.86 (4.14) | 0.74 |
| Intention | 4.22 (1.37) | 5.95 (1.46) | **<0.001** | 14.81 (4.97) | 13.36 (3.66) | 0.25 |

We further drilled down to check what concepts or mechanisms caused that differences between the comprehensions of the two idioms set.

Table 4 shows the results with respect to the categories defined in Table 1. It seems that the most significant concepts that caused the difference in understanding the specification is the breaking out concept (RWBR-E), that also appeared in the more complex specifications (RWBLBR-I).

**Table 4.** Comprehension average scores (and standard deviation) on BP specification questions with respect to BP concepts

|            | RW- E       | RWBL- E     | RWBR- E     | RWBL-I      | RWBR-I      | RWBLBR-I    |
|------------|-------------|-------------|-------------|-------------|-------------|-------------|
| Structured | 2.14 (1.13) | 1.27 (0.77) | 1.55 (0.67) | 1.77 (0.53) | 1.45 (0.51) | 2.73 (0.88) |
| bSync      | 1.89 (0.93) | 1.04 (0.81) | 0.26 (0.45) | 1.67 (0.48) | 1.19 (0.74) | 1.37 (0.93) |
| Sig. (T-test) | 0.41     | 0.30        | **0.00**    | 0.47        | 0.14        | **0.00**    |

\* E- Execution, I- Intention

## 3.3 Discussion

The results confirmed our conjecture regarding the intention comprehension but not our conjecture regarding the execution semantics. As we further look for explanations for the results, we opt for ontological analysis of language grammars [18] in which the mapping process of the language grammar (BP version, in our case) to the ontological world (the execution semantics and intention, in our case) may suffer from various deficiencies. One such deficiency is the construct overload: "Construct overload occurs when one design construct maps into two or more ontological constructs". In bSync (a design construct) this is exactly the case in which one statement is mapped into several event types (ontological constructs). This deficiency, that affects the mapping to the actual execution of the program, seems, according to our findings, to be the root cause for the results we get in the experiment.

Another alternative for interpreting the results is to look at cognitive analysis frameworks. The COGEVAL is one such framework [19]. We find it appropriate for our analysis as it refers to various cognitive aspects of modeling and because the framework has been demonstrated to be useful in many cases.

The framework consists of several propositions among which we found the following well fitted to our case:

P1: "The greater the degree of chunking supported by a model, the greater the modeling effectiveness."

The results suggest that the structured BP increases the degree of chunking with respect of treating events as it has a unique concept that treats each event type separately. Thus, in simple cases of request, wait-for, and blocking no chunking was required (as these were simple to understand), no statistically significant differences were found between the comprehension of the two sets of BP idioms. However, in the case of the more complex tasks, consisting the breaking out, chunking was beneficial and as the **Structured** BP increases the degree of chunking and using it was found useful in terms of effectiveness (correctness).

As for the other way around, considering that increased chunking may be of a disadvantage in some aspects, COGEVAL suggest that:

P2: "The greater the number of simultaneous items required (over seven) to create schema segments or chunks, the lower the modeling effectiveness of the model."

In our case, the **Structured** BP uses a limited number (three) of simultaneous items to specify the same concept as in the **bSync** BP. This explains the reason that the **Structured** BP did not negatively affect the effectiveness.

### 3.4   Threat to Validity

Several threats to the validity may be encountered when discussing the experiment.

**Conclusion validity** concerns with issues that affect the ability to infer the correct conclusion regarding the relations between the treatment and the outcome of the experiment. As we believe that the only variable that was changed during the experiment was the used version of BP, we believe that our conclusions are valid and no major treat exists.

**Internal validity** is the degree to which conclusions can be drawn about the causal effect of the independent variables on the dependent variables. By randomly assigning the subjects to the two versions, we neutralized most of the possible effects that may have influenced the independent variable of participants, such as experience, training, and personal characteristics. An additional threat to internal validity is the quality of training, which in our case was the tutorial. It might be that such a training is not enough; yet, the scope of the training for both groups was the same.

**External validity** concerns with the ability to generalize experimental results outside the experimental settings. An external validity threat is always present when experimenting with students, as the issue of whether they are representative of software professionals is raised. However, in this experiment, we checked differences among similar groups, the experiment theme is not familiar to professionals, and as the students are in their third year, they have already gained some experience. Another external validity issue, which is unfortunately inherent to controlled experiments, is the size and complexity of the tasks used. The size of the various tasks is small; nevertheless, controlled experiments require that subjects complete the assigned task in a limited amount of time and without interruption to keep variables under control.

## 4   Conclusions

We addressed the concern of behavioral specification abstraction. In particular, we referred to a specific approach to behavioral specification called behavioral programming (BP) that was equipped with modeling capabilities of Blockly. Within the context of that language we compared existing idioms (bSync) with a new set of structured idioms. Our comparison was in terms of understanding behavioral specification. The results of the controlled experiment indicated that abstracting the specification leads to a higher level of understanding. This was evident in particular in cases when a main flow allows for breaking out.

The results of the evaluation performed in this research indicate that it is desirable to abstract specification constructs (i.e., modeling or programming idioms) without scarifying their expressiveness as their usability is better than their low-level counterparts. This is particularly relevant when complex constructs are introduced.

Clearly, such results should be taken with caution and further examination is required. Thus, in the future, we plan to further experiment the two versions (and maybe other alternatives) to further understand the conceptual differences among them so to better design the right abstractions, in BP and in other languages.

**Acknowledgement.** This research was partially supported by the Israel Science Foundation, the Philip M. Klutznick Research Fund, and the Dora Joachimowicz research grant.

# Appendix

While the focus of this work is on empirical evaluation of the idioms, in terms of their usability to programmers, we hereby provide a proof for the expressiveness equivalence of the two sets of idioms.

**Claim 1:** Every b-thread developed with the structured idioms can be translated to a semantically equivalent b-thread that applies only the bSync idiom using If last_event==x {} and break.

**Proof:** By structural induction.

Induction base: if there is no Break-upon or Blocking structures in the program, replace each request(x) and each wait-for(y) with, respectively, a bSync(x,none,none) and a bSync(none,y,none).

Induction step: Assume, by induction, that the claim is true for programs with at most $n$ levels of nesting of the Break-upon or Blocking structures. Given a program with $n + 1$ levels of nesting we can replace each block of maximal nesting level as follows. If the nesting level of the block is less than $n + 1$, it can be replaced by a code that uses only bSync by the induction assumption. For a block of the form blocking(x){P}, where P is some code with $n$ levels of nesting, let $P'$ be a code, given by the induction assumption, that is semantically equivalent to P and uses only the bSync idiom. Let $P''$ be the code obtained by adding x to the list of blocked events in every bSync in $P'$. We can now replace the code Blocking (x) {P} with $P''$. Similarly, for a block of the form {P} break-upon(x), where P is some code with $n$ levels of nesting, let $P'$ be a code, given by the induction assumption, that is semantically equivalent to P. Let $P''$ be the code obtained by adding x to the list of waited-for events in each bSync in $P'$. Let *label* be a name that does not appear as a label in $P''$ and let $P'''$ be the code obtained by adding the commands If last_event==x {break *label* } after each bSync in $P''$. We can now replace the code {P} break-upon(x) with *label*: {P''}. Clearly, the code obtained after all the above replacements contains only bSync, with no application of the structured idioms, and is semantically equivalent to the original code. This proves our claim. ■

In fact, the above proof follows the way we have implemented the structured idioms.

Another issue that should be clarified in the above proof is the semantics of waiting-for or requesting an event while, at the same time, blocking it. This can be done with bSync, when some event is specified both in the waited-for or in the requested lists and in the `blocked` list. It can also be done with the structured idioms, when an event is requested or waited-for in the scope where it is specified as blocked or a `break` `upon` event. In this case, one must decide which specification takes priority – whether to ignore the blocking or to ignore the request or wait-for. It easy to verify that the above proof is correct as long as we use the same priority order in both the `bSync` and in the structured idioms.

**Claim 2** Every b-thread developed with `bSync` idiom can be translated to a semantically equivalent b-thread that uses only the structured idioms.

**Proof** Replace each `bSync(x,y,z)` with `blocking(x){break-upon(y)` `{request(x)}}`. ∎

# References

1. Hendrix, T.D., Cross II, J.H., Maghsoodloo, S., McKinney, M.L.: Do visualizations improve program comprehensibility? experiments with control structure diagrams for Java. ACM SIGCSE Bull. **32**(1), 382–386 (2000)
2. Briand, L.C., Bunse, C., Daly, J.W., Differding, C.: An experimental comparison of the maintainability of object-oriented and structured design documents. Empirical Softw. Eng. **2**(3), 291–312 (1997)
3. Feo, J.T.: A Comparative Study of Parallel Programming Languages: The Salishan Problems. Elsevier, North Holland (2014)
4. Gamma, E., Helm, R., Johnson, R., Vlissides, J.: Design Patterns. Addison-Wesley, Boston (1995)
5. Beck, K., Crocker, R., Meszaros, G., Vlissides, J., Coplien, J.O., Dominick, L., Paulisch, F.: Industrial experience with design patterns. In: Proceedings of the 18th International Conference on Software Engineering (1996)
6. Budinsky, F.J., Finnie, M.A., Vlissides, J.M., Yu, P.S.: Automatic code generation from design patterns. IBM Syst. J. **35**(2), 151–171 (1996)
7. Buschmann, F., Meunier, R., Rohnert, H., Sommerlad, P., Stal, M.: Pattern-Oriented Software Architecture: A System of Patterns. Wiley, New York (1996)
8. Florijn, G., Meijers, M., Winsen, P.: Tool support for object-oriented patterns. In: Akşit, M., Matsuoka, S. (eds.) ECOOP 1997. LNCS, vol. 1241, pp. 472–495. Springer, Heidelberg (1997). doi:10.1007/BFb0053391
9. Prechelt, L., Unger, B., Philippsen, M., Tichy, W.: Two controlled experiments assessing the usefulness of design pattern information during program maintenance. IEEE Trans. Software Eng. **28**(6), 595–606 (2002)
10. Prechelt, L., Unger, B., Tichy, W.F., Brossler, P., Votta, L.G.: A controlled experiment in maintenance: comparing design patterns to simpler solutions. IEEE Trans. Softw. Eng. **27**(12), 1134–1144 (2001)
11. Harel, D., Marron, A., Weiss, G.: Behavioral programming. Commun. ACM **55**(7), 90–100 (2012)
12. Damm, W., Harel, D.: LSCs: breathing life into message sequence charts. J. Formal Methods Syst. Des. **19**(1), 45–80 (2001)
13. Harel, D., Marelly, R.: Come, Let's Play: Scenario-Based Programming Using LSCs and the Play-Engine. Springer, Heidelberg (2003)

14. Harel, D., Marron, A., Weiss, G.: Programming coordinated behavior in Java. In: D'Hondt, T. (ed.) ECOOP 2010. LNCS, vol. 6183, pp. 250–274. Springer, Heidelberg (2010). doi: 10.1007/978-3-642-14107-2_12

15. Ashrov, A., Marron, A., Weiss, G., Wiener, G.: A use-case for behavioral programming: an architecture in JavaScript and Blockly for interactive applications with cross-cutting scenarios. Sci. Comput. Program. **98**(Part 2), 268–292 (2015)

16. Resnick, M., Maloney, J., Monroy-Hernández, A., Rusk, N., Eastmond, E., Brennan, K., Millner, A., Rosenbaum, E., Silver, J., Silverman, B., et al.: Scratch: Programming for all. Comm. ACM **52**(11), 60–67 (2009)

17. Maoz, S., Harel, D., Kleinbort, A.: A compiler for multi-modal scenarios: transforming LSCs into AspectJ. ACM Trans. Softw. Eng. Methodol. (TOSEM) **20**(4) (2011). Article 18

18. Wand, Y., Weber, R.: On the ontological expressiveness of information systems analysis and design grammars. Inform. Syst. J. **3**, 217–237 (1993)

19. Bajaj, A., Rockwell, S.: COGEVAL: applying cognitive theories to evaluate conceptual models. In: Advanced Topics in Database Research, pp. 255–282 (2005)

# Modelling Languages and Methods in Evolving Context

# A Security Requirements Modelling Language to Secure Cloud Computing Environments

Shaun Shei[✉], Haralambos Mouratidis, and Aidan Delaney

School of Computing, Engineering and Mathematics,
Secure and Dependable Software Systems (SenSe) Research Cluster,
University of Brighton, Brighton, UK
{S.Shei,H.Mouratidis,A.J.Delaney}@brighton.ac.uk

**Abstract.** This paper presents a cloud-enhanced modelling language for capturing and describing cloud computing environments, enabling developers to model and reason about security issues in cloud systems from a security requirements engineering perspective. Our work builds upon concepts from the Secure Tropos methodology, where in this paper we introduce novel cloud computing concepts, relationships and properties in order to carry out analysis and produce cloud security requirements. We illustrate our concepts through a case study of a cloud-based career office system from the University of the Aegean. Finally we discuss how our cloud modelling language enriches cloud models with security concepts, guiding developers of cloud systems in understanding cloud vulnerabilities and mitigation strategies through semi-automated security analysis.

**Keywords:** Cloud modelling language · Meta-model · Cloud security requirements · Security requirements engineering

## 1 Introduction

The premise of the cloud computing paradigm is that computing resources are offered by third party providers as a form of commodity accessed through network connections [1]. In comparison to traditional IT solutions, this lowers capital costs and abstracts away implementation and infrastructure details by allowing cloud users to select from pre-configured computing services. However one of the prerequisites for cloud computing; outsourcing data and processes to third parties, raises several security and legal questions [2]. Multi-tenancy in cloud computing refers to multiple cloud users running independent logical processes through virtualisation, while sharing physical components such as CPU, RAM and storage. However from a cloud computing context, the mutual distrust in multi-tenancy environments brings up questions about the security of user data when sharing physical infrastructure [3]. For example consider the scenario where two companies are using virtual machines(VM) hosted on the same physical server. A VM escape vulnerability can be exploited, enabling one company to

© Springer International Publishing AG 2017
I. Reinhartz-Berger et al. (Eds.): BPMDS/EMMSAD 2017, LNBIP 287, pp. 337–345, 2017.
DOI: 10.1007/978-3-319-59466-8_21

access the sensitive data of another company. This attack has been practically demonstrated in [4], in order to extract information from a target co-residing virtual machine.

In this paper we present a cloud modelling language to capture cloud computing concepts from a security requirements engineering perspective, with enhanced properties and attributes to describe the cloud environment as a system as-is and a system to-be. This work builds upon the modelling language proposed in previous work [5], and is part of an on-going research effort to create a framework for holistically modelling secure cloud computing systems, grounded in security requirements engineering and cloud computing security concepts. Our contributions in this paper are:

- *C1*: An updated cloud meta-model aligning concepts from security requirements engineering and cloud computing.
- *C2*: Definitions for cloud concepts, relationships and properties to holistically model secure cloud computing environments.

The rest of the paper is structured as follows. The cloud meta-model, cloud modelling language and security-enhanced cloud computing concepts are defined in Sect. 2. A motivating case study based on a cloud system for the University of the Aegean Career Office is presented in Sect. 3. In Sect. 4 we discuss the respective related work. Finally we conclude the paper in Sect. 5, noting the on-going work and contributions.

## 2    The Secure Cloud Modelling Language

In this section we present our secure cloud modelling language in order to define the concepts and relationships required to model cloud computing systems from a security requirements perspective. This work is part of an on-going thesis and has been refined through several iterations of published work, the latest appearing in [5]. Our cloud meta-model is shown in Fig. 1, illustrating the concepts as boxes, relationships as shaded boxes and properties as attributes inside boxes. The novel cloud computing concepts and relationships proposed in this paper are boxes with thick outlines. Concepts extended from the Secure Tropos methodology [6] is shown as boxes with thin outlines. Boxes with dashed outlines denote existing concepts which has been extended in our research. We now present our novel cloud computing concepts.

### 2.1    Proposed Cloud Computing Concepts

In this subsection we introduce our concepts for modelling cloud computing systems, in the context of security requirements engineering.

**Cloud Service:** *A cloud service provides a specific computing capability, is managed and owned by actors and requires virtual and physical resources in order to deliver its capability.* The cloud service concept is a specialisation of the goal

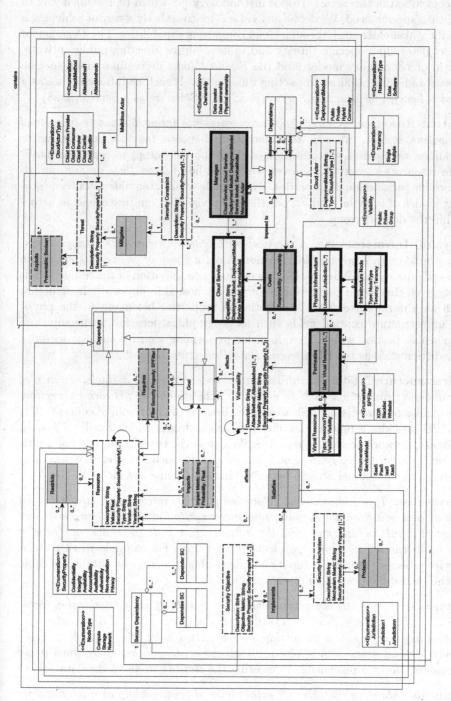

**Fig. 1.** The cloud meta-model with security requirements engineering and cloud computing concepts

concept found in the Secure Tropos methodology [6], which represents a way to achieve a specific need. We define a cloud service to embody a way of achieving a specific stakeholder need, through cloud computing capabilities. The *Deployment Model* determines specific threats and vulnerabilities affecting public, private, hybrid or community models and the *Service Model* determines cloud-specific threats and vulnerabilities impacting different levels such as Infrastructure as a Service(IaaS), Platform as a Service(PaaS) and Software as a Service(SaaS).

**Virtual Resource:** *A virtual resource represents intangible assets in a cloud computing system.* In order to differentiate between tangible and intangible resources, we create a specialisation of the resource concept to represent intangible resources as virtual resources which can be of *Type Data* or *Software* to determine jurisdictional properties. An example of an intangible resource is student grades of type *data*, which has the *group* visibility limiting access to actors within the defined group.

**Physical Infrastructure:** *A physical infrastructure represents a tangible system which, given a geographical location, hosts a group of physical assets within its local proximity.* We define this concept as a specialisation of the resource concept, given that cloud computing resources are hosted in physical infrastructure such as a data-centre. This is essential as properties belonging to the physical infrastructure contain fields such as geographical location, ownership and responsible parties; which is required for performing security analysis within a jurisdiction such as the EU *General Data Protection Regulation*.

**Infrastructure Node:** *An infrastructure node represents a single instance of a computing component such as a server, data storage or network connection.* A tangible resource is defined as a specialisation of the resource concept. The *NodeID* provides a unique identifier for each instance, which can be a *type* of compute, network or storage resource. We define the tenancy as single or multi-tenant, in order to determine cloud-specific threats such as hypervisor weakness leading to side-channel attacks between virtual machine instances [4].

**Permeates:** *This indicates the relationship which interrelates data-in-transit and data-at-rest from the virtual resource concept to the infrastructure node and physical infrastructure, and from the infrastructure node to another instance of the infrastructure node or a physical infrastructure.* For example when a cloud service processes user data stored on a physical hard drive, the data is traceable to the hard drive from a computation node.

**Owns:** *Owns indicates an actors level of responsibility as a relationship where the initiating actor possess ownership over a physical asset, is the creator of a virtual asset or has data ownership over a virtual asset.* For example in cases where a cloud users data is physically stored on assets owned by third party providers, who are responsible in meeting the security needs of the data.

**Manages:** *Manages indicates an actors level of responsibility as a relationship, in the configuration and delivery of a cloud service.* Actors managing cloud services inherit the responsibility for meeting the security needs of resources required from the cloud service and its dependencies.

## 2.2    Extended Concepts and Relationships

In this subsection we outline the extensions to existing concepts in the Secure Tropos methodology, bridging concepts from cloud computing to the security requirements engineering domain. These extensions include definition properties to existing concepts, allowing the language to express richer levels of information.

Several concepts have an associated **Security property**, which for the security constraint, security mechanism and security objective concepts, describes specific security needs such as confidentiality, integrity or availability on the concept. In the case of threats and vulnerabilities, this represents the impact of a breach in security, for example a threat with the integrity security property indicates an impact on the integrity of targeted concepts.

**Cloud Actor:** *The cloud actor concept has two properties; DeploymentModel representing deployment model and CloudActorType representing the cloud actor role.* NIST defines five types of cloud actors; Cloud Service Provider, Cloud Consumer, Cloud Broker, Cloud Carrier and Cloud Auditor [1]. The type of cloud actor determines the set of responsibilities and also constrains the validity of relationships with other concepts. For example a cloud consumer who isn't also a CSP cannot provide physical infrastructure to another CSP actor.

**Requires:** *A goal, cloud service or resource requires a cloud service or resource, in order to satisfy a stakeholder need, fulfil a capability or collaborate with other resources or cloud services.* This relationship indicates the resource or cloud service instances required by a goal, cloud service or resource. The *Filter Security Property* property can whitelist or blacklist specific security needs as security properties on associated concepts.

**Impacts:** *A goal, cloud service or resource is impacted by a threat, which threaten their security properties.* This relationship indicates a resource or cloud service is impacted by a specific instance of a threat, where a *Impact Metric* denotes the security consequences of a breach as a qualitative or quantitative value and the *Probability* indicates the likelihood of a threat impacting the concept.

**Exploits:** *A threat is able to exploit a vulnerability.* This relationship indicates that the specific instance of a threat exploits one or more vulnerabilities.

The *Preventable* property denotes if the relationship of an instance of a threat exploiting a vulnerability is preventable. This allows the analysis to determine if mitigation strategies exist.

## 3    Career Office System Case Study

In this paper we present a case study based on the University of the Aegean Career Office, which is an existing cloud-based system. This case study was

presented in a previous collaborative publication by the author in [8]. The main
objective of the University of the Aegean Career Office system is boundary management, i.e. helping students to manage the choices and transitions they need
to make upon completing their studies. The Career Office creates the survey and
outsources its hosting and the gathering of responses to a cloud service provider.
There are several existing security needs, specifically that only authorised university members are able to access the survey system and that the data should
have guaranteed availability. The objective of the case study is to model the
security implications of outsourcing to a third party cloud service provider.

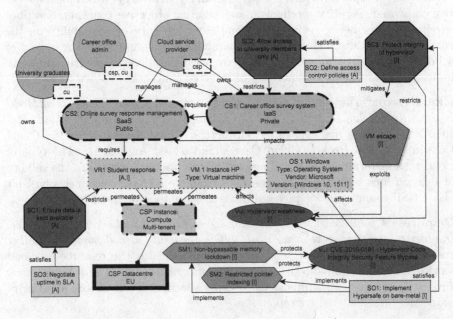

**Fig. 2.** A security enhanced cloud model of the University of the Aegean Career Office
System

Due to space constraints we have modelled the cloud concepts concerning
one specific organisational goal of the system, the conduction of a survey of the
university's graduates. The cloud model generated using our cloud modelling
language proposed in this paper is shown in Fig. 2. We are able to see that the
cloud service *"CS2: Online survey response management"* requires the virtual
resource *"VR1 student response"*, which is owned by the actor *"University graduates"*. The security constraint *"SC1 Ensure data is kept available"* restricts
*"VR1"* and due to the requires relationship from CS2, we can infer that the
actor responsible for managing *"CS2"* is also responsible for ensuring the security constraint *"SC1"* is addressed. We then describe the resources required by
the cloud services, identifying the properties of a virtual machine instance in
order to examine vulnerabilities which affects the system given a specification

of resources used. Specifically the virtual resource "VM 1 Instance HP" of type *Virtual machine* has the virtual resource "*OS 1 Windows*" associated, which provides additional levels of detail. Thus given the type, vendor and version properties in the virtual resource "*OS 1 Windows*", we are able to describe and model the vulnerability affecting this particular configuration. At the high level we model the vulnerability "*Vul: Hypervisor weakness*" which affects the virtual resource "VM 1 Instance HP" due to the type *Virtual machine*. But as the model provides more information in "*OS 1 Windows*", we are able to model at a lower level of granularity the vulnerability "Hypervisor Code Integrity Security Feature Bypass" with the Common Vulnerabilities and Exposures(CVE) ID "*CVE-2016-0181*" which affects *version 1511* of the type *Operating System Windows 10* by the vendor *Microsoft*. We then model two alternative security mechanisms "*SM1: Npn-bypassable memory lockdown*" and "*SM2: Restricted pointer indexing*", which protects the vulnerability "*CVE-2016-0181*". These vulnerabilities are implemented through the security objective "*SO1: Implement Hypersafe on bare-metal*". The "*[I]*" property in the concepts discussed previously indicates that the security property *Integrity* is associated with these concepts. Thus given a threat "*VM escape [I]*", this threat exploits the *integrity* property of the vulnerability "*Hypervisor weakness*", which itself affects the *integrity* property.

Therefore we are able to model the data required by cloud service, how the data permeates through the physical components in the cloud system, jurisdiction and cloud characteristics such as multi-tenancy and virtualisation. We then identify cloud-specific vulnerabilities and mitigation strategies through security mechanisms and security objectives.

# 4   Related Work

One of the primary research directions in cloud security focuses on the mitigating mechanisms and software solutions at the implementation level, targeting existing and operational software systems [9]. We argue that security is a factor that is most effective when integrated as early as possible in the software development life-cycle [7]. However existing requirements engineering approaches such as [6,10] lack the expressive power to support the developers understanding when modelling relationships between organisational, business and security needs in a cloud computing environment. Specifically existing approaches lack a language expressive enough to model cloud-specific concepts such as multi-tenancy, virtualisation and cloud services in the context of cloud security. Beckers et al. proposes a pattern-based method eliciting cloud security requirements, guiding cloud customers during the process of modelling cloud systems [11]. However their approach focuses on establishing an Information Security Management System (ISMS) without considering the propagation of users cloud security needs. Li et al. provides a holistic security requirements-eliciting approach towards socio-technical systems [12]. However their work lacks expressive power for capturing cloud-specific properties, which is essential for inferring cloud security issues. Review efforts indicates that while most work only target cloud computing issues in isolation, for example considering security properties in software systems or human factors on a social level but failing to provide direct correlation between different conceptual layers [13].

Our proposed approach ensures that the system-under-design incorporates security from the early requirements stage, by providing an expressive modelling language able to capture cloud computing concepts and characteristics. Thus our modelling language captures essential cloud characteristics such as multi-tenancy and security implications in order to progress towards addressing the security problem in cloud computing [2].

## 5 Conclusion

The proposed cloud modelling language in this paper enables developers to realise organisational needs in a cloud computing context, capturing the needs of the system as-is and expressing the system to-be. Addressing the contribution points *C1* and *C2*, we have defined a cloud modelling language to capture cloud security concepts. We argue that by enhancing the proposed cloud concepts with detailed relationships and properties, the language is able to represent cloud computing systems through both abstract and fine-grained perspectives. Future work will focus on enhancing the support for semi-automated analysis techniques, using information from vulnerability databases and expert security knowledge to generate a security mitigation strategy given a cloud model.

## References

1. Mell, P., Grance, T.: The NIST definition of cloud computing (2011)
2. Almorsy, M., Grundy, J., Mller, I.: An analysis of the cloud computing security problem. In: Proceedings of APSEC 2010 Cloud Workshop, November 2010
3. Li, Y., Cuppens-Boulahia, N., Crom, J.-M., Cuppens, F., Frey, V.: Expression and enforcement of security policy for virtual resource allocation in IaaS cloud. In: Hoepman, J.-H., Katzenbeisser, S. (eds.) SEC 2016. IAICT, vol. 471, pp. 105–118. Springer, Cham (2016). doi:10.1007/978-3-319-33630-5_8
4. Ristenpart, T., Tromer, E., Shacham, H., Savage, S.: Exploring information leakage in third-party compute clouds. In: Proceeding of 16th ACM Conference on Computer and Communications Security, pp. 199–212. ACM (2009)
5. Shei, S., Kalloniatis, C., Mouratidis, H., Delaney, A.: Modelling secure cloud computing systems from a security requirements perspective. In: Katsikas, S., Lambrinoudakis, C., Furnell, S. (eds.) TrustBus 2016. LNCS, vol. 9830, pp. 48–62. Springer, Cham (2016). doi:10.1007/978-3-319-44341-6_4
6. Mouratidis, H., Giorgini, P.: Secure Tropos: a security-oriented extension of the tropos methodology. Int. J. Software Eng. Knowl. Eng. **17**(02), 285–309 (2007)
7. Kissel, R., Stine, K., Scholl, M., Rossman, H., Fahlsing, J., Gulick, J.: Security considerations in the system development lifecycle (NIST 800-64 rev. 2) (2008)
8. Argyropoulos, N., Shei, S., Kalloniatis, C., Mouratidis, H., et al.: A semi-automatic approach for eliciting cloud security and privacy requirements. In: Proceeding of 50th Hawaii International Conference on System Sciences (2017)

9. Modi, C., Patel, D., Borisaniya, B., Patel, A., Rajarajan, M.: A survey on security issues and solutions at different layers of Cloud computing. J. Supercomputing **63**(2), 561–592 (2013)

10. Yu, E.S.: Social modeling and i*. In: Borgida, A.T., Chaudhri, V.K., Giorgini, P., Yu, E.S. (eds.) Conceptual Modeling: Foundations and Applications. LNCS, vol. 5600, pp. 99–121. Springer, Heidelberg (2009). doi:10.1007/978-3-642-02463-4_7

11. Beckers, K., Côté, I., Fabender, S., Heisel, M., Hofbauer, S.: A pattern-based method for establishing a cloud-specific information security management system. Requirements Eng. **18**(4), 343–395 (2013)

12. Li, T., Horkoff, J., Beckers, K., Paja, E., Mylopoulos, J.: A holistic approach to security attack modeling and analysis. In: Proceeding of the Eighth International i* Workshop (2015)

13. Iankoulova, I., Daneva, M.: Cloud computing security requirements: a systematic review. In: Sixth International Conference on Research Challenges in Information Science (RCIS), pp. 1–7. IEEE (2012)

# On Valuation of Smart Grid Architectures: An Enterprise Engineering Perspective

Iván S. Razo-Zapata[1]([✉]), Anup Shrestha[2], and Erik Proper[1]

[1] Luxembourg Institute of Science and Technology (LIST),
Esch-Sur-Alzette, Luxembourg
{ivan.razo.zapata,erik.proper}@list.lu
[2] School of Management and Enterprise,
University of Southern Queensland, Toowoomba, Australia
anup.shrestha@usq.edu.au

**Abstract.** This paper presents the initial design of a method to value smart grid (SG) architectures from a business point of view. The proposed design relies on the use of the Smart Grid Architecture Model (SGAM) and an adapted version of Bedell's method to assess the strategic importance and effectiveness of SG elements. As an attempt to automate such valuation, we also propose the use of a survey and a decision support system (DSS) that can determine the overall value of SG architectures.

**Keywords:** Smart grid · Enterprise architecture · Valuation · Decision support system

## 1 Introduction

Since a smart grid (SG) is an electricity network system that uses digital technology to monitor and manage the transport of electricity from all generation sources to meet the varying electricity demands of end users [7], it can facilitate the integration of renewable sources into the traditional energy value chain [2], e.g. virtual power plants based on solar or wind energy. Despite the benefits, SGs currently face several barriers (e.g. legal, economic and operational) [7]. Among those barriers, the unknown impact of information and communication technology (ICT) is one of the most important (i.e. the shorter life expectancy of some ICT components as well as security and privacy) [7].

Current methods to value renewable energy projects rely mostly on assessing cost-related issues, e.g. Levelized Cost of Electricity (LCOE), Levelized Avoided Cost of Electricity (LACE), System LCOE and System Value [8,14]. These approaches, however, overlook or simplify valuation issues related to the impact of ICT that usually supports and increasingly influences the functioning of such SG projects [2,7]. A complete valuation of these projects, therefore, needs to be complemented with an assessment that also takes into account the impact of ICT aspects. Such an assessment should not only cover costs related to software

© Springer International Publishing AG 2017
I. Reinhartz-Berger et al. (Eds.): BPMDS/EMMSAD 2017, LNBIP 287, pp. 346–353, 2017.
DOI: 10.1007/978-3-319-59466-8_22

& hardware installation, maintenance and operation but also business-oriented issues such as strategic importance and effectiveness of ICT elements, which are significant and relevant to achieve SG goals (e.g. $CO_2$ reductions).

To achieve this assessment, enterprise architecture (EA) models can be applied since they provide a holistic approach that simultaneously looks at business and ICT aspects. Although these architectural models provide tools for supporting design and modeling, they usually lack tools to perform thorough analysis of the architectures.

As a first attempt to fill such gap, we **sketch the design** of a method that allows to assess the value of smart grid projects using EA models. The method adapts Bedell's method [13] to value the strategic importance and effectiveness of SG architectures that are designed using EA models. The method also foresees the use of a decision-support system (DSS) to implement a survey-based approach that exploits the information encoded in the EA models. Likewise, the approach is inspired by valuation techniques that have been already applied in enterprise architecture. Furthermore, in this work, we only focus on the valuation of business issues related to the strategic importance and effectiveness of the ICT elements that compose SG architectures, which are representations/models of real-world SG projects.

The rest of the paper is structured in the following way. Section 2 presents some related work, whereas Sect. 3 briefly describes the methodology we follow and presents the design of a proposed solution. Later on, Sect. 4 provides some discussion and Sect. 5 finishes the paper with general conclusions and future research directions.

## 2   Related Work

There are several methods to value renewable energy projects. Among the most relevant, LCOE, measures the overall cost of a power generating technology [1]. Although LCOE is widely used, it presents some drawbacks. For instance, as highlighted in [8], LCOE is unable to compute information about *when, where* and *how* power is generated, which is specially relevant for DERs [8]. To overcome some of its drawbacks, several metrics have been recently proposed. For instance, LACE [15], System LOCE [14] and System Value [8]. All these traditional (economic) methods, nonetheless, mostly assess cost-related issues while simplifying or neglecting business issues related to the impact of ICT (e.g. strategic importance of components).

There have been, nonetheless, recent efforts trying to economically assess SG architectures using architectural models that include ICT. The European project DISCERN has partially used the so-called Smart Grid Architecture Model (SGAM) to assess the "economic viability" of SG solutions [5].

In a similar vein, Quartel et al. have adapted Bedell's method for the valuation of IT portfolios [12,13]. Managers are expected to provide information not only on the (perceived) importance of business processes to the organization (IBO) and business activities to business processes (IBA) but also on the effectiveness of information systems in supporting business activities (ESA) [12]. Once the information is obtained, the method can estimate the value and cost of a given architecture [12].

In our design, we aim to also adapt Bedell's method to value SG architectures based on SGAM. The later provides a "standardized" way to describe SG architectures, whereas the former offers a step-wise method to value the strategic importance and effectiveness of ICT elements. Understanding the importance and effectiveness of ICT elements is of utmost relevance to stakeholders (e.g. energy utilities and retailers) as both measures provide insights on whether ICT investments might be needed to support new or current operations and which operations might need "extra" support [13]. For instance, demand-side management (DSM) is a paradigm within SGs that aims to intelligently match energy demand and supply by mostly influencing consumption using among other things smart components (e.g. smart meters, controllers) at the customer premises [2]. The addition of all new components, nonetheless, requires understanding the impact they bring to other operations within current SG architectures (e.g. new forms of energy billing to influence consumption).

Furthermore, to gather the information on the importance of ICT elements, we foresee the use of a DSS that will provide a (semi) automated way of collecting data via surveys and facilitate decision making by generating reports on the overall value of the SG architecture under analysis. In this way, the final objective is to provide a "holistic" method to value smart grid (SG) projects based on information collected from experts via surveys.

## 3   Methodology and Proposed Solution

To design our solution, we follow a design science research (DSR) approach [6,10]. Out of the traditional six steps (problem identification and motivation, definition of the objectives for a solution, design and development, demonstration, evaluation and communication), we only cover the first three as the main goal of this paper is to sketch the design of a potential solution. In this way, Sect. 1 has already identified the need to provide a complementary way to assess the value of SG projects by taking into account the impact of ICT. Likewise, Sect. 2 has defined the objective of a solution, which is presented in the following paragraphs.

To achieve our objective, we propose adapting Bedell's method [13] to value SG architectures that are designed based on SGAM [3]. SGAM supports a holistic description of all the elements within an SG architecture, whereas Bedell's method allows to value the importance and effectiveness of such architecture. By the same token, to collect information required by Bedell's method, we also propose the use of a tailored survey. The following paragraphs elaborate on each one of these elements.

## 3.1  SGAM

The Smart Grid Architecture Model (SGAM) proposes an enterprise-wide, service-oriented approach to describe an SG architecture [3]. SGAM relies on *domains*, *zones* and *interoperability* layers. SGAM domains support the specification of elements related to the electrical conversion/supply chain (from generation, transformation, transportation all the way to customers). SGAM zones support the definition of different levels of power system management (automated management mostly). SGAM interoperability layers integrate all aspects related to business objectives, functionality, information exchange, communication protocols and ultimately the technical infrastructure of SGs [3].

The main advantage of using SGAM to value SG architectures is twofold: communication and analysis. First, SGAM provides a "holistic language" that facilitates the communication among stakeholders (e.g. it sufficiently covers business and ICT elements). For example, to value the importance of technical elements, one can use the elements from the component and communication layers, whereas business and function layers can be used to value the importance of operational elements. Second, since SGAM has been designed by experts in the electricity domain, it focuses on the elements that are ultimately needed to operationalize SG projects [3].

## 3.2  Adaptation to Bedell's Method

Bedell's method was originally designed to analyze the contribution of information systems to organizations' business value [13]. The method, nonetheless, has been also adapted to analyze IT portfolios based on EA models [12]. The main idea behind the method can be summarized in three steps. First, to gather information about the *importance* of the elements within an architecture by asking questions to people in charge of the architecture. Second, to use the collected information to compute the *effectiveness* of such architectural elements. Finally, by combining information about importance and effectiveness, we can obtain a holistic valuation of the overall SG architecture.

Figure 1 illustrates the main idea behind using Bedell's method to value SG architectures based on SGAM. As one can see, information related to the Importance of elements is obtained by a survey, whereas information about Effectiveness can be computed using formulas.

**Computing Importance Based on a Survey.** To compute the importance of bottom layers to upper layers, we propose to conduct a survey that will collect information about the strategic importance of elements *per layer*. In short, as proposed in Bedell's method, we must score the importance of each element within the system by means of a set of questions. Figure 2 shows such a set of questions. Briefly, the idea is to analyze the strategic importance of the following elements (see also Fig. 1).

– Importance of **C**omponents to **C**ommunication protocols (ICC).

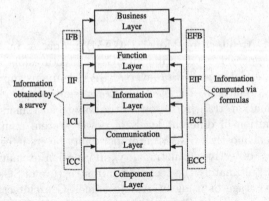

**Fig. 1.** Overall picture of Bedell's method adapted to value SG architectures based on the five SGAM layers. The Importance of elements at each layer is obtained via a survey, whereas the Effectiveness is computed via formulas.

- Importance of Communication protocols to Information sharing models (ICI).
- Importance of Information sharing models to Business Functions (IIF).
- Importance of Business Functions to Business Services (IFB).

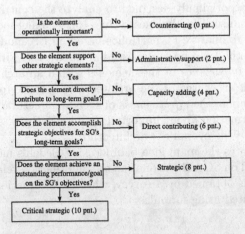

**Fig. 2.** Determining the strategic importance of elements within the SG architecture, adapted from [13]. Note: it might be needed to (re)adapt these questions per layer.

**Computing Effectiveness.** As seen in Table 1, the information regarding the effectiveness of each layer can be computed using formulas that use the information gathered in the previous steps (i.e. information about the strategic importance of each element).

**Table 1.** Formulas to compute the effectiveness per layer (see also Fig. 1)

| Effectiveness of | Formula |
|---|---|
| Component to Communication | $ECC = \sum ICC$ |
| Communication element to Information | $ECI = ECC \times \sum ICI$ |
| Information element to Function | $EIF = ECI \times \sum IIF$ |
| Function to Business | $EFB = EIF \times \sum IFB$ |

### 3.3 A Survey to Combine Importance and Effectiveness

We discuss the integration of survey data regarding strategic importance with a decision-support system (DSS). A DSS framework, potentially combined with a rules engine and statistical analysis tools, can be used to analyze the collected survey data and identify individual data that exceed predetermined or adaptive thresholds. A responsive DSS has been proven to enhance decision performance [4]. Moreover, a business process engine can be used to manage the core DSS knowledge base of strategic value of the SG architectures to the business.

A DSS design model for complex domains such as SG architecture requires broader and more integrated viewpoints from different layers of the architecture [9]. The primary role for DSS assessment of survey data is to provide an effective means to reduce the data overload and to provide a means of strategic view to allow appropriate measurement of the importance of the SGAM elements (across layers) to best assess the value of SG architectures. In this way, the DSS system may ultimately influence improvements in the way SG architectures are designed and implemented. Figure 3 illustrates a DSS workflow to compute strategic importance and effectiveness of elements within the layers of the SG architecture. The workflow has been developed based on the BPMN 2.0 notation using Innovator for Business Analysts software.

As depicted in Fig. 3, there are three key stakeholders involved during the assessment of the strategic importance and effectiveness of the SG architecture: *assessment facilitator, survey participants* and *decision maker*. The assessment facilitator initiates the process by capturing details of the stakeholders and their roles in the survey. The survey questionnaire is then allocated to the relevant stakeholders (experts) from the DSS database via an interface (web browser or mobile app). As the participants respond to the survey questions, the assessment facilitator can track the survey status. The strategic importance and effectiveness scores are then computed based on the questions described in Fig. 2 and the set of formulas presented in Table 1. Based on associated business rules, the DSS can map questions with associated recommendations when the scores are below an established parameter, i.e. when risks are identified. The scores and associated recommendations are then compiled to generate an assessment report by DSS which is sent to the decision makers by the assessment facilitator.

Finally, the decision makers study the assessment report to determine the value of SG architecture to the business in terms of strategic importance.

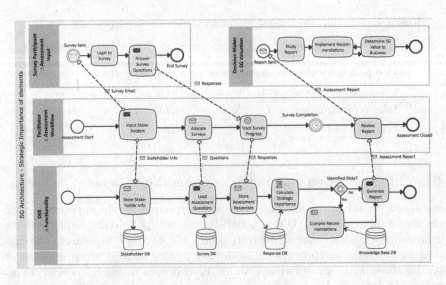

**Fig. 3.** Determination of Strategic Importance and effectiveness of SG Architectures using SGAM, a DSS and Bedell's method.

Additionally, recommended guidelines from the DSS may be actioned to improve the strategic importance of the architecture to the business. Such recommendations provide a transparent, evidence-based approach while taking a course of action to determine strategic value. We believe that in decision situations where perceptual factors from key stakeholders of a system must be captured, such as the quantitative models illustrated in Fig. 2, a DSS workflow (such as Fig. 3) can be optimized to embed such models, and this can ultimately help managers make better decisions [11].

## 4   Discussion

We do not call for ignoring LCOE, LACE, System LCOE or System Value but rather aim to complement the valuation of SG architectures by providing an approach that assess the strategic importance and effectiveness of ICT elements, which are key resources to achieve the goals of SG architectures. In this way, the main stakeholders (e.g. energy utilities, retailers) can have a more holistic view on how ICT elements impact SG architectures. For instance, how new paradigms such as DSM can impact current and new operations. In our design we have made several assumptions that might need to be revised in future versions. We have adapted Bedell's method to a different setting for which its value still needs to be validated within real-world cases. In concrete, we assume that strategic importance of SG elements can be assessed adapting the same questions described by the original Bedell's method. By the same token, we also assume that the formulas to compute effectiveness can be easily applied to SG architectures.

# 5  Conclusions and Future Work

We have described the initial design of a method to value smart grid SG architectures that focuses on the strategic importance and effectiveness of SG elements. Our method uses a DSS and a survey to collect information about the strategic importance and effectiveness of SG elements within SG architectures. It also assumes that SG architectures are described using SGAM.

As next steps we plan to perform four tasks: (1) refine our design by asking potential stakeholders to provide feedback on our current assumptions, (2) develop our DSS using standardized technology, and (3) demonstrate and evaluate our method within a real-world setting in which an energy utility or retailer needs to value an SG architecture.

# References

1. Borenstein, S.: The private and public economics of renewable electricity generation. J. Econ. Perspect. **26**(1), 67–92 (2012)
2. Bush, S.F.: Communication-Enabled Intelligence for the Electric Power Grid. IEEE Press, London (2014)
3. CEN-CENELEC-ETSI. Smart grid coordination group: Smart grid reference architecture, European Committee for Standardization, Brussels, Belgium, Technical report (2012)
4. Chan, S.H., et al.: Decision motivation and its antecedents. Information & Management (2017)
5. DISCERN Project. WP8 D8.1 Business Case on Use Cases and Sensitivity Analysis (2017). https://www.discern.eu/. Accessed 27 Feb 2017
6. Gregor, S., Hevner, A.R.: Positioning and presenting design science research for maximum impact. MIS Q. **37**(2), 337–355 (2013)
7. Technology Roadmap: How2Guide for Smart Grids in Distribution Networks, International Energy Agency (IEA). Technical report OECD/IEA (2015)
8. Next Generation Wind and Solar Power - From Cost to Value, International Energy Agency (IEA). Technical report, OECD/IEA (2016)
9. Klashner, R., Sabet, S.: A DSS Design Model for complex problems: Lessons from mission critical infrastructure. Decis. Support Syst. **43**(3), 990–1013 (2007)
10. Peffers, K., et al.: A design science research methodology for information systems research. J. Manage. Inf. Syst. **24**(3), 45–77 (2007)
11. Power, D.J., Sharda, R.: Model-driven decision support systems: concepts and research directions. Decis. Support Syst. **43**(3), 1044–1061 (2007)
12. Quartel, D., Steen, M.W., Lankhorst, M.: Using enterprise architecture and business requirements modeling. In: 14th IEEE International Enterprise Distributed Object Computing Conference (EDOC), pp. 3–13 (2010)
13. Schuurman, P., Egon, W.B., Philip, P.: Calculating the importance of information systems: the method of Bedell revisited (2008)
14. Ueckerdt, F., et al.: System LCOE: what are the costs of variable renewables? Energy **63**, 61–75 (2013)
15. U.S. Energy Information Administration. Levelized Cost and Levelized Avoided Cost of New Generation Resources in the Annual Energy Outlook 2016, Technical report, August 2016

# Author Index

Abrishamkar, Sadra  272
Argyropoulos, Nikolaos  19
Ashrov, Adiel  319
Aveiro, David  220
Awadid, Afef  239

Bachhofner, Stefan  3
Banjac, Danijela  289
Banjac, Goran  289
Batoulis, Kimon  68
Bider, Ilia  171
Brdjanin, Drazen  289

Delaney, Aidan  337
Di Ciccio, Claudio  3

Evron, Yotam  305

Ferme, Vincenzo  103
Fish, Andrew  19

Ghannouchi, Sonia Ayachi  239
Gordon, Michal  319
Gouveia, Duarte  220
Guerreiro, Sérgio  257

Hadar, Irit  189

Ivanchikj, Ana  103

Kis, Isabella  3
Koutsopoulos, Georgios  171

Leymann, Frank  103
Lübke, Daniel  119

Mandal, Sankalita  68
Mangler, Juergen  34
Maric, Slavko  289
Marron, Assaf  319

Mendling, Jan  3
Mouratidis, Haralambos  19, 337

Nurcan, Selmin  239

Pautasso, Cesare  103
Probst, Thomas  137
Proper, Erik  346
Pryss, Rüdiger  137, 153
Pufahl, Luise  68, 85

Razo-Zapata, Iván S.  346
Reichert, Manfred  137, 153
Rinderle-Ma, Stefanie  34

Sandkuhl, Kurt  204
Schlee, Winfried  137
Schobel, Johannes  153
Seigerroth, Ulf  204
Shei, Shaun  337
Shrestha, Anup  346
Skouradaki, Marigianna  103
Soffer, Pnina  305
Stertz, Florian  34
Sturm, Arnon  272, 319
Syamsiyah, Alifah  51

van der Aalst, Wil M.P.  51
van der Linden, Dirk  189
van Dongen, Boudewijn F.  51
van Lessen, Tammo  119

Weiss, Gera  319
Weske, Mathias  68, 85

Yu, Eric  272

Zamansky, Anna  189, 305
Zimoch, Michael  137, 153

Printed in the United States
By Bookmasters